PERSPECTIVES
IN
AESTHETICS

PERSPECTIVES

IN

AESTHETICS

Plato to Camus

EDITED BY

PEYTON E. RICHTER

BOSTON UNIVERSITY

THE ODYSSEY PRESS, INC. NEW YORK

ACKNOWLEDGMENTS

For permission to reprint material from copyrighted works, the editor is grateful to the following:

G. BELL & SONS, LTD.—for selection from Hegel's Philosophy of Fine Art, translated by F. P. B. Osmaston, 1920. THE BODLEY HEAD, LTD.—for selection from Beauty and Ugliness and Other Studies in Psychological Aesthetics by Vernon Lee and Clementina Anstruther-Thomson, 1912. THE LITERARY ESTATE OF ROGER FRY and CHATTO & WINDUS, LTD.—for selections from "An Essay in Aesthetics" in Vision and Design I (1920) and from "Some Questions in Esthetics" in Transformations: Critical and Speculative Essays in Art (1926) by Roger Fry. THE CLARENDON PRESS, OXFORD—for selection from Aristotle's Politica translated by Benjamin Jowett, revised edition by W. D. Ross, 1921. ENCYCLOPAEDIA BRITANNICA—for selection from the article "Aesthetics" by Benedetto Croce in the Encyclopaedia Britannica, 14th edition. FABER & FABER, LTD.—for selection from Plotinus: The Enneads translated by Stephen MacKenna, third edition, 1962. ALFRED A. KNOPF, INC.—for selection from The Rebel by Albert Camus. Copyright, 1956 by Alfred A. Knopf, Inc. Reprinted from The Rebel, Vintage Edition, by Albert Camus, translated by Anthony Bower, by permission of the publisher. THE OPEN COURT PUBLISHING COMPANY (1307 Seventh Street, La Salle, Illinois)—for selection from Experience and Nature by John Dewey, second edition, 1929. PANTHEON BOOKS, INC.—for selection from Plotinus' Enneads. Reprinted from The Enneads by Plotinus, 3rd edition (Stephen MacKenna, trans.) by permission of Pantheon Books, A Division of Random House, Inc. All rights reserved. G. P. PUTNAM'S SONS—for selection from John Dewey's Art as Experience. Reprinted by permission of G. P. Putnam's Sons from Art as Experience by John Dewey. Copyright 1934 by John Dewey. G. P. PUTNAM'S SONS AND COWARD-McCANN—for selection from Transformations; Critical and Speculative Essays on Art by Roger Fry, Chatto & Windus, Ltd., copyright 1926. THE WORLD PUBLISHING COMPANY—for selection from Vision and Design by Roger Fry, Meridian Books, 1957. YALE UNIVERSITY PRESS—for selection from An Essay on Man: An Introduction to a Philosophy of Human Culture by Ernst Cassirer, copyright 1944 by Yale University Press.

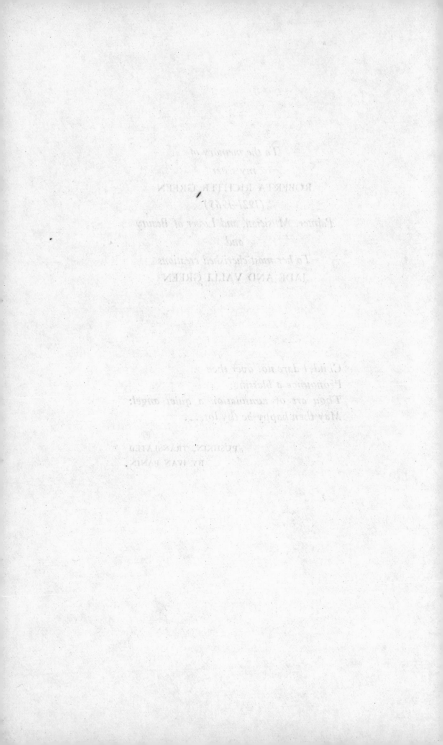

PREFACE

The purpose of this book is to introduce its readers to some of the most important theories of art and beauty from ancient times to the present through selections from original sources beginning with Plato and ending with Camus. Prefacing each selection or group of selections from a given author is a biographical sketch of that author and a succinct exposition of his aesthetic perspective. Where two or more selections are presented, they are connected by interpretive or transitional passages provided by the editor, thus making it possible to include the cardinal portions of a major work or portions of two works by the same author without losing a sense of continuity. This method of presenting primary material is not new; it has been applied by previous editors to fields other than aesthetics, for example, by Sheldon P. Peterfreund in his *Introduction to American Philosophy*. It seems to me to be a particularly valuable method for introducing newcomers to the literature of aesthetics, a literature which has not usually been noteworthy for its clarity, brevity, and simplicity. By applying this method here, I hope to provide students with a general orientation to aesthetic theories and with a guide through some of their complexities which may promote the study of these theories as they are here presented through selections and also facilitate the later study of some of the complete works in which they are fully expounded.

Although the editorial text preceding each group of selections has for the most part been limited to giving an exposition of the background and the basic tenets of the perspective under consideration, a "Guide to Supplementary Reading," which lists some of the best criticism and discussion, has been included at the end of each chapter to assist the student in making a critical evaluation of the perspective. This "Guide" should also be useful to students pursuing any of the topics suggested for further study which are listed in each chapter after the questions for review and discussion. The entire book has been planned in such a way that it can have a variety of different uses—as a basic or adjunct text in introductory courses in aesthetics, as a source book in the history of aesthetics and art criticism, and as a means for adding new dimensions to courses in art history, art appreciation, and general education courses in the humanities. It may also be of use to readers who are exploring the field of aesthetics on their own.

But however the book be used, the reader should not expect to find in it more than a fair sampling, a collection of representative types, of aesthetic speculation and analysis. If he will find some of the outstanding figures in the history of aesthetics included here, he will not find others (e.g. Schelling, Shaftesbury, Collingwood). Although a number of the most influential intellectual movements which have affected the development of aesthetics are represented, some, equally important (e.g. Thomism, Marxism, Analytic Philosophy) are only mentioned in passing. Moreover, the book contains no perspectives in Eastern Aesthetics. Had my space, time, energy, and knowledge been unlimited, perhaps I might have been able to produce a far more comprehensive and satisfactory book, Perspectives in World Aesthetics. But for the present I will be content if I have succeeded in presenting some perspectives in Western aesthetics in a way that will make them more accessible and comprehensible to the beginning student. After having put this book to good use, this student should not only find it easier to become better acquainted with the perspectives included in it, but should also find himself better prepared to study other perspectives on his own. I hope that he will want to do both, and that the completion of a book and of a course in aesthetics will mark the beginning rather than the end of a student's inquiry into the field.

Finally, although I assume full responsibility for whatever shortcomings or imperfections this book may have, I want to take this opportunity to express my appreciation to those who have been instrumental, directly or indirectly, in its production. I am grateful to Professor Joseph H. Wellbank of Northeastern University for having read portions of the manuscript and for having made several valuable suggestions for improving it; to Dean Horatio LaFauci, Professors Marx Wartofsky, James Fisher, Joseph Jurich, and Harry Crosby, all of Boston University, for having given me the benefits of their expert advice on several matters pertaining to the form and content of the envisaged work;

to Miss Carol Morris of Boston University for her kindness in having been willing to help me read the galley proofs; and to Professor John Lavely, Chairman of the Philosophy Department at Boston University, for having arranged for me to offer courses in aesthetics frequently during the years in which I was engaged in research for this book. I am also grateful to my former teachers, Professor-Emeritus Anna Forbes Liddell of Florida State University and Professor Glenn R. Negley of Duke University, for having encouraged me while I was a graduate student to continue my study of aesthetics; to my friends Professor and Mrs. Horace Armistead of Boston University, Mrs. Elizabeth Ann Hiscox of Brooklyn College, Mrs. Ivy Winterton of Russell Sage College, and Miss Wessie Connell of the Roddenbery Memorial Library (Cairo, Georgia) for many years of stimulating and diverting conversation about literary and aesthetic topics; and to my students in humanities and aesthetics courses at Boston University whose questions, comments, and papers have continually provoked me to further research and reflection. In addition, I want to thank Miss Christa Frank, Miss Hildegard Bárány, Miss Octavia Hughes, Mrs. Jacqueline Swain, Mrs. Barbara Saunders, Mrs. Colene Dodsworth, Mrs. Annabel MacDonald, Mrs. Adele McLaughlin, and Mr. and Mrs. David Black for having helped me in various ways which expedited my labors during the period in which I was working on the manuscript. A special debt of gratitude I owe to my friend Miss Dionne Demarest, who heard a great deal about this book before it came into existence. Another of my friends, Mrs. Ilona Ricardo Kinzer, who did the translations from Guyau and Fechner especially for this book, has been a source not only of invaluable assistance and advice but also of inspiration. And last of all (in sequence but not in precedence), I am deeply grateful to my mother, Mary B. Richter, my sister, Mary Bell Richter, and my nephew, Karl Frederick Richter, for their continuing interest, encouragement, and devotion which helped me considerably in bringing this book to completion.

PEYTON E. RICHTER

Boston University,
College of Basic Studies

CONTENTS

xi

A NOTE ON THE SOURCES

The readings included in the chapters are as follows. Complete references are found in the chapter notes.

PLATO: selections from the *Republic* and the *Symposium*, translated by Benjamin Jowett.

ARISTOTLE: selections from the *Poetics*, translated by S. H. Butcher, and the *Politics*, translated by Benjamin Jowett, revised by W. D. Ross.

PLOTINUS: selections from *The Enneads*, translated by Stephen MacKenna, revised by B. S. Page.

EDMUND BURKE: selections from *A Philosophical Inquiry into the Origin of Our Ideas of the Sublime and the Beautiful.*

G. E. LESSING: selections from the *Laocoön*, translated by Ellen Frothingham.

IMMANUEL KANT: selections from the *Critique of Judgment*, translated by J. H. Bernard.

G. W. F. HEGEL: selections from *The Introduction to Hegel's Philosophy of Fine Art*, translated by Bernard Bosanquet; selections from the *Philosophy of Fine Art*, translated by F. P. B. Osmaston.

ARTHUR SCHOPENHAUER: selections from *The World as Will and Idea*, translated by R. B. Haldane and J. Kemp.

EUGÈNE VÉRON: selections from *Aesthetics*, translated by W. H. Armstrong.

JEAN MARIE GUYAU: selections from *L'Art au point de vue sociologique*, translated by Ilona Ricardo.

LEO TOLSTOY: selections from *What Is Art?* translated by Aylmer Maude.

HIPPOLYTE TAINE: selections from *The Philosophy of Art*, translated by J. Durand.

GUSTAV FECHNER: selections from *Vorschule der Aesthetik*, translated by Ilona Ricardo.

VERNON LEE: selections from Vernon Lee and Clementina Anstruther-Thomson's *Beauty and Ugliness*.

MAX DESSOIR: selections from "The Fundamental Questions of Contemporary Aesthetics," translated by Ethel D. Puffer.

GEORGE SANTAYANA: selections from *The Sense of Beauty* and *Reason in Art*.

BENEDETTO CROCE: selections from the article "Aesthetics" in the fourteenth edition of the *Encyclopaedia Britannica*.

ROGER FRY: selections from *Vision and Design* and *Transformations*.

ERNST CASSIRER: selections from *An Essay on Man*.

JOHN DEWEY: selections from *Experience and Nature*, second edition, and *Art as Experience*.

ALBERT CAMUS: selections from *The Rebel*, translated by Anthony Bower.

PERSPECTIVES
IN
AESTHETICS

INTRODUCTION

THE ORIGIN OF AESTHETICS

Aesthetics had a history long before it had a name. It was born in Greece and—more than two thousand years later—it was christened in Germany. But even though aesthetics as a critical inquiry into beauty and art began with the ancient Greeks and as a philosophical "science" began with the eighteenth-century Germans, some degree of aesthetic reflectiveness based upon the appreciation of natural and artistic beauty has been characteristic of human life ever since our earliest ancestors began to appraise the pleasantness or unpleasantness of their perception of various lights, colors, movements, shapes, textures, tastes, and odors and ever since they began to create, to reflect upon, and to judge as good or bad various works of art, from highly polished spears to well-drawn wooly mammoths. Aesthetics from one point of view has prehistoric origins. Later advances in aesthetic reflectiveness went hand in hand with advances in the arts. We can scarcely imagine the astonishing artistic achievements of the ancient Egyptians, Assyrians, Babylonians, Persians, Indians, and Chinese without the presence of some theoreticians possessing high sensitivity to beauty, definite artistic ideals, and discriminating taste. But be that as it may, if by aesthetics we mean the sustained and self-critical inquiry into the meaning and value of our experiences of beauty and art, an inquiry contained within that larger sphere of critical inquiry called philosophy, which is stimulated primarily by intellectual curiosity and consummated in better substantiated beliefs and clearer conceptions, then aesthetics really began with the Greeks.

Why it began with the Greeks is a question which we can leave to the historians of aesthetics to answer in detail.[1] Most of them agree that it was highly appropriate if not inevitable that aesthetics should have had its origin in the land that had already given birth

1

to its mother, philosophy. There were many factors that contributed to the growth of aesthetic consciousness in Greek thinkers. The long history of philosophical speculation on the nature of reality; the poetic imagination at work in Greek religion; the high premium put on physical beauty and games; the advanced understanding and enjoyment of geometrical forms; the leisure to appreciate and the wealth to accumulate beautiful things; the sheer genius exemplified in Greek art, particularly in its temples, statues, and paintings, its dramatic, lyric, and epic poems; and perhaps even the stark Greek landscape flooded with light—all of these factors helped to make certain questions, aesthetic questions, seem natural and appropriate. How ought beauty to be defined? What kind of knowledge, if any, can be obtained from works of art? What should be the functions of art in an ideal city-state? What is the relationship between the good, the true, and the beautiful? Such questions became subjects for lively controversy and rigorous thinking among Greek philosophers. And in attempting to answer them they unwittingly invented aesthetics. It was, like democracy and epic poetry, a typically Greek invention.

Aesthetics, then, began in Greece; more specifically, it began when the Greek philosopher Socrates—that fascinating, controversial, persistently curious individual who believed there was virtue in knowing—turned his attention in the fifth century B.C. to what was then probably a new and intriguing question, What is Beauty? Fortunately we have several accounts of how Socrates dealt with this question and arrived at tentative answers to it. One was recorded by the Athenian general Xenophon, an admirer of Socrates, who in his *Memorabilia* passed down to us one of the three surviving contemporary literary portraits of Socrates. (The other two are found in Aristophanes' comedy *The Clouds* and in Plato's *Dialogues*.) According to Xenophon's account,[2] Socrates taught that there is no such thing as absolute beauty. Like goodness, beauty is to be defined with reference to the end a thing serves, the purpose it fulfills. Something is properly called beautiful and good, or ugly and bad, to the extent to which it performs, or fails to perform, the function for which it was designed. Even a dung basket, Socrates admitted, should be called beautiful if it is well adapted to be useful in its way, and a golden shield ugly if it is poorly designed to serve its end. Socrates was convinced, Xenophon tells us, that the beautiful is basically the useful.

Plato's account of Socrates' views on beauty, while not always inconsistent with Xenophon's, presents quite a different, more dramatically interesting picture, perhaps because Plato, artistic genius that he was, understood far better than Socrates' honest but mundane military admirer the complexities of the issue under discussion and its subtle ramifications. But since Plato's account appears in a number of dialogues written at different periods of his life, we can never be quite sure how much of what Socrates is reported to have said actually came from the fertile imagination of Plato in various stages of his development. Nevertheless, in the *Hippias Major*, one of the fullest and possibly the earliest of Plato's accounts, we can get some notion of the searching manner in which Socrates dealt with a problem that was to perplex thinkers for centuries afterwards and that was eventually to become one of the main preoccupations of thinkers called "aestheticians." In this dialogue,[3] Socrates shows up the ignorance of Hippias of Elis, a conceited Sophist windbag. When Socrates asks for a definition of beauty, Hippias in his muddle-headed way thinks that he can define it by giving an example (viz., a beautiful girl) or by referring to a characteristic of something he considers to be beautiful (viz., the gilt on a sword). Guided by Socrates' dialectical maneuvering, Hippias is slowly led toward a more precise definition, which emerges only after a number of preliminary definitions—that beauty is the fitting or the appropriate, that it is the useful, that it is the profitable, that it is the pleasurable—have been proposed, examined, and discredited. The definition given at the end of the discussion—that the beautiful is that which is both profitable and pleasurable—is not completely satisfactory to Socrates, and he is willing to keep on searching for a better one, but at least he has shown Hippias (and us) that the problem of beauty is much more difficult than it might at first seem and that it is important for a person to know precisely what he really means when he calls an object or an action beautiful. If he doesn't know, at least he doesn't have to claim that he knows, as Hippias at first did.

Plato gives us accounts of several occasions on which Socrates discussed the problem of Beauty. In the *Symposium* (or the *Banquet*), one of Plato's finest dialogues, the central issue is love, but the dialogue concludes with Socrates' presentation of a soothsayer's views (actually his own or Plato's) on the relation between love and beauty. Socrates is convinced that beyond the world of appearances there is an ideal Beauty worthy of being loved above everything else. This and this alone is capable of satisfying the philosopher's passion. In another of Plato's dialogues, his most famous, the *Republic,* Socrates returns to the problem of beauty, which here becomes part of a larger problem, that of envisaging an ideal city-state in which the best men rule and individual and collective justice are achieved. As in the *Symposium,* ideal beauty (or goodness or truth) is still the philosopher's paramount concern, but in his role as legislator the philosopher must deal with the kind of aesthetic environment which will nurture good men. For this reason, Socrates discusses the role art can play in the new social order, and considers its origin, its utility, and its limitations. He eventually proposes sweeping reforms in the domain of the arts. Homer and Hesiod will be discarded as teachers of religion and morality, the Athenian equivalents of our rock-and-roll and sentimental sound-track music will be banned, as will be all those disconcerting tragedies and comedies so popular with the Athenians but which either make men suffer too vicariously or laugh too outrageously. The philosopher-legislator will see to it that the arts, by giving expression to the highest moral and aesthetic standards, promote the public welfare, and if the artist should object that these reforms curtail his freedom of expression and sterilize his imagination, then he will be told that he, being an artist, and a mere imitator of things, is incapable of knowing his own best interests. For only a philosopher, the philosophers Socrates and Plato insist, can know true realities, perfect truth and beauty and goodness.

We will return to Socrates and Plato later, having said enough about them here to indicate to the reader that what we call "aesthetic inquiry" today was already a going concern over two thousand years ago in ancient Greece. These philosophers formulated some of the major aesthetic problems and offered solutions to them; they attempted to clarify the functions of the various arts, to understand artistic creativity, and to reach a satisfactory definition of beauty.

"OUR FOUNDER"

The beginning of aesthetics has now been sketched, but the question still remains, how did aesthetics get its name as a philosophical "science" on which treatises and textbooks could be written, lectures delivered, and examinations given? The answer to this question may come as a slight disappointment to those whose imaginations have been stirred by the Socratic search for Beauty with which aesthetics began. For aesthetics was named by an eighteenth-century philosopher whose own name would probably be forgotten today, except by rare scholars, had he not thought of a new name for an old subject. ALEXANDER GOTTLIEB BAUMGARTEN was his name, he lived from 1714 to 1762, and during the last twenty years of his life he was a professor of philosophy at the university of Frankfurt-on-the-Oder. Professor Baumgarten was an ambitious system builder, a skillful logician and metaphysician, and, as Immanuel Kant (who used his textbooks) characterized him, an "excellent analyst."

Like his rationalistic predecessors, Descartes, Leibniz, and Wolff,[4] Baumgarten had faith in the primacy of reason, under the guidance of which "clear and distinct ideas" could be attained and rigorous logical deductions could be made. But fortunately for the history of aesthetics, he was also a passionate lover of poetry, and this presented him with a problem. For poetry, which was in his opinion a "perfect sensuous language," expressed ideas that were clear without being distinct. Indeed, the idea or representation presented by a poem must be by its very nature confused (i.e. fused into a unity which could be sensuously experienced but not intellectually conceived), otherwise it would not achieve its poetical effect. Baumgarten's problem, then, was to find a rational explanation for poetry which would fit into his rationalistic *Weltanschauung*. While he was still an advanced graduate student in philosophy, he wrestled with this problem, and in his doctoral dissertation, *Reflections on Poetry*,[5] which was published in Halle in 1735 when Baumgarten was only twenty-one years old, he gave his solution to it. In doing so, he gave aesthetics its proper name. According to his early view, which he never changed essentially, poetry and the other arts differ from philosophy in that they aim at perceptual vividness rather than at conceptual distinctness. But just as we apprehend truth by the use of our higher cognitive faculty of reason, so do we apprehend beauty by the use of our lower cognitive faculty of sensuous perception. In order to make beauty intelligible, however, we need a science of the things we perceive to accompany and supplement the science of the things we know. We need, that is, a science of perception—aesthetics, he called it—as well as a science of logic.[6] This new science, by providing us with a much needed "analogue of reason," will allow us to bring the arts into the domain of rational philosophy. Such were the conclusions, in brief, of young Baumgarten's doctoral dissertation.

Fifteen years later, after he had become an established professor and had had chance to think further and to lecture on his "new" science, Baumgarten gave an extensive exposition of this "science of sensuous knowledge" or "theory of art." He presented his conclusions in his AESTHETICA (1750), the first book of that title in the history of literature.[7] Aesthetics, according to Baumgarten, has as its object the attainment of beauty, which is the "perfection of sensuous knowledge as such." When there is a defect of sensuous knowledge, when it is imperfect, the result is ugliness. However, since aesthetics is also the "art of thinking beautifully," we may think of ugly things in beautiful ways and beautiful things in ugly ways. The aesthetician must first of all give an explanation of how beautiful thoughts are discovered; he must probe into the subjective processes by means of which the artistically beautiful is created; he must present a logic of the creative imagination in order to account for the "phenomenal perfection," the sensuous vitalization of knowledge, which comes from works of art. Baumgarten has a high opinion of the artistic genius for, in presenting clear and vivid aesthetic perceptions, he is accomplishing something as important in his own domain as the philosopher is accomplishing in his domain of "clear and distinct ideas." Acute sensitivity, powerful imagination, delicate taste, and preoccupation with the texture of sensuous appearance are as essential to the artist as rational appraisal, patient analysis, and preoccupation with the structure of appearance are to the philosopher. But theoretical aesthetics as envisaged by Baumgarten was not only to be a science useful in explaining the nature of artistic discovery; it was also to be a science concerned with the means by which artistic values are presented and communicated. He himself never lived to complete the development of his system of aesthetics, however, nor did he expect to do so. Like Moses, having led others to the promised land, and having glimpsed its outlines, he left to others the tasks of conquering and developing it.

Although scholars still debate the originality and significance of Baumgarten's contributions to aesthetics,[8] they seem to agree that he made an important contribution to the field by giving it a name (even though some claim they could have thought of a better one) and by bringing the subject to the attention of others. Innumerable volumes dealing with the same subject were to appear in the future, eventually enough to fill whole libraries, but the first on the shelf (and one of the driest and least read), that ponderous Latin tome entitled simply AESTHETICA, was the one that gave the whole section its name. Whether or not he laid the foundations of a new science, as some claim, or merely obfuscated aesthetic ideas, as others claim he did, Baumgarten was undoubtedly the Adam to aesthetics.

AESTHETICS IN REVIEW:
BEFORE BAUMGARTEN

From what has been said thus far, it might seem that there is an uneventful gap of over two thousand years in the history of aesthetics, between the Greek initiators of aesthetics, Socrates and Plato, in the fifth century B.C., to the German founding father, Baumgarten, in the middle of the eighteenth century. Even the briefest historical survey will show that this certainly was not the case!

In Greek times, Aristotle, one of Plato's former pupils who had become a great philosopher in his own right, wrote a work that may well have been in part intended as an answer to his master's criticisms of art. An analysis of the nature of tragic and epic poetry, Aristotle's *Poetics* is considered by most critics to be the greatest and certainly the most influential treatise ever written in the entire history of aesthetics. Aristotle's definition of tragedy, his account of the origin of imitative art, his discussion of the elements of a good play, his doctrine of catharsis, his distinction between poetical and historical truth, were to have never ending repercussions on later generations of aestheticians, literary critics, and practicing dramatists; to some, such as the eighteenth-century critic and playwright Lessing, Aristotle's teachings in the *Poetics* were as infallible as the *Elements* of Euclid. Another important ancient Greek contribution to aesthetics was made by the philosopher Plotinus, a mystical Neoplatonist, who, like Aristotle, seems to have thought of a good answer to Plato's debasement of imitative art. Plotinus's conception of a sublime, ineffable, but intelligible Beauty which shines through material appearances and which gives a higher significance to artistic imitations has had an influence almost equal to that of Aristotle's on later aestheticians. The treatise "Beauty," in his *Enneads,* might even be called the Magna Carta of metaphysical aesthetics.

The Roman contributions to aesthetics were for the most part derived from and inferior to the original contributions of the Greeks, yet during Roman times three works were produced which were to have great influence on future aesthetic thought. The first of these was a poetic epistle, *The Art of Poetry,* written by the great Roman poet Horace. This work, while not profound, is filled with a good deal of practical wisdom and sensible advice about the content, technique, and creation of poetry. Baumgarten frequently referred to it in his own later discussion of poetry. A second major work written during the Roman era was a treatise *On the Sublime* (or *On Literary Excellence*) by a Greek critic known traditionally as "Longinus." According to this author, inspired feeling and creative genius are necessary to the achievement of artistic greatness; sublime expression is, in his opinion, "the echo of a great soul."[9] Finally, there was a highly-influential treatise, *On Architecture,* written by a practicing Roman architect, Vitruvius. Along with a detailed discussion of many practical problems of construction, Vitruvius presented several definite principles of composition—order, symmetry, propriety, and economy—which he believed should govern architectural creation.

During the early Christian and medieval period, when aesthetics suffered an extended but not a total eclipse—someone has said that the sun of human beauty was temporarily obscured by the moon of divine beauty—St. Augustine and St. Thomas Aquinas formulated Christian conceptions of beauty which fused the traditional classical emphasis on unity and proportion with the traditional Christian (and Neo-Platonic) emphasis on higher spiritual significance. A Neo-Platonist converted to Christianity, St. Augustine (354–430) attempted to find an appropriate place for sensuous as well as spiritual satisfaction, for art as well as for religion, in his supernaturalistic perspective. God, he taught, is the ultimate principle of all the goodness, measure, beauty, and order in the world, and only in so far as the human arts lead the soul upward to God are they useful and good. Music, in that it is less tied to the senses, can promote this spiritual ascension better than the other arts. And it is in his treatise *On Music* that St. Augustine gave his fullest treatment of his views on beauty. Although St. Thomas Aquinas (1227–1274) did not write extensively on aesthetic problems, his definition of beauty as "that which when seen pleases," his insistence on the ultimate identity of beauty and goodness, his emphasis on "the splendor of form," and his statement of three conditions of beauty—integrity, harmony, and clarity— provided the basic tenets for later, more fully articulated aesthetic theories developed in the nineteenth and twentieth centuries by Neo-Scholastic thinkers.[10]

In the Renaissance aesthetics was revitalized and humanized by the increasing curiosity about the purely human realm, by the expansion of scientific knowledge and the exploration of the natural world, by the renewal of interest in classical art and thought, and by the new creative ventures of individual artists such as Leonardo da Vinci, Michelangelo, and Raphael. In Italy, numerous treatises on painting, architecture, and sculpture appeared; the resurgence of interest in the aesthetic views of Plato and Aristotle inspired dialogues on Beauty and commentaries on Tragedy; and the results of "applied aesthetics" were everywhere to be seen in the splendid buildings, statues, and paintings which were worthy of comparison with the greatest works of antiquity. But it was in England that the greatest dramatist of the Renaissance, Shakespeare, was produced and the greatest work on poetry was written. A work embued with the spirit of the Renaissance, Sir Philip Sidney's *Defense of Poesie* (1583) praised "the planet-like music of poetry," its "virtue-breeding delightfulness," and extolled the poet for his ability to know, move, and teach man.

If Italy was the cradle of aesthetics in the Renaissance, France, in the seventeenth century, was its throne. For during "*le grand siècle*," France, under its "Sun King," Louis XIV, not only produced three dramatic geniuses, Corneille, Racine, and Molière, as well as a number of outstanding architects, painters, sculptors, musicians, and literary artists through whom she rose to a position of dominance over European taste, she also produced a philosopher, René Descartes, whose rationalism provided a focus for the Neo-Classical age. Descartes (1596–1650) was mainly concerned with applying a method based on intuition and proceeding according to deduction in order to attain "clear and distinct ideas" in the various fields of knowledge. Although he never formulated an aesthetic theory as such, he firmly believed in the aesthetic value of purity of diction, simplicity and clarity of expression, sincerity of feeling, nobility of thought, and rational control of passion. Under the influence of Cartesianism, the poet Nicolas Boileau (1636–1711) later wrote the greatest and most characteristic didactic poem of the century, *The Art of Poetry* (1674). Boileau's work—"a poet's Discourse on Method" it has been called[11]—summed up and propagandized the Neo-Classical ideals of his age—clarity, good sense, and rational order. The aspiring poet is advised to love reason above everything else, to seek truth under its guidance, and to borrow from it the "beauty, force, and light" which he should seek to capture in his works.

The seeds of Neo-Classical ideals, which had been so widely sown by Boileau and other Frenchmen, drifted to England where they took root and sprang up during the latter half of the seventeenth and flowered during the first half of the eighteenth century. Alexander Pope in poetry, Christopher Wren in architecture, Henry Purcell in music, Sir Joshua Reynolds in painting were among the major representatives of the "new taste." Adherence to rules could produce polished perfection in art. But the home-grown empiricism, stemming from the seventeenth-century English philosopher John Locke (1632–1710), with its reliance on sense-impressions and mental associations, provided a psychological basis for the new aesthetic ideas developed by Joseph Addison, David Hume, and Edmund Burke as they (among many others) set out during the course of the eighteenth century to investigate "the primary pleasures of the imagination," "the standard of taste," and "the origin of our ideas of the sublime and the beautiful." And it was Neo-Platonism, with its spiritual shimmer and its mystical optimism, that inspired Lord Shaftesbury (1671–1713) as he explored the three domains of the True, the Beautiful, and the Good.

While English, French, and Italian thinkers were continuing to discuss problems arising from their reflection on the various arts and were dealing with such topics as taste, imagination, genius, beauty, the sublime, and the picturesque, in Germany the rationalist Baumgarten was formulating and developing the "new science" of aesthetics which, he hoped, would bring rational understanding, coherent order, and increased attention to the investigation of aesthetic experience. Thus, in an age of criticism and enlightenment, aesthetics emerged at last as a recognized and independent philosophical discipline having relatively definite boundaries and distinctive problems of its own.

AESTHETICS IN REVIEW:
AFTER BAUMGARTEN

Having been christened by a German, aesthetics seemed for decades to be "the German science." The Golden Age of German aesthetics, heralded by Immanuel Kant's *Critique of Judgment* (1790), reached its full maturity in the idealist theories of Schiller, Schelling, Hegel, and Schopenhauer. Schiller (1759–1805), influenced by Kant's explanation of beauty as the free play and harmony of our cognitive faculties, developed an aesthetic theory according to which the living forms of beauty are created by a play-instinct in man. Schelling (1775–1854) explained beauty as the revelation of the Infinite in the Finite; Hegel, as the realization of Absolute Spirit in sensuous medium; and Schopenhauer, as an objectification of Platonic Idea by the Cosmic Will to Live. This was the great age of metaphysical empire building, but while the sky was all aglow with luminous insights, the ground was fog-bound with obscure metaphysical notions. Beauty, with a capital B, seemed to become more of an abstract idea as it became more of a "concrete reality" in the philosophers' architectonic systems. Hegel's philosophy of art, with its elaborate explanations of how the Absolute Spirit unfolds itself in the various stages and kinds of art, exerted an almost hypnotic influence on German aesthetics during the nineteenth century, until it was supplanted by the newer and less metaphysically ambitious approaches developed by later thinkers—again Germans—among which were Robert Zimmermann, the formalist, Gustav Fechner, the father of experimental aesthetics, and Theodor Lipps, chief formulator of the *Einfühlung* (empathy) theory of aesthetic experience.

Despite the Germans' great contributions to aesthetics, they never held a real monopoly on the field, not even in the nineteenth century. In France, the traditions of German metaphysical aesthetics were perpetuated by the illustrious eclectic philosopher Victor Cousin, a personal friend of Hegel, and by his humble disciple, Théodore Jouffroy. Sociological theories of art were developed by the positivist Auguste Comte, who held that science explains and art ideally represents facts; by Hippolyte Taine, who started the rage for interpreting art in terms of *race, milieu,* and *moment*; and, finally, by the poet-philosopher Jean Marie Guyau, usually called "the father of sociological aesthetics," who held that the highest aim of art is to express qualities of life in such a way that social sympathy and solidarity are promoted. And French thinkers made many other contributions to aesthetics during the century in which French artists were transforming modern art. Expressionist theories of art were formulated by Eugène Véron and Sully-Prudhomme; the utopian socialist P. J. Proudhon, inspired by his friend Courbet, stressed the social responsibilities of art; Charles Baudelaire wrote in prose as well as in poetry about "aesthetic correspondences" and, under the influence of the painter Delacroix, presented his theory of artistic imagination; artistic genius was probed by Gabriel Séailles; and, finally, scientific approaches to aesthetics were promoted by Paul Souriau, one of the first thinkers to give a detailed analysis of the aesthetics of movement.

Turning now from France to other countries in our brief look at nineteenth-century aesthetics, in England John Ruskin and William Morris were preaching the importance of practical and fine arts in revitalizing morality and in reforming society, while Oscar Wilde and Walter Pater were lauding "art for art's sake." Spokesmen for biological, psychological, and physiological approaches to aesthetics were also heard from. Herbert Spencer presented a play theory of art based on evolutionary theory; "Vernon Lee" (Violet Paget) and her colleague, Clementina Anstruther-Thomson, performed innumerable psychological "self-experiments" in order to explore responses to aesthetic forms; and Grant Allen produced *Physiological Aesthetics* (1877). Nor was Hegelian Idealism without its adherents. Bernard Bosanquet's famous *History of Aesthetic* (1892) remains a monument to the influence of Hegel on nineteenth-century English aesthetics. Shifting southward to Italy, Benedetto Croce was, before the end of the century, turning his attention from antiquarian studies to research on aesthetic problems, from which he was to emerge as the dominant figure in twentieth-century Italian philosophy. From the New World, in the last decade of the century, came George Santayana's *Sense of Beauty* (1896), a prelude to American naturalistic aesthetics which glowed with poetic images and pulsated with that thinker's unique sensibility. And, finally, from Czarist Russia, Leo Tolstoy, novelist turned prophet, launched a guided missile entitled *What Is Art?* (1898) aimed at destroying the whole edifice of what he considered to be decadent, pleasure-obsessed Western aesthetics.

Instead of continuing into our own century this satellite view of specific features in the history of aesthetics, let us conclude this section (which has been intended not as a survey but as a synopsis to help the beginning student get some orientation to a vast and unfamiliar field) with a few general remarks about twentieth-century aesthetics.[12] Aesthetics has in this century, as in centuries past, reflected the intellectual and ideational as well as the emotional and religious concerns of its time. Pragmatism and phenomenology, logical positivism and existentialism, Marxism and Fascism, Freudian and Jungian psychology, naturalistic humanism and personalistic idealism, Neo-Thomism and Neo-Orthodoxy—all of these have given rise to, or have exerted an influence upon, the formulation of various aesthetic theories. Some theories have been directly related to new developments in twentieth-century art—for example, to cubism and futurism, dadaism and surrealism, abstract expressionism and nonobjectivism, popism and opism. Others have been proposed because they were needed by certain political or religious authorities or because they were required by accepted metaphysical systems.

Progress in aesthetics has not been unaffected by the social turmoils of our century. Research on aesthetic problems has sometimes been disrupted and curtailed by economic crises, revolutions, and wars. In Germany, for example, the rise of Nazism and later the Second World War put an end to several decades of brilliant aesthetic research under the guidance of the Jewish philosopher of art Max Dessoir. In Russia, the triumph of the Bolsheviks after the Revolution of 1917 gave the official sanction to Marxist aesthetics and eventually led to the restriction, if not the annihilation, of other approaches. And, today, the continuing "cold war" between the United States, Russia, and China at times impedes the free exchange of ideas about art and makes impartial appraisal of aesthetic research difficult if not impossible.

But despite the difficulties aesthetics sometimes encounters, today it is far less provincial than it ever was in the past, for interest in its problems is international. Professional societies of aesthetics are active in the United States, Great Britain, France, Italy, and Japan; journals devoted primarily to aesthetic problems are published in those countries and in Spain and Poland; an International Congress on Aesthetics has been held every four years since 1956; an International Association of Empirical Aesthetics was founded as recently as 1965; the contributions of Eastern aesthetics are at last being recognized and studied in the West; and for the first time surveys of world aesthetics are being undertaken.[13] Moreover, courses in aesthetics have proliferated in colleges and universities; the classics of aesthetics are appearing in paper editions; and, most important, new and outstanding contributions to the field are being made by thinkers convinced that aesthetics is relevant to knowledge, to art, and to life. Finally, aesthetics in the twentieth century is no longer considered to be primarily the philosophy of the beautiful or the philosophy of art, or even necessarily a branch of philosophy at all. The newer and broader definition of the field is that formulated and adhered to by the American *Journal of Aesthetics and Art Criticism* (founded in 1941), according to which aesthetics includes "all studies of the arts and related types of experience from a philosophic, scientific, or other theoretical standpoint, including those of psychology, sociology, anthropology, cultural history, art criticism, and education."[14]

Thus broadened, deepened, challenged, and enriched, aesthetics today seems indeed to have a bright future. Barring an all-out atomic war, it may have a history as long after, as before Baumgarten gave it a name.

WHY PERSPECTIVES IN AESTHETICS DIFFER

As you become acquainted with the various perspectives in aesthetics presented in this book you will undoubtedly be struck by certain similarities among them, but you will also perhaps be perplexed to discover how radically they sometimes differ. Instead of thinking of them as forming a kind of dialogue, you may find yourself thinking of them as a Babelogue! There are several reasons why aesthetic theories differ. First of all, their authors have sometimes disagreed with one another as to what their major task should be and how their field of inquiry ought to be de-limited. To some thinkers, Hegel for example, aesthetics is the science of the beautiful in fine art; the task of the aesthetician, therefore, is to explain how the beauty manifest in works of art comes about, or, in more Hegelian terms, how a sensuous form is made to express a spiritual content. In accomplishing this task, Hegel discusses the various arts within the context of his elaborate metaphysics, the basic tenet of which is that Reality is Absolute Spirit or Mind. Art, he believes, passes dialectically through three stages—symbolic, classical, and romantic—in its attempt to express the Absolute more absolutely, but since it can never do this as well as religion and philosophy can, these forms of Absolute Spirit eventually must replace art, making it a thing of the past. But despite Hegel's arguments that his is the only complete, consistent, and true philosophy of art and despite the fact that he brought to its elaboration a knowledge of the arts perhaps unprecedented in the history of aesthetics up to that time, many of his fellow aestheticians found his views unconvincing.

To be sure, some of those who called Hegel's philosophy absolute nonsense and the work of a charlatan, as his arch-enemy Schopenhauer did, offered as an alternative a metaphysical aes-thetics as difficult to substantiate (although perhaps not as elaborate and as difficult to fathom) as Hegel's. But other thinkers, Eugène Véron and Leo Tolstoy, for example, refused to accept the view that aesthetics is basically to be concerned with the beautiful in art and hastily passed by the entrance to the Hegelian labyrinth. Véron argued that the conception of beauty and the conception of art are not "co-terminous"; art may be a broad enough con-ception to include all works of beauty, but beauty is not a broad enough conception to encompass all works of art. Art, for Véron, is not the dialectical manifestation of Absolute Spirit, it is "the direct and spontaneous manifestation of human personality."[15] Rejecting aesthetics as the science of beauty, he argues that it can only have meaning and relevance as the study of the manifesta-tions of artistic genius. Tolstoy is more vehement than Véron in his denunciation of all philosophies of beauty. Beauty is, he holds, a meaningless term (or an "emotive term" in contemporary jargon); it is only used by the ruling snobs, including philosophers of beauty, to justify their own personal preferences. Not beauty but Art, the expression and communication of emotion, should be the concern of the aesthetician, Tolstoy insists.

Aesthetics has been defined in various other ways by thinkers represented in this book. Benedetto Croce defined it from the standpoint of his "spiritual monism" as the philosophical science of art, art being defined as intuition-expression. Aesthetics is not, however, merely a branch of philosophy for Croce; it is the whole of philosophy brought to bear on the understanding of art. For the naturalist John Dewey, on the other hand, aesthetics is the theory of aesthetic experience. The task of the aesthetician is not, according to Dewey, that of defining beauty or "spiritualizing" art or of compartmentalizing the various types of artistic expression; his task is to show the continuity of aesthetic experience with ordinary experience, to explain how art grows out of human activities and makes them more meaningful and valuable. Starting as they do from different conceptions of aesthetics, which in turn spring from different conceptions of philosophy and of reality, it is not surprising that Croce's and Dewey's perspectives in aesthetics are at odds with one another. Other conceptions of aesthetics, Max Dessoir's, for example, which proposes to restrict the domain of aesthetics to the theory of beauty and to create a "General Science of Art" in order to deal with numerous other problems relating to art, and Ernst Cassirer's, which conceives aesthetics to be the philosophy of art as symbolic form, also result in wide divergences of approach and conclusion.

This fact, that aestheticians first of all have disagreed as to precisely what aesthetics is or should be, explains some of the differences among the perspectives. But there are other reasons why aesthetic perspectives differ, at times radically. As was suggested earlier in a remark about nineteenth-century German aesthetics, some thinkers (e.g. Kant, Hegel, and Schopenhauer) have come to the consideration of beauty and art with a metaphysical axe to grind. Having worked out a theory of reality which to them at least is absolutely convincing, they fit beauty into a prefabricated system of ideas; the body of art is put on a Procrustean bed and cut accordingly. If a transition is needed between will and desire in order to complete a system of thought which neatly corresponds to our mental faculties, then aesthetic feeling can serve quite nicely in bridging a gap. If reality is the unfolding of the

Idea, or if it is Will and Representation, then art must be shown to share somehow in this unfolding or be related in some way to Will and Representation. Besides sometimes performing feats of metaphysical thaumaturgy, aestheticians (being human) have sometimes pontificated their prejudices. Tolstoy is a good case in point. Despite his great contribution to aesthetics through his expressionist definition of art, Tolstoy's attack on French symbolist poetry and on Wagner in *What Is Art?*[16] is little more than criticism by ridicule, and in attempting to show that these works of art are incapable of expressing and of communicating genuine emotion to everyone, he really only succeeds in convincing the reader that one aesthetician, namely Leo Tolstoy, is incapable of appreciating works of art that do not happen to conform to his moralistic standards or that do not aim at achieving the aesthetic effects he considers admirable. Even the great Plato, in his scathing discussion of tragedy and comedy, revealed the extent to which an unfavorable prejudice against malpracticing artists can block objective appraisal of an art form.

Another fact that may help account for differences among aesthetic perspectives is that their authors have had different levels of competency in dealing with the various forms of art. Although outstanding contributions to aesthetics have sometimes been made by thinkers concerned with only one or two of the arts,[17] the construction of an aesthetic theory which attempts to encompass and to explain the whole domain of the arts (assuming that such an undertaking is feasible) presupposes that the theoretician has at his disposal enough relevant data on which to construct his hypothesis for explaining the general nature of art. Of course often metaphysical dogma has been substituted for empirical data. This is one reason why the junk heap of discarded aesthetic theories is so high! But as Gustav Fechner (himself a conscientious student of the arts) pointed out,[18] there must be an empirical basis for aesthetics, which must include extensive experience of works of art, if an "aesthetics from below" is to support and corroborate an "aesthetics from above." Most of the thinkers included in this book were well prepared to generalize about art. Of the modern thinkers included, probably Hegel and Dessoir had the most extensive knowledge (for their time) of the various art forms, although they lacked the advantages enjoyed by others—Lessing, Guyau, Lee, Tolstoy, Santayana, Fry, and Camus—who were able to draw from their own personal experience as creators of works of art when they came to the creation of an aesthetic theory. Among our representatives, probably Kant's acquaintance with the arts (except for literature) was the most limited. However, Taine revealed that he had little grasp of the nature of music and architecture when he interpreted them according to the aesthetic theory he had applied to painting, sculpture, and poetry, arts in which he was well versed. Not that we should expect an aesthetician to have the kind of expert knowledge of all of the arts which practitioners of each of them possess. But, if a thinker is bold enough to tackle the question "What is Art?" we do expect him to have a broad and varied enough knowledge of the arts to give to his generalizations a foundation and to make them applicable.[19] Considering the demands made upon the aesthetician in this respect, we can well understand why some have held—Charles Lalo, for example—that aesthetics is among the most difficult of all human disciplines.

Having seen, then, that aesthetic perspectives differ from one another because their authors have had different conceptions of the task of aesthetics, different interests in the field, and different qualifications to deal with it, let us call attention, finally, to one other factor, or rather set of factors, that has affected the formulation of aesthetic theories and that helps account for further differences among them. Like a work of art, an aesthetic theory not only reflects the aims, interests, and abilities of its creator, it also reflects the cultural milieu and the historical circumstances in which it was conceived; it bears witness to the direct and indirect influence upon its creator of a configuration of economic, political, technological, scientific, educational, racial, religious, psychological, artistic, and numerous other factors which existed in a certain period of history. Aesthetic perspectives must be seen in perspective. We must not forget, for example, that Plato formulated his aesthetic views in fifth-century Athens, Burke in eighteenth-century England, Fechner in nineteenth-century Germany, Camus in twentieth-century France. The major aesthetic problems with which these thinkers were concerned—Plato's problem of determining the role of art in a well-governed city-state, Burke's problem of discovering the origin of aesthetic ideas, Fechner's problem of explaining the psychological basis of aesthetic appreciation, Camus's problem of finding a purpose for artistic creation in an age of crisis—these problems had arisen, for various reasons, in the cultural milieu in which these thinkers were living. And, as a careful study of these and other thinkers will reveal, they relied heavily on the materials already available to them in finding solutions to their problems. Although the importance of the influence of cultural and historical conditions on aesthetic thought has sometimes been exaggerated (e.g. by Taine and the Marxists) with the result that the interpretation of aesthetic theories has been oversociologized and the question of the validity of aesthetic theories overlooked, certainly such influences are important and should be kept in mind in attempting to understand why they differ.

Since aesthetic perspectives have had so many reasons to differ during the history of aesthetics, it is not easy to find points which all of them have in common. Although we refer to them as perspectives in *aesthetics,* aesthetics, as we have seen, has not always been defined in the same way (e.g. as philosophy of beauty or as philosophy of art) and has not been concerned with the same tasks in the various perspectives. Consequently, we cannot say that all aesthetic perspectives are philosophies of beauty, or that all of them are philosophies of art. We cannot even say that all of them are philosophies any more, since in recent years the definition of aesthetics has been broadened to include theoretical approaches other than the philosophical. But despite the differences among aesthetic perspectives, they do seem to have at least three essential traits in common: they have a common basis, aesthetic experience; a common aim, the theoretical understanding of some aspects of that experience; and a common domain, the domain of objects which have been created in order to bring about such experience, namely, works of art. Differences arise again, however, when it comes to explaining how "aesthetic experience" is to be defined and approached, what methods are to be used in understanding it, and what are the characteristics of works of art which make them suitable objects of aesthetic experience, "aesthetic objects."

AESTHETIC PROBLEMS

From all that has been said, the beginning student may conclude (and rightly) that Baumgarten's "new science" is certainly problem-besieged. Just to mention some of the major problems with which aesthetics has been traditionally concerned should excite the student who likes intellectual challenges. There is, first of all, the problem of defining beauty and its "modifications" or of distinguishing the "aesthetic types"—the beautiful, the ugly, the sublime, the tragic, the comic, the grotesque, etc. Then there is the problem of defining art, with its related problems of discovering the similarities and differences among the various arts and of ranking them according to some principle (i.e. classifying them or giving them systematic order). Next there is the problem of understanding the nature of aesthetic experience, which involves also the problems of distinguishing it from other kinds of experience, of explaining its value, the kind of emotion it evokes, and the attitude appropriate to it. In addition, there is the problem of understanding the constitution of the aesthetic object, its unique characteristics, its structure and texture, its form, content, and functions, and its ontological status. Another problem is that of fathoming the nature of artistic creativity, of discovering the kind of motivation, skill, technique, imagination, knowledge, taste, and genius that go into the creation of an aesthetic object. There is also the problem of elucidating the aesthetic judgment, of distinguishing it from other kinds of judgment, and of considering whether or not it can be verified. Finally, there is the problem of determining the role the arts ought to play in society, their relation to other human activities and institutions, their use or uselessness.

We can stop our list there without having exhausted by any means the problems which beset aestheticians.[20] Within the confines of the present volume, you should not expect any one of the thinkers included to deal with all of these problems. As you will soon discover, usually in our selections a thinker deals with only one or two of the problems (e.g. Kant with aesthetic judgment, Tolstoy with the definition of art, Dewey with aesthetic experience, Aristotle with tragedy, Santayana with beauty) but in the course of his discussion he usually gets involved in a discussion of other related problems. In several of the selections presented, a thinker (e.g. Taine, Fechner, or Dessoir) deals with the method (or methods) he proposes to use in solving aesthetic problems rather than with the answers he proposes to give to them.

Now you are ready (and we hope eager) to begin your study of perspectives in aesthetics. From a study of aesthetics you may not learn a great deal about any one of the art forms, but you will learn a great deal about what is involved in your experience of all of them. A study of aesthetics may not change your artistic preferences, although it should make you more aware of them and affect the ways in which you articulate and defend them. A study of aesthetics may not give you any final, satisfactory answers to questions such as "What is beauty?" and "What is art?" but it should stimulate you to think more critically about these questions, and the answers which have been given to them, and perhaps help you to arrive at your own tentative answers. It would be foolish to claim that a study of aesthetics makes artists more creative, critics more accurate, and perceivers more sensitive, but it is not foolish to claim that a study of aesthetics can make artists less pontifical, critics less dogmatic, and perceivers less naive. And, finally, in so far as aesthetics, as a field of critical investigation, can foster the habits of critical analysis and rational speculation, it can contribute to the growth of more reflective, more intellectually curious, more tolerant, and, ultimately, perhaps even more fully enlightened individuals.

NOTES

1. See the accounts in Katharine Gilbert and Helmut Kuhn, *A History of Esthetics*, revised edition (Bloomington, Indiana University Press, 1953), Chap. I and Bernard Bosanquet, *A History of Aesthetic* (New York, Meridian Books, 1957), Chap. II.

2. Xenophon, *Memorabilia*, Bk. III, Chap. 8.

3. Plato's authorship of the *Hippias Major* has been disputed by some Platonic scholars (e.g. Benjamin Jowett). There are selections from it in E. F. Carritt (ed.), *Philosophies of Beauty* (New York, Oxford University Press, 1931), pp. 3-16. For a summary of the argument of the dialogue see A. E. Taylor, *Plato, the Man and his Work* (Cleveland, Meridian Books, 1956), pp. 29-34.

4. For an account of the aesthetic views of René Descartes (1596-1650) and Gottfried Wilhelm Leibniz (1661-1716), see

Gilbert and Kuhn, *A History of Esthetics,* cited above, Chap. VII. An exposition of the philosophy of the Leibnizian Christian Wolff (1679–1754), which formed the immediate background of Baumgarten's speculations, may be found in J. E. Erdmann, *A History of Philosophy,* translated by Williston S. Hough (London, Swan Sonnenschein, 1892), Vol. II, pp. 219–235.

5. This work, the original title of which was *Meditationes philosophicae de nonnullis ad poema pertinentibus,* has been translated into English by Karl Aschenbrenner and William B. Holther under the title *Reflections on Poetry* (Berkeley, University of California Press, 1954).

6. Baumgarten derived the name from the Greek word *aisthetikos,* which originally meant "perceptible by the senses."

7. *Aesthetica* has never been translated into English.

8. For accounts and evaluations of Baumgarten's aesthetics see Gilbert and Kuhn, *A History of Esthetics,* cited above, pp. 289–295; Benedetto Croce, *Aesthetic as Science of Expression and General Linguistic,* translated by Douglas Ainslie (New York, The Noonday Press, 1953), pp. 212–219; and Ernst Cassirer, *The Philosophy of the Enlightenment,* translated by F. C. A. Koelln and J. P. Pettegrove (Boston, Beacon Press, 1955), pp. 338–357. Of these, Cassirer places the highest value on Baumgarten's contributions to aesthetics.

9. E. F. Carritt (ed.), *Philosophies of Beauty* (New York, Oxford University Press, 1931), p. 37.

10. For example, by Jacques Maritain and Etienne Gilson.

11. Gilbert and Kuhn, *A History of Esthetics,* cited above, p. 214.

12. The student interested in twentieth-century aesthetics will find a gold mine of material in the cumulative volumes of the *Journal of Aesthetics and Art Criticism,* which began publication in 1941. For accounts of the development of aesthetics during the first half of this century, see Thomas Munro, *Toward Science in Aesthetics* (New York, Liberal Arts Press, 1956), pp. 85–150, and Gilbert and Kuhn, *A History of Esthetics,* cited above, Chap. XIX.

13. One of the recent surveys was undertaken by the late French aesthetician Raymond Bayer, in his *L'esthétique mondiale au XXᵉ siecle* (Paris, Presses Universitaires de France, 1961).

14. This statement appears on the inside cover of the *Journal of Aesthetics and Art Criticism.*

15. Eugène Véron, *Aesthetics*, translated by W. H. Armstrong (London, Chapman & Hall, 1879), p. 389.

16. Leo Tolstoy, *What Is Art?* translated by Aylmer Maude (New York, Thomas Y. Crowell & Co., 1899), Chap. X ("On the Symbolists and Decadents") and Chap. XIII ("On Wagner").

17. To name a few, Eduard Hanslick (music), Frank Lloyd Wright (architecture), Adolf Hildebrand (sculpture), Sir Joshua Reynolds (painting), and Samuel T. Coleridge (poetry).

18. Fechner discussed aesthetics "from below" and "from above" in the first chapter of his *Vorschule der Aesthetik* (Leipzig, Breitkopf & Hartel, 1876).

19. For a modern view of the ideal educational background for an aesthetician, see Thomas Munro, "A College Program in Aesthetics and the Arts," *Journal of Aesthetics and Art Criticism*, IV (December, 1945), 115–118.

20. Among the recent works which deal with the problems of aesthetics are the following: F. H. Sparshott, *The Structure of Aesthetics* (Toronto, University of Toronto Press, 1963), Jerome Stolnitz, *Aesthetics and Philosophy of Art Criticism* (Boston, Houghton Mifflin & Co., 1960), James L. Jarrett, *The Quest for Beauty* (Englewood Cliffs, N.J., Prentice-Hall, 1957), Hunter Mead, *An Introduction to Aesthetics* (New York, The Ronald Press Co., 1952), Monroe C. Beardsley, *Aesthetics* (New York, Harcourt, Brace & World, 1958), and Morris Weitz, *Philosophy of the Arts* (New York, Russell & Russell, 1964). Among the problem-oriented anthologies are: Melvin Rader, *A Modern Book of Esthetics*, 3rd edition (New York, Holt, Rinehart, 1953), Morris Weitz, *Problems in Aesthetics* (New York, The Macmillan Co., 1959), John Margolis, *Philosophy Looks at the Arts* (New York, Charles Scribner's Sons, 1962), and W. E. Kennick, *Art and Philosophy* (New York, St. Martin's Press, 1964). The most recent history of aesthetics in English is Monroe C. Beardsley's *Aesthetics from Classical Greece to the Present: A Short History* (New York, The Macmillan Co., 1966).

CHAPTER 1

Art Under Scrutiny

PLATO

The drama of Plato's life (427–347 B.C.), as we can imagine it now, unfolded in three acts. In the first, the brilliant and poetical Athenian aristocrat, having been born toward the close of the golden age of Pericles, grew up during the Peloponnesian War to witness the decline of his native city-state through political mismanagement, class struggle, and military disaster and its eventual surrender to Sparta in 404 B.C. But for Plato a redeeming feature of the times was his idol, Socrates, that ironic, self-appointed gadfly to the state who in the midst of social upheaval and moral decline continued to encourage young men to undertake an intensive, critical examination of their lives and beliefs. Socrates was convinced that rational inquiry would lead eventually to the virtue that *is* knowledge—knowledge of the perfect, ideal Goodness by which moral character could be transformed and states reformed. Although Socrates himself managed to remain detached from the political intrigues of his day, some of his former associates, including the irrepressible Alcibiades and the ambitious Critias, played important roles in furthering the downfall of the Athenian state. Not long after a democratic government was restored following the end of the war, Socrates, brought to trial by his enemies on charges of impiety and corrupting Athenian youth, was condemned and put to death.

The death of Socrates in 399 B.C. marked the end of the first and the beginning of the second act of Plato's life. Profoundly disillusioned with Athenian democracy, he left Athens for Megara where he continued his philosophical studies and began to write dialogues in which the central speaker was his beloved Socrates.

Later, while traveling in Italy and in Sicily, he broadened his philosophical knowledge and became for a time influential in the court of Dionysius I, king of Syracuse, through his friendship with Dion, the king's brother-in-law. Plato's efforts to convert the pleasure-loving king to philosophy ended in failure, however, and brought suffering to himself.[1]

The third and final act in Plato's life began when he returned from Sicily to Athens and founded a school, the Academy, dedicated to the formation of statesmen through the pursuit of philosophical, mathematical, and scientific studies. There he spent the rest of his life teaching and writing, except for two later (and also unsuccessful) visits to Syracuse to aid his old friend, Dion. Throughout his old age Plato continued to develop and to refine his philosophical views, embodying them in dialogues unmatched in the history of Western literature for their fertility of thought and brilliance of style. The young Plato's views are found in such early Socratic dialogues as the *Apology*, *Crito*, *Ion*, and *Charmides;* his maturer views, in the *Symposium*, *Republic*, *Phaedo*, and *Phaedrus;* and his later, most seasoned wisdom, in such works as the *Parmenides*, *Philebus*, *Timaeus*, and *Laws*.[2]

For Plato's fullest treatment of art we must go to the *Republic*, the dialogue in which he presents his conception of the good life and envisages the kind of ideal society in which this life, a life of overall moral goodness or justice, could perhaps be achieved. Basic to Plato's ethical and social philosophy is his conviction that individual and state alike should be under the governance of reason. As in the just state rational men, philosophers, should govern the workers with the aid of soldiers, each group performing its different functions in harmony with the others for the welfare of the whole state, so in the good or just individual the faculty of reason should govern the appetites with the aid of the spirited faculty or will, each faculty performing its different functions in harmony with the others for the welfare of the whole individual. Plato holds that we can envisage and emulate this ideal of a perfectly just state, and the individuals composing it, even if it is not realizable now, or perhaps ever, in experience. We can also envisage, he believes, a perfectly unjust state, a diabolic tyranny which would result from the losing of the harmonious balance essential to justice. When the political power which rational men ought to wield is usurped by subordinate factors, the results will be states dominated by selfish ambition, by avarice, by lawless individualism, and, eventually, by unrestrained brute force.

Plato gives a detailed account of the kind of education he deems necessary in order to produce good rulers and reliable guardians of his ideal city-state. From its very beginning this education, which stresses both physical training and appreciation of literature and of the other arts, would aim at producing individuals strong and graceful in body as well as morally sound and aesthetically sensitive. In its advanced stages, apart from periods of time devoted to physical training and to military and public service, education would give the future philosophers thorough discipline in mathematical sciences, including arithmetic, geometry, astronomy, and "harmonics," and, finally, in dialectics, the ultimate philosophical discipline through which one gets to know by pure intelligence the essential nature of knowledge, reality, and goodness. It is not surprising, then, that the ideal rulers would be fifty years old before they would be qualified to rule.

Plato recognized, of course, that more than academic education would be necessary to produce ideal rulers. The whole state, the entire complex of institutions, the total educational environment, must be carefully ordered so as to promote unity of purpose and harmony of parts. To achieve this end, Plato is prepared to impose strict state control, not just on education but on all the activities of individual citizens, whether these activities be political, economic, sexual, or aesthetic. Men and women will have equal access to educational and political opportunity; the guardians will not be allowed to possess private property and money; they will not be allowed to marry, but their mating and reproduction will be regulated by the state and their offspring reared in state nurseries; and the literature and music, which play such essential parts in educating and in molding good citizens, Plato believes, must be carefully censored by state authorities.

In later life Plato modified somewhat his views on the structure of the ideal society, but in the course of doing so in his last dialogue, the *Laws*, he retained the policy of censorship which he would have imposed on the arts, particularly on poetry. The lawgivers will see to it, he urges, by persuasion whenever possible but by force whenever necessary, that poets produce works that are morally appropriate both in content and form. Seasoned men of wisdom, truly discriminating critics, and not the unreliable public, will be the proper judges of what is fitting and right in

dance, music, and poetry; they will be the only competent judges
of artistic imitation because they will know what a work is
supposed to represent and whether it is an accurate, well-executed
representation; they and only they can repress the lawless in-
novations of irresponsible artists and mold the taste of the public
by feeding it with the purest aesthetic fare.[3]

We shall see in our selections from the *Republic* how important
Plato considered the arts to be in educating and nurturing the
guardians of the ideal state. We shall also see why he proposed
strict censorship of the literature used in the initial stages of
education and why he held that the imitative artist, particularly
the poet, is so much inferior to the philosopher in his access to
truth, his relation to reality and—this comes out most strikingly
in the concluding section of the *Symposium*—in his insight into
the ultimate nature of goodness and beauty. Indeed, Plato believes
the poet is more akin to the madman than to the philosopher.
As he has Socrates point out in two other dialogues, the *Phaedrus*
and the *Ion*, possession by the Muses *is* a kind of madness.
Self-control, rationality, detachment, are incompatible with
genuine poetic creativity, which requires sensitivity, genius,
divine inspiration. "For the poet," says Socrates in the *Ion*, "is a
light and winged and holy thing, and there is no invention in
him until he has been inspired and is out of his senses, and the
mind is no longer in him: when he has not attained to this state,
he is powerless and is unable to utter his oracles."[4]

Because Plato had such harsh things to say about the misuse of
poetry in education and because he concluded his criticisms of
art by banishing the bad artists from his ideal city-state and by
restricting the freedom to create of remaining artists, it is easy
to misunderstand Plato's own view of poetry. Allowing for a
certain ambivalence in a man who renounced poetry for philosophy
in his youth, perhaps Plato's real aim, as a number of critics have
pointed out,[5] was not to attack but to defend poetry, for which
he always retained a passion, from those who misunderstand its
genuine aesthetic merits and overestimate its didactic and intellectual elements, seeing in it something more than what it can
actually provide: highly pleasurable, purely aesthetic enjoyment,
inspiration captured in words. In any case, there is no doubt that
Plato recognized that purely aesthetic values could be enjoyed
through the contemplation of form, sound, and color. As he has
Socrates point out in the *Philebus*, a straight line, a circle, a

well-drawn geometrical figure, a pure tone, a pleasing patch of color, a sweet smell—these are enjoyable in themselves; their sheer sensuous quality pleases with a harmless pleasure which is intrinsically valuable.[6]

But despite the pleasures that poetry and the other arts may bring, be these pleasures harmless or harmful, the end of life for Plato is not pleasure, but something to him much higher: enlightenment through rational inquiry and, ultimately, through direct encounter with Absolute Truth. To him the most sublime experience a person can have—and that person must be a philosopher to have it—is the direct confrontation with the Idea of the Good, the perfect Beauty, Symmetry, and Truth: the ideal eternal Measure which is the sun of the intelligible world, the world of eternal, self-subsisting forms transcending the transitory, relative, and imperfect particular things of everyday experience. At this higher level of insight into Measure, the moral and the aesthetic and the intellectual perspectives converge and coalesce; the philosopher then truly knows, attaining at last the wisdom which he has always loved and sought after. But even at the lower level, in a world of appearances which contains among other imperfect things works of art, Plato insists that "the excellence or beauty of every work of art is due to this observance of measure."[7]

Art Under Scrutiny

1. *In his dialogue the* Republic, *Plato in the role of Socrates discusses aesthetic problems first in connection with the education of the guardians of his ideal city-state. While his proposed curriculum begins, as it did in Plato's day, with music (in its broadest sense, including poetry and letters as well as song and melody) and gymnastics, the literary material presented to children is to be carefully censored so that it will promote virtue rather than vice among citizens. The fables used in the primary stage of education must always represent the gods as just, good, and constant; heroes, as brave and temperate; and the afterlife as nothing dreadful. As the writings of Homer and Hesiod, those staples of Greek education, are found by Socrates to be filled with lies about moral and religious matters, they are detrimental,*

he claims, to the proper education of highly impressionable young minds. Socrates is equally concerned with the manner or style in which these stories are to be presented. He prefers a straightforward narrative method to an imitation or mimicking of the various parts by the author. Here he explains why he believes it would be morally hazardous for the future guardians of his ideal state to become habituated to imitating or mimicking diverse and contradictory roles, as they might well learn to do should they be exposed to volatile and versatile, but amoral and pernicious, imitative artists and mimics. In the following passage, Socrates, who is the first speaker, is interrogating the young Adeimantus, one of Plato's brothers.

Then, Adeimantus, let me ask you whether our guardians ought to be imitators; or rather, has not this question been decided by the rule already laid down that one man can only do one thing well, and not many; and that if he attempt many, he will altogether fail of gaining much reputation in any?[8]

Certainly.

And this is equally true of imitation; no one man can imitate many things as well as he would imitate a single one?

He cannot.

Then the same person will hardly be able to play a serious part in life, and at the same time to be an imitator and imitate many other parts as well; for even when two species of imitation are nearly allied, the same persons cannot succeed in both, as, for example, the writers of tragedy and comedy—did you not just now call them imitations?

Yes, I did; and you are right in thinking that the same persons cannot succeed in both.

Any more than they can be rhapsodists and actors at once?

True.

Neither are comic and tragic actors the same; yet all these things are but imitations.

They are so.

And human nature, Adeimantus, appears to have been coined into yet smaller pieces, and to be as incapable of imitating many things well, as of performing well the actions of which the imitations are copies.

Quite true, he replied.

If then we adhere to our original notion and bear in mind that our guardians, setting aside every other business, are to dedicate themselves wholly to the maintenance of freedom in the State, making this their craft, and engaging in no work which does not bear on this end, they ought not to practise or imitate anything else; if they imitate at all, they should imitate from youth upward only those characters which are suitable to their profession—the courageous, temperate, holy, free, and the like; but they should not depict or be skillful at imitating any kind of illiberality or baseness, lest from imitation they should come to be what they imitate. Did you never observe how imitations, beginning in early youth and continuing far into life, at length grow into habits and become a second nature, affecting body, voice, and mind?

Yes, certainly, he said.

Then, I said, he will not allow those for whom we profess a care and of whom we say that they ought to be good men, to imitate a woman, whether young or old, quarrelling with her husband, or striving and vaunting against the gods in conceit of her happiness, or when she is in affliction, or sorrow, or weeping; and certainly not one who is in sickness, love, or labour.

Very right, he said.

Neither must they represent slaves, male or female, performing the offices of slaves?

They must not.

And surely not bad men, whether cowards or any others, who do the reverse of what we have just been prescribing, who scold or mock or revile one another in drink or out of drink, or who in any other manner sin against themselves and their neighbours in word or deed, as the manner of such is. Neither should they be trained to imitate the action or speech of men or women who are mad or bad; for madness, like vice, is to be known but not to be practised or imitated.

Very true, he replied.

Neither may they imitate smiths or other artificers, or oarsmen, or boatswains, or the like?

How can they, he said, when they are not allowed to apply their minds to the callings of any of these?

Nor may they imitate the neighing of horses, the bellowing of bulls, the murmur of rivers and roll of the ocean, thunder, and all that sort of thing?

Nay, he said, if madness be forbidden, neither may they copy the behaviour of madmen.

You mean, I said, if I understand you aright, that there is one sort of narrative style which may be employed by a truly good man when he has anything to say, and that another sort will be used by a man of an opposite character and education.

And which are these two sorts? he asked.

Suppose, I answered, that a just and good man in the course of a narration comes on some saying or action of another good man, —I should imagine that he will like to personate him, and will not be ashamed of this sort of imitation; he will be most ready to play the part of the good man when he is acting firmly and wisely; in a less degree when he is overtaken by illness or love or drink, or has met with any other disaster. But when he comes to a character which is unworthy of him, he will not make a study of that; he will disdain such a person, and will assume his likeness, if at all, for a moment only when he is performing some good action; at other times he will be ashamed to play a part which he has never practised, nor will he like to fashion and frame himself after the baser models; he feels the employment of such an art, unless in jest, to be beneath him, and his mind revolts at it.

So I should expect, he replied.

Then he will adopt a mode of narration such as we have illustrated out of Homer, that is to say, his style will be both imitative and narrative; but there will be very little of the former, and a great deal of the latter. Do you agree?

Certainly, he said; that is the model which such a speaker must necessarily take.

But there is another sort of character who will narrate anything, and, the worse he is, the more unscrupulous he will be; nothing will be too bad for him: and he will be ready to imitate anything, not as a joke, but in right good earnest, and before a large company. As I was just now saying, he will attempt to represent the roll of thunder, the noise of wind and hail, or the creaking of wheels, and pulleys, and the various sounds of flutes, pipes, trumpets, and all sorts of instruments: he will bark like a dog, bleat like a sheep, or crow like a cock; his entire art will consist in imitation of voice and gesture, and there will be very little narration.

That, he said, will be his mode of speaking.

These, then, are the two kinds of style?

Yes.

And you would agree with me in saying that one of them is simple and has but slight changes; and if the harmony and rhythm are also chosen for their simplicity, the result is that the speaker, if he speaks correctly, is always pretty much the same in style, and he will keep within the limits of a single harmony (for the changes are not great), and in like manner he will make use of nearly the same rhythm?

That is quite true, he said.

Whereas the other requires all sorts of harmonies and all sorts of rhythms, if the music and the style are to correspond, because the style has all sorts of changes.

That is also perfectly true, he replied.

And do not the two styles, or the mixture of the two, comprehend all poetry, and every form of expression in words? No one can say anything except in one or other of them or in both together.

They include all, he said.

And shall we receive into our State all the three styles, or one only of the two unmixed styles? or would you include the mixed?

I should prefer only to admit the pure imitator of virtue.

Yes, I said, Adeimantus; but the mixed style is also very charming: and indeed the pantomimic, which is the opposite of the one chosen by you, is the most popular style with children and their attendants, and with the world in general.

I do not deny it.

But I suppose you would argue that such a style is unsuitable to our State, in which human nature is not twofold or manifold, for one man plays one part only?

Yes; quite unsuitable.

And this is the reason why in our State, and in our State only, we shall find a shoemaker to be a shoemaker and not a pilot also, and a husbandman to be a husbandman and not a dicast also, and a soldier a soldier and not a trader also, and the same throughout?

True, he said.

And therefore when any one of these pantomimic gentlemen, who are so clever that they can imitate anything, comes to us, and makes a proposal to exhibit himself and his poetry, we will fall down and worship him as a sweet and holy and wonderful being; but we must also inform him that in our State such as he

are not permitted to exist; the law will not allow them. And so
when we have anointed him with myrrh, and set a garland of
wool upon his head, we shall send him away to another city. For
we mean to employ for our souls' health the rougher and severer
poet or story-teller, who will imitate the style of the virtuous
only, and will follow those models which we prescribed at first
when we began the education of our soldiers.

We certainly will, he said, if we have the power.[9]

2. *Turning now to music in its narrower sense (viz., song and
melody), Socrates proposes to restrict the "harmonies" or tunes
and scales to those which would be, he holds, conducive to behavior consistent with the best interests of the ideal state. The
so-called Lydian, Mixed Lydian, and Ionian harmonies would be,
for various reasons, eliminated as unfitting, leaving the warlike
Dorian and the sober Phrygian harmonies. Throughout his discussion Socrates' (or Plato's) main concern is that the future
guardians receive the kind of aesthetical education, or cultivation
of feelings and perceptions, which will instill in them a sense of
harmony, proportion, and gracefulness, providing thereby an
appropriate basis for later intellectual education. Socrates, who
speaks first in the following passage, is now interrogating Glaucon,
another of Plato's brothers who participates in the discussion.*

Then now, my friend, I said, that part of music or literary
education which relates to the story or myth may be considered to be finished; for the matter and manner have both been
discussed.

I think so too, he said.

Next in order will follow melody and song.

That is obvious.

Every one can see already what we ought to say about them, if
we are to be consistent with ourselves.

I fear, said Glaucon, laughing, that the word 'every one' hardly
includes me, for I cannot at the moment say what they should be;
though I may guess.

At any rate you can tell that a song or ode has three parts—the
words, the melody, and the rhythm; that degree of knowledge I
may presuppose?[10]

Yes, he said; so much as that you may.

And as for the words, there will surely be no difference between words which are and which are not set to music; both will conform to the same laws, and these have been already determined by us?

Yes.

And the melody and rhythm will depend upon the words?

Certainly.

We were saying, when we spoke of subject-matter, that we had no need of lamentations and strains of sorrow?

True.

And which are the harmonies expressive of sorrow? You are musical, and can tell me.

The harmonies which you mean are the mixed or tenor Lydian, and the full-toned or bass Lydian, and such like.

These then, I said, must be banished; even to women who have a character to maintain they are of no use, and much less to men.

Certainly.

In the next place, drunkenness and softness and indolence are utterly unbecoming the character of our guardians.

Utterly unbecoming.

And which are the soft or drinking harmonies?

The Ionian, he replied, and the Lydian; they are termed 'relaxed.'

Well, and are these of any military use?

Quite the reverse, he replied; and if so the Dorian and the Phrygian are the only ones which you have left.

I answered: Of the harmonies I know nothing, but I want to have one warlike, to sound the note or accent which a brave man utters in the hour of danger and stern resolve, or when his cause is failing, and he is going to wounds or death or is overtaken by some other evil, and at every such crisis meets the blows of fortune with firm step and a determination to endure; and another to be used by him in times of peace and freedom of action, when there is no pressure of necessity, and he is seeking to persuade God by prayer, or man by instruction and admonition, or on the other hand, when he is expressing his willingness to yield to persuasion or entreaty or admonition, and which represents him when by prudent conduct he has attained his end, not carried away by his success, but acting moderately and wisely under the circumstances, and acquiescing in the event. These two harmonies I ask you to leave; the strain of necessity and the strain of freedom, the strain of the unfortunate and the strain of the fortunate, the strain of courage, and the strain of temperance; these, I say, leave.

And these, he replied, are the Dorian and Phrygian harmonies of which I was just now speaking.

Then, I said, if these and these only are to be used in our songs and melodies, we shall not want multiplicity of notes or a pan-harmonic scale?

I suppose not.

Then we shall not maintain the artificers of lyres with three corners and complex scales, or the makers of any other many-stringed curiously harmonised instruments?

Certainly not.

But what do you say to flute-makers and flute-players? Would you admit them into our State when you reflect that in this composite use of harmony the flute is worse than all the stringed instruments put together; even the panharmonic music is only an imitation of the flute?

Clearly not.

There remains then only the lyre and the harp for use in the city, and the shepherds may have a pipe in the country.

That is surely the conclusion to be drawn from the argument.

The preferring of Apollo and his instruments to Marsyas and his instruments is not at all strange, I said.

Not at all, he replied.

And so, by the dog of Egypt, we have been unconsciously purging the State, which not long ago we termed luxurious.

And we have done wisely, he replied.

Then let us now finish the purgation, I said. Next in order to harmonies, rhythms will naturally follow, and they should be subject to the same rules, for we ought not to seek our complex systems of metre, or metres of every kind, but rather to discover what rhythms are the expressions of a courageous and harmonious life; and when we have found them, we shall adapt the foot and the melody to words having a like spirit, not the words to the foot and melody. To say what these rhythms are will be your duty—you must teach me them, as you have already taught me the harmonies.

But, indeed, he replied, I cannot tell you. I only know that there are some three principles of rhythm out of which metrical systems are framed, just as in sounds there are four notes[11] out of which all the harmonies are composed; that is an observation which I have made. But of what sort of lives there are severally the imitations I am unable to say....

But there is no difficulty in seeing that grace or the absence of grace is an effect of good or bad rhythm.

None at all.

And also that good and bad rhythm naturally assimilate to a good and bad style; and that harmony and discord in like manner follow style; for our principle is that rhythm and harmony are regulated by the words, and not the words by them.

Just so, he said, they should follow the words.

And will not the words and the character of the style depend on the temper of the soul?

Yes.

And everything else on the style?

Yes.

Then beauty of style and harmony and grace and good rhythm depend on simplicity—I mean the true simplicity of a rightly and nobly ordered mind and character, not that other simplicity which is only an euphemism for folly?

Very true, he replied.

And if our youth are to do their work in life, must they not make these graces and harmonies their perpetual aim?

They must.

And surely the art of the painter and every other creative and constructive art are full of them,—weaving, embroidery, architecture, and every kind of manufacture; also nature, animal and vegetable,—in all of them there is grace or the absence of grace. And ugliness and discord and inharmonious motion are nearly allied to ill words and ill nature, as grace and harmony are the twin sisters of goodness and virtue and bear their likeness.

That is quite true, he said.

But shall our superintendence go no further, and are the poets only to be required by us to express the image of the good in their works, on pain, if they do anything else, of expulsion from our State? Or is the same control to be extended to other artists, and are they also to be prohibited from exhibiting the opposite forms of vice and intemperance and meanness and indecency in sculpture and building and the other creative arts; and is he who cannot conform to this rule of ours to be prevented from practising his art in our State, lest the taste of our citizens be corrupted by him? We would not have our guardians grow up amid images of moral deformity, as in some noxious pasture, and there browse and feed upon many a baneful herb and flower day by day, little by little, until they silently gather a festering mass of corruption in their own soul. Let our artists rather be those who are gifted to discern the true nature of the beautiful and graceful; then will our youth dwell in a land of health, amid fair sights and sounds, and receive the good in everything; and beauty, the effluence of fair works, shall flow into the eye and ear, like a health-giving breeze from a purer region, and insensibly draw the soul from earliest years into likeness and sympathy with the beauty of reason.

There can be no nobler training than that, he replied.

And therefore, I said, Glaucon, musical training is a more potent instrument than any other, because rhythm and harmony find their way into the inward places of the soul, on which they mightily fasten, imparting grace, and making the soul of him who is rightly educated graceful, or of him who is ill-educated ungraceful; and also because he who has received this true education of the inner being will most shrewdly perceive omissions or faults in art and nature, and with a true taste, while he praises and rejoices over and receives into his soul the good, and becomes noble and good, he will justly blame and hate the bad, now in the days of his youth, even before he is able to know the reason why; and when reason comes he will recognise and salute the friend with whom his education has made him long familiar.[12]

3. *Toward the end of his* Republic, *having completed the exposition of his ideal city-state, in which justice will prevail, Plato returns to the discussion of imitative art. Here he has Socrates set forth his view that the artist who imitates objects is inferior both to the craftsman who makes objects according to his conceptions of their forms or archetypes, and to God or the Idea of the Good, the source of their forms. Presupposed throughout this discussion is Plato's metaphysical view that particular sensible things are not true realities but only appearances or copies of universal, eternal realities, the divine Ideas or Forms. Since the artist presents in his work a copy of what is itself a copy, he is far removed from truth and reality. The speakers, as before, are first Socrates, then Glaucon.*

Can you tell me what imitation[13] is? for I really do not know.
A likely thing, then, that I should know.

Why not? for the duller eye may often see a thing sooner than
the keener.

Very true, he said; but in your presence, even if I had any faint
notion, I could not muster courage to utter it. Will you enquire
yourself?

Well then, shall we begin the enquiry in our usual manner:
Whenever a number of individuals have a common name, we
assume them to have also a corresponding idea or form:—do you
understand me?[14]

I do.

Let us take any common instance; there are beds and tables in
the world—plenty of them, are there not?

Yes.

But there are only two ideas or forms of them—one the idea of
a bed, the other of a table.

True.

And the maker of either of them makes a bed or he makes a
table for our use, in accordance with the idea—that is our way of
speaking in this and similar instances—but no artificer makes the
ideas themselves: how could he?

Impossible.

And there is another artist,—I should like to know what you
would say of him.

Who is he?

One who is the maker of all the works of all other workmen.

What an extraordinary man!

Wait a little, and there will be more reason for your saying so.
For this is he who is able to make not only vessels of every kind,
but plants and animals, himself and all other things—the earth and
heaven, and the things which are in heaven or under the earth; he
makes the gods also.

He must be a wizard and no mistake.

Oh, you are incredulous, are you? Do you mean that there is no
such maker or creator, or that in one sense there might be a maker
of all these things but in another not? Do you see that there is a
way in which you could make them all yourself?

What way?

An easy way enough; or rather, there are many ways in which
the feat might be quickly and easily accomplished, none quicker

than that of turning a mirror round and round—you would soon enough make the sun and the heavens, and the earth and yourself, and other animals and plants, and all the other things of which we were just now speaking, in the mirror.

Yes, he said; but they would be appearance only.

Very good, I said, you are coming to the point now. And the painter too is, as I conceive, just another—a creator of appearances, is he not?

Of course.

But then I suppose you will say that what he creates is untrue. and yet there is a sense in which the painter also creates a bed?

Yes, he said, but not a real bed.

And what of the maker of the bed? were you not saying that he too makes, not the idea which, according to our view, is the essence of the bed, but only a particular bed?

Yes, I did.

Then if he does not make that which exists he cannot make true existence, but only some semblance of existence; and if any one were to say that the work of the maker of the bed, or of any other workman, has real existence, he could hardly be supposed to be speaking the truth.

At any rate, he replied, philosophers would say that he was not speaking the truth.

No wonder, then, that his work too is an indistinct expression of truth.

No wonder.

Suppose now that by the light of the examples just offered we enquire who this imitator is?

If you please.

Well then, here are three beds: one existing in nature, which is made by God, as I think that we may say—for no one else can be the maker?

No.

There is another which is the work of the carpenter?

Yes.

And the work of the painter is a third?

Yes.

Beds, then, are of three kinds, and there are three artists who superintend them: God, the maker of the bed, and the painter?

Yes, there are three of them.

God, whether from choice or from necessity, made one bed in

nature and one only; two or more such ideal beds neither ever have been nor ever will be made by God.

Why is that?

Because even if He had made but two, a third would still appear behind them which both of them would have for the idea, and that would be the ideal bed and not the two others.

Very true, he said.

God knew this, and He desired to be the real maker of a real bed, not a particular maker of a particular bed, and therefore He created a bed which is essentially and by nature one only.

So we believe.

Shall we, then, speak of Him as the natural author or maker of the bed?

Yes, he replied; inasmuch as by the natural process of creation He is the author of this and of all other things.

And what shall we say of the carpenter—is not he also the maker of the bed?

Yes.

But would you call the painter a creator and maker?

Certainly not.

Yet if he is not the maker, what is he in relation to the bed?

I think, he said, that we may fairly designate him as the imitator of that which the others make.

Good, I said; then you call him who is third in the descent from nature an imitator?

Certainly, he said.

And the tragic poet is an imitator, and therefore, like all other imitators, he is thrice removed from the King and from the truth?

That appears to be so.[15] ...

4. *The imitative arts, then, according to Plato, give us copies of copies, fleeting images, rather than substantial realities, and the practitioner of these arts, whether painter, tragedian, or epic poet is at best a deceiver and at worst a charlatan. In any event, such an artist does not know the difference between knowledge and ignorance, Plato claims, otherwise he would seek to make actual things (if indeed he could do so) rather than to fabricate copies of them. When we strip off the delightful manner in which these imitations are presented, as in Homer's poetry, for example, we soon discover their lack of substance. Moreover, the imitative*

artist is invariably somewhat of a rabble rouser, for he appeals to the irrational part of men's souls, arousing their passions and appetites by emotional appeals rather than inculcating self-control by strengthening reason, as a wise man, a philosopher, would do. In light of all these accusations that can be substantiated against imitative artists, particularly against Homer, Socrates feels compelled to banish them from his envisaged city-state, and to limit those poets who are allowed to remain primarily to writing works in which the gods are praised and the virtues of heroes extolled. Knowing full well the pleasure poetry brings, Socrates regrets having to curtail it so drastically, and he would be willing to reopen its case should anyone be able to convince him that he has misjudged its moral utility; but at present justice is far dearer to him than pleasure, and he must side with philosophy in its ancient quarrel with poetry. The discussion between Socrates, who speaks first here, and Glaucon continues.

Thus far then we are pretty well agreed that the imitator has no knowledge worth mentioning of what he imitates. Imitation is only a kind of play or sport, and the tragic poets, whether they write in Iambic or in Heroic verse, are imitators in the highest degree?

Very true.

And now tell me, I conjure you, has not imitation been shown by us to be concerned with that which is thrice removed from the truth?

Certainly.

And what is the faculty in man to which imitation is addressed?

What do you mean?

I will explain: The body which is large when seen near, appears small when seen at a distance?

True.

And the same object appears straight when looked at out of the water, and crooked when in the water; and the concave becomes convex, owing to the illusion about colours to which the sight is liable. Thus every sort of confusion is revealed within us; and this is that weakness of the human mind on which the art of conjuring and of deceiving by light and shadow and other ingenious devices imposes, having an effect upon us like magic.[16]

True.

And the arts of measuring and numbering and weighing come to the rescue of the human understanding—there is the beauty of them—and the apparent greater or less, or more or heavier, no longer have the mastery over us, but give way before calculation and measure and weight?

Most true.

And this, surely, must be the work of the calculating and rational principle in the soul?[17]

To be sure.

And when this principle measures and certifies that some things are equal, or that some are greater or less than others, there occurs an apparent contradiction?

True.

But were we not saying that such a contradiction is impossible —the same faculty cannot have contrary opinions at the same time about the same thing?

Very true.

Then that part of the soul which has an opinion contrary to measure is not the same with that which has an opinion in accordance with measure?

True.

And the better part of the soul is likely to be that which trusts to measure and calculation?

Certainly.

And that which is opposed to them is one of the inferior principles of the soul?

No doubt.

This was the conclusion at which I was seeking to arrive when I said that painting or drawing, and imitation in general, when doing their own proper work, are far removed from truth, and the companions and friends and associates of a principle within us which is equally removed from reason, and that they have no true or healthy aim.

Exactly.

The imitative art is an inferior who marries an inferior, and has inferior offspring.

Very true.

And is this confined to the sight only, or does it extend to the hearing also, relating in fact to what we term poetry?

Probably the same would be true of poetry.

Do not rely, I said, on a probability derived from the analogy of painting; but let us examine further and see whether the faculty with which poetical imitation is concerned is good or bad.

By all means.

We may state the question thus:—Imitation imitates the actions of men, whether voluntary or involuntary, on which, as they imagine, a good or bad result has ensued, and they rejoice or sorrow accordingly. Is there anything more?

No, there is nothing else.

But in all this variety of circumstances is the man at unity with himself—or rather, as in the instance of sight there was confusion and opposition in his opinions about the same things, so here also is there not strife and inconsistency in his life? Though I need hardly raise the question again, for I remember that all this has been already admitted; and the soul has been acknowledged by us to be full of these and ten thousand similar oppositions occurring at the same moment?

And we were right, he said.

Yes, I said, thus far we were right; but there was an omission which must now be supplied.

Were we not saying that a good man, who has the misfortune to lose his son or anything else which is most dear to him, will bear the loss with more equanimity than another.

Yes.

But will he have no sorrow, or shall we say that although he cannot help sorrowing, he will moderate his sorrow?

The latter, he said, is the truer statement.

Tell me: will he be more likely to struggle and hold out against his sorrow when he is seen by his equals, or when he is alone?

It will make a great difference whether he is seen or not

When he is by himself he will not mind saying or doing many things which he would be ashamed of any one hearing or seeing him do?

True.

There is a principle of law and reason in him which bids him resist, as well as a feeling of his misfortune which is forcing him to indulge his sorrow?

True.

But when a man is drawn in two opposite directions, to and from the same object, this, as we affirm, necessarily implies two distinct principles in him?

Certainly.

One of them is ready to follow the guidance of the law?

How do you mean?

The law would say that to be patient under suffering is best, and that we should not give way to impatience, as there is no knowing whether such things are good or evil; and nothing is gained by impatience; also, because no human thing is of serious importance, and grief stands in the way of that which at the moment is most required.

What is most required? he asked.

That we should take counsel about what has happened, and when the dice have been thrown order our affairs in the way which reason deems best; not, like children who have had a fall, keeping hold of the part struck and wasting time in setting up a howl, but always accustoming the soul forthwith to apply a remedy, raising up that which is sickly and fallen, banishing the cry of sorrow by the healing art.

Yes, he said, that is the true way of meeting the attacks of fortune.

Yes, I said; and the higher principle is ready to follow this suggestion of reason?

Clearly.

And the other principle, which inclines us to recollection of our troubles and to lamentation, and can never have enough of them, we may call irrational, useless, and cowardly?

Indeed, we may.

And does not the latter—I mean the rebellious principle— furnish a great variety of materials for imitation? Whereas the wise and calm temperament, being always nearly equable, is not easy to imitate or to appreciate when imitated, especially at a public festival when a promiscuous crowd is assembled in a theatre. For the feeling represented is one to which they are strangers.

Then the imitative poet who aims at being popular is not by nature made, nor is his art intended, to please or to affect the rational principle in the soul; but he will prefer the passionate and fitful temper, which is easily imitated?

Clearly.

And now we may fairly take him and place him by the side of the painter, for he is like him in two ways: first, inasmuch as his creations have an inferior degree of truth—in this, I say, he is like him; and he is also like him in being concerned with an inferior part of the soul; and therefore we shall be right in refusing to admit him into a well-ordered State, because he awakens and nourishes and strengthens the feelings and impairs the reason. As in a city when the evil are permitted to have authority and the good are put out of the way, so in the soul of man, as we maintain, the imitative poet implants an evil constitution, for he indulges the irrational nature which has no discernment of greater and less, but thinks the same thing at one time great and at another small—he is a manufacturer of images and is very far removed from the truth.

Exactly.

But we have not yet brought forward the heaviest count in our accusation:—the power which poetry has of harming even the good (and there are very few who are not harmed), is surely an awful thing?

Yes, certainly, if the effect is what you say.

Hear and judge: The best of us, as I conceive, when we listen to a passage of Homer, or one of the tragedians, in which he represents some pitiful hero who is drawling out his sorrows in a long oration, or weeping, and smiting his breast—the best of us, you know, delight in giving way to sympathy, and are in raptures at the excellence of the poet who stirs our feelings most.

Yes, of course I know.

But when any sorrow of our own happens to us, then you may observe that we pride ourselves on the opposite quality—we would fain be quiet and patient; this is the manly part, and the other which delighted us in the recitation is now deemed to be the part of a woman.

Very true, he said. . . .

And the same may be said of lust and anger and all the other affections, of desire and pain and pleasure, which are held to be inseparable from every action—in all of them poetry feeds and waters the passions instead of drying them up; she lets them rule, although they ought to be controlled, if mankind are ever to increase in happiness and virtue.

I cannot deny it.

Therefore, Glaucon, I said, whenever you meet with any of the eulogists of Homer declaring that he has been the educator of Hellas, and that he is profitable for education and for the ordering of human things, and that you should take him up again and again and get to know him and regulate your whole life according to him, we may love and honour those who say these things—they are excellent people, as far as their lights extend; and we are ready to acknowledge that Homer is the greatest of poets and first of tragedy writers; but we must remain firm in our conviction that hymns to the gods and praises of famous men are the only poetry which ought to be admitted into our State. For if you go beyond this and allow the honeyed muse to enter, either in epic or lyric verse, not law and the reason of mankind, which by common consent have ever been deemed best, but pleasure and pain will be the rulers in our State.

That is most true, he said.

And now since we have reverted to the subject of poetry, let this our defence serve to show the reasonableness of our former judgment in sending away out of our State an art having the tendencies which we have described; for reason constrained us. But that she may not impute to us any harshness or want of politeness, let us tell her that there is an ancient quarrel between philosophy and poetry.... Notwithstanding this, let us assure our sweet friend and the sister arts of imitation, that if she will only prove her title to exist in a well-ordered State we shall be delighted to receive her—we are very conscious of her charms; but we may not on that account betray the truth.[18] I dare say, Glaucon, that you are as much charmed by her as I am, especially when she appears in Homer?

Yes, indeed, I am greatly charmed.

Shall I propose, then, that she be allowed to return from exile, but upon this condition only—that she make a defence of herself in lyrical or some other metre?

Certainly.

And we may further grant to those of her defenders who are lovers of poetry and yet not poets the permission to speak in prose on her behalf: let them show not only that she is pleasant but also useful to States and to human life, and we will listen in a kindly spirit; for if this can be proved we shall surely be the gainers—I mean, if there is a use in poetry as well as a delight?

Certainly, he said, we shall be the gainers.

If her defense fails, then, my dear friend, like other persons who are enamoured of something, but put a restraint upon themselves when they think their desires are opposed to their interests, so too must we after the manner of lovers give her up, though not without a struggle. We too are inspired by that love of poetry which the education of noble States has implanted in us, and therefore we would have her appear at her best and truest; but so long as she is unable to make good her defence, this argument of ours shall be a charm to us, which we will repeat to ourselves while we listen to her strains; that we may not fall away into the childish love of her which captivates the many. At all events we are well aware that poetry being such as we have described is not to be regarded seriously as attaining to the truth; and he who listens to her, fearing for the safety of the city which is within him, should be on his guard against her seductions and make our words his law.[19] ...

5. *If Plato's treatment of art in the* Republic *seems to us narrow and even puritanical, we must remember that he considered himself to be above everything else a philosopher, a lover of wisdom, and he was convinced that the end he sought was not to be found in transitory, material things or in copies of them, but in permanent, immaterial forms. Although he expected a philosopher to appreciate the beauty and goodness he might find exemplified in individuals, he also expected him to look beyond these imperfect exemplifications to that higher realm in which Beauty and Goodness and Truth, as divine essences or archetypes, are eternal. These, and these alone, are the objects of the philosopher's passion. In Plato's dialogue the* Symposium, *Socrates and several of his friends discuss the nature of love. When Socrates' turn comes to contribute, he narrates a speech which he had supposedly heard sometime before from a prophetess, Diotima of Mantineia. The following passage, taken from the latter part of Diotima's (or Socrates') speech, is one of the most important and influential in Plato's entire dialogues. It is, in essence, Plato's aesthetic credo.*

'These are the lesser mysteries of love, into which even you, Socrates, may enter; to the greater and more hidden ones which are the crown of these, and to which, if you pursue them in a right spirit, they will lead, I know not whether you will be able to attain. But I will do my utmost to inform you, and do you follow if you can. For he who would proceed aright in this matter should begin in youth to visit beautiful forms; and first, if he be guided by his instructor aright, to love one such form only—out of that he should create fair thoughts; and soon he will of himself perceive that the beauty of one form is akin to the beauty of another; and then if beauty of form in general is his pursuit, how foolish would he be not to recognize that the beauty in every form is one and the same! And when he perceives this he will abate his violent love of the one, which he will despise and deem a small thing, and will become a lover of all beautiful forms; in the next stage he will consider that the beauty of the mind is more honourable than the beauty of the outward form. So that if a virtuous soul have but a little comeliness, he will be content to love and tend him, and will search out and bring to the birth thoughts which may improve the young, until he is compelled to contemplate and see the beauty of institutions and laws, and to understand that the beauty of them all is of one family, and that personal beauty is a trifle; and after laws and institutions he will go on to the sciences, that he may see their beauty, being not like a servant in love with the beauty of one youth or man or institution, himself a slave mean and narrow-minded, but drawing towards and contemplating the vast sea of beauty, he will create many fair and noble thoughts and notions in boundless love of wisdom; until on that shore he grows and waxes strong, and at last the vision is revealed to him of a single science, which is the science of beauty everywhere. To this I will proceed; please give me your very best attention:

'He who has been instructed thus far in the things of love, and who has learned to see the beautiful in due order and succession, when he comes towards the end will suddenly perceive a nature of wondrous beauty (and this, Socrates, is the final cause of all our former toils)—a nature which in the first place is everlasting, not growing and decaying, or waxing and waning; secondly, not fair in one point of view and foul in another, or at one time or in one relation or at one place fair, at another time or in another relation or at another place foul, as if fair to some and foul to others, or in the likeness of a face or hands or any other part of the bodily frame, or in any form of speech or knowledge, or existing in any other being, as for example, in an animal, or in heaven, or in earth, or in any other place; but beauty absolute, separate, simple, and everlasting, which without diminution and without increase, or any change, is imparted to the ever-growing and perishing beauties of all other things. He who from these ascending under the influence of true love, begins to perceive that beauty, is not far from the end. And the true order of going, or being led by another, to the things of love, is to begin from the beauties of earth and mount upwards for the sake of that other beauty, using these as steps only, and from one going on to two, and from two to all fair forms, and from fair forms to fair practices, and from fair practices to fair notions, until from fair notions he arrives at the notion of absolute beauty, and at last knows what the essence of beauty is. This, my dear Socrates,' said the stranger of Mantineia, 'is that life above all others which man should live, in the contemplation of beauty absolute; a beauty which if you once beheld, you would see not to be after the measure of gold, and garments, and fair boys and youths, whose presence now entrances you; and you and many a one would be content to live seeing them only and conversing with them without meat or drink, if that were possible—you only want to look at them and to be with them. But what if man had eyes to see the true beauty—the divine beauty, I mean, pure and clear and unalloyed, not clogged with the pollutions of mortality and all the colours and vanities of human life—thither looking, and holding converse with the true beauty simple and divine? Remember how in that communion only, beholding beauty with the eye of the mind, he will be enabled to bring forth, not images of beauty, but realities (for he has hold not of an image but of a reality), and bringing forth and nourishing true virtue to become the friend of God and be immortal, if mortal man may.[20] Would that be an ignoble life?'[21] ...

NOTES

1. Plato's trials and tribulations while in Syracuse are related in letters. See Plato's *Epistles*, translated by Glenn R. Morrow (New York, Library of Liberal Arts, Bobbs-Merrill Co., 1962).

2. Two books on Plato which discuss the contemporary relevance of his views are Robert S. Brumbaugh's *Plato for the Modern Age* (New York, Collier Books, 1964) and R. H. S. Crossman's *Plato Today* (New York, Oxford University Press, 1939). Excellent analyses of the various dialogues are contained in A. E.

Taylor's *Plato: The Man and His Work* (New York, Meridian Books, 1956).

3. See *Laws*, II, 660, 668–671; VII, 801. For a recent article on Plato's final treatment of art, see Edith W. Schipper's "Mimesis in the Arts in Plato's *Laws*," *Journal of Aesthetics and Art Criticism*, (Winter, 1963), 199–202.

4. Plato, *Ion*, 534, in *The Dialogues of Plato*, translated by Benjamin Jowett, 3rd edition (New York, Oxford University Press, 1892), Vol. I, p. 502. See also *Phaedrus*, 245.

5. For example, Allan Gilbert in "Did Plato Banish the Poets or the Critics?" (listed in our "Guide to Supplementary Reading").

6. See Plato, *Philebus*, 51.

7. Plato, *Statesman*, 284, in *The Dialogues of Plato*, translated by Benjamin Jowett, cited above, Vol. IV, p. 484.

8. Socrates had taken the position previously (in the second book of the *Republic*) that since men differ in their natural endowments or aptitudes they are suited to different occupations. The division of labor or the specialization of function is one of the fundamental principles upon which Plato founded his ideal city-state.

9. Plato, *Republic*, Bk. III, 394–398, in *The Dialogues of Plato*, translated by Benjamin Jowett, cited above, Vol. III, pp. 78–83.

10. Accounts of ancient Greek music are given in the following works: Cecil Gray, *The History of Music*, 2nd edition (London, 1931); D. B. Monro, *The Modes in Ancient Greek Music* (Oxford, 1894); R. P. Winnington-Ingram, *Mode in Ancient Greek Music* (Cambridge, 1936); and Curt Sachs, *The Rise of Music in the Ancient World* (New York, 1943).

11. As Jowett points out, Socrates refers here to the four notes of the tetrachord.

12. Plato, *Republic*, Bk. III, 398–402, in *The Dialogues of Plato*, translated by Benjamin Jowett, cited above, Vol. III, pp. 83–88.

13. In his earlier discussion of art, Plato used the word "imitation" (*mimesis*) to refer to a poetical manner or style in which the author "acts out" the various parts rather than narrates them. Henceforth, however, "imitation" will refer more generally to what the artist does when he attempts to copy the objects of sensory experience or to represent the "realities" of appearance.

14. The Idea or Form of a thing is, for Plato, the thing's essence —its universal, subsisting character. It is a metaphysical not a

mental object, and it depends neither upon human concepts nor upon the characteristics of physical things, which may copy it, for its reality.

15. Plato, *Republic*, Bk. X, 595–597, in *The Dialogues of Plato*, translated by Benjamin Jowett, cited above, Vol. III, pp. 306–310.

16. Elsewhere, in his analogy of the Divided Line (*Republic*, Bk. VI, 509–511), Plato puts imagining or conjecturing at the very lowest level of cognition as it has to do only with images in the world of sensible experience rather than with higher objects of thought.

17. According to Plato (*Republic*, Bk. IV, 434–441), the soul has three parts or elements: reason, will or the spirited element, and appetite or craving. To show the advantages of cultivating reason as the ruling principle in the individual and in the state is one of his major concerns in the *Republic* and in his other dialogues.

18. This challenge may have been taken up by Aristotle and Plotinus, both of whom gave later, as we shall see, answers to Plato's criticisms of imitative art.

19. Plato, *Republic* (Bk. X, 602–608) in *The Dialogues of Plato*, translated by Benjamin Jowett, cited above, Vol. III, pp. 316–323.

20. Plato expresses this conviction also in his famous Allegory of the Cave in the *Republic*, Bk. VII, 514–521.

21. Plato, *Symposium*, 210–212, in *The Dialogues of Plato*, translated by Benjamin Jowett, cited above, Vol. I, pp. 580–582.

QUESTIONS AND TOPICS FOR FURTHER STUDY

1. In what respects and by what means can works of art affect human beings, according to Plato? What specific proposals does he make to ensure that the effects of art will be beneficial rather than detrimental to the development of citizens of an ideal city-state?

2. What is the principle upon which Plato criticizes the indiscriminate emulation or imitation of various types of character and behavior? Why is this principle so important in Plato's view?

3. Why does Plato consider musical training to be a more powerful instrument than any other in education? Which harmonies in Greek music does he accept and reject? Why?

4. Explain why Plato holds that an imitative artist is three times removed from the truth. Why does the philosopher succeed while the artist fails in attaining truth?

5. What are the criteria according to which Plato would censor the arts? What would be the results of the application of these criteria, according to Plato?

6. Why would tragedy and comedy appeal more to the mass of men than to the wise individual, according to Plato? Do you agree with him? Why or why not?

7. Why does Plato single out Homer as his primary target in his attacks on imitative poetry? What might have been the basis for the ancient quarrel between poetry and philosophy mentioned by Socrates?

8. What arguments, if any, can you think of which could be brought forward in answer to Socrates' attacks on poetry?

9. What different kinds of beauty does Socrates refer to in the passage from the *Symposium?* According to what standards are some to be ranked higher than others?

10. Topics for further study: (a) Plato's view of artistic creation (cf. particularly the *Phaedrus*); (b) Plato's view of literary criticism (cf. the *Ion*); (c) the relationship of moral and aesthetic values in Plato's philosophy; (d) Plato as a literary artist; (e) Plato's view of beauty (cf. *Hippias Major*).

GUIDE TO SUPPLEMENTARY READING

(Works marked with asterisks are available in paperbound editions.)

I. PRIMARY SOURCES

Plato, *The Dialogues of Plato*, translated into English with analyses and introductions by Benjamin Jowett, 3rd edition, 5 volumes (New York, Oxford University Press, 1892).

————*The Republic*, translated with an introduction by H. D. P. Lee (Baltimore, Maryland, Penguin Books, Inc., 1955).

————*The Republic of Plato*, translated with introduction and notes by Francis M. Cornford (New York and London, Oxford University Press, 1945).

————*Great Dialogues of Plato*, translated by W. H. D. Rouse (New York, Mentor Books, New American Library, 1956).

II. SECONDARY WORKS

Collingwood, R. G., "Plato's Philosophy of Art" in *Essays in the Philosophy of Art*, edited with an introduction by Alan Donagan (Bloomington, Indiana University Press, 1964).

Demos, Raphael, *The Philosophy of Plato* (New York, Charles Scribner's Sons, 1939).

Gilbert, Allan H., "Did Plato Banish the Poets or the Critics?" *Studies in Philology*, XXXVI (1939), 1–19.

Gilbert, Katharine, "The Relation of the Moral to the Aesthetic Standard in Plato," in *The Philosophical Review*, XLIII (1934), 279–94.

Gilbert, Katharine, and Helmut Kuhn, *A History of Esthetics*, revised edition (Bloomington, Indiana University Press, 1953), Chap. II.

Grube, G. M. A., *Plato's Thought* (London, Methuen and Co., Ltd., 1935), Chap. VI.

Lodge, Rupert Clendon, *Plato's Theory of Art* (London, Routledge and Paul, 1953).

Nettleship, Richard Lewis, *Lectures on the Republic of Plato* (London, Macmillan and Company, 1937).

Warry, J. G., *Greek Aesthetic Theory* (New York, Barnes and Noble, 1962), Chaps. 1–4.

Wimsatt, William K., Jr., and Cleanth Brooks, *Literary Criticism: A Short History* (New York, Alfred A. Knopf, 1957), Chap. 1.

CHAPTER 2

In Defense of Art

ARISTOTLE AND PLOTINUS

Plato had prepared his brief, presented his evidence, summed up his case, and called for a verdict of "Guilty" against the imitative artist since he supposedly misrepresented reality and catered to the irrational in man. But the philosopher's strictures on poetry and his challenge for others to prove him wrong did not fail to elicit strong critical responses from his contemporaries, as it did from all later "defenders of poesy." In ancient times, two of the most convincing and influential "answers" to Plato were provided by his former pupil, Aristotle, and his later idolizer, Plotinus.[1] Aristotle is said to have based his defense of dramatic poetry on his own direct knowledge of hundreds of Greek tragedies and comedies, which he had either seen or read, and his observation of the often beneficial effects which the performance of these works had on audiences and on himself.[2] And along with the knowledge he had acquired of Greek dramatic, epic, and lyric poetry, he had developed metaphysical and psychological views which were significantly different from Plato's and according to which the nature and function of art could be reinterpreted more positively. Plotinus, for his part, viewed art, as he viewed all human phenomena, from the perspective of his own deep mystical experience of a unitary metaphysical principle, an absolute Goodness-Beauty-Truth, which he saw reflecting itself in all reality, including the creations of the imitative artist. These two great thinkers, so different in many respects, agreed that art has an important role to play in human experience: for Aristotle, it can bring pleasure and lead toward a clearer understanding of the universals in experience, and for Plotinus, it can direct our minds upward toward Ideal Perfection.[3]

ARISTOTLE

Aristotle (384–322 B.C.) was the son of a physician, the protégé of a metaphysician, and the tutor of a world conqueror.[4] Born in Stagira, Macedonia, Aristotle grew up in the Macedonian capital of Pella, where his father practiced medicine in the court of King Amyntas II, father of Philip and grandfather of Alexander of Macedonia. At the age of eighteen he went to Athens to study philosophy in Plato's Academy, remaining there for perhaps as long as twenty years, until Plato's death in 347 B.C. During this time the young genius became thoroughly imbued with Platonism, pursued independent scientific research, and began to critically evaluate his master's teachings in order to formulate a philosophy of his own. Later, he left Athens to seek knowledge elsewhere— it was during this period that he married, and served as tutor to Prince Alexander of Macedonia—but he returned twelve years later to found another Athenian school of philosophy, the Lyceum. He spent the next twelve years there, teaching, directing research, and continuing his scientific investigations. His work was disrupted in 323, however, when in the wake of Alexander the Great's death an anti-Macedonian uprising occurred in Athens. Finding himself in grave danger because of his old connections with the royal court of Macedonia, Aristotle decided to withdraw rather than allow the Athenians "to sin against philosophy a second time." A year later he died of acute indigestion at his country home in Euboea, leaving behind in his unedited writings ample evidence of his ambitious attempt to analyze all the realms of human knowledge and action and to speculate on the nature of reality as a whole. Besides his important contributions to the fields of logic, natural science, metaphysics, psychology, ethics, political science, and rhetoric, he made a lasting contribution to aesthetics in his world-famous *Poetics*.[5]

Although Aristotle was undoubtedly greatly influenced by Plato in his aesthetic views—for example, in his view that poetry is by its very nature imitative and emotion-arousing—he differs considerably from his teacher in his explanation of the nature of artistic imitation and the value of aesthetic experience. Whereas Plato had questioned the reality of works of imitative art and had cast aspersions on their value, Aristotle takes for granted their reality and proceeds to explain their nature and to justify their value. Unhampered by Plato's theory of forms, which he rejected as a useless duplication of sensible things,[6] Aristotle is able to view art objects not as copies of real things, but as things real in their own right, things which he can understand once he has grasped their essential characteristics, examined the materials out of which they are made, and reconstructed the techniques through which they have come into existence.[7] Using this empirical and inductive approach to the study of art, Aristotle re-interprets and finds reason to appreciate diverse artistic representations which his master would have condemned. For, unlike Plato, Aristotle holds that the imitative poet can express universal truths in his works and can also guide emotions to constructive rather than destructive ends.

To Aristotle, art is, first of all, a capacity to make something come into being; it is the capacity to transform the potential into the actual, the capacity to create something that otherwise would not have been. The work of art originates in its maker; it does not occur inevitably like an eclipse or grow up naturally like a mushroom. Art is the result of rational deliberation and of imaginative vision, the result of a process of fitting means to ends in order to bring into existence the thing intended by the artist.[8] And were the artist unable to conceptualize the end, envisage the work he intended to create, he would never be able to proceed to the realization of that work in material form.[9] Aristole is appreciative of the aptitude, the skill, the genius that go into the constitution of a work of art. He admires the knowledge which the artist must possess in order to create a convincing representation. The poet, in his view, must be somewhat of a philosopher in creating his works, and somewhat of a psychologist in fathoming their highest end or purpose.

Furthermore, Aristotle argues that purposive activity is inherent in all living things. It is in their very nature to strive toward the fulfillment of some end. At the human level this purposive striving, this action directed toward an end, finds its highest fulfillment in man's intelligence, the capacity which makes it possible for man to seek and to achieve ends—in ethics, politics, and art—far beyond what nature could ever achieve. This does not mean, however, that human art goes against nature; on the contrary, it means that art imitates or emulates nature in its essential purposive striving.

Art, as intelligent discriminating activity, can bring to satisfying completion, to fruition, what nature might have attempted but failed to accomplish. If nature were able to create a work of art, Aristotle holds, it would do so the way art does; and if art were able to create a natural thing, it would proceed the way nature proceeds. So if art would imitate nature, nature, given conscious intelligence, would imitate art.[10]

Turning from what Aristotle has to say about the nature of art to what he says about the nature of the beautiful, we find that although he says very little, what he does say—in the *Poetics* and in other works— is very much to the point. He conceives of the beautiful thing as having certain formal properties of order, symmetry, definiteness, and magnitude, properties which would lend themselves to mathematical measurement. A thing of beauty, to Aristotle, whether it be a work of art or a living creature, will manifest a unity in variety, an integration of parts into a harmonious whole which becomes such that from the whole nothing can be added or subtracted without spoiling its total effectiveness. Aristotle also recognizes that beauty as it is manifested in human beings is relative to the function appropriate to the body at various stages of life; in youth it would be seen as fitness for athletics, in maturity, for warfare, in old age as freedom from deformity. Thus in his aesthetics, as in his ethics, he recognizes the governing principle of the mean, the principle of measure and proportion.[11]

Aristotle's *Poetics*, from which the following selections have been taken, deals chiefly with tragedy and epic poetry. (It may have contained originally a treatment of comedy which has not come down to us.)[12] This work has undoubtedly exerted more influence, elicited more comment and criticism, and guided (or misguided) more actual production than any other work in the entire history of aesthetics and literary criticism.[13]

The Imitative Arts of Poetry and Music

1. *Aristotle undertakes in his* Poetics *to answer such questions as "What is poetry?" "What are the different kinds of poetry?" and "What constitutes a good poem, be it a tragedy or an epic?" Beginning with what he considers fundamental, he states his gen-*

*eral view that art is imitation and proceeds to explain how various
arts differ in terms of the media or means they use in imitating, the
objects which they imitate, and the ways or manner in which they
accomplish imitation. Since some artists aim at depicting the objects they imitate as either better or worse than they are in
actuality, imitation is not to be interpreted narrowly as a mere
copying or re-duplication of what already exists.*

Epic poetry and Tragedy, Comedy also and Dithyrambic
poetry,[14] and the music of the flute and of the lyre in most of their
forms, are all in their general conception modes of imitation. They
differ, however, from one another in three respects,—the medium,
the objects, the manner or mode of imitation, being in each case
distinct.

For as there are persons who, by conscious art or mere habit,
imitate and represent various objects through the medium of
colour and form, or again by the voice; so in the arts above mentioned, taken as a whole, the imitation is produced by rhythm,
language, or 'harmony,' either singly or combined.

Thus in the music of the flute and of the lyre, 'harmony' and
rhythm alone are employed; also in other arts, such as that of the
shepherd's pipe, which are essentially similar to these. In dancing,
rhythm alone is used without 'harmony'; for even dancing imitates
character, emotion, and action, by rhythmical movement.

There is another art which imitates by means of language alone,
and that either in prose or verse—which verse, again, may either
combine different metres or consist of but one kind—but this has
hitherto been without a name. . . .

There are, again, some arts which employ all the means above
mentioned,—namely, rhythm, tune, and metre. Such are Dithyrambic and Nomic poetry,[15] and also Tragedy and Comedy; but
between them the difference is, that in the first two cases these
means are all employed in combination, in the latter, now one
means is employed, now another.

Such, then, are the differences of the arts with respect to the
medium of imitation.

Since the objects of imitation are men in action, and these men
must be either of a higher or a lower type (for moral character
mainly answers to these divisions, goodness and badness being the
distinguishing marks of moral differences), it follows that we

must represent men either as better than in real life, or as worse, or as they are. It is the same in painting. Polygnotus depicted men as nobler than they are, Pauson as less noble. Dionysius drew them true to life.[16]

Now it is evident that each of the modes of imitations above mentioned will exhibit these differences, and become a distinct kind in imitating objects that are thus distinct. Such diversities may be found even in dancing, flute-playing, and lyre-playing. So again in language, whether prose or verse unaccompanied by music. Homer, for example, makes men better than they are; Cleophon as they are; Hegemon the Thasian, the inventor of parodies, and Nicochares, the author of the Deiliad, worse than they are.[17] The same thing holds good of Dithyrambs and Nomes; here too one may portray different types. . . . The same distinction marks off Tragedy from Comedy; for Comedy aims at representing men as worse, Tragedy as better than in actual life.

There is still a third difference—the manner in which each of these objects may be imitated. For the medium being the same, and the objects the same, the poet may imitate by narration—in which case he can either take another personality as Homer does, or speak in his own person, unchanged—or he may present all his characters as living and moving before us.

These, then, as we said at the beginning, are the three differences which distinguish artistic imitation,—the medium, the objects, and the manner. So that from one point of view, Sophocles is an imitator of the same kind as Homer—for both imitate higher types of character; from another point of view, of the same kind as Aristophanes—for both imitate persons acting and doing. Hence, some say, the name of 'drama' is given to such poems, as representing action.[18] . . .

2. *Aristotle now attempts to trace the imitation which is poetry back to its sources in human nature and experience. Man is an imitative animal, he believes, and gains pleasure from seeing something accurately represented even when he would not enjoy seeing that thing in real life. Add to this imitative instinct the human instinct for harmony and rhythm, for metrical language, along with the special aptitudes and individual character of artists, and one can understand, Aristotle is convinced, why poetry would originate among human beings.*

Poetry in general seems to have sprung from two causes, each of them lying deep in our nature. First, the instinct of imitation is implanted in man from childhood, one difference between him and other animals being that he is the most imitative of living creatures, and through imitation learns his earliest lessons; and no less universal is the pleasure felt in things imitated. We have evidence of this in the facts of experience. Objects which in themselves we view with pain, we delight to contemplate when reproduced with minute fidelity; such as the forms of the most ignoble animals and of dead bodies. The cause of this again is, that to learn gives the liveliest pleasure, not only to philosophers but to men in general; whose capacity, however, of learning is more limited. Thus the reason why men enjoy seeing a likeness is, that in contemplating it they find themselves learning or inferring, and saying perhaps, 'Ah, that is he.' For if you happen not to have seen the original, the pleasure will be due not to the imitation as such, but to the execution, the colouring, or some such other cause.

Imitation, then, is one instinct of our nature. Next, there is the instinct for 'harmony' and rhythm, metres being manifestly sections of rhythm. Persons, therefore, starting with this natural gift developed by degrees their special aptitudes, till their rude improvisations gave birth to Poetry.[19] . . .

3. *Aristotle's paramount concern in his* Poetics *is with the nature of tragedy; here he gives his formal definition of tragedy and explains its various parts: plot, character, diction, thought, spectacle, and song. Of these parts, plot is considered by Aristotle to be the most important, since it, unlike character, is indispensable in achieving the tragic effect of arousing and purging pity and fear.*

Tragedy, then, is an imitation of an action that is serious, complete, and of a certain magnitude; in language embellished with each kind of artistic ornament, the several kinds being found in separate parts of the play; in the form of action, not of narrative; through pity and fear effecting the proper purgation of these emotions.[20] By 'language embellished,' I mean language into which rhythm, 'harmony,' and song enter. By 'the several kinds in separate parts,' I mean, that some parts are rendered through the medium of verse alone, others again with the aid of song.

Now as tragic imitation implies persons acting, it necessarily follows, in the first place, that Spectacular equipment will be a part of Tragedy. Next, Song and Diction, for these are the medium of imitation. By 'Diction' I mean the mere metrical arrangement of the words: as for 'Song,' it is a term whose sense every one understands.

Again, Tragedy is the imitation of an action; and an action implies personal agents, who necessarily possess certain distinctive qualities both of character and thought; for it is by these that we qualify actions themselves, and these—thought and character—are the two natural causes from which actions spring, and on actions again all success or failure depends. Hence, the Plot is the imitation of the action:—for by plot I here mean the arrangement of the incidents. By Character I mean that in virtue of which we ascribe certain qualities to the agents. Thought is required wherever a statement is proved, or, it may be, a general truth enunciated. Every Tragedy, therefore, must have six parts, which determine its quality—namely, Plot, Character, Diction, Thought, Spectacle, Song.[21] Two of the parts constitute the medium of imitation, one the manner, and three the objects of imitation. And these complete the list. . . .

But most important of all is the structure of the incidents. For Tragedy is an imitation, not of men, but of an action and of life, and life consists of action, and its end is a mode of action, not a quality. Now character determines men's qualities, but it is by their actions that they are happy or the reverse. Dramatic action, therefore, is not with a view to the representation of character: character comes in as subsidiary to the actions. Hence the incidents and the plot are the end of a tragedy; and the end is the chief thing of all. Again, without action there cannot be a tragedy; there may be without character. The tragedies of most of our modern poets fail in the rendering of character; and of poets in general this is often true. It is the same in painting; and here lies the difference between Zeuxis[22] and Polygnotus. Polygnotus delineates character well: the style of Zeuxis is devoid of ethical quality. Again, if you string together a set of speeches expressive of character, and well finished in point of diction and thought, you will not produce the essential tragic effect nearly so well as with a play which, however deficient in these respects, yet has a plot and artistically constructed incidents. Besides which, the most powerful elements of emotional interest in Tragedy—Peripeteia or Reversal of the Situation, and Recognition scenes—are parts of the plot. A further proof is, that novices in the art attain to finish of diction and precision of portraiture before they can construct the plot. It is the same with almost all the early poets.

The Plot, then, is the first principle, and, as it were, the soul of a tragedy: Character holds the second place. A similar fact is seen in painting. The most beautiful colours, laid on confusedly, will not give as much pleasure as the chalk outline of a portrait. Thus Tragedy is the imitation of an action, and of the agents mainly with a view to the action.[23] ...

4. *In considering the nature of the tragic plot, Aristotle distinguishes its essential parts, its characteristic unity, and its appropriate magnitude. Of the so-called "Aristotelian unities," only one, unity of action, is held by Aristotle himself to be essential to achieving the tragic effect.*

Now, according to our definition, Tragedy is an imitation of an action that is complete, and whole, and of a certain magnitude; for there may be a whole that is wanting in magnitude. A whole is that which has a beginning, a middle, and an end. A beginning is that which does not itself follow anything by causal necessity, but after which something naturally is or comes to be. An end, on the contrary, is that which itself naturally follows some other thing, either by necessity, or as a rule, but has nothing following it. A middle is that which follows something as some other thing follows it. A well-constructed plot, therefore, must neither begin nor end at haphazard, but conform to these principles.

Again, a beautiful object, whether it be a living organism or any whole composed of parts, must not only have an orderly arrangement of parts, but must also be of a certain magnitude; for beauty depends on magnitude and order. Hence a very small animal organism cannot be beautiful; for the view of it is confused, the object being seen in an almost imperceptible moment of time. Nor, again, can one of vast size be beautiful; for as the eye cannot take it all in at once, the unity and sense of the whole is lost for the spectator; as for instance if there were one a thousand miles long. As, therefore, in the case of animate bodies and organisms a certain magnitude is necessary, and a magnitude which may be easily embraced in one view; so in the plot, a certain length is necessary, and a length which can be easily embraced by the memory. The limit of length in relation to dramatic competition and sensuous presentment, is no part of artistic theory. For had it been the rule for a hundred tragedies to compete together, the performance would have been regulated by the water-clock,—as indeed we are told was formerly done. But the limit as fixed by the nature of the drama itself is this:—the greater the length, the more beautiful will the piece be by reason of its size, provided that the whole be perspicuous. And to define the matter roughly, we may say that the proper magnitude is comprised within such limits, that the sequence of events, according to the law of probability or necessity, will admit of a change from bad fortune to good, of from good fortune to bad.

Unity of plot does not, as some persons think, consist in the unity of the hero. For infinitely various are the incidents in one man's life which cannot be reduced to unity; and so, too, there are many actions of one man out of which we cannot make one action. . . . As, therefore, in the other imitative arts, the imitation is one when the object imitated is one, so the plot, being an imitation of an action, must imitate one action and that a whole, the structural union of the parts being such that, if any one of them is displaced or removed, the whole will be disjointed and disturbed. For a thing whose presence or absence makes no visible difference, is not an organic part of the whole.[24]

5. *Aristotle brings out the true function of the poet, who is essentially the plot-maker, by a comparison of poetry and history. Whereas the poet aims at imitating credible actions which can be seen to have a universal significance, the historian is limited to recording particular events which actually occurred no matter how incredible they might seem. In constructing his plots, then, the poet should so interrelate the incidents that the outcome, even though a surprise, seems credible and probable.*

It is, moreover, evident from what has been said, that it is not the function of the poet to relate what has happened, but what may happen,—what is possible according to the law of probability or necessity. The poet and the historian differ not by writing in verse or in prose. The work of Herodotus might be put into verse, and it would still be a species of history, with metre no less than without it. The true difference is that one relates what has happened, the other what may happen. Poetry, therefore, is a more philosophical and a higher thing than history: for poetry tends to express the universal, history the particular. By the universal I mean how a person of a certain type will on occasion speak or act, according to the law of probability or necessity; and it is this universality at which poetry aims in the names she attaches to the personages. The particular is—for example—what Alcibiades did or suffered. In Comedy this is already apparent: for here the poet first constructs the plot on the lines of probability, and then inserts characteristic names;—unlike the lampooners who write about particular individuals. But tragedians still keep to real names, the reason being that what is possible is credible: what has not happened we do not at once feel sure to be possible: but what has happened is manifestly possible: otherwise it would not have happened. Still there are even some tragedies in which there are only one or two well known names, the rest being fictitious. In others, none are well known,—as in Agathon's Antheus, where incidents and names alike are fictitious, and yet they give none the less pleasure. We must not, therefore, at all costs keep to the received legends, which are the usual subjects of Tragedy. Indeed, it would be absurd to attempt it; for even subjects that are known are known only to a few, and yet give pleasure to all. It clearly follows that the poet or 'maker' should be the maker of plots rather than of verses; since he is a poet because he imitates, and what he imitates are actions. And even if he chances to take an historical subject, he is none the less a poet; for there is no reason why some events that have actually happened should not conform to the law of the probable and possible, and in virtue of that quality in them he is their poet or maker.[25] ...

6. *Aristotle now comes to the defense of poetry against those who misunderstand its nature and apply wrong standards in judging its worth. Since the poet is of necessity an imitator of actions, he certainly can err when he fails through ineptitude; however, when he makes errors of fact or presents impossibilities within his works he is not necessarily wrong in doing so. The nature of poetic truth must be understood and defended. For*

Aristotle, the total artistic effect, the overall convincing quality of the work of art is paramount; it is indeed poetry's ultimate justification.

The poet being an imitator, like a painter or any other artist, must of necessity imitate one of three objects,—things as they were or are, things as they are said or thought to be, or things as they ought to be. The vehicle of expression is language,—either current terms or, it may be, rare words or metaphors. There are also many modifications of language, which we concede to the poets. Add to this, that the standard of correctness is not the same in poetry and politics, any more than in poetry and any other art. Within the art of poetry itself there are two kinds of faults,—those which touch its essence, and those which are accidental. If a poet has chosen to imitate something, [but has imitated it incorrectly] through want of capacity, the error is inherent in the poetry. But if the failure is due to a wrong choice—if he has represented a horse as throwing out both his off legs at once, or introduced technical inaccuracies in medicine, for example, or in any other art—the error is not essential to the poetry. These are the points of view from which we should consider and answer the objections raised by the critics.

First as to matters which concern the poet's own art. If he describes the impossible, he is guilty of an error; but the error may be justified, if the end of the art be thereby attained (the end being that already mentioned),—if, that is, the effect of this or any other part of the poem is thus rendered more striking. A case in point is the pursuit of Hector. If, however, the end might have been as well, or better, attained without violating the special rules of the poetic art, the error is not justified: for every kind of error should, if possible, be avoided.

Again, does the error touch the essentials of the poetic art, or some accident of it? For example,—not to know that a hind has no horns is a less serious matter than to paint it inartistically.

Further, if it be objected that the description is not true to fact, the poet may perhaps reply,—'But the objects are as they ought to be': just as Sophocles said that he drew men as they ought to be; Euripides, as they are. In this way the objection may be met. If, however, the representation be of neither kind, the poet may answer,—'This is how men say the thing is.' This applies to tales about the gods. It may well be that these stories are not higher than fact nor yet true to fact: they are, very possibly, what Xenophanes[26] says of them. But anyhow, 'this is what is said.' Again, a description may be no better than the fact: 'still, it was the fact'; as in the passage about the arms: 'Upright upon their butt-ends stood the spears,' [27] This was the custom then, as it now is among the Illyrians.

Again, in examining whether what has been said or done by some one is poetically right or not, we must not look merely to the particular act or saying, and ask whether it is poetically good or bad. We must also consider by whom it is said or done, to whom, when, by what means, or for what end; whether, for instance, it be to secure a greater good, or avert a greater evil. . . .

In general, the impossible must be justified by reference to artistic requirements, or to the higher reality, or to received opinion. With respect to the requirements of art, a probable impossibility is to be preferred to a thing improbable and yet possible. Again, it may be impossible that there should be men such as Zeuxis painted. 'Yes,' we say, 'but the impossible is the higher thing; for the ideal type must surpass the reality.' To justify the irrational, we appeal to what is commonly said to be. In addition to which, we urge that the irrational sometimes does not violate reason; just as 'it is probable that a thing may happen contrary to probability.' [28]

7. *Like Plato, Aristotle is aware of the important role the arts can play in the education of youth and in the daily lives of citizens of a city-state. In his* Politics, *he discusses the influence which music, which is to him the most imitative of all the arts, can have in forming the character of citizens. Since he holds music to have such a wide variety of uses, Aristotle (unlike Plato) is willing to admit all the modes practiced by Greek musicians into his ideal city-state, as long as each mode is used for the purpose appropriate to it and all modes are regulated by judicious philosophers.*

But music is pursued, not only as an alleviation of past toil, but also as providing recreation. And who can say whether, having this use, it may not also have a nobler one? In addition to this common pleasure, felt and shared in by all (for the pleasure given by music is natural, and therefore adapted to all ages and characters), may it not have also some influence over the character and the soul? It must have such an influence if characters are affected by it. And that they are so affected is proved in many ways, and not least by the power which the songs of Olympus exercise; for beyond question they inspire enthusiasm, and enthusiasm is an emotion of the ethical part of the soul. Besides, when men hear imitations, even apart from the rhythms and tunes themselves, their feelings move in sympathy. Since then music is a pleasure, and virtue consists in rejoicing and loving and hating aright, there is clearly nothing which we are so much concerned to acquire and to cultivate as the power of forming right judgements, and of taking delight in good dispositions and noble actions. Rhythm and melody supply imitations of anger and gentleness, and also of courage and temperance, and of all the qualities contrary to these, and of the other qualities of character, which hardly fall short of the actual affections, as we know from our own experience, for in listening to such strains our souls undergo a change. The habit of feeling pleasure or pain at mere representations is not far removed from the same feeling about realities; for example, if any one delights in the sight of a statue for its beauty only, it necessarily follows that the sight of the original will be pleasant to him. The objects of no other sense, such as taste or touch, have any resemblance to moral qualities; in visible objects there is only a little, for there are figures which are of a moral character, but only to a slight extent, and all do not participate in the feeling about them. Again, figures and colours are not imitations, but signs, of moral habits, indications which the body gives of states of feeling. The connexion of them with morals is slight, but in so far as there is any, young men should be taught to look, not at the works of Pauson, but at those of Polygnotus, or any other painter or sculptor who expresses moral ideas. On the other hand, even in mere melodies there is an imitation of character, for the musical modes differ essentially from one another, and those who hear them are differently affected by each. Some of them make men sad and grave, like the so-called Mixolydian, others enfeeble the mind, like the relaxed modes, another, again, produces a moderate and settled temper, which appears to be the peculiar effect of the Dorian; the Phrygian inspires enthusiasm. . . . The same principles apply to rhythms; some a character of rest, others of motion, and of these latter again, some have a more vulgar, others a nobler movement. Enough has been said to show that music has a power of forming the character, and should therefore be introduced into the education of the young. The study is suited to the stage of youth, for young persons will not, if they can help, endure anything which is not sweetened by pleasure, and music has a natural sweetness. There seems to be in us a sort of affinity to musical modes and rhythms, which makes some philosophers say that the soul is a tuning, others, that it possesses tuning. . . .

We accept the division of melodies proposed by certain philosophers into ethical melodies, melodies of action, and passionate or inspiring melodies, each having, as they say, a mode corresponding to it. But we maintain further that music should be studied, not for the sake of one, but of many benefits, that is to say, with a view to (1) education, (2) purgation . . .; music may also serve (3) for intellectual enjoyment, for relaxation, and for recreation after exertion. It is clear, therefore, that all the modes must be employed by us, but not all of them in the same manner. In education the most ethical modes are to be preferred, but in listening to the performances of others we may admit the modes of action and passion also. For feelings such as pity and fear, or, again, enthusiasm, exist very strongly in some souls, and have more or less influence over all. Some persons fall into a religious frenzy, whom we see as a result of the sacred melodies—when they have used the melodies that excite the soul to mystic frenzy—restored as though they had found healing and purgation. Those who are influenced by pity or fear, and every emotional nature, must have a like experience, and others in so far as each is susceptible to such emotions, and all are in a manner purged and their souls lightened and delighted. The purgative melodies likewise give an innocent pleasure to mankind. Such are the modes and the melodies in which those who perform music at the theatre should be invited to compete. But since the spectators are of two kinds—the one free and educated, and the other a vulgar crowd composed of mechanics, labourers, and the like—there ought to be contests and exhibitions instituted for the relaxation of the second class also. And the music will correspond to their minds; for as their minds are perverted from the natural state, so there are perverted modes and highly strung and unnaturally coloured melodies. A man receives pleasure from what is natural to him, and therefore professional musicians may be allowed to practise this lower sort

of music before an audience of a lower type. But, for the purposes
of education, as I have already said, those modes and melodies
should be employed which are ethical, such as the Dorian, as we
said before; though we may include any others which are approved
by philosophers who have had a musical education.[29] . . .

PLOTINUS

The great Neoplatonist, Plotinus, (A.D. 205–270) "seemed ashamed
of being in the body"—or so his biographer, the philosopher
Porphyry, tells us.[30] Plotinus never told even his closest associates
when and where and to whom he was born; nor did he allow his
likeness to be struck, pointing out platonically that any portrait
of him would reflect not his real being but only an image of an
image. We learn from Porphyry, however, that Plotinus was born
in Egypt; that in his early twenties he developed a passion for
philosophy; that he studied with Ammonius Saccas in Alexandria;
and that after an unsuccessful attempt to get to Persia to study
Eastern philosophy, at the age of forty he settled permanently in
Rome to teach his own philosophy. From then on Plotinus lived
a quiet and ascetic existence, attracting by his inspired teaching
and personal magnetism a wide variety of followers, including
doctors, politicians, orators, critics, and poets, not to mention
philosophers. He even won the admiration of the Roman emperor
and empress. At one time it seemed likely that the emperor, whose
name was Gallienus, would assist Plotinus in establishing a utopian
community, patterned on Plato's ideals, but the plan never ma-
terialized. Although Plotinus himself later set down his own
teachings, poor vision prevented him from rereading and editing
his manuscripts once he had composed them. However, his disciple
Porphyry was chosen to edit the fifty-two treatises after his
master's death, and divided them into six parts of nine treatises
each (hence the *Enneads*). As Plotinus lay dying of diphtheria at
the age of sixty-four, his last words to his doctor were characteristic of the mystical philosophy he had lived and was dying by:
"I am striving to give back the Divine in myself to the Divine in
All."[31]

The aesthetics of Plotinus is intimately bound up with a highly complex and subtle metaphysical system which supports and is supported by a profound mysticism.[32] The major tenet of this system is that everything that is emanates or flows from a dynamic spiritual principle, an ineffable and transcendent Godhead which Plotinus calls The One. We cannot say what the One is, however, nor can we have knowledge of it, since it transcends being and knowledge, and has no form, personality, or intelligence. Yet we can be sure that were there no One, no ultimate Divine Unity, there would be no multiplicity of being, no life, intelligence, soul, or nature. The One or The Good is the Supreme Source, Plotinus believes, without which there would be nothing, nothing at all.

From the superabundance of the One, from its overflow, so to speak, the various levels of being are generated. First there is emanated the all-encompassing Divine Intellect, the realm of Platonic Forms, which provides the archetypal patterns for cosmic creation. From this is derived the Universal or World Soul, which, following the Divine patterns, forms and governs and animates the material universe. Individual souls are manifestations of the Universal Soul. Finally, at the furtherest remove from the generative perfection of the One, there is Matter—unlimited, formless, pure nonbeing—which is, according to Plotinus, the source of evil and of ugliness.[33]

These emanations represent for Plotinus the stages of the descent from the One. It is also possible, he believes, to return to the One, from whence we came; the soul can ascend to the intelligible world and ultimately be reunited with its ultimate Source. Plotinus is convinced that some men—musicians, lovers, and philosophers —are better suited than others to reach the supreme goal of reunification.[34] A musician, already sensitive to the beauty of tones and appreciative of harmony and rhythm, can be taught that it is the intelligible harmony in music, not just purely sensuous quality, which excites his admiration. And when he learns, further, to separate the material from the ideal elements in music, he is well on his way to loving and understanding the higher intelligible Beauty. As for the lover, he is readily excited by the beautiful things he perceives around him, but he must be taught to look beyond these corporeal things to the incorporeal forms which things exemplify and to the ultimate Ideal Beauty from which they are derived. Finally, the philosopher finds it even easier than the musician or the lover to ascend to the intelligible world, for it is his nature to look for the universal in the particular and to contemplate incorporeal things. Still, the philosopher also may need some guidance, as well as further mathematical and dialectical training, before he can reach the "land of the Blessed One."

Although Plotinus certainly does not denigrate the beauties that appear to the senses—they are after all copies of an ideal realm—he would have us direct our attention to the beauties that transcend the sensible world, the beauties that are to be "seen" only through an inner spiritual vision and which, when seen, will inspire in us the most exalted love imaginable. Noble conduct, justice, moral purity, righteousness, courage—these manifest to us in everyday life the spiritual qualities for which we have reverence and esteem; they are, therefore, rightly called beautiful.[35] But realization of spiritual beauty is impossible so long as we remain encrusted in alien matter, degraded and ugly. We must, then, strip away the material coils which bind us; we must discipline our desires, purify our passions; we must withdraw from the ugliness that weighs us down and ascend toward the higher realm lying within us in the very "center of our souls."[36] Until we renounce our material nature and recognize the Divine in all, we can never know and cherish the highest Beauty of all, the Divine Absolute Beauty. This intelligible Beauty is ineffable, to be sure, but it is nonetheless supremely, preeminently real and accessible to all those who learn how to reach "the beloved Fatherland." Plotinus believes he has found the Way and can direct others to it, providing they are willing and capable of undergoing the rigorous intellectual and moral discipline necessary to the task, and are inspired by an insatiable desire to reach the goal. The lovers of Intelligible Beauty, and they alone, can have a vision of the First Beauty, the One, which lies beyond Intellectual Being. And when they join the single source of all that is, their joy, he believes, will be perfect ecstasy.[37]

Beauty

1. *Plotinus begins his inquiry into the nature of beauty by point-ing to the variety of things we call beautiful and raising the question as to what, if anything, they have in common that might*

*account for this attribution. After giving reasons for rejecting
attempts to explain beauty in terms of symmetry, he suggests
that we seek a higher spiritual principle which might explain the
kinship our souls feel with certain things.*

Beauty addresses itself chiefly to sight; but there is a beauty for
the hearing too, as in certain combinations of words and in all
kinds of music, for melodies and cadences are beautiful; and minds
that lift themselves above the realm of sense to a higher order
are aware of beauty in the conduct of life, in actions, in character, in the pursuits of the intellect; and there is the beauty of
the virtues. What loftier beauty there may be, yet, our argument
will bring to light.

What, then, is it that gives comeliness to material forms and
draws the ear to the sweetness perceived in sounds, and what is
the secret of the beauty there is in all that derives from Soul?

Is there some One Principle from which all take their grace,
or is there a beauty peculiar to the embodied and another for
the bodiless? Finally, one or many, what would such a Principle be?

Consider that some things, material shapes for instance, are
gracious not by anything inherent but by something communicated, while others are lovely of themselves, as, for example, Virtue.

The same bodies appear sometimes beautiful, sometimes not; so
that there is a good deal between being body and being beautiful.

What, then, is this something that shows itself in certain material forms? This is the natural beginning of our inquiry.

What is it that attracts the eyes of those to whom a beautiful
object is presented, and calls them, lures them, towards it, and fills
them with joy at the sight? If we possess ourselves of this, we
have at once a standpoint for the wider survey.

Almost everyone declares that the symmetry of parts towards
each other and towards a whole, with, besides, a certain charm
of colour, constitutes the beauty recognized by the eye, that in
visible things, as indeed in all else, universally, the beautiful thing
is essentially symmetrical, patterned.

But think what this means.

Only a compound can be beautiful, never anything devoid of
parts; and only a whole; the several parts will have beauty, not in

themselves, but only as working together to give a comely total. Yet beauty in an aggregate demands beauty in details: it cannot be constructed out of ugliness; its law must run throughout.

All the loveliness of colour and even the light of the sun, being devoid of parts and so not beautiful by symmetry, must be ruled out of the realm of beauty. And how comes gold to be a beautiful thing? and lightning by night, and the stars, why are these so fair?

In sounds also the simple must be proscribed, though often in a whole noble composition each several tone is delicious in itself.

Again since the one face, constant in symmetry, appears sometimes fair and sometimes not, can we doubt that beauty is something more than symmetry, that symmetry itself owes its beauty to a remoter principle?

Turn to what is attractive in methods of life or in the expression of thought; are we to call in symmetry here? What symmetry is to be found in noble conduct, or excellent laws, in any form of mental pursuit?

What symmetry can there be in points of abstract thought?

The symmetry of being accordant with each other? But there may be accordance or entire identity where there is nothing but ugliness: the proposition that honesty is merely a generous artlessness chimes in the most perfect harmony with the proposition that morality means weakness of will; the accordance is complete.

Then again, all the virtues are a beauty of the Soul, a beauty authentic beyond any of these others; but how does symmetry enter here? The Soul, it is true, is not a simple unity, but still its virtue cannot have the symmetry of size or of number: what standard of measurement could preside over the compromise or the coalescence of the Soul's faculties or purposes?

Finally, how by this theory would there be beauty in the Intellectual-Principle,[38] essentially the solitary? ...

Let us, then, go back to the source, and indicate at once the Principle that bestows beauty on material things.

Undoubtedly this Principle exists; it is something that is perceived at the first glance, something which the Soul names as from an ancient knowledge, and, recognizing, welcomes it, enters into unison with it.

But let the Soul fall in with the Ugly and at once it shrinks within itself, denies the thing, turns away from it, not accordant, resenting it.

Our interpretation is that the Soul—by the very truth of its nature, by its affiliation to the noblest Existents in the hierarchy of Being—when it sees anything of that kin, or any trace of that kinship, thrills with an immediate delight, takes its own to itself, and thus stirs anew to the sense of its nature and of all its affinity.

But, is there any such likeness between the loveliness of this world and the splendours in the Supreme? Such a likeness in the particulars would make the two orders alike: but what is there in common between beauty here and beauty There? [39]

2. *Plotinus now gives his own theory of beauty. The beauty of things results from their communion in an ideal formal realm. The spiritual principle which manifests itself in a beautiful object is what gives that object its unity and coherence; the object's parts are fused together by the indivisible unity of an indwelling idea. Plotinus believes that we, as spiritual beings, possess an aesthetic faculty which perceives and appreciates beauty in those things in which the unity of the Idea is evident.*

We hold that all the loveliness of this world comes by communion in Ideal-Form.

All shapelessness whose kind admits of pattern and form, as long as it remains outside of Reason and Idea, is ugly by that very isolation from the Divine-Thought. And this is the Absolute Ugly: an ugly thing is something that has not been entirely mastered by pattern, that is by Reason, the Matter not yielding at all points and in all respects to Ideal-Form.

But where the Ideal-Form has entered, it has grouped and coordinated what from a diversity of parts was to become a unity: it has rallied confusion into co-operation: it has made the sum one harmonious coherence: for the Idea is a unity and what it moulds must come to unity as far as multiplicity may.

And on what has thus been compacted to unity, Beauty enthrones itself, giving itself to the parts as to the sum: when it lights on some natural unity, a thing of like parts, then it gives itself to that whole. Thus, for an illustration, there is the beauty, conferred by craftsmanship, of all a house with all its parts, and the beauty which some natural quality may give to a single stone.

This, then, is how the material thing becomes beautiful—by communicating in the thought (Reason, Logos) that flows from the Divine....

And the Soul includes a faculty peculiarly addressed to Beauty—one incomparably sure in the appreciation of its own, when Soul entire is enlisted to support its judgement.

Or perhaps the Soul itself acts immediately, affirming the Beautiful where it finds something accordant with the Ideal-Form within itself, using this Idea as a canon of accuracy in its decision.

But what accordance is there between the material and that which antedates all Matter?

On what principle does the architect, when he finds the house standing before him correspondent with his inner ideal of a house, pronounce it beautiful? Is it not that the house before him, the stones apart, is the inner idea stamped upon the mass of exterior matter, the indivisible exhibited in diversity?

So with the perceptive faculty: discerning in certain objects the Ideal-Form which has bound and controlled shapeless matter, opposed in nature to Idea, seeing further stamped upon the common shapes some shape excellent above the common, it gathers into unity what still remains fragmentary, catches it up and carries it within, no longer a thing of parts, and presents it to the Ideal-Principle as something concordant and congenial, a natural friend: the joy here is like that of a good man who discerns in a youth the early signs of a virtue consonant with the achieved perfection within his own soul.

The beauty of colour is also the outcome of a unification: it derives from shape, from the conquest of the darkness inherent in Matter by the pouring-in of light, the unembodied, which is a Rational-Principle and an Ideal-Form.

Hence it is that Fire itself is splendid beyond all material bodies, holding the rank of Ideal-Principle to the other elements, making ever upwards, the subtlest and sprightliest of all bodies, as very near to the unembodied; itself alone admitting no other, all the others penetrated by it: for they take warmth but this is never cold; it has colour primally; they receive the Form of colour from it: hence the spendour of its light, the splendour that belongs to the Idea. And all that has resisted and is but uncertainly held by its light remains outside of beauty, as not having absorbed the plenitude of the Form of colour.

And harmonies unheard in sound create the harmonies we hear
and wake the Soul to the consciousness of beauty, showing it the
one essence in another kind: for the measures of our sensible
music are not arbitrary but are determined by the Principle whose
labour is to dominate Matter and bring pattern into being.

Thus far of the beauties of the realm of sense, images and
shadow-pictures, fugitives that have entered into Matter—to
adorn, and to ravish, where they are seen.[40]

3. *Plotinus' ultimate aim is to direct us to the Highest Beauty
which transcends the senses, the Beauty inherent in the Divine
Intellect and, above that, in the One. This Divine Beauty is pure,
omnipotent, and primary, unlike all its derivative manifestations,
valuable though they may be. Making explicit his disagreement
with Plato's strictures on art, Plotinus points out that the artist
does not merely copy existing sensible things, but aims at giving
sensuous representation to the forms of things which he inwardly envisages.*

It is a principle with us that one who has attained to the vision
of the Intellectual Cosmos and grasped the beauty of the Authentic
Intellect will be able also to come to understand the Father and
Transcendent of that Divine Being. It concerns us, then, to try to
see and say, for ourselves and as far as such matters may be told,
how the Beauty of the divine Intellect and of the Intellectual
Cosmos may be revealed to contemplation.

Let us go to the realm of magnitudes:—suppose two blocks of
stone lying side by side: one is unpatterned, quite untouched by
art; the other has been minutely wrought by the craftsman's hands
into some statue of god or man, a Grace or a Muse, or if a human
being, not a portrait but a creation in which the sculptor's art has
concentrated all loveliness.

Now it must be seen that the stone thus brought under the
artist's hand to the beauty of form is beautiful not as stone—for so
the crude block would be as pleasant—but in virtue of the Form
or Idea introduced by the art. This form is not in the material; it
is in the designer before ever it enters the stone; and the artificer
holds it not by his equipment of eyes and hands but by his

participation in his art. The beauty, therefore, exists in a far higher state in the art; for it does not come over integrally into the work; that original beauty is not transferred; what comes over is a derivative and a minor: and even that shows itself upon the statue not integrally and with entire realization of intention but only in so far as it has subdued the resistance of the material.

Art, then, creating in the image of its own nature and content, and working by the Idea or Reason-Principle of the beautiful object it is to produce, must itself be beautiful in a far higher and purer degree since it is the seat and source of that beauty, indwelling in the art, which must naturally be more complete than any comeliness of the external. In the degree in which the beauty is diffused by entering into matter, it is so much the weaker than that concentrated in unity: everything that reaches outwards is the less for it, strength less strong, heat less hot, every power less potent, and so beauty less beautiful.

Then again every prime cause must be, within itself, more powerful than its effect can be: the musical does not derive from an unmusical source but from music; and so the art exhibited in the material work derives from an art yet higher.

Still the arts are not to be slighted on the ground that they create by imitation of natural objects; for, to begin with, these natural objects are themselves imitations; then, we must recognize that they give no bare reproduction of the thing seen but go back to the Reason-Principles from which Nature itself derives, and, furthermore, that much of their work is all their own; they are holders of beauty and add where nature is lacking. Thus Pheidias wrought the Zeus upon no model among things of sense but by apprehending what form Zeus must take if he chose to become manifest to sight.[41]

4. *Turning from the consideration of beauty in art to beauty in nature, Plotinus finds additional evidence there to support his belief that the beauty of appearance presupposes a higher essential beauty.*

But let us leave the arts and consider those works produced by Nature and admitted to be naturally beautiful which the creations of art are charged with imitating, all reasoning life and unreasoning things alike, but especially the consummate among them, where the moulder and maker has subdued the material and given the form he desired. Now what is the beauty here? It has nothing to do with the blood or the menstrual process: either there is also a colour and form apart from all this or there is nothing unless sheer ugliness or (at best) a bare recipient, as it were the mere Matter of beauty.

Whence shone forth the beauty of Helen, battle-sought; or of all those women like in loveliness to Aphrodite; or of Aphrodite herself; or of any human being that has been perfect in beauty; or of any of these gods manifest to sight, or unseen but carrying what would be beauty if we saw.

In all these is it not the Idea, something of that realm but communicated to the produced from within the producer, just as in the works of art, we held, it is communicated from the arts to their creations? Now we can surely not believe that, while the made thing and the Idea thus impressed upon Matter are beautiful, yet the Idea not so alloyed but resting still with the creator—the Idea primal, immaterial, firmly a unity—is not Beauty.

If material extension were in itself the ground of beauty, then the creating principle, being without extension, could not be beautiful: but beauty cannot be made to depend upon magnitude since, whether in a large object or a small, the one Idea equally moves and forms the mind by its inherent power. A further indication is that as long as the object remains outside us we know nothing of it; it affects us by entry; but only as an Idea can it enter through the eyes which are not of scope to take an extended mass: we are, no doubt, simultaneously possessed of the magnitude which, however, we take in not as mass but by an elaboration upon the presented form.

Then again the principle producing the beauty must be, itself, ugly, neutral, or beautiful: ugly, it could not produce the opposite; neutral, why should its product be the one rather than the other? The Nature, then, which creates things so lovely must be itself of a far earlier beauty; we, undisciplined in discernment of the inward, knowing nothing of it, run after the outer, never understanding that it is the inner which stirs us; we are in the case of one who sees his own reflection but not realizing whence it comes goes in pursuit of it.

But that the thing we are pursuing is something different and that the beauty is not in the concrete object is manifest from the beauty there is in matters of study, in conduct and custom; briefly, in soul and mind. And it is precisely here that the greater beauty lies, perceived whenever you look to the wisdom in a man and delight in it, not wasting attention on the face, which may be hideous, but passing all appearance by and catching only at the inner comeliness, the truly personal; if you are still unmoved and cannot acknowledge beauty under such conditions, then looking to your own inner being you will find no beauty to delight you and it will be futile in that state to seek the greater vision, for you will be questing it through the ugly and impure.

This is why such matters are not spoken of to everyone; you, if you are conscious of beauty within, remember....

Thus there is in the Nature-Principle itself an Ideal archetype of the beauty that is found in material forms and, of that archetype again, the still more beautiful archetype in Soul, source of that in Nature. In the proficient soul this is brighter and of more advanced loveliness: adorning the soul and bringing to it a light from that greater light which is Beauty primally, its immediate presence sets the soul reflecting upon the quality of this prior, the archetype which has no such entries, and is present nowhere but remains in itself alone, and thus is not even to be called a Reason-Principle but is the creative source of the very first Reason-Principle which is the Beauty to which Soul serves as Matter.[42] ...

5. *According to Plotinus, wisdom governs the creation of an art object just as it governs all creation. This wisdom operates as a dynamic, integrative principle which contains and coordinates all multiple elements, whether in a work of art or in an universe. Matter, Nature, the World Soul, the Divine Intellect with its archetypal forms—all of these levels of being are emanations of the self-same Source, the ineffable One, from which Beauty radiates.*

All that comes to be, work of nature or of craft, some wisdom has made: everywhere a wisdom presides at a making.

No doubt the wisdom of the artist may be the guide of the work; it is sufficient explanation of the wisdom exhibited in the arts; but the artist himself goes back, after all, to that wisdom in Nature which is embodied in himself; and this is not a wisdom built up of theorems but one totality, not a wisdom consisting of manifold detail co-ordinated into a unity but rather a unity working out into detail. . . .

Consider the universe: we are agreed that its existence and its nature come to it from beyond itself; are we, now, to imagine that its maker first thought it out in detail—the earth, and its necessary situation in the middle; water and, again, its position as lying upon the earth; all the other elements and objects up to the sky in due place and order; living beings with their appropriate forms as we know them, their inner organs and their outer limbs —and that having thus appointed every item beforehand, he then set about the execution?

Such designing was not even possible; how could the plan for a universe come to one that had never looked outward? Nor could he work on material gathered from elsewhere as our craftsmen do, using hands and tools; feet and hands are of the later order.

One way, only, remains: all things must exist in something else; of that prior—since there is no obstacle, all being continuous within the realm of reality—there has suddenly appeared a sign, an image, whether given forth directly or through the ministry of soul or of some phase of soul matters nothing for the moment: thus the entire aggregate of existence springs from the divine world, in greater beauty There because There unmingled but mingled here.

From the beginning to end all is gripped by the Forms of the Intellectual Realm: Matter itself is held by the Ideas of the elements and to these Ideas are added other Ideas and others again, so that it is hard to work down to crude Matter beneath all that sheathing of Idea. Indeed since Matter itself is, in its degree, an Idea—the lowest—all this universe is Idea and there is nothing that is not Idea as the archetype was. And all is made silently, since nothing had part in the making but Being and Idea—a further reason why creation went without toil. The Exemplar was the Idea of an All and so an All must come into being.

Thus nothing stood in the way of the Idea, and even now it dominates, despite all the clash of things: the creation is not hindered on its way even now; it stands firm in virtue of being All. To me, moreover, it seems that if we ourselves were archetypes, Ideas, veritable Being, and the Idea with which we construct here were our veritable Essence, then our creative power, too, would toillessly effect its purpose: as man now stands, he does not produce in work a true image of himself: become man, he has ceased to be the All; ceasing to be man—we read—'he soars aloft and administers the Cosmos entire';[43] restored to the All he is maker of the All.

But—to our immediate purpose—it is possible to give a reason why the earth is set in the midst and why it is round and why the ecliptic runs precisely as it does, but, looking to the creating principle, we cannot say that because this was the way therefore things were so planned: we can say only that because the Exemplar is what it is, therefore the things of this world are good; the causing principle, we might put it, reached the conclusion before all formal reasoning and not from any premises, not by sequence or plan but before either, since all of that order is later, all reason, demonstration, persuasion.

Since there is a Source, all the created must spring from it and in accordance with it; and we are rightly told not to go seeking the causes impelling a Source to produce, especially when this is the perfectly sufficient Source and identical with the Term: a Source which is Source and Term must be the All-Unity, complete in itself....

This then is Beauty primally: it is entire and omnipresent as an entirety; and therefore in none of its parts or members lacking in beauty; beautiful thus beyond denial. Certainly it cannot be anything (be, for example, Beauty) without being wholly that thing; it can be nothing which it is to possess partially or in which it utterly fails (and therefore it must entirely be Beauty entire).

If this principle were not beautiful, what other could be? Its prior does not deign to be beautiful; that which is the first to manifest itself—Form and object of vision to the intellect—cannot but be lovely to see. It is to indicate this that Plato,[44] drawing on something well within our observation, represents the Creator as approving the work he has achieved; the intention is to make us feel the lovable beauty of the archetype and of the Divine Idea; for to admire a representation is to admire the original upon which it was made.

It is not surprising if we fail to recognize what is passing within us: lovers, and those in general that admire beauty here, do not stay to reflect that it is to be traced, as of course it must be, to the Beauty There....

And indeed if the divine did not exist, the transcendantly beautiful, in a beauty beyond all thought, what could be lovelier than the things we see? Certainly no reproach can rightly be brought against this world save only that it is not That.[45] ...

NOTES

1. We cannot be sure that Aristotle and Plotinus actually intended what they said about art to be direct answers to Plato's challenge; there is no doubt, however, that they were aware of it.

2. Beneficial primarily because of the pleasurable catharsis they apparently brought about.

3. The contributions which Aristotle and Plotinus made in providing alternatives to the "copy theory" of visual art is very well discussed in Frances B. Blanshard's *Retreat from Likeness in the Theory of Painting* (New York, Columbia University Press, 1949).

4. The chief source of information about the life of Aristotle is Diogenes Laertius's brief biography in his *Lives of Eminent Philosophers* (English translation by R. D. Hicks, two volumes, Cambridge, Harvard University Press, 1925) Vol. I, Bk. V, upon which the following account is mainly based.

5. See Philip Wheelwright's *Aristotle* (New York, Odyssey Press, 1951) for well chosen and newly translated selections from seven of Aristotle's most important works—*Natural Science*, the *Metaphysics, Zoology, Psychology*, the *Nicomachean Ethics, On Statecraft*, and *The Art of Poetry* (the *Poetics*). For brief treatments of Aristotle's philosophy as a whole see A. E. Taylor's *Aristotle* (New York, Dover Publications, 1955) and G. R. G. Mure's *Aristotle* (New York, Oxford University Press, 1964). For a recent, more extensive treatment from a naturalistic viewpoint, see John Herman Randall, Jr.'s, *Aristotle* (New York, Columbia University Press, 1960). All of these works are available in paperbound editions.

6. In his *Metaphysics* (Bk. I, Chap. 9), Aristotle gives several other reasons why he found Plato's theory of forms unacceptable.

7. Aristotle believes that we can never understand anything that exists until we have grasped its reasons for being—the causes or "determining factors" which account for its existence. In his *Physics* or *Natural Science*, Bk. II, Chap. 3, he distinguishes four factors or causes which taken together will allow us, he believes, to explain the existence of things: (1) the material cause or material factor—the stuff out of which the thing is made; (2) the formal cause or formal factor—the essential or distinctive character of the thing, its organizational structure or ideal pattern; (3) the efficient cause or "propelling factor"—"the immediate source of change or of cessation from change"; and (4) the final cause or

"telic factor"—"the end or purpose for the sake of which a thing is done." (See Wheelwright, op. cit., p. 26). In making a marble statue of a god, for example, the marble is (1); the idea of the god in the sculptor's mind is (2); the sculptor is (3); and the finished statue is (4).

8. See Aristotle, *Metaphysics*, Bk. VII, Chap. 7.

9. See Aristotle, *Parts of Animals*, Bk. I.

10. See Aristotle, *Physics*, Bk. II.

11. The above account of Aristotle's conception of beauty is based on his remarks on it in the *Metaphysics*, Bk. XIII; the *Poetics*, Chap. 7; the *Nichomachean Ethics*, Bk. II; and the *Rhetoric*, Bk. I.

12. For an interesting attempt to reconstruct Aristotle's theory of comedy from the *Poetics* and from other sources, including a later Peripatetic document, the "Coislinian Tractate," see Lane Cooper's *Aristotelian Theory of Comedy* ... listed in our "Guide to Supplementary Reading." According to the "Coislinian Tractate," comedy imitates imperfect and ludicrous actions, and arouses and purges the emotions of pleasure and laughter.

13. Lane Cooper and Alfred Gudeman in their *Bibliography of the Poetics of Aristotle* (New Haven, Yale University Press, 1928) listed over 1500 items, and since then interest in the *Poetics* has by no means waned. One of the most recent and important critical commentaries, Gerald F. Else's *Aristotle's Poetics: The Argument* (Cambridge, Harvard University Press, 1957), runs to 670 pages.

14. Dithyrambs were choral hymns sung to musical accompaniment and associated originally with the worship of Dionysius, god of wine. Aristotle believed that tragedy owed its origin to the early authors of dithyrambs.

15. A Nome was a hymn written for a single voice and lyre.

16. Polygnotus, Pauson, and Dionysius were well-known painters of the fifth century B.C. Aristotle admired Polygnotus's ability to express moral ideas in painting.

17. Among these authors' works, only Homer's have survived.

18. These and the following selections from Aristotle's *Poetics* are taken from S. H. Butcher's *Aristotle's Theory of Poetry and Fine Art with a Critical Text and Translation of The Poetics*, 4th edition (London, MacMillan and Co., 1911). The preceding selections are from Chaps. I–III. Hereafter Butcher's translation in the above edition will be cited as *Poetics* (S.H.B.)

19. *Poetics* (S.H.B.), Chap. IV.

20. Aristotle's conception of the "catharsis" or purgation of the emotions of pity and fear, which comes from tragedy, has been the subject of interminable and inconclusive discussion among critics since the Renaissance. Does Aristotle use "catharsis" as a medical or as a religious metaphor, or perhaps as both? Does tragedy achieve, as Milton and later S. H. Butcher believed, a homeopathic cure of painful emotions by applying to them similar emotions? Does Aristotle mean, as W. H. Fyfe believes, that tragedy provides "a good clearance," "an emotional aperient"; or, as Humphry House interprets him, that tragedy exercises and directs our emotions toward proper moral ends; or, as J. G. Warry interprets him, that the effect of tragedy is to sublimate and ameliorate emotion through hypnotic influence? These are only a few of the questions and possible answers evoked by Aristotle's use of the word "catharsis." Unfortunately, Aristotle himself never explained the term fully anywhere in his works, although he seems to have intended to do so. He does, however, refer to the cathartic effect of music in the *Politics*, Book VIII, Chaps. 5–7, portions of which conclude the present selections, and he discusses pity and fear in the *Rhetoric*, Book II, Chaps. 5 and 8. These passages are the crucial primary aids to the study of his view of the tragic catharsis so briefly mentioned in the *Poetics*. But practically every one of the secondary works listed under "Aristotle" in our "Guide to Supplementary Reading" contains some discussion of "catharsis."

21. These parts are discussed in further detail in other sections of the *Poetics* not included in the present selections.

22. Zeuxis was a famous Greek painter of the late fifth and early fourth century. He was noted for his ability to achieve extremely realistic effects in his painting.

23. *Poetics* (S.H.B.), Chap. VI.

24. *Poetics* (S.H.B.), Chaps. VII–VIII.

25. *Poetics* (S.H.B.), Chap. IX.

26. Xenophanes, sixth-century Greek philosopher and poet, believed that no man can know the truth about the gods and criticized the Greeks' anthropomorphic conceptions of deity.

27. Homer, *Iliad*, X, 152.

28. *Poetics* (S.H.B.), Chap. XXV. Aristotle is quoting Agathon, a fifth-century tragedian, who is mentioned several times in the *Poetics*. The same Agathon appears in Plato's *Symposium*.

29. The preceding selections are taken from Aristotle's *Politica*, translated by Benjamin Jowett, revised edition (Oxford, Clarendon Press, 1921), Bk. VIII, Chaps. 5 and 7.

30. Porphyry's "Life of Plotinus," on which the following account is based, is included in Stephen MacKenna's translation of the *Enneads* (New York, Pantheon Books, 1962).

31. Porphyry, "One the Life of Plotinus...," *Enneads*, Chap. 2 (MacKenna translation, op. cit.).

32. Beauty and art are discussed primarily in the First Ennead, Sixth Tractate ("Beauty") and in the Fifth Ennead, Eighth Tractate ("On the Intellectual Beauty") from which our selections in this chapter are taken. Although these two tractates are not contained in Jerome Katz's *Philosophy of Plotinus* (New York, Appleton-Century-Crofts, 1950), Katz's book, containing new translations of twelve representative tractates as well as an excellent introduction, should be useful to the student undertaking for the first time a study of Plotinus' system. (It is available in a paperbound edition.)

33. Plotinus discusses the nature of matter in the Second Ennead, Fourth Tractate.

34. Plotinus discusses these three types of men in the First Ennead, Third Tractate ("Dialectic"), Chaps. 1–3, upon which the rest of this paragraph is based.

35. See the Fifth Ennead, Sixth Tractate, Chap. 6.

36. On the ugly soul, see the First Ennead, Sixth Tractate, Chap. 5. Plotinus' conception of the "soul-center," a highly influential conception in the later history of mystical thought, is discussed in the Sixth Ennead, Ninth Tractate, Chap. 8.

37. Plotinus' discussion of the ascent of the soul from material to spiritual beauty is strongly influenced by Socrates' speech on love and beauty in Plato's *Symposium*, with which our selections from Plato concluded. Porphyry claims that it was through meditating on and following the methods suggested in Plato's dialogue that Plotinus himself was able to ascend to God. See Porphyry's "Life of Plotinus," Chap. 23.

38. The Intellectual-Principle is the Divine Mind, Intellect, or Thought, which emanates from the One.

39. I.e., between earthly and Divine or Intelligible Beauty. These and the following selections are taken from *Plotinus: The Enneads* translated by Stephen MacKenna, 3rd edition revised by B. S. Page

(New York, Pantheon Books, 1962). The preceding selections are from the First Ennead, Sixth Tractate, Chaps. 1–2 (pp. 56–57). Citations henceforth will run: *Enneads*, (MacKenna translation).

40. *Enneads* (MacKenna translation), First Ennead, Sixth Tractate, Chaps. 2–3 (pp. 57–59).

41. *Enneads* (MacKenna translation), Fifth Ennead, Eighth Tractate, Chap. 1 (pp. 422–423).

42. *Enneads* (MacKenna translation), Fifth Ennead, Eighth Tractate, Chaps. 2–3 (pp. 423–424).

43. Plato, *Phaedrus*, 246c.

44. Plato, *Timaeus*, 37c.

45. *Enneads* (MacKenna translation), Fifth Ennead, Eighth Tractate, Chaps. 5, 7–8 (p. 426, pp 427–429).

QUESTIONS AND TOPICS FOR
FURTHER STUDY

1. Explain how Aristotle differentiates the various imitative arts. What is the origin of imitative art, according to him?

2. Give Aristotle's definition of tragedy. Which of its elements is most important in his view? Why? Do you agree with him on this point? Why or why not?

3. What are the characteristics of a beautiful object, according to Aristotle? How can we determine whether or not a work of art possesses unity, in his view?

4. Explain why Aristotle considers poetry to be "a more philosophical and higher thing than history." What would be his answer to Plato's strictures on imitative art?

5. Compare Aristotle's and Plato's views of the role of music in the life of citizens in an ideal city-state.

6. Why does Plotinus reject symmetry as the basic principle for explaining the nature of beauty?

7. What is the common basis of all beautiful things, according

to Plotinus? How does he explain our ability to perceive beauty? How does an ugly thing differ from one that is beautiful, in his view?

8. What is Plotinus' view of the value of works of imitative art? How do you account for his differences from Plato in his evaluation?

9. Does Plotinus rank the beauty of nature or the beauty of art higher? What considerations lead him to this view?

10. Topics for further study: (a) Aristotle's theory of comedy; (b) Aristotle's doctrine of catharsis; (c) Aristotle's views on epic poetry; (d) the relationship of aesthetic and moral values in the philosophy of Plotinus; (e) Plotinus' influence on Byzantine art.

GUIDE TO SUPPLEMENTARY READING

(Works marked with asterisks are available in paperbound editions.)

ARISTOTLE

I. PRIMARY SOURCES

Aristotle, *Aristotle's Theory of Poetry and Fine Art, with a critical text and translation of The Poetics, by S. H. Butcher, with a prefatory essay, Aristotelian Literary Criticism, by John Gassner, 4th edition (New York, Dover Publications, 1951).

———The Poetics of Aristotle, translated by Ingram Bywater (Oxford, Oxford University Press, 1920).

———Aristotle's Art of Poetry, with introduction and explanations by W. Hamilton Fyfe (Oxford, The Clarendon Press, 1940).

———*Aristotle's Poetics; Translation and Analysis, by Kenneth A. Telford (Chicago, Henry Regnery Co., 1961).

II. SECONDARY WORKS

Bosanquet, Bernard, *A History of Aesthetic (New York, Meridian Books, 1957), Chapter IV, pp. 56–76.

Cooper, Lane, An Aristotelian Theory of Comedy, with an Adaptation of the Poetics and a Translation of the Tractatus Coislinianas (New York, Harcourt, Brace, 1922).

———The Poetics of Aristotle: Its Meaning and Influence (New York, Longmans, Green, 1927).

Gilbert, Allan H., "The Aristotelian Catharsis," The Philosophical Review, XXXV (1926), 301–314.

Gilbert, Katharine E., "Aesthetic Imitation and Imitators in Aristotle," The Philosophical Review, XLV (1936), 558–573.

Gilbert, Katharine E., and Helmut Kuhn, A History of Esthetics (Bloomington, Indiana University Press, 1953), Chapter III.

House, Humphry, Aristotle's Poetics, revised with a preface by Colin Hardie (London, Rupert Hart-Davis, 1956).

Ingarden, Roman, "A Marginal Commentary on Aristotle's Poetics," Journal of Aesthetics and Art Criticism, XX (Winter, 1961), 163–173; (Spring, 1962), 273–285.

Lucas, F. L., Tragedy in Relation to Aristotle's Poetics (London, Hogarth Press, 1949).

McKeon, Richard, "Literary Criticism and the Concept of Imitation in Antiquity," Modern Philology, XXXIV (1936), 1–35.

Olson, Elder, *Aristotle's Poetics and English Literature (Chicago and London, University of Chicago Press, 1965).

Ross, W. D., *Aristotle, 5th edition, revised (London, Methuen and Company, 1949), Chap. IX.

Warry, J. G., Greek Aesthetic Theory; A Study of Callistic and Aesthetic Concepts in the Works of Plato and Aristotle (New York, Barnes and Noble, 1962), Chaps. V–VIII.

Wilson, Robert N., "Aristotle and Modern Literature," JAAC, XV (September, 1956), 74–84.

Wimsatt, William K., Jr., and Cleanth Brooks, Literary Criticism: A Short History (New York, Alfred A. Knopf, 1957), Chaps. 2 and 3.

PLOTINUS

I. PRIMARY SOURCES

Plotinus, *The Enneads*, translated by Stephen MacKenna and B. S. Page, 3rd edition (London, Faber and Faber, 1962).

——*The Essential Plotinus: Representative Treatises from The Enneads*, selected and translated with introduction and commentary by Elmer O'Brien, S.J. (New York, Mentor Books, New American Library, 1964).

——*The Essence of Plotinus*, edited by Grace H. Turnbull (New York, Oxford University Press, 1934).

II. SECONDARY WORKS

Anton, John P., "Plotinus' Refutation of Beauty as Symmetry," *JAAC*, XXIII (Winter, 1964), 233–237.

Inge, W. R., *The Philosophy of Plotinus*, 3rd edition, two volumes (London, New York and Toronto, Longmans Green and Company, 1948).

Michelis, P. A., "Neo-Platonic Philosophy and Byzantine Art," *JAAC*, XI (September, 1952), 21–45.

Pistorius, Philippus V., *Plotinus and Neoplatonism, An Introductory Study* (Cambridge, Bowes & Bowes, 1952), Chap. VII.

Whittaker, T., *The Neoplatonists*, 2nd edition (Cambridge, Cambridge University Press, 1918).

Wimsatt, William K., Jr., and Cleanth Brooks, *Literary Criticism: A Short History* (New York, Alfred A. Knopf, 1957), Chap. 7.

CHAPTER 3

Explorations of the Aesthetic Field

BURKE AND LESSING

While there may still be disagreement among historians of aesthetics as to whether modern aesthetics actually began in England with the Earl of Shaftesbury's Neo-Platonic rhapsodizing on ideal beauty, goodness, and truth, or in Italy with Giambattista Vico's "New Science," which elevated poetical imagination to the same level of significance as scientific intellect, or in Germany with Alexander Baumgarten's attempt to understand how sensuous knowledge could be brought to perfection, the historians seem to be in agreement that, in any event, modern aesthetics began in the eighteenth century, the "Age of Criticism" and the "Age of Enlightenment."[1] For this was also the age of aesthetic exploration.

In England, early in the century, Joseph Addison was exploring in the *Spectator* (1712) "the pleasures of the imagination" as they arise from our perception of "what is great, uncommon, or beautiful." Later, William Hogarth, painter and engraver, in his *Analysis of Beauty* (1753), claimed that he had discovered in the serpentine line "the line of beauty," and that he could now explain how certain principles—"fitness, variety, uniformity, simplicity, intricacy, and quantity"—cooperate in producing beauty. A few years later (1757), Edmund Burke opened up a new aesthetic realm, the sublime, to rational consideration.[2] And Sir Joshua Reynolds, the great portrait painter and the president of the Royal Academy, delivered from 1769 to 1790 a series of lucid *Discourses on Art* so that students could have the benefits of his long and arduous explorations of the aesthetic field in attempting to create ideal beauty. Throughout the century, other English

90

thinkers pursued inquiries into the origin of our ideas of beauty, the basis of our standards of taste, the fundamental principles of art and literary criticism, and the nature of artistic genius.[3]

Nor were French thinkers any less active than English in launching out on aesthetic explorations. Early in the century, Abbé Dubos, through his *Critical Reflections on Painting and Sculpture* (1719), explored the immediate sensory effects of works of art and brought into currency lively discussions of "les Beaux-Arts" or Fine Arts. Père André, inspired like Shaftesbury by Neo-Platonism, in his *Essay on Beauty* (1741), claimed he had discovered a new and useful way of classifying the types of beauty which would bring order to standards of taste by clearly distinguishing between Divine or essential, natural, and artificial beauty. Abbé Batteau, the author of *The Fine Arts Reduced to One Principle* (1746), believed he had found the unifying principle among the arts in the principle of imitation of nature, and proceeded to classify arts according to whether they deal primarily with space or time. Later, Denis Diderot, the greatest of the French Encyclopedists and one of the most brilliant critics of the century, tried to explain aesthetic phenomena on strictly empirical grounds, without resorting to *a priori* conceptions or ideal types.[4] The philosophy of the Enlightenment was being brought to bear on aesthetic, as well as on social, political, and moral issues.

Finally, the Germans, who had lagged behind the English and the French in their attention to aesthetic exploration during the first half of the century, made up for lost time during the latter half. For, in that amazingly productive period from 1750 to 1790, Alexander Baumgarten published the first treatise on Aesthetics, giving a name to the whole field; J. J. Winckelmann,[5] inspired with a passion for Greek sculpture, wrote the first real history of art, initiating a new discipline; G. E. Lessing freed German authors from the shackles of French Neo-Classical ideals through his critical works and plays, making possible the new forms of literary creativity pursued by Herder, Schiller, and Goethe; and, in 1790, Immanuel Kant crowned four decades of German aesthetic exploration with his *Critique of Judgment*, the greatest contribution to aesthetic enlightenment of the entire century.

From the wide variety of explorations of the aesthetic field prior to Kant, Edmund Burke and G. E. Lessing have been chosen as representative of some of the aesthetic and critical problems under consideration during this pioneering period in the history of modern aesthetics.

BURKE

Long before he won fame as a brilliant orator and political thinker, Edmund Burke (1729–1797) was known for his contribution to aesthetic theory. Burke was born in Dublin, where he attended a Quaker school and Trinity College before going on to London in 1750 in order to study law. Although he allowed his literary and social activities to interfere with his legal studies, his early years in London were not unproductive. Before he was thirty, he had three published works to his credit, the *Vindication of Natural Society* (1756), which was a satirical work written in the manner of Bolingbroke, *Account of the European Settlements in America*, a revision of a work written previously by William Burke, and *A Philosophical Enquiry into the Origins of Our Ideas of the Sublime and the Beautiful* (1757), the work which first brought him fame as an author at home and abroad.[6] Not long afterwards, however, Burke's interests turned from literature back to law, and his energies were increasingly absorbed in politics. The rest of his illustrious career—his effort to conciliate the American colonies, his role in the impeachment proceedings against Warren Hastings, and his grave concern over the repercussions of the French Revolution—has little if any real bearing on the aesthetic theory which he formulated in his youth and never saw reason to change.

Throughout his *Philosophical Enquiry into the Origins of Our Ideas of the Sublime and the Beautiful* Burke follows what he considers to be a completely empirical method. His conclusions, he promises, will be drawn "from a diligent examination of our passions in our own breasts; from a careful survey of the properties of things which we find by experience to influence these passions; and from a sober and attentive investigation of the laws of nature, by which those properties are capable of affecting the body, and thus of exciting our passions."[7] He is undertaking, he reminds us, not a complete study of the sublime and the beautiful in all their ramifications into the fine arts, but is limiting his inquiry primarily to the origin of these ideas in sensation, convinced as he is that "when we go but one step beyond the immediate sensible qualities of things, we go out of our depth."[8] Following in the British empirical tradition of Bacon, Hobbes, and Locke, Burke aims at building up a theory based on sensation and induction, analyzing the complex entity into its simple ingredients, cautiously but confidently reading "the characters of nature," and learning first "to crawl before attempting to fly."

Burke's main purpose in his *Enquiry* is to discover valid principles of taste, principles which are common to all men and which can be applied in making aesthetic judgments. Taste is, in his view, "that faculty or those faculties of the mind which are affected with, or form a judgment of, the works of imagination and the elegant arts."[9] Despite the diversity of tastes, which seems on the surface to give support to the wide-spread belief that there is no arguing about tastes, Burke is convinced that sound principles which should govern taste can be discovered, and that anarchy in aesthetic matters can be shown to be unjustifiable. In arguing against the unlicensed relativity of tastes, he begins with a consideration of the role that the three "natural powers"—the senses, the imagination, and the judgment—play in human experience. Since all normal human beings have the same sense organs, which reveal to them the same appearances of objects, by our very nature, Burke argues, there is a common basis at least for the similarity, if not for the identity of tastes. Everyone would agree, he believes, that honey is sweet and vinegar, sour, and that the taste of one is naturally pleasant while the taste of the other is unpleasant, even though habit and acquired taste might cause a man to come to prefer a bitter to a sweet taste. At the fundamental level of essential human nature, then, there *is* a real disputing about tastes. "I believe no man thinks a goose to be more beautiful than a swan," Burke says, "or imagines that what they call a Friezland hen excels a peacock."[10] The level at which there is no real disputing, however, is the level at which habits, prejudices, and social conditions have molded various preferences in various individuals.

Nor does Burke find extreme relativism in matters of taste any more justified essentially at the level of imagination. Imagination is, for him, the creative power the mind evidences "either in representing at pleasure the images of things in the order and manner in which they were received by the senses, or in combining those images in a new manner, and according to a different order."[11] Depending on the senses for its material and consequently unable to produce anything "absolutely new," the imagination finds pleasing or displeasing the very images which initially pleased or displeased sense; therefore, we should not be surprised to find a basis for agreement, a common principle, in the realm of imagination, just as we found one in the realm of sense. Whatever differences exist are differences not in kind but in degree, Burke holds, and these differences arise "either from a greater degree of natural sensibility, or from a closer and longer attention to the object."[12] Two men may agree that several marble tables are highly polished, but may not be able to agree as to which one is the most highly polished. In this case, Burke points out, there would be no common measure to which they could appeal; there is in fact a qualitative difference which only the expert, in this case a marble polisher, can judge with competence.

Finally, with reference to judgment, the reliability of this mental power in matters of taste will depend, Burke thinks, upon the degree of experience, refinement, attention, and knowledge possessed by the individual judging. Burke concludes his discussion of taste in the Introduction to his *Enquiry* by asserting that taste "is not a simple idea, but is partly made up of a perception of the primary pleasures of sense, of the secondary pleasures of the imagination, and of the conclusions of the reasoning faculty, concerning the various relations of these, and concerning the human passions, manners, and actions."[13] He believes that all of these factors contribute to the formation of taste, and that their common basis lies in the human mind, which derives its ideas, as well as its pleasures, through the senses.

In the first three parts of his *Enquiry*, from which our selections are taken, Burke presents the major tenets of his aesthetic theory. In the fourth part, he speculates on how the immediate sensible qualities of objects actually evoke in us the "delightful horror" which is the feeling of the sublime and the blissful delight which is the feeling of the beautiful.[14] His explanation, in brief, is that those sensible qualities which tend to cause a contraction or a tension of our nerve fibers to a degree short of pain evoke in us the feeling of the sublime, whereas those qualities which relax and soothe our nerve fibers evoke the sense of beauty. Objects which we call sublime—those which are vast or rugged, massive, gloomy, etc.—bring pleasure because they arouse and exercise the "finer parts" of our organic system by causing our nerve fibers to contract and to strain. Objects which are called beautiful—those which are small, smooth, clear, light, delicate, etc.—bring pleasure because they relax and tranquilize our nervous system.

Although today Burke's efforts to explain sublimity and beauty in such simple physiological terms might seem to us far too simple, he was charting a course which others a century later would follow in reaching more fully elaborated physiological and experimental approaches to aesthetics. Apart from the insights and speculations it contains, which may still be of interest to the student of aesthetics, and apart from its importance as a highly influential treatise in the history of aesthetics, Burke's *Enquiry* remains significant as an early attempt at which Fechner called "aesthetics from below."[15]

The Origin of Our Ideas of the Sublime and the Beautiful

1. *Burke's explanation of the psychological basis of our ideas of the beautiful and the sublime may first be stated synoptically.*

The passions which belong to self-preservation, turn on pain and danger; they are simply painful when their causes immediately affect us; they are delightful when we have an idea of pain and danger, without being actually in such circumstances; this delight I have not called pleasure, because it turns on pain, and because it is different enough from any idea of positive pleasure. Whatever excites this delight, I call *sublime*. The passions belonging to self-preservation are the strongest of all the passions.

The second head to which the passions are referred, with relation to their final cause, is society. There are two sorts of societies. The first is the society of sex. The passion belonging to this is called love, and it contains a mixture of lust; its object is the beauty of women. The other is the great society with man and all other animals. The passion subservient to this is called likewise love, but it has no mixture of lust, and its object is beauty; which is a name I shall apply to all such qualities in things as induce in us a sense of affection and tenderness, or some other passion the most nearly resembling these. The passion of love has its rise in positive pleasure; it is, like all things which grow out of pleasure, capable of being mixed with a mode of uneasiness, that is, when an idea of its object is excited in the mind, with an idea at the same time of having irretrievably lost it. This mixed sense of pleasure I have not called *pain*, because it turns upon actual pleasure, and because it is, both in its cause and in most of its effects, of a nature altogether different.

Next to the general passion we have for society, to a choice in which we are directed by the pleasure we have in the object, the particular passion under this head, called sympathy, has the greatest extent. The nature of this passion is, to put us in the place of another in whatever circumstance he is in, and to affect us in a like manner; so that this passion may, as the occasion requires, turn either on pain or pleasure.[16] . . .

2. *Burke thinks that the social passion of sympathy plays an important role in accounting for the pleasures we derive from works of art, particularly from those in which suffering is depicted, for example, in tragedy, as well as from the observation of the misfortunes of others in real life. Tragedy pleases, Burke holds, not because it is a mere imitation or because we feel safe from misfortune while pleasurably witnessing it; tragedy pleases because in arousing pity and fear it satisfies to some extent—though not as completely and powerfully as real life situations might—our sympathetic nature.*

It is a common observation, that objects, which in reality would shock, are in tragical, and such like representations, the source of a very high species of pleasure. This, taken as a fact, has been the cause of much reasoning. The satisfaction has been commonly attributed, first to the comfort we receive in considering that so melancholy a story is no more than a fiction; and next, to the contemplation of our own freedom from the evils which we see represented. I am afraid it is a practice much too common in inquiries of this nature, to attribute the cause of feelings which merely arise from the mechanical structure of our bodies, or from the natural frame and constitution of our minds, to certain conclusions of the reasoning faculty on the objects presented to us; for I should imagine, that the influence of reason in producing our passions is nothing near so extensive as it is commonly believed. . . .

To examine this point concerning the effect of Tragedy in a proper manner, we must previously consider how we are affected by the feelings of our fellow-creatures in circumstances of real distress. I am convinced we have a degree of delight, and that no small one, in the real misfortunes and pains of others: for let the affection be what it will in appearance, if it does not make us shun such objects, if on the contrary it induces us to approach them, if it makes us dwell upon them, in this case I conceive we must have a delight or pleasure of some species or other in contemplating objects of this kind. Do we not read the authentic histories of scenes of this nature with as much pleasure as romances or poems, where the incidents are fictitious? . . . Our delight, in cases of this kind, is very greatly heightened, if the sufferer be some excellent person who sinks under an unworthy fortune. Scipio and Cato are both virtuous characters; but we are more deeply affected by the violent death of the one, and the ruin of the great cause he adhered to, than with the deserved triumphs and uninterrupted prosperity of the other; for terror is a passion which always produces delight when it does not press too close; and pity is a passion accompanied with pleasure, because it arises from love and social affection. . . . If this passion was simply painful, we would shun with the greatest care all persons and places that could excite such a passion; as some, who are so far gone in indolence as not to endure any strong impression, actually do. But the case is widely different with the greater part of mankind; there is no spectacle we so eagerly pursue as that of some uncommon and grievous calamity; so that whether the misfortune is before our eyes, or whether they are turned back to it in history, it always touches with delight. This is not an unmixed delight, but blended with no small uneasiness. The delight we have in such things hinders us from shunning scenes of misery; and the pain we feel prompts us to relieve ourselves in relieving those who suffer; and all this antecedent to any reasoning, by an instinct that works us to its own purposes without our concurrence. . . .

It is thus in real calamities. In imitated distresses, the only difference is the pleasure resulting from the effects of imitation: for it is never so perfect but we perceive it is an imitation, and on that principle are somewhat pleased with it. And indeed in some cases we derive as much or more pleasure from that source than from the thing itself. But then, I imagine, we shall be much mistaken if we attribute any considerable part of our satisfaction in tragedy in the consideration that tragedy is a deceit, and its representations no realities. The nearer it approaches the reality, and the further it removes us from all idea of fiction, the more perfect is its power. But be its power of what kind it will, it never approaches to what it represents. Choose a day on which to represent the most sublime and affecting tragedy we have; appoint the most favourite actors; spare no cost upon the scenes and decorations; unite the greatest efforts of poetry, painting, and music; and when you have collected your audience, just at the moment when their minds are erect with expectation, let it be reported that a state criminal of high rank is on the point of being executed in the adjoining square; in a moment the emptiness of the theatre would demonstrate the comparative weakness of the imitative arts, and proclaim the triumph of the real sympathy. I believe that this notion of our having a simple pain in the reality, yet a delight in the representation, arises from hence, that we do not sufficiently distinguish what we should be eager enough to see if it was once done. We delight in seeing things, which so far from doing, our heartiest wishes would be to see redressed. . . .

Nor is it, either in real or fictitious distresses, our immunity from them which produces our delight; in my own mind I can discover nothing like it. I apprehend that this mistake is owing to a sort of sophism, by which we are frequently imposed upon; it arises from our not distinguishing between what is indeed a necessary condition to our doing or suffering any thing in general, and what is the *cause* of some particular act. If a man kills me with a sword, it is a necessary condition to this that we should have been both of us alive before the fact; and yet it would be absurd to say, that our being both living creatures was the cause of his crime and of my death. So it is certain, that it is absolutely necessary my life should be out of any imminent hazard before I can take a delight in the sufferings of others, real or imaginary, or indeed in any thing else, from any cause whatsoever. But then it is a sophism to argue from thence, that this immunity is the cause of my delight either on these or any occasions. No one can

distinguish such a cause of satisfaction in his own mind I believe;
nay, when we do not suffer any very acute pain, nor are exposed
to any imminent danger of our lives, we can feel for others,
whilst we suffer ourselves; and often then most when we are
softened by affliction; we see with pity even distresses which we
would accept in the place of our own.[17]

*3. Having dealt with sympathy and its role in aesthetic expe-
rience, Burke turns to the two other social passions, imitation and
ambition, explaining how each of these contributes its share in
producing aesthetic satisfaction. In discussing imitation, Burke
sets forth a rule by means of which, he believes, one can ascertain
whether sympathy or imitation is paramount in the appreciation
of a given work of art.*

The second passion belonging to society is imitation, or, if you
will, a desire of imitating, and consequently a pleasure in it. This
passion arises from much the same cause with sympathy; for, as
sympathy makes us take a concern in whatever men feel, so this
affection prompts us to copy whatever they do; and consequently
we have a pleasure in imitating, and in whatever belongs to
imitation merely as it is such, without any intervention of the
reasoning faculty, but solely from our natural constitution, which
Providence has framed in such a manner as to find either pleasure
or delight, according to the nature of the object, in whatever
regards the purposes of our being. . . . Herein it is that painting,
and many other agreeable arts, have laid one of the principal
foundations of their power. And since, by its influence on our
manners and our passions, it is of such great consequence, I shall
here venture to lay down a rule, which may inform us, with a
good degree of certainty, when we are to attribute the power of
the arts to imitation, or to our pleasure in the skill of the imitator
merely, and when to sympathy, or some other cause in conjunction with it. When the object represented in poetry or painting
is such as we could have no desire of seeing in the reality, then
I may be sure that its power in poetry or painting is owing to the
power of imitation, and to no cause operating in the thing itself.
So it is with most of the pieces which the painter call still-life.
In these a cottage, a dunghill, the meanest and most ordinary

utensils of the kitchen, are capable of giving us pleasure. But when the object of the painting or poem is such as we should run to see if real, let it affect us with what odd sort of sense it will, we may rely upon it, that the power of the poem or picture is more owing to the nature of the thing itself, than to the mere effect of imitation, or to a consideration of the skill of the imitator, however excellent. . . .

Although imitation is one of the great instruments used by Providence in bringing our nature towards its perfection, yet if men gave themselves up to imitation entirely, and each followed the other, and so on in an eternal circle, it is easy to see that there never could be any improvement amongst them. . . . To prevent this, God has planted in man a sense of ambition, and a satisfaction arising from the contemplation of his excelling his fellows in something deemed valuable amongst them. . . . Now, whatever, either on good or upon bad grounds tends to raise a man in his own opinion, produces a sort of swelling and triumph that is extremely grateful to the human mind; and this swelling is never more perceived, nor operates with more force, than when without danger we are conversant with terrible objects, the mind always claiming to itself some part of the dignity and importance of the things which it contemplates. Hence proceeds what Longinus has observed of that glorying and sense of inward greatness, that always fills the reader of such passages in poets and orators as are sublime; it is what every man must have felt in himself upon such occasions.[18]

4. *Burke now proceeds to analyze the causes and effects of the sublime in nature. The effects, ranging from astonishment to respect, may be produced, he believes, by a variety of causes including: obscurity, power, privation, and greatness or smallness of dimension.*

The passion caused by the great and sublime in *nature,* when those causes operate most powerfully, is astonishment; and astonishment is that state of the soul in which all its motions are suspended with some degree of horror. In this case the mind is so entirely filled with its object, that it cannot entertain any other, nor by consequence reason on that object which employs it. Hence arises the great power of the sublime, that, far from being produced by them, it anticipates our reasonings, and hurries us on by an irresistible force. Astonishment, as I have said, is the effect of the sublime in its highest degree; the inferior effects are admiration, reverence and respect. . . .

No passion so effectually robs the mind of all its powers of acting and reasoning as fear; for fear being an apprehension of pain or death, it operates in a manner that resembles actual pain. Whatever therefore is terrible, with regard to sight, is sublime too, whether this cause of terror, be endued with greatness of dimensions or not; for it is impossible to look on any thing as trifling or contemptible that may be dangerous. . . .

To make any thing very terrible, obscurity seems in general to be necessary. When we know the full extent of any danger, when we can accustom our eyes to it, a great deal of the apprehension vanishes. . . .

It is one thing to make an idea clear, and another to make it *affecting* to the imagination. . . . In reality, a great clearness helps but little towards affecting the passions, as it is in some sort an enemy to all enthusiasms whatever. . . .

So that poetry, with all its obscurity, has a more general as well as a more powerful dominion over the passions than the other art [i.e., painting]. And I think there are reasons in nature, why the obscure idea, when properly conveyed, should be more affecting than the clear. It is our ignorance of things that causes all our admiration, and chiefly excites our passions. Knowledge and acquaintance makes the most striking causes affect but little. . . .

Besides those things which *directly* suggest the idea of danger, and those which produce a similar effect from a mechanical cause, I know of nothing sublime which is not some modification of power. And this branch rises, as naturally as the other two branches, from terror, the common stock of every thing that is sublime. . . .

All *general* privations are great, because they are all terrible; *Vacuity, Darkness, Solitude,* and *Silence.* . . .

Greatness of dimension is a powerful cause of the sublime. This is too evident, and the observation too common, to need any illustration; it is not so common to consider in what ways greatness of dimension, vastness of extent, or quantity, has the most striking effect: for certainly these are ways and modes wherein the same quantity of extension shall produce greater effects than it is found to do in others. Extension is either in length, height, or depth. Of these the length strikes least; and hundred yards of even ground will never work such an effect as a tower an hundred yards high, or a rock or mountain of that altitude. I am apt to imagine likewise, that height is less grand than depth; and that we are more struck at looking down from a precipice, than at looking up at an object of equal height: but of that I am not very positive. A perpendicular has more force in forming the sublime, than an inclined plane; and the effects of a rugged and broken surface seem stronger than where it is smooth and polished. It would carry us out of our way to enter in this place into the cause of these appearances; but certain it is they afford a large and fruitful field of speculation. However, it may not be amiss to add to these remarks upon magnitude, that as the great extreme of dimension is sublime, so the last extreme of littleness is in some measure sublime likewise; when we attend to the infinite divisibility of matter, when we pursue animal life into these excessively small, and yet organized beings, that escape the nicest inquisition of the sense; when we push our discoveries yet downward, and consider those creatures so many degrees yet smaller, and the still diminishing scale of existence, in tracing which the imagination is lost as well as the sense, we become amazed and confounded at the wonders of minuteness; nor can we distinguish in its effect this extreme of littleness from the vast itself; for division must be infinite, as well as addition; because the idea of a perfect unity can no more be arrived at than that of a complete whole to which nothing may be added.[19]

5. *Continuing his survey of the causes of sublimity, Burke discusses infinity, difficulty, magnificence, and light, all of which, under certain circumstances, can produce the emotional effects characteristic of the sublime. (Burke also believes that colors, sounds, and even smells and tastes can sometimes be capable of conveying sublimity.)*

Another source of the sublime is *Infinity*; if it does not rather belong to the last. Infinity has a tendency to fill the mind with that sort of delightful horror which is the most genuine effect, and truest test of the sublime. There are scarce any things which can become the objects of our senses, that are really and in their own nature infinite; but the eye not being able to perceive the bounds of many things, they seem to be infinite, and they produce the same effects as if they were really so. We are deceived in the like manner, if the parts of some large object are so continued to any indefinite number, that the imagination meets no check which may hinder its extending them at pleasure. . . .

Infinity, though of another kind, causes much of our pleasure in agreeable, as well as of delight in sublime images. The spring is the pleasantest of the seasons; and the young of most animals, though far from being completely fashioned, afford a more agreeable sensation than the full grown, because the imagination is entertained with the promise of something more, and does not acquiesce in the present object of the sense. In unfinished sketches of drawing, I have often seen some things which pleased me beyond the best finishing; and this, I believe, proceeds from the cause I have just assigned. . . .

Another source of greatness is *Difficulty*. When any work seems to have required immense force and labour to effect it, the idea is grand. . . .

Magnificence is likewise a source of the sublime. A great profusion of things, which are splendid or valuable in themselves, is *magnificent*. The starry heaven, though it occurs so very frequently to our view, never fails to excite an idea of grandeur. This cannot be owing to any thing in the stars themselves, separately considered. The number is certainly the cause. The apparent disorder augments the grandeur; for the appearance of care is highly contrary to our ideas of magnificence. Besides, the stars lie in such apparent confusion as makes it impossible, on ordinary occasions, to reckon them. This gives them the advantage of a sort of infinity. In works of art, this kind of grandeur, which consists in multitude, is to be very cautiously admitted; because, a profusion of excellent things is not to be attained, or with too much difficulty; and because in many cases this splendid confusion would destroy all use, which should be attended to, in most of the works of art, with the greatest care; besides, it is to be considered, that unless you can produce an appearance of infinity by your disorder, you will have disorder only, without magnificence. . . .

With regard to light, to make it a cause capable of producing the sublime, it must be attended with some circumstances besides its bare faculty of showing other objects. Mere light is too common a thing to make a strong impression on the mind; and without a strong impression nothing can be sublime. But such a light as that of the sun, immediately exerted on the eye, as it overpowers the sense, is a very great idea. Light of an inferior strength to this, if it moves with great celerity, has the same power; for lightning is certainly productive of grandeur, which it owes chiefly to the extreme velocity of its motion. A quick transition from light to darkness, or from darkness to light, has yet a greater effect. But darkness is more productive of sublime ideas than light. . . .

Having thus run through the causes of the sublime with reference to all the senses, my first observation . . . will be found very nearly true; that the sublime is an idea belonging to self-preservation; that it is therefore one of the most affecting we have; that its strongest emotion is an emotion of distress; and that no pleasure from a positive cause belongs to it.[20] . . .

6. *Turning now from the sublime to the beautiful, Burke begins by distinguishing the love aroused by beauty from the desire which aims at possessing, not merely contemplating, its object. He then proceeds to characterize the beautiful object in terms of seven sensible qualities. Finally, in concluding his discussion of the beautiful, Burke asserts that although in some cases the qualities characteristic of the beautiful and the sublime may seem to coalesce, beauty and sublimity are nonetheless basically different kinds of aesthetic experience.*

It is my design to consider beauty as distinguished from the sublime; and in the course of the enquiry, to examine how far it is consistent with it. . . . By beauty, I mean that quality, or those qualities in bodies by which they cause love, or some passion similar to it. I confine this definition to the merely sensible qualities of things, for the sake of preserving the utmost simplicity in a subject which must always distract us, whenever we take in those various causes of sympathy which attach us to any persons or things from secondary considerations, and not from the direct force which they have merely on being viewed. I likewise distinguish love, by which I mean that satisfaction which arises to the mind upon contemplating any thing beautiful, or whatsoever nature it may be, from desire or lust, which is an energy of the mind that hurries us on to the possession of certain objects that do not affect us as they are beautiful, but by means altogether different. . . .

Beauty hath usually been said to consist in certain proportions of parts. On considering the matter, I have great reason to doubt whether beauty be at all an idea belonging to proportion. Proportion relates almost wholly to convenience, as every idea of order seems to do; and it must therefore be considered as a creature of the understanding, rather than a primary cause acting on the senses and imagination. It is not by the force of long attention and inquiry that we find any object to be beautiful: beauty demands no assistance from our reasoning; even the will is unconcerned: the appearance of beauty as effectually causes some degree of love in us, as the application of ice or fire produces the ideas of heat and cold. . . .

Beauty is a thing much too affecting not to depend upon some positive qualities. And, since it is no creature of our reason, since it strikes us without any reference to use, and even where no use at all can be discerned, since the order and method of nature is generally very different from our measures and proportions, we must conclude that beauty is, for the greater part, some quality in bodies acting mechanically upon the human mind by the intervention of the senses. We ought therefore to consider attentively in what manner those sensible qualities are disposed, in such things as, by experience, we find beautiful, or which excite in us the passion of love, or some correspondent affection. . . .

The most obvious point that presents itself to us in examining any object, is its extent or quantity. And what degree of extent prevails in bodies that are held beautiful may be gathered from the usual manner of expression concerning it. I am told that in most languages, the objects of love are spoken of under diminutive epithets. . . . A great beautiful thing is a manner of expression scarcely ever used; but that of a great ugly thing, is very common. There is a wide difference between admiration and love. The sublime, which is the cause of the former, always dwells on great objects, and terrible; the latter on small ones, and pleasing: we submit to what we admire, but we love what submits to us; in one case we are forced, in the other we are flattered, into compliance. In short, the ideas of the sublime and the beautiful stand on foundations so different, that it is hard, I had almost said impossible, to think of reconciling them in the same subject, without considerably lessening the effect of the one or the other upon the passions: so that, attending to their quantity, beautiful objects are comparatively small. . . .

The next property constantly observable in such objects is *smoothness*: a quality so essential to beauty, that I do not now recollect any thing beautiful that is not smooth. . . . A very considerable part of the effect of beauty is owning to this quality; indeed the most considerable; for, take any beautiful object, and give it a broken and rugged surface, and, however well-formed it may be in other respects, it pleases no longer: whereas, let it want ever so many of the other constituents, if it wants not this, it becomes more pleasing than almost all the others without it. . . .

But, as perfectly beautiful bodies are not composed of angular parts, so their parts never continue long in the same right line. They vary their direction every moment, and they change under the eye by a deviation continually carrying on, but for whose beginning or end you will find it difficult to ascertain a point. The view of a beautiful bird will illustrate this observation. . . . In this description, I have before me the idea of a dove; it agrees very well with most of the conditions of beauty. It is smooth and downy; its parts are (to use that expression) melted into one another: you are presented with no sudden protuberance through the whole, and yet the whole is continually changing. . . .

An air of robustness and strength is very prejudicial to beauty. An appearance of *delicacy*, and even of fragility, is almost essential to it. Whoever examines the vegetable or animal creation, will find this observation to be founded in nature. . . . The beauty of women is considerably owing to their weakness or delicacy, and is even enhanced by their timidity, a quality of mind analogous to it. . . .

As to the colours usually found in beautiful bodies, it may be somewhat difficult to ascertain them, because, in the several parts of nature, there is an infinite variety. However, even in this variety we may mark out something on which to settle. First, the colours of beautiful bodies must not be dusky or muddy, but clean and fair. Secondly, they must not be of the strongest kind. Those which seem most appropriate to beauty are the milder of every sort; light greens; soft blues; weak whites; pink reds, and violets. Thirdly, if the colours be strong and vivid, they are always diversified, and the object is never of one strong colour; they are almost always such a number of them (as in variegated flowers), that the strength and glare of each is considerably abated....

On closing this general view of beauty, it naturally occurs that we should compare it with the sublime; and, in this comparison, there appears a remarkable contrast; for sublime objects are vast in their dimensions, beautiful ones comparatively small: beauty should be smooth, and polished; the great, rugged and negligent: beauty should shun the right line, yet deviate from it insensibly; the great, in many cases, loves the right line; and, when it deviates, it often makes a strong deviation: beauty should not be obscure; the great ought to be solid and even massive. They are, indeed, ideas of a very different nature, one being founded on pain, the other on pleasure; and, however they may vary afterwards from the direct nature of their causes, yet these causes keep up an eternal distinction between them, a distinction never to be forgotten by any whose business it is to affect the passions.[21] ...

LESSING

Gotthold Ephraim Lessing (1729–1781) was one of the greatest literary critics and most influential dramatists in the history of German literature.[22] A Lutheran pastor's son, Lessing intended to follow his father's profession when he enrolled in the University of Leipzig at the age of seventeen, but his interests soon turned to the theatre. Developing his talents first in Leipzig and later in Berlin, within a few years he became well known as a playwright, critic, journalist, and polemicist. His first dramatic hit was *Miss Sara Sampson* (1755), a domestic tragedy; his first major critical work, *Letters Concerning Recent German Literature* (1759). In order to support himself later while he continued writing, he served five years as secretary to a Silesian general in Breslau, where he completed his major work on aesthetics, *Laocoön* (published in 1766), and a sentimental comedy, *Minna von Barnhelm* (produced in 1767). In 1767, Lessing went to Hamburg as drama critic and consultant for the recently founded National Theatre. Although this change stimulated him to write an important series of critical articles on drama, *The Hamburg Drama-turgy*, when the theatre closed in 1769, he was forced to look for another position. Accepting an appointment as librarian to the Duke of Brunswick, he moved to Wolfenbüttel where he resided for the rest of his life and continued his writing. Among the major works of this, his last period were two new plays, *Emilia Galotti* (1767) and *Nathan the Wise* (1779), and a prose work, *The Education of Mankind* (1780). At the age of forty-seven he married the widow of one of his old friends, but his marital happiness was short lived as his wife died in childbirth less than two years later. Lonely, dejected, poor, broken in health and in spirit, Lessing himself survived her for only three years.

Lessing begins *Laocoön*, his essay on the limits of the arts of poetry and painting, by reflecting on the art historian Winckel-mann's explanation of why, on the one hand, the Greek sculptors of the Laocoön statuary group depicted Laocoön in such a way that he does not seem to cry out while he and his sons are being crushed by enormous snakes, whereas, on the other hand, in Virgil's *Aeneid* he is described as raising a terrible cry. Winckel-mann had explained the restraint exercised by the Greek sculptors as another example of the "noble simplicity and quiet grandeur" which he found to be characteristic of Greek but not of Roman art. Lessing, citing several examples in Homer and in Greek tragedy where heroes and even gods cry out, finds reason to disagree with Winckelmann. He goes on to argue that if the sculptors chose to depict Laocoön in the way they did it was not because they felt that screaming was unworthy of a hero under such circumstances but rather because they were being consistent with the end of their art, which above all was to achieve beauty. And beauty, they must have believed, could only be achieved by eliminating all extraneous and distracting elements which might stand in its way. The sculptors could not let Laocoön scream, Lessing believes, not because this would be inconsistent with his character, but because it would distort his countenance, making him repulsive and producing an ugly rather than a beautiful aesthetic effect. Moreover, since the sculptors were aware of the limitations of their art, which necessitated their confining them-selves to the expression of a single moment in a temporal process, they chose "the most fruitful moment," the moment in which Laocoön sighs before crying out, leaving the observer's imagination free to supply the culminating moment, the climax of the action. It is therefore in the very nature of the sculptor's art, and not in Winckelmann's "noble simplicity and quiet grandeur" that we can find the true explanation for Laocoön's half-open mouth.[23]

Against this background of critical controversy, Lessing presents his own theory of the arts, defining and defending their separation and autonomy, and opposing all those who hold that a poet is a painter in words or a painter is a poet in pigments. He argues that the poet is freer from limitation than the sculptor or painter in that his art does not need to concern itself with one single moment. Poetry can depict action progressively: the events leading up to Laocoön's predicament can be narrated, his and his sons' horrible fate—their piercing screams and death agonies—can be described, and subsequent events presented. The poet Virgil was right, then, in allowing Laocoön to cry out, Lessing believes, just as right as were the sculptors of the Laocoön group in having him suppress the cry.

But if the stress in Lessing's *Laocoön* is on the differences among the arts, this does not mean that he fails to recognize and to appreciate their similarities and common basis in man's attempt to represent and to interpret life and nature. In his *Hamburg Dramaturgy*, the collection of newspaper articles in which he applies the principles of Aristotle (in his mind "as infallible as the *Elements* of Euclid") to prove the shortcomings of French Neo-Classical drama and to show the need for a revitalized, truly classical ideal for drama, Lessing has something of importance to say about the central purpose of all the arts and about their relation to nature and man. The complexity of nature is such, Lessing holds, that it would take an infinite spirit to comprehend and to enjoy its coherent design, its interconnected, perpetually changing patterns. Although no finite spirit, no individual man, can grasp the total scheme, he does have the power to impose limits on what he will pay attention to and enjoy in nature and is able to eliminate all that distracts from his attention and enjoyment. If man lacked this power of attention and concentration, he would not be fully alive or conscious; he would be so open to sense impressions, he would be unimpressionable; he would feel so many feelings, he would be incapable of feeling deeply. We must be able to abstract, Lessing points out, otherwise we would be constantly abstracted. And this is why art is so important to man's life. Its purpose is to do the abstracting for us in the aesthetic realm, and by doing this, to facilitate and to increase our attention and enjoyment. By the means which the arts provide us, we are able to experience things as purely and as concentratedly as they could be, in reality, experienced were we ourselves artists.[24]

The Limits of the Arts of Painting and Poetry

1. *Lessing, in his* Laocoön, *tries to justify what seems to him to be the necessary and aesthetically appropriate limits of poetry and painting. In reflecting on these arts, many questions have arisen in his mind. What, if anything, do the two have in common? How do they differ? Can poetry achieve some aesthetic effects so much better than painting that painting should not even attempt them? What are the actual results in practice of recognizing, and of ignoring, the limitations which seem to be inherent in the medium of each art? In answering these questions, Lessing appeals to the following fundamental principles.*

If it be true that painting employs wholly different signs or means of imitation from poetry,—the one using forms and colors in space, the other articulate sounds in time,—and if signs most unquestionably stand in convenient relation with the thing signified, then signs arranged side by side can represent only objects existing side by side, or whose parts so exist, while consecutive signs can express only objects which succeed each other, or whose parts succeed each other, in time.

Objects which exist side by side, or whose parts so exist, are called bodies. Consequently bodies with their visible properties are the peculiar subjects of painting.

Objects which succeed each other, or whose parts succeed each other in time, are actions. Consequently actions are the peculiar subjects of poetry.

All bodies, however, exist not only in space, but also in time. They continue, and, at any moment of their continuance, may assume a different appearance and stand in different relations. Every one of these momentary appearances and groupings was the result of a preceding, may become the cause of a following, and is therefore the centre of a present, action. Consequently painting can imitate actions also, but only as they are suggested through forms.

Painting, in its coexistent compositions, can use but a single moment of an action, and must therefore choose the most pregnant one, the one most suggestive of what has gone before and what is to follow.

Poetry, in its progressive imitations, can use but a single attribute of bodies, and must choose that one which gives the most vivid picture of the body as exercised in this particular action.

Hence the rule for the employment of a single descriptive epithet, and the cause of the rare occurrence of descriptions of physical objects.

I should place less confidence in this dry chain of conclusions did I not find them fully confirmed by Homer, or, rather, had they not been first suggested to me by Homer's method. These principles alone furnish a key to the noble style of the Greek, and enable us to pass just judgment on the opposite method of many modern poets who insist upon emulating the artist in a point where they must of necessity remain inferior to him.[25]

2. *An ardent admirer of Homer, Lessing adduces that poet's practice as evidence for the validity of his principles on the limits of poetry and painting. After explaining in some detail how the poet and painter should proceed, the first by imitating objects as they succeed one another in time, and the second, as they coexist in space, Lessing urges that poetry and painting be kept separate but equal.*

I find that Homer paints nothing but progressive actions. All bodies, all separate objects, are painted only as they take part in such actions, and generally with a single touch. No wonder, then, that artists find in Homer's pictures little or nothing to their purpose, and that their only harvest is where the narration brings together in a space favorable to art a number of beautiful shapes in graceful attitudes, however little the poet himself may have painted shapes, attitudes, or space. . . .

But, it may be urged, the signs employed in poetry not only follow each other, but are also arbitrary; and, as arbitrary signs, they are certainly capable of expressing things as they exist in space. Homer himself furnishes examples of this. We have but to call to mind his shield of Achilles to have an instance of how circumstantially and yet poetically a single object can be described according to its coexistent parts.

I will proceed to answer this double objection. I call it double, because a just conclusion must hold, though unsupported by examples, and on the other hand the example of Homer has great weight with me, even when I am unable to justify it by rules.

It is true that since the signs of speech are arbitrary, the parts of a body can by their means be made to follow each other as readily as in nature they exist side by side. But this is a property of the signs of language in general, not of those peculiar to poetry. The prose writer is satisfied with being intelligible, and making his representations plain and clear. But this is not enough for the poet. He desires to present us with images so vivid, that we fancy we have the things themselves before us, and cease for the moment to be conscious of his words, the instruments with which he effects his purpose. That was the point made in the definition given above of a poetical picture. But the poet must always paint; and now let us see in how far bodies, considered in relation to their parts lying together in space, are fit subjects for this painting.

How do we obtain a clear idea of a thing in space? First we observe its separate parts, then the union of these parts, and finally the whole. Our senses perform these various operations with such amazing rapidity as to make them seem but one. This rapidity is absolutely essential to our obtaining an idea of the whole, which is nothing more than the result of the conception of the parts and of their connection with each other. Suppose now that the poet should lead us in proper order from one part of the object to the other; suppose he should succeed in making the connection of these parts, perfectly clear to us; how much time will he have consumed?

The details, which the eye takes in at a glance, he enumerates slowly one by one, and it often happens that, by the time he has brought us to the last, we have forgotten the first. Yet from these details we are to form a picture. When we look at an object the various parts are always present to the eye. It can run over them again and again. The ear, however, loses the details it has heard, unless memory retain them. And if they be so retained, what pains and effort it costs to recall their impressions in the proper order and with even the moderate degree of rapidity necessary to the obtaining of a tolerable idea of the whole. . . .

I do not deny that language has the power of describing a corporeal whole according to its parts. It certainly has, because its signs, although consecutive, are nevertheless arbitrary. But I deny that this power exists in language as the instrument of poetry. For illusion, which is the special aim of poetry, is not produced by these verbal descriptions of objects, nor can it ever be so produced. The coexistence of the body comes into collision with the sequence of the words, and although while the former is getting resolved into the latter, the dismemberment of the whole into its parts is a help to us, yet the reunion of these parts into a whole is made extremely difficult, and not infrequently impossible.

Where the writer does not aim at illusion, but is simply addressing the understanding of his readers with the desire of awakening distinct and, as far as possible, complete ideas, then these descriptions of corporeal objects, inadmissible as they are in poetry, are perfectly appropriate. Not only the prose writer, but the dogmatic poet (for in as far as he dogmatizes he is no poet) may use them with good effect. . . .

And shall Homer nevertheless have fallen into those barren descriptions of material objects?

Let us hope that only a few such passages can be cited. And even those few, I venture to assert, will be found really to confirm the rule, to which they appear to form an exception.

The rule is this, that succession in time is the province of the poet, coexistence in space that of the artist.

To bring together into one and the same picture two points of time necessarily remote, as Mazzuoli does the rape of the Sabine women and the reconciliation effected by them between their husbands and relations; or as Titian does, representing in one piece the whole story of the Prodigal Son,—his dissolute life, his misery, and repentance,—is an encroachment of the painter on the domain of the poet, which good taste can never sanction.

To try to present a complete picture to the reader by enumerating in succession several parts or things which in nature the eye necessarily takes in at a glance, is an encroachment of the poet on the domain of the painter, involving a great effort of the imagination to very little purpose.

Painting and poetry should be like two just and friendly neighbors, neither of whom indeed is allowed to take unseemly liberties in the heart of the other's domain, but who exercise mutual forbearance on the borders, and effect a peaceful settlement for all the petty encroachments which circumstances may compel either to make in haste on the rights of the other.[26]

3. *Lessing also thinks that poets should not attempt to describe in detail beautiful objects or beautiful persons; these can be far better represented by painters directly through visual forms. This does not mean, however, that poets cannot elicit images of beauty by describing the emotional effects of beautiful things upon the beholder and by transforming beauty into charm.*

The true justification of both poet and painter shall not, however, be left to rest upon this analogy of two friendly neighbors. A mere analogy furnishes neither proof nor justification. I justify them in this way. As in the picture the two moments of time follow each other so immediately that we can without effort consider them as one, so in the poem the several touches answering to the different parts and properties in space are so condensed, and succeed each other so rapidly, that we seem to catch them all at once. . . .

What I have been saying of bodily objects in general applies with even more force to those which are beautiful.

Physical beauty results from the harmonious action of various parts which can be taken in at a glance. It therefore requires that these parts should lie near together; and, since things whose parts lie near together are the proper subjects of painting, this art and this alone can imitate physical beauty.

The poet, who must necessarily detail in succession the elements of beauty, should therefore desist entirely from the description of physical beauty as such. He must feel that these elements arranged in a series cannot possibly produce the same effect as in juxtaposition; that the concentrating glance which we try to cast back over them immediately after their enumeration, gives us no harmonious picture; and that to conceive the effect of certain eyes, a certain mouth and nose taken together, unless we can recall a similar combination of such parts in nature or art, surpasses the power of human imagination.

Here again Homer is the model of all models. He says, Nireus
was fair; Achilles was fairer; Helen was of godlike beauty. But
he is nowhere betrayed into a more detailed description of these
beauties. Yet the whole poem is based upon the loveliness of
Helen. How a modern poet would have revelled in descriptions of it! . . .

But are we not robbing poetry of too much by taking from her
all pictures of physical beauty?

Who seeks to take them from her? We are only warning her
against trying to arrive at them by a particular road, where she
will blindly grope her way in the footsteps of a sister art without
ever reaching the goal. We are not closing against her other roads
whereon art can follow only with her eyes. . . .

What Homer could not describe in its details, he shows us by
its effect. Paint us, ye poets, the delight, the attraction, the love,
the enchantment of beauty, and you have painted beauty itself.
Who can think of Sappho's beloved, the sight of whom, as she
confesses, robs her of sense and thought, as ugly? We seem to be
gazing on a beautiful and perfect form, when we sympathize with
the emotions which only such a form can produce. . . .

Yet another way in which poetry surpasses art in the description
of physical beauty, is by turning beauty into charm. Charm is
beauty in motion, and therefore less adapted to the painter than
the poet. The painter can suggest motion, but his figures are
really destitute of it. Charm therefore in a picture becomes
grimace, while in poetry it remains what it is, a transitory beauty,
which we would fain see repeated. It comes and goes, and since
we can recall a motion more vividly and easily than mere forms
and colors, charm must affect us more strongly than beauty under
the same conditions.[27] . . .

4. *Lessing next considers the question as to whether or not
ugliness as well as beauty can provide appropriate subject matter
for the poet and painter.*

A single incongruous part may destroy the harmonious effect of
many beauties, without, however, making the object ugly. Ugliness
requires the presence of several incongruous parts which we must
be able to take in at a glance if the effect produced is to be the
opposite of that which we call beauty.

Accordingly ugliness in itself can be no subject for poetry. Yet Homer has described its extreme in Thersites, and described it by its coexistent parts. Why did he allow himself in the case of ugliness what he wisely refrained from as regards beauty? Will not the effect of ugliness be as much hindered by the successive enumeration of its elements, as the effect of beauty is neutralized by a similar treatment?

Certainly it will, and therein lies Homer's justification. The poet can make ugliness his theme only because it acquires through his description a less repulsive aspect, and ceases in a measure to produce the effect of ugliness. What we cannot employ by itself, he uses as an ingredient to excite and strengthen certain mixed impressions, with which he must entertain us in the absence of those purely agreeable.

These mixed sensations are those of the ridiculous and the horrible.

Homer makes Thersites ugly in order to make him ridiculous. Mere ugliness, however, would not have this effect. Ugliness is imperfection, and the ridiculous requires a contrast between perfections and imperfections. This is the explanation of my friend,[28] to which I would add that this contrast must not be too sharp and decided, but that the opposites must be such as admit of being blended into each other. . . .

Such is the use which the poet makes of ugliness of form. How can the painter legitimately employ it?

Painting as imitative skill can express ugliness; painting as fine art will not express it. In the former capacity its sphere extends over all visible objects; in the latter it confines itself to those which produce agreeable impressions.

But do not disagreeable impressions please in the imitation? Not all . . . .

We wish to see neither Thersites himself nor his image. If his image be the less displeasing, the reason is not that ugliness of shape ceases to be ugly in the imitation, but that we possess the power of diverting our minds from this ugliness by admiration of the artist's skill. But this satisfaction is constantly disturbed by the thought of the unworthy use to which art has been put, and our esteem for the artist is thereby greatly diminished.[29]

5. *After expressing his dissatisfaction with Aristotle's treatment of the problem of the imitation of ugliness in art, Lessing argues*

that ugliness of form and loathsomeness should be excluded from painting and only used in poetry in order to achieve by contrast emotional effects which would otherwise be unachievable.

Aristotle adduces another reason for the pleasure we take in even the most faithful copy of what in nature is disagreeable. He attributes this pleasure to man's universal desire for knowledge. We are pleased when we can learn from a copy of τὶ ἕχαστον, what each and everything is, or when we can conclude from it ὅτι οντος ἐχἐινος, that it is the very thing we already know. But this is no argument in favor of the imitation of ugliness. The pleasure which arises from the gratification of our desire for knowledge is momentary and only incidental to the object with regard to which it has been satisfied, whereas the discomfort which accompanies the sight of ugliness is permanent, and essential to the object causing it. How, then, can one counterbalance the other? Still less can the trifling entertainment of tracing a likeness overcome the unpleasant impression produced by ugliness. The more closely I compare the ugly copy with the ugly original, the more I expose myself to this influence, so that the pleasure of the comparison soon disappears, leaving nothing behind but the painful impression of this twofold ugliness.

From the examples given by Aristotle he appears not to include ugliness of form among the disagreeable things which may give pleasure in the imitation. His examples are wild beasts and dead bodies. Wild beasts excite terror even when they are not ugly; and this terror, not their ugliness, may be made to produce sensations of pleasure through imitation. So also of dead bodies. Keeness of sympathy, the dreadful thought of our own annihilation, make a dead body in nature an object of aversion. In the imitation the sense of illusion robs sympathy of its sharpness, and, by the addition of various palliating circumstances, that disturbing element may be either entirely banished or so inseparably interwoven with these softening features, that terror is almost lost in desire.

Since, then, ugliness of form, from its exciting sensations of pain of a kind incapable of being converted by imitation into pleasurable emotions, cannot in itself be a fitting subject for painting as a fine art, the question arises whether it may not be employed in painting as in poetry as an ingredient for strengthening other sensations.

May painting make use of deformity in the attainment of the ridiculous and horrible?

I will not venture to answer this question absolutely in the negative. Unquestionably, harmless ugliness can be ridiculous in painting also, especially when united with an affectation of grace and dignity. Equally beyond question is it that hurtful ugliness excites terror in a picture as well as in nature, and that the ridiculous and the terrible, in themselves mixed sensations, acquire through imitation an added degree of fascination.

But I must call attention to the fact that painting and poetry do not stand upon the same footing in this respect. In poetry, as I have observed, ugliness of form loses its disagreeable effect almost entirely by the successive enumeration of its coexistent parts. As far as effect is concerned it almost ceases to be ugliness, and can thus more closely combine with other appearances to produce new and different impressions. But in painting ugliness is before our eyes in all its strength, and affects us scarcely less powerfully than in nature itself. Harmless ugliness cannot, therefore, long remain ridiculous. The disagreeable impression gains the mastery, and what was at first amusing becomes at last repulsive. Nor is the case different with hurtful ugliness. The element of terror gradually disappears, leaving the deformity unchanging and unrelieved....

The same rules hold of things loathsome as of things ugly, in respect of imitation. Indeed, since the disagreeable effect of the former is the more violent, they are still less suitable subjects of painting or poetry. Only because the effect is softened by verbal expression, did I venture to assert that the poet might employ certain loathsome traits as an ingredient in such mixed sensations as can with good effect be strengthened by the use of ugliness.

The ridiculous may be heightened by an element of disgust; representations of dignity and propriety likewise become ludicrous when brought into contrast with the disgusting. Examples of this abound in Aristophanes....

I come now to objects of disgust in painting. Even could we prove that there are no objects directly disgusting to the eye, which painting as a fine art would naturally avoid, it would still be obliged to refrain from loathsome objects in general, because they become through the association of ideas disgusting also to the sense of sight.... But painting does not employ loathsomeness for its own sake, but, like poetry, to give emphasis to the ludicrous and the terrible. At its peril! What I have already said of ugliness in this connection applies with greater force to loathsomeness. This also loses much less of its effect in a visible representation than in a description addressed to the ear, and can therefore unite less closely with the elements of the ludicrous and terrible in painting than in poetry. As soon as the surprise passes and the first curious glance is satisfied, the elements separate and loathsomeness appears in all its crudity.[30] ...

NOTES

1. Since he formally christened it, Baumgarten is usually considered the founder of the "science of aesthetics." But Benedetto Croce claims that Vico (1668–1744) "invented" it at least ten years before Baumgarten. See Croce's "History of Aesthetic" (Part II of *Aesthetic, as Science of Expression and General Linguistic*), Chapter V. More recently, Anthony Ashley Cooper, the third Earl of Shaftesbury (1671–1713), author of *Characteristics of Men, Man, Manners, Opinions, Times*, etc. (1711), has had a number of supporters as the true originator of aesthetics. See Jerome Stolnitz, "On the Significance of Lord Shaftesbury in Modern Aesthetic Theory," *Philosophical Quarterly*, 11 (1961), 97–113.

2. The problem of the sublime had been dealt with, in relation primarily to rhetoric, since ancient times, since Longinus's treatise *On the Sublime* or *On Literary Excellence*. Burke, however, broke with the traditional approach to the problem. See S. H. Monk's *The Sublime*, listed in our "Guide to Supplementary Reading."

3. To mention only the most important ones, Francis Hutcheson's *Inquiry into the Original of Our Ideas of Beauty and Virtue* (1725), David Hume's essay "Of the Standard of Taste" (1757), Henry Home's (Lord Kames) *Elements of Criticism* (1761), Alexander Gerard's *Essay on Genius* (1774), and Archibald Alison's *Essays on the Nature and Principles of Taste* (1790).

4. Diderot (1713–1784) wrote the article on beauty in the famous French *Encyclopedia*. Among his other important works

on aesthetics are his essays on painting and dramatic poesy, his *Salons*, and his "Paradox of the Actor." On his aesthetic theory see Thomas J. Durkin's "Three Notes to Diderot's Aesthetic," *Journal of Aesthetics and Art Criticism*, XV (March, 1957), 331–339; and George Boas's "The Arts in the *Encyclopedia*," *JAAC*, XXIII (Fall, 1964), 97–107.

5. Johann Joachim Winckelmann (1717–1768), German art historian and antiquarian, was the author of *Thoughts on the Imitation of Greek Works in Painting and Sculpture* (1759), one of the books which evoked Lessing's *Laocoön*, and the *History of Ancient Art* (1764). Walter Pater has an essay on Winckelmann in his *Renaissance*. For a discussion of his influence on his contemporaries, see Henry C. Hatzfeld's *Winckelmann and His German Critics: 1755–1781* (New York, King's Crown Press, 1943).

6. Burke's *Enquiry* was first published without the use of his name, but he was soon known to be its author. For one of the fullest and best discussions of the *Enquiry*, its composition, content, and influence, see J. T. Boulton's Introduction to his recent edition of the work, listed in our "Guide to Supplementary Reading."

7. Preface to the first edition (1757) of Burke's *Enquiry*, reprinted in J. T. Boulton's recent edition of the second edition (1759) of this work. All subsequent quotations and selections are taken from a reprint of Burke's second edition, *A Philosophical Enquiry into the Origin of Our Ideas of the Sublime and the Beautiful, With an Introductory Discourse Concerning Taste and Several Other Additions* (Philadelphia, J. Watts, 1806). This edition will henceforth be cited as *Enquiry*.

8. *Enquiry*, p. 194 (Part IV, Sec. I).

9. *Enquiry*, p. 5 (Introduction).

10. *Enquiry*, p. 10 (Introduction).

11. *Enquiry*, p. 13 (Introduction).

12. *Enquiry*, p. 21 (Introduction).

13. *Enquiry*, p. 25 (Introduction).

14. In the fifth and final part of his *Enquiry*, Burke discusses the aesthetic and emotional effects of words in poetry. Some recent critics have considered this to be the best part of the whole work.

15. Among the English admirers of Burke's *Enquiry* were Dr. Samuel Johnson, Sir Joshua Reynolds, David Hume, and, much

later, Thomas Hardy. In France, Diderot was influenced by it, and, in Germany, Lessing, Moses Mendelssohn, and Kant recognized its importance in understanding the beautiful and the sublime. Fechner, in the introduction to his *Vorschule der Aesthetik*, specifically mentions Burke among those who had pursued "aesthetics from below."

16. *Enquiry*, pp. 68–70 (Part I, Sec. XVIII).

17. *Enquiry*, pp. 57–64 (Part I, Secs. XIII–XV).

18. *Enquiry*, pp. 64–68 (Part I, Secs. XVI–XVII).

19. *Enquiry*, pp. 77–78 (Part II, Secs. I–II); p. 80 (Part II, Sec. III); pp. 82, 84–85 (Part II, Sec. IV); p. 89 (Part II, Sec. V); p. 100 (Part II, Sec. VI); pp. 102–103 (Part II, Sec. VII).

20. *Enquiry*, p. 104 (Part II, Sec. VIII); pp. 110–113 (Part II, Secs. XI–XIII); pp. 115–116 (Part II, Sec. XIV); pp. 127–128 (Part II, Sec. XXII).

21. *Enquiry*, pp. 129–132 (Part III, Secs. I–II); pp. 167–172 (Part III, Secs. XII–XV); pp. 174–176 (Part III, Secs. XVI–XVII); pp. 189–190 (Part III, Sec. XXVII).

22. According to H. B. Garland, Lessing altered the entire course of German literature through his critical and constructive contributions, and deserves the title "founder of modern German literature." See Garland's book on Lessing listed in our "Guide to Supplementary Literature." For an excellent, succinct statement of Lessing's contribution to eighteenth-century criticism, see Ernst Cassirer's *Philosophy of the Enlightenment*, translated by F. C. A. Koelln and J. P. Pettegrove (Boston, Beacon Press, 1955), pp. 357–360.

23. There have been innumerable interpretations of the Laocoön statuary group, created by Rhodian sculptors of the late Hellenistic period, since it was rediscovered in Rome in 1506. Besides Winckelmann and Lessing, Herder, Diderot, Goethe, Schopenhauer, and Taine attempted to explain its aesthetic significance. For a brief account of changing views of the statuary group, see Margaret Bieber's *Laocoön: The Influence of the Group Since Its Rediscovery*, with photographs by Ernest Nash (New York, Columbia University Press, 1942).

24. See *Hamburg Dramaturgy*, Letter 70.

25. Gotthold Ephraim Lessing, *Laocoön, An Essay upon the Limits of Painting and Poetry*, translated by Ellen Frothingham (Boston, Roberts Brothers, 1874), pp. 91–92 (Sec. XVI). All subsequent selections are taken from this edition, which will henceforth be cited as *Laocoön*.

26. *Laocoön*, pp. 92–93 (Sec. XVI); pp. 101–103; 105–106 (Sec. XVII); pp. 109–110 (Sec. XVIII).

27. *Laocoön*, p. 112 (Sec. XVIII); pp. 126–127 (Sec. XX); pp. 136–138 (Sec. XXI).

28. Lessing is referring to the German author and aesthetician Moses Mendelssohn (1739–1809), whose works influenced both Lessing and Kant.

29. *Laocoön*, pp. 148–149, 153–154 (Sec. XXIII).

30. *Laocoön*, pp. 154–156 (Sec. XXIV); pp. 160–161, 167 (Sec. XXV).

QUESTIONS AND TOPICS FOR FURTHER STUDY

1. What are some of the psychological assumptions underlying Burke's aesthetic theory?

2. How does Burke explain the fact that we get enjoyment from a work in which we see others suffer (i.e. the tragic paradox)?

3. How does Burke's view of imitation in art resemble and differ from Aristotle's?

4. What are some of the causes which produce the feeling of the sublime in nature, according to Burke? Give an illustration of each of the causes you mention. What are the psychological effects of these phenomena?

5. Compare the beautiful and the sublime from Burke's point of view. Why does he hold that they are basically different kinds of aesthetic experience? What objections, if any, would you raise to his view of the beautiful?

6. Recapitulate the differences between poetry and painting from Lessing's point of view. Why does he think that it is important to the poet and to the painter to keep these differences in mind?

7. What does Lessing advise the poet to do in order to achieve a sense of beauty in his work? To what extent does he think a poet can deal with ugliness?

8. For what reason does Lessing differ from Aristotle on the subject of imitating ugliness and loathsomeness in works of art?

9. Do you find any similarities between Lessing's and Burke's solutions to aesthetic problems?

10. Topics for further study: (a) Burke's views on poetry; (b) Burke on standards of taste; (c) the influence of Burke on Lessing; (d) Lessing's and Plato's views of Homer's poetry; (d) Lessing's theory of tragedy.

GUIDE TO SUPPLEMENTARY READING

(Works marked with asterisks are available in paperbound editions.)

BURKE

I. PRIMARY SOURCE

Burke, Edmund, *A Philosophical Enquiry into the Origin of Our Ideas of the Sublime and Beautiful,* edited with an introduction and notes by J. T. Boulton (London, Routledge and Kegan Paul; New York, Columbia University Press, 1958).

II. SECONDARY WORKS

Hipple, Walter, Jr., *The Beautiful, the Sublime and the Picturesque in Eighteenth Century British Aesthetic Theory* (Carbondale, Illinois, Southern Illinois University Press, 1957), Chapter 6.

Howard, William Gould, "Burke Among the Forerunners of Lessing," *PMLA,* XXII (1907), 608–632.

Hussey, Christopher, *The Picturesque: Studies in a Point of View* (London, Putnam, 1927).

Monk, Samuel H., **The Sublime: A Study of Critical Theories in Eighteenth Century England,* (Ann Arbor, Ann Arbor Paperbacks, University of Michigan Press, 1960), Chapter V.

Wichelns, Herbert A., "Burke's Essay on the Sublime and its Reviewers," *Journal of English and Germanic Philology,* XXI (1922), 645–661.

LESSING

I. PRIMARY SOURCES

Lessing, Gotthold Ephraim, *Laocoön: An Essay upon the Limits of Painting and Poetry, translated by Ellen Frothingham (New York, Noonday Press, 1957).

——*Hamburg Dramaturgy, with a new introduction by Victor Lange (New York, Dover Publications, 1962).

II. SECONDARY WORKS

Bosanquet, Bernard, *A History of Aesthetic (New York, Meridian Books, 1957), Chapter IX, pp. 217–239.

Butler, Eliza Marian, *The Tyranny of Greece over Germany: A Study of the Influence Exercised by Greek Art and Poetry over the Great German Writers of the Eighteenth, Nineteenth, and Twentieth Centuries (Boston, Beacon Press, 1958).

Garland, H. B., Lessing: The Founder of Modern German Literature (London, Macmillan and Co., Ltd.; New York, St. Martin's Press, 1962).

Gilbert, Katharine, and Helmut Kuhn, A History of Esthetics, revised edition (Bloomington, Indiana University Press, 1953), Chapter X.

Robertson, John George, Lessing's Dramatic Theory, Being an Introduction to and Commentary on His "Hamburgische Dramaturgie" (Cambridge, The University Press, 1939).

Rolleston, T. W., "Lessing and Modern German Literature," in Studies in European Literature (Oxford, 1900), pp. 93–130.

Vail, Curtis C. D., Lessing's Relation to the English Language and Literature (New York, Columbia University Press, 1936).

Wellek, René, A History of Modern Criticism: 1750–1950, Volume I The Late Eighteenth Century (New Haven, Yale University Press, 1955), Chapter 8.

Wimsatt, William K., Jr., and Cleanth Brooks, Literary Criticism: A Short History (New York, Alfred A. Knopf, 1957).

Zimmern, Helen, Gotthold Ephraim Lessing: His Life and Works (London, Longmans, Green and Co., 1878).

CHAPTER 4

Aesthetic Judgment

KANT

The son of a hard-working harness maker and a deeply pious housewife, Immanuel Kant (1724–1804) was born in Königsberg, a seaport in East Prussia where he was to spend most of his life. After finishing at a Pietist school, the Collegium Fridericianum, Kant went on to the University of Königsberg where he studied mathematics, natural sciences, and philosophy. A lack of funds forced him to postpone his advanced education for seven years, during which time he earned money by serving as a private tutor away from the city. Eventually he returned to the university and completed his doctorate in philosophy in 1755. He then occupied a position as lecturer in the university for fifteen years before he finally was awarded his long-awaited professorship in 1770. By this time, having made a reputation for himself through his scientific and philosophical writings, among which were *General Natural History and Theory of the Heavens* (1755) and *Observations on the Feeling of the Beautiful and Sublime* (1764),[1] he was beginning to receive offers to teach elsewhere. His preference was always, however, to teach at the University of Königsberg, and it was during his tenure there that he produced his most important works dealing with epistemology (*Critique of Pure Reason*, 1781), moral philosophy (*Critique of Practical Reason*, 1788), and aesthetics and teleology (*Critique of Judgment*, 1790). These were the works which brought Kant renown as one of the greatest philosophers of all time and which profoundly affected the development of modern philosophy. Later in his career, his cooly rational but by no means irreverent treatment of religion evoked criticism from Prussian authorities, who extracted from him a promise not to write further on religious subjects; he did, however, continue to write works on jurisprudence, moral philosophy, anthropology, and metaphysics. Throughout his life, Kant preached and practiced a rational self-discipline, which, with his quiet and cautious way of living, probably aided him in living to a ripe old age despite his physical fragility. But far from being a dry and rigid character, he was in real life a popular lecturer, an affable host, a much-beloved professor, and a man of good will.

The *Critique of Judgment*, the work in which Kant gives us his aesthetic theory, is one of the most baffling works in the entire history of aesthetics. It is also one of the most rewarding. It is baffling partly because Kant chose to organize his material according to a rigid and complicated plan; partly because he assumed that his readers would be familiar with the contents of his earlier works, which were by no means easy to comprehend; and partly because of the difficult and sometimes obscure terminology he employed in expressing his ideas. It is rewarding, however, in that it encourages its readers to think critically and systematically about the fundamental problems of aesthetics; it leads them to a better understanding of what is presupposed and implied by their aesthetic judgments; and it gives them different and unusual perspectives from which they can reevaluate their most familiar aesthetic experiences. Although Hegel exaggerated when he said that "Kant spoke the first rational word on aesthetics"—we must not underestimate the rationality of the founding father, Baumgarten, and of other pre-Kantian aestheticians— Kant's *Critique of Judgment* is unquestionably a substantial and seminal work, one of the great masterpieces in the history of aesthetics.[2]

In this third and final of his *Critiques*, Kant brought to a conclusion the formidable task he had begun in the *Critique of Pure Reason* and had continued in the *Critique of Practical Reason*, the task of explaining how it is possible to have *a priori* synthetic knowledge, or knowledge which is universally and necessarily applicable to every experience but which is absolutely independent of all experience for its origin and validity.[3] Kant had called upon reason in his *Critique of Pure Reason* "again to undertake the most laborious of all tasks—that of self-examination" and to answer the basic question "what and how much can reason and understanding, apart from experience, cognize?"[4] To find an answer to this question, Kant thought it necessary to institute a "Copernican revolution in philosophy." Instead of assuming "that all our knowledge must conform to objects," let us assume, he suggested boldly, "that objects must conform to our knowledge." Proceeding from this assumption, Kant explained how the faculty of sensibility, through its *a priori* forms of intuition (viz. space and time), gives us the content of the objects we experience, and the faculty of understanding, through its system of concepts or categories, provides their form. Were it not for this complex interpenetration, this harmonious union, of understanding and sensibility, he claims, knowledge would be impossible. Thoughts, deprived of their content, would be empty; intuitions, lacking concepts, would be blind.[5] The mind is, for Kant, active and constructive, not just receptive and reproductive; it is "the lawgiver of nature." However, when reason, in its purely cognitive functions, attempts to know the nature of non-sensible things, things as they are in themselves (*noumena*), not just things as they appear (*phenomena*), it inevitably falls into contradictions and errors. Pure theoretical reason can never provide us with a valid basis for our most fundamental moral and religious beliefs; God, freedom, and immortality transcend its reach.

But Kant did not stop there. He was convinced that there must be room for faith as well as for reason in his critical philosophy. Having shown the limits of reason in its theoretical functions in his first *Critique,* in his second, the *Critique of Practical Reason,* he tried to show how reason in its practical or moral functions can indeed provide a sound foundation for our most cherished beliefs. Inherent in human nature and springing from the human will itself is a universally valid "categorical imperative" or moral law, a rational, absolutely binding sense of moral obligation without which the moral and religious life would be unintelligible. It is on the basis of this inner-determined moral law that we can feel absolutely justified in postulating the existence of God, the reality of freedom, and the certainty of immortality. To his own satisfaction, Kant thought he had proven that in its practical or moral functions reason prescribes laws *a priori* for the realm of freedom just as surely as in its theoretical functions it prescribes laws *a priori* for the realm of nature.

Yet his task was not finished. He had examined the cognitive faculties of reason in his first *Critique* and the faculties of desire in his second; now, in his third *Critique,* he turned to an examination of the faculties of feeling pleasure and pain. While his scrutiny of the understanding had revealed the *a priori* principle of conformity to law which, he believed, was applicable to nature, and his scrutiny of reason had revealed the *a priori* principle of final purpose which was applicable to freedom, he still needed "a mediating link between the realm of the natural concept and that of the concept of freedom in its effects." [6] He was determined "to throw a bridge" across "the great gulf that separates the supersensible from phenomena," [7] a bridge over which he could pass from the philosophy of nature to moral philosophy. He had become convinced that an examination of the faculty of judgment, "the faculty of thinking the particular as contained under the universal," [8] would reveal a principle of purposiveness which would have important application to art and nature. In the first part of the *Critique of Judgment*, he considers the judgment of taste or the aesthetical judgment and discusses the subjective purposiveness presupposed in our experiences of the beautiful and the sublime; in the second part, which was probably the most important part to Kant, he examines the teleological judgment and discusses the objective purposiveness presupposed in our experience of nature. Since we are concerned only with Kant's aesthetic views, we do not need to follow him further than through the first part of his last *Critique*. [9]

But before turning to what Kant has to say about the aesthetic judgment of the beautiful and the sublime, let us take a brief look at some of his other related views.

Art, for Kant, is "production through freedom." [10] It comes about not through the ordinary course of natural events, but as the result of human effort, human skill, and rational deliberation. Like science, it involves theory, but it is predominantly practical. Like handicraft, it involves work, but its end is free rather than mercenary. Aesthetical arts differ from mechanical arts in that their aim is only to give pleasure. If the pleasure derived from an aesthetical art is merely sensuous, that art is properly called pleasant; but if an aesthetical art is capable of providing cognitive pleasure, then, and only then, should it be called a beautiful art. Kant suggests, somewhat tentatively, that the aesthetical or fine arts might be conveniently classified according to an analogy drawn between them and the various ways in which we express our thoughts and feelings—through words, gestures, and tones of voice. There are, analogically, three kinds of fine art: arts of speech (viz. rhetoric and poetry); formative arts (viz. sculpture, architecture, painting, and landscape gardening) and, finally, the art of the play of sensations or of "external sensible impressions" which includes music and the art of color. Poetry Kant considers to be the highest of all the arts in aesthetic value because of its capacity to stimulate the imagination, to enlighten the understanding, and to direct the mind to the comprehension of ineffable "aesthetical ideas" [11] and to "the supersensible," the reality that lies beyond. Music, on the other hand, while it might well be the highest of all arts in terms of sheer pleasantness and universal communicability, is far inferior to poetry, in Kant's opinion, and he ranks it as the lowest of all arts because of its ephemeral effect, its purely pleasurable nature, and its inability to satisfy the understanding.[12]

Kant recognizes, however, the value that merely pleasant arts can have in the life of man, even if these arts do not (and by their very nature, cannot) satisfy man's highest practical and intellectual needs. To be sure, music, games, and laughter may be only forms of play—of tone, of chance, or of thought—but they are nonetheless valuable in that they provide a harmless release to animal impulses, aid in restoring psychic equilibrium at times, and, by heightening vitality, favorably influence health. The experience of the beautiful and the sublime play important roles in the life of a rational man, but there is also an appropriate place in that life for laughter which, as Kant defines it, is "an affection arising from the sudden transformation of a strained expectation into nothing." [13]

In discussing art, Kant has much to say about artistic genius. It is "the innate mental disposition (*ingenium*) through which Nature gives the rule to Art." [14] The artistic genius is "a favorite of nature," "a rare phenomenon," who has the unique ability to express the ineffable aspects of existence through aesthetical ideas, rendering these aspects universally communicable. The works of artistic geniuses are never mere imitations; they are original creations, exemplary models. The process by which such works are created can never be fully explained or successfully reduced to rules and formulas. For this reason Kant thinks that the process of artistic creativity differs completely from that of scientific discovery, the procedures of which can be explained, reconstructed, and repeated. Unlike the scientific genius, the artistic genius is different in kind, not just in degree, from his imitator.[15]

Through experience the artistic genius may increase his skill in giving form to matter, but were it not for his unique natural endowment, he could never create the works he does. Still, Kant does not favor the works of unrestrained geniuses, such as those produced by some of his contemporary *Sturm und Drang* artists.[16] The free vital spirit of genius, its soaring imagination, must be disciplined by sound critical judgment and by discriminating taste. Imagination and spirit, understanding and taste—all of these, Kant holds, are required of the genius if he is to create truly beautiful works of art.

Analytic of the Aesthetical Judgment

1. *When we judge an object to be beautiful, when we judge it aesthetically or by the faculty of taste, what characteristics do we attribute to the object? What mental faculties are involved? What logical and metaphysical presuppositions are made? What are the "moments" or essential phases of the judgment of taste? For guidance in answering such questions as these, Kant refers back to the logical functions of judgment—their quality, quantity, modality, and relation—by means of which he had worked out the categories of the understanding in the* Critique of Pure Reason.[17] *He first considers the judgment of taste in terms of quality because that is what, he says, the judgment "first pays attention to." According to quality, he holds, the judgment of taste is aesthetical rather than logical and subjective rather than objective—i.e. it has reference to the feelings of pleasure and pain evoked in the subject rather than to the actual characteristics of the object itself. When we judge an object to be beautiful, we mean, Kant argues, that we gain pleasure merely from contemplating it; we are not concerned with its existence or nonexistence or with its usefulness or uselessness: the satisfaction which we have in the object is completely disinterested.*

The satisfaction which we combine with the representation of the existence of an object is called interest. Such satisfaction always has reference to the faculty of desire, either as its determining ground or as necessarily connected with its determining ground. Now when the question is if a thing is beautiful, we do not want to know whether anything depends or can depend on the existence of the thing either for myself or for any one else, but how we judge it by mere observation (intuition or reflection). If any one asks me if I find that palace beautiful which I see before me, I may answer: I do not like things of that kind which are made merely to be stared at. Or I can answer like that Iroquois *Sachem*, who was pleased in Paris by nothing more than by the cook-shops. Or again after the manner of *Rousseau* I may rebuke the vanity of the great who waste the sweat of the people on such superfluous things. In fine I could easily convince myself that if I found myself on an uninhabited island without the hope of ever again coming among men, and could conjure up just such a splendid building by my mere wish, I should not even give myself the trouble if I had a sufficiently comfortable hut. This may all be admitted and approved; but we are not now talking of this. We wish only to know if this mere representation of the object is accompanied in me with satisfaction, however indifferent I may be as regards the existence of the object of this representation. We easily see that in saying it is *beautiful* and in showing that I have taste, I am concerned, not with that in which I depend on the existence of the object, but with that which I make out of this representation in myself. Every one must admit that a judgment about beauty, in which the least interest mingles, is very partial and is not a pure judgment of taste. We must not be in the least prejudiced in favour of the existence of the things, but be quite indifferent in this respect, in order to play the judge in things of taste....

Whatever by means of Reason pleases through the mere concept is GOOD. That which pleases only as a means we call *good for something* (the useful); but that which pleases for itself is *good in itself*. In both there is always involved the concept of a purpose, and consequently the relation of Reason to the (at least possible) volition, and thus a satisfaction in the *presence* of an Object or an action, i.e. some kind of interest.

In order to find anything good, I must always know what sort of a thing the object ought to be, i.e. I must have a concept of it. But there is no need of this to find a thing beautiful. Flowers, free delineations, outlines intertwined with one another without design and called [conventionally] foliage, having no meaning,

depend on no definite concept, and yet they please. The satisfaction in the beautiful must depend on the reflection upon an
object, leading to any concept (however indefinite); and it
is thus distinguished from the pleasant which rests entirely
upon sensation. . . .

The pleasant and the good have both a reference to the faculty
of desire; and they bring with them—the former a satisfaction
pathologically conditioned (by impulses, *stimuli*)—the latter a
pure practical satisfaction, which is determined not merely by
the representation of the object, but also by the represented
connection of the subject with the existence of the object. [It is
not merely the object that pleases, but also its existence.*] [18] On
the other hand, the judgment of taste is merely *contemplative*; i.e.
it is a judgment which, indifferent as regards the existence of an
object, compares its character with the feeling of pleasure and
pain. But this contemplation itself is not directed to concepts; for
the judgment of taste is not a cognitive judgment (either
theoretical or practical), and thus is not *based* on concepts, nor
has it concepts as its *purpose*.

The Pleasant, the Beautiful, and the Good, designate then, three
different relations of representations to the feeling of pleasure
and pain, in reference to which we distinguish from each other
objects or methods of representing them. . . . That which
GRATIFIES a man is called *pleasant*; that which merely PLEASES
him is *beautiful*; that which is ESTEEMED [or approved*] by
him, i.e. that to which he accords an objective worth, is *good*. . . .
We may say that of all these three kinds of satisfaction, that of
taste in the Beautiful is alone a disinterested and *free* satisfaction;
for no interest, either of Sense or of Reason, here forces our assent.
Hence we may say of satisfaction that it is related in the three
aforesaid cases to *inclination*, to *favour*, or to *respect*. Now *favour*
is the only free satisfaction. . . .

Taste is the faculty of judging of an object or a method of
representing it by an *entirely disinterested* satisfaction or dissatisfaction. The object of such satisfaction is called *beautiful*. [19]

2. *The second "moment" or determination of the judgment of
taste, its quantity, has to do with the universality and nonconceptual nature of the beautiful. The judgment of taste, implying
as it does an entirely disinterested satisfaction in the aesthetic*

experience, also implies a universality of satisfaction. When a person judges an object to be beautiful, he does not mean merely that he finds it to be beautiful, but that all men ought to find it beautiful too. Sensory pleasures are highly variable and are relative to individuals, Kant points out, but aesthetic satisfactions have a universal, though completely subjective, ground. When an object is such that it stimulates the free play of the apprehending faculty, the imagination, and the comprehending faculty, the understanding, we feel aesthetic pleasure and are convinced that everyone else experiencing the object will also feel as we do about it.

As regards the Pleasant everyone is content that his judgment, which he bases upon private feeling, and by which he says of an object that it pleases him, should be limited merely to his own person. Thus he is quite contented that if he says, "Canary wine is pleasant," another man may correct his expression and remind him that he ought to say "It is pleasant *to me*." And this is the case not only as regards the taste of the tongue, the palate, and the throat, but for whatever is pleasant to any one's eyes and ears. To one violet colour is soft and lovely, to another it is washed out and dead. One man likes the tone of wind instruments, another that of strings. To strive here with the design of reproving as incorrect another man's judgment which is different from our own, as if the judgments were logically opposed, would be folly. As regards the pleasant therefore the fundamental proposition is valid: *everyone has his own taste* (the taste of Sense).

The case is quite different with the Beautiful. It would (on the contrary) be laughable if a man who imagined anything to his own taste, thought to justify himself by saying: "This object (the house we see, the coat that the person wears, the concert we hear, the poem submitted to our judgment) is beautiful *for me*." For he must not call it *beautiful* if it merely pleases him. Many things may have for him charm and pleasantness; no one troubles himself at that; but if he gives out anything as beautiful, he supposes in others the same satisfaction—he judges not merely for himself, but for every one, and speaks of beauty as if it were a property of things. Hence he says "the *thing* is beautiful;" and he does not count on the agreement of others with this his judgment of satisfaction, because he has found this agreement several times before, but he *demands* it of them. He blames them if they judge otherwise and he denies them taste, which he nevertheless requires from them. Here then we cannot say that each man has his own particular taste. For this would be as much as to say that there is no taste whatever, i.e. no aesthetical judgment, which can make a rightful claim upon every one's assent. . . .

If we judge Objects merely according to concepts, then all representation of beauty is lost. Thus there can be no rule according to which any one is to be forced to recognize anything as beautiful. We cannot press [upon others] by the aid of any reasons or fundamental propositions our judgment that a coat, a house, or a flower is beautiful. People wish to submit the Object to their own eyes, as if the satisfaction in it depended on sensation; and yet if we then call the object beautiful, we believe that we speak with a universal voice, and we claim the assent of every one, although on the contrary all private sensations can only decide for the observer himself and his satisfaction.

We may see now that in the judgment of taste nothing is postulated but such a *universal voice*, in respect of the satisfaction without the intervention of concepts; and thus the *possibility* of an aesthetical judgment that can, at the same time, be regarded as valid for every one. The judgment of taste itself does not *postulate* the agreement of every one (for that can only be done by a logically universal judgment because it can adduce reasons); it only *imputes* this agreement to every one, as a case of the rule in respect of which it expects, not confirmation by concepts, but assent from others. . . .

If the pleasure in the given object precedes, and it is only its universal communicability that is to be acknowledged in the judgment of taste about the representation of the object, there would be a contradiction. For such pleasure would be nothing different from the mere pleasantness in the sensation, and so in accordance with its nature could have only private validity, because it is immediately dependent on the representation through which the object *is given*.

Hence, it is the universal capability of communication of the mental state in the given representation which, as the subjective condition of the judgment of taste, must be fundamental, and must have the pleasure in the object as its consequent. But nothing can be universally communicated except cognition and representation, so far as it belongs to cognition. For it is only thus that this latter can be objective; and only through this has it a universal point of reference, with which the representative power of every one is compelled to harmonize. If the determining ground of our judgment as to this universal communicability of the representation is to be merely subjective, i.e. is conceived independently of any concept of the object, it can be nothing else than the state of mind, which is to be met with in the relation of our representative powers to each other, so far as they refer a given representation to *cognition in general.*

The cognitive powers, which are involved by this representation, are here in free play, because no definite concept limits them to a definite rule of cognition. Hence, the state of mind in this representation must be a feeling of the free play of the representative powers in a given representation with reference to a cognition in general. Now a representation by which an object is given, that is to become a cognition in general, requires *Imagination,* for the gathering together the manifold of intuition, and *Understanding,* for the unity of the concept uniting the representations. This state of *free play* of the cognitive faculties in a representation by which an object is given, must be universally communicable; because cognition, as the determination of the Object with which given representations (in whatever subject) are to agree, is the only kind of representation which is valid for every one.

The subjective universal communicability of the mode of representation in a judgment of taste, since it is to be possible without presupposing a definite concept, can refer to nothing else than the state of mind in the free play of the Imagination and the Understanding (so far as they agree with each other, as is requisite for *cognition in general.*) We are conscious that this subjective relation, suitable for cognition in general, must be valid for every one, and thus must be universally communicable, just as if it were a definite cognition, resting always on that relation as its subjective condition.

This merely subjective (aesthetical) judging of the object, or of the representation by which it is given, precedes the pleasure in the same, and is the ground of this pleasure in the harmony of the cognitive faculties; but on that universality of the subjective conditions for judging of objects is alone based the universal subjective validity of the satisfaction bound up by us with the representation of the object that we call beautiful. . . .

The *beautiful* is that which pleases universally without [requiring] a concept.[20]

3. *Kant begins his exposition of the third moment of the judgment of taste, the moment of relation, by explaining what he means by purposiveness in general. When we have a concept of a thing's function, we think we know its final cause, its purpose, and can understand it as striving to attain this end, i.e. as being purposive. But when we appreciate a beautiful thing we do not need to know (nor do we care) what its purpose is; we do not need to have a concept of what sort of thing it is or what end it might be designed to achieve. We find it satisfying merely to contemplate. Yet, since this contemplation brings about the harmony of our cognitive faculties and with this harmony, pleasure, we tend to attribute to the object a kind of subjective purposiveness, but without any definite purpose.*

If we wish to explain what a purpose is according to its transcendental determinations (without presupposing anything empirical like the feeling of pleasure) [we say that] the purpose is the object of a concept, in so far as the concept is regarded as the cause of the object (the real ground of its possibility); and the causality of a *concept* in respect of its *Object* is its purposiveness *(forma finalis)*. Where then not merely the cognition of an object, but the object itself (its form and existence) is thought as an effect only possible by means of the concept of this latter, there we think a purpose....

The faculty of desire, so far as it is determinable to act only through concepts, i.e. in conformity with the representation of a purpose, would be the Will. But an Object, or a state of mind, or even an action, is called purposive, although its possibility does not necessarily presuppose the representation of a purpose, merely because its possibility can be explained and conceived by us only so far as we assume for its ground a causality according to purposes, i.e. in accordance with a will which has regulated it according to the representation of a certain rule. There can be, then, purposiveness without purpose, so far as we do not place the causes of this form in a Will, but yet can only make the explanation of its possibility intelligible to ourselves by deriving it from a Will. Again, we are not always forced to regard what we observe (in respect of its possibility) from the point of view of Reason. Thus we can at least observe a purposiveness according to form, without basing it on a purpose (as the material of the *nexus finalis*), and remark it in objects, although only by reflection. . . .

Every purpose, if it be regarded as a ground of satisfaction, always carries with it an interest—as the determining ground of the judgment—about the object of pleasure. Therefore no subjective purpose can lie at the basis of the judgment of taste. But also the judgment of taste can be determined by no representation of an objective purpose, i.e. of the possibility of the object itself in accordance with principles of purposive combination, and consequently by no concept of the good; because it is an aesthetical and not a cognitive judgment. It therefore has to do with no *concept* of the character and internal or external possibility of the object by means of this or that cause, but merely with the relation of the representative powers to one another, so far as they are determined by a representation.

Now this relation in the determination of an object as beautiful is bound up with the feeling of pleasure, which is declared by the judgment of taste to be valid for every one; hence a pleasantness, [merely] accompanying the representation, can as little contain the determining ground [of the judgment] as the representation of the perfection of the object and the concept of the good can. Therefore it can be nothing else than the subjective purposiveness in the representation of an object without any purpose (either objective or subjective); and thus it is the mere form of purposiveness in the representation by which an object is *given* to us, so far as we are conscious of it, which constitutes the satisfaction that we without a concept judge to be universally communicable; and, consequently, this is the determining ground of the judgment of taste.[21] . . .

4. *What Kant means by purposiveness without purpose becomes clearer when he goes on to distinguish and illustrate two kinds of beauty, only one of which, free beauty, gives us purely aesthetic enjoyment unconditioned by concepts or by an objective purpose. The other kind, adherent beauty, since it presupposes a concept or a definite purpose in order to be fully appreciated, is only conditionally beautiful. As a result of his examination of the judgment of taste in terms of its third moment, its relation to purpose, Kant reaches the paradoxical conclusion that the beautiful essentially involves only purposiveness without purpose.*

There are two kinds of beauty: free beauty *(pulchritudo vaga)* or merely dependent beauty *(pulchritudo adhaerens)*. The first presupposes no concept of what the object ought to be; the second does presuppose such a concept and the perfection of the object in accordance therewith. The first is called the (self-subsistent) beauty of this or that thing; the second, as dependent upon a concept (conditioned beauty), is ascribed to objects which come under the concept of a particular purpose.

Flowers are free natural beauties. Hardly anyone but a botanist knows what sort of a thing a flower ought to be; and even he, though recognizing in the flower the reproductive organ of the plant, pays no regard to this natural purpose if he is passing judgment on the flower by Taste. There is, then, at the basis of this judgment no perfection of any kind, no internal purposiveness, to which the collection of the manifold is referred. Many birds (such as the parrot, the humming bird, the bird of paradise), and many sea shells are beauties in themselves, which do not belong to any object determined in respect of its purpose by concepts, but please freely and in themselves. So also delineations *à la grecque,* foliage for borders or wall-papers, mean nothing in themselves; they represent nothing—no Object under a definite concept,—and are free beauties. We can refer to the same class what are called in music phantasies (i.e. pieces without any theme), and in fact all music without words.

In judging of a free beauty (according to the mere form) the judgment of taste is pure. There is presupposed no concept of any purpose, which the manifold of the given object is to serve, and which therefore is to be represented in it. By such a concept the freedom of the Imagination which disports itself in the contemplation of the figure would be only limited.

But human beauty (i.e. of a man, a woman, or a child), the beauty of a horse, or a building (be it church, palace, arsenal, or summer-house), presupposes a concept of the purpose which determines what the thing is to be, and consequently a concept of its perfection; it is therefore adherent beauty. Now as the combination of the Pleasant (in sensation) with Beauty, which properly is concerned with form, is a hindrance to the purity of the judgment of taste; so also is its purity injured by the combination with Beauty of the Good (viz. that manifold which is good for the thing itself in accordance with its purpose).

We could add much to a building which would immediately

please the eye, if only it were not to be a church. We could adorn a figure with all kinds of spirals and light but regular lines, as the New Zealanders do with their tattooing, if only it were not the figure of a human being. And again this could have much finer features and a more pleasing and gentle cast of countenance provided it were not intended to represent a man, much less a warrior.

Now the satisfaction in the manifold of a thing in reference to the internal purpose which determines its possibility is a satisfaction grounded on a concept; but the satisfaction in beauty is such as presupposes no concept, but is immediately bound up with the representation through which the object is given (not through which it is thought). If now the judgment of Taste in respect of the beauty of a thing is made dependent on the purpose in its manifold, like a judgment of Reason, and thus limited, it is no longer a free and pure judgment of Taste. . . .

A judgment of taste, then, in respect of an object with a definite internal purpose, can only be pure, if either the person judging has no concept of this purpose, or else abstracts from it in his judgment. Such a person, although forming an accurate judgment of taste in judging of the object as a free beauty, would yet by another who considers the beauty in it only as a dependent attribute (who looks to the purpose of the object) be blamed, and accused of false taste; although both are right in their own way, the one in reference to what he has before his eyes, the other in reference to what he has in his thought. By means of this distinction we can settle many disputes about beauty between judges of taste; by showing that the one is speaking of free, the other of dependent, beauty,—that the first is making a pure, the second an applied, judgment of taste. . . .

Beauty is the form of the *purposiveness* of an object, so far as this is perceived in it *without any representation of a purpose.*[22]

5. *So far Kant has argued that the judgment of taste refers to an object which in terms of quality brings a disinterested satisfaction, in terms of quantity gives a universal satisfaction, and in terms of relation involves a purposiveness without purpose. Now, in treating of the final moment or determination of the judgment of taste, he discusses it in terms of its modality, and argues that the experience of the beautiful implies a necessary*

satisfaction. The argument here is very much like that by which Kant supported his view that the beautiful gives a universal satisfaction. As before, Kant argues that in making a judgment of taste we must presuppose a common sense, a principle of universal communicability, which is subjective and indeterminate but nonetheless essential if we are to explain why we feel that others necessarily ought to agree with us when we judge an object to be beautiful.

I can say of every representation that it is at least *possible* that (as a cognition) it should be bound up with a pleasure. Of a representation that I call *pleasant* I say that it *actually* excites pleasure in me. But the *beautiful* we think as having a *necessary* reference to satisfaction. Now this necessity is of a peculiar kind. It is not a theoretical objective necessity; in which case it would be cognized *a priori* that everyone *will feel* this satisfaction in the object called beautiful by me. It is not a practical necessity, in which case, by concepts of a pure rational will serving as a rule for freely acting beings, the satisfaction is the necessary result of an objective law and only indicates that we absolutely (without any further design) ought to act in a certain way. But the necessity which is thought in an aesthetical judgment can only be called *exemplary,* i.e. a necessity of the assent of *all* to a judgment which is regarded as the example of a universal rule that we cannot state. Since an aesthetical judgment is not an objective cognitive judgment, this necessity cannot be derived from definite concepts, and is therefore not apodictic. Still less can it be inferred from the universality of experience (of a complete agreement of judgments as to the beauty of a certain object). For not only would experience hardly furnish sufficiently numerous vouchers for this; but also, on empirical judgments we can base no concept of the necessity of these judgments. . . .

The judgment of taste requires the agreement of everyone; and he who describes anything as beautiful claims that everyone *ought* to give his approval to the object in question and also describe it as beautiful. The *ought* in the aesthetical judgment is therefore pronounced in accordance with all the data which are required for judging and yet is only conditioned. We ask for the agreement of every one else, because we have for it a ground that is common to all; and we could count on this agreement, provided we were always sure that the case was correctly subsumed under that ground as rule of assent....

If judgments of taste (like cognitive judgments) had a definite objective principle, then the person who lays them down in accordance with this latter would claim an unconditioned necessity for his judgment. If they were devoid of all principle, like those of the mere taste of sense, we would not allow them in thought any necessity whatever. Hence they must have a subjective principle which determines what pleases or displeases only by feeling and not by concepts, but yet with universal validity. But such a principle could only be regarded as a *common sense*, which is essentially different from common Understanding which people sometimes call common Sense *(sensus communis)*; for the latter does not judge by feeling but always by concepts, although ordinarily only as by obscurely represented principles.

Hence it is only under the presupposition that there is a common sense (by which we do not understand an external sense, but the effect resulting from the free play of our cognitive powers)—it is only under this presupposition, I say, that the judgment of taste can be laid down....

Cognitions and judgments must, along with the conviction that accompanies them, admit of universal communicability; for otherwise there would be no harmony between them and the Object, and they would be collectively a mere subjective play of the representative powers, exactly as scepticism desires. But if cognitions are to admit of communicability, so must also the state of mind,—i.e. the accordance of the cognitive powers with a cognition generally, and that proportion of them which is suitable for a representation (by which an object is given to us) in order that a cognition may be made out of it—admit of universal communicability. For without this as the subjective condition of cognition, cognition as an effect could not arise. This actually always takes place when a given object by means of Sense excites the Imagination to collect the manifold, and the Imagination in its turn excites the Understanding to bring about a unity of this collective process in concepts. But this accordance of the cognitive powers has a different proportion according to the variety of the Objects which are given. However, it must be such that this internal relation, by which one mental faculty is excited by another, shall be generally the most beneficial for both faculties in respect of cognition (of given objects); and this accordance can only be determined by feeling (not according to concepts). Since now this accordance itself must admit of universal communicability, and consequently also our feeling of it (in a given representation), and since the universal communicability of a feeling presupposes a common sense, we have grounds for assuming this latter. And this common sense is assumed without relying on psychological observations, but simply as the necessary condition of the universal communicability of our knowledge, which is presupposed in every Logic and in every principle of knowledge that is not sceptical. . . .

In all judgments by which we describe anything as beautiful, we allow no one to be of another opinion; without, however, grounding our judgment on concepts but only on our feeling, which we therefore place at its basis not as a private, but as a common, feeling. Now this common sense cannot be grounded on experience; for it aims at justifying judgments which contain an *ought*. It does not say that everyone *will* agree with my judgment, but that he *ought*. And so common sense, as an example of whose judgment I here put forward my judgment of taste and on account of which I attribute to the latter an *exemplary* validity, is a mere ideal norm, under the supposition of which I have a right to make into a rule for everyone a judgment that accords therewith, as well as the satisfaction in an Object expressed in such judgment. For the principle, which concerns the agreement of different judging persons, although only subjective, is yet assumed as subjectively universal (an Idea necessary for everyone); and thus can claim universal assent (as if it were objective) provided we are sure that we have correctly subsumed [the particulars] under it.

This indeterminate norm of a common sense is actually presupposed by us; as is shown by our claim to lay down judgments of taste. . . .

The *beautiful* is that which without any concept is cognized as the object of a *necessary* satisfaction.[23]

6. *In his aesthetic theory, Kant discusses our judgments of the sublime as well as our judgments of the beautiful. After noting the similarities between the sublime and the beautiful, he distinguishes*

one from the other in terms of differences in the form of the
objects they represent, their different effects on the mental
faculties, and the different kinds of pleasures they evoke. Since
the sublime is, in Kant's view, that which is absolutely great, and
since we cannot have sense experience of an object in nature that
can be so characterized, the feeling of the sublime can be made
intelligible only through reference to a higher, supersensible faculty
within us.

The Beautiful and the Sublime agree in this, that both please in
themselves. Further, neither presupposes a judgment of sense nor
a judgment logically determined, but a judgment of reflection.
Consequently the satisfaction [belonging to them] does not depend
on a sensation, as in the case of the Pleasant, nor on a definite
concept, as in the case of the Good; but it is nevertheless referred
to concepts although indeterminate ones. . . .

But there are also remarkable differences between the two. The
Beautiful in nature is connected with the form of the object,
which consists in having [definite] boundaries. The Sublime, on
the other hand, is to be found in a formless object, so far as in it
or by occasion of it *boundlessness* is represented, and yet its totality
is also present to thought. Thus the Beautiful seems to be regarded
as the presentation of an indefinite concept of Understanding, the
Sublime as that of a like concept of Reason. Therefore the satisfaction in the one case is bound up with the representation of
quality, in the other with that of *quantity*. And the latter satisfaction is quite different in kind from the former, for this [the
Beautiful*] directly brings with it a feeling of the furtherance of
life, and thus is compatible with charms and with the play of the
Imagination. But the other [the feeling of the Sublime] is a
pleasure that arises only indirectly; viz. it is produced by the
feeling of a momentary checking of the vital powers and a
consequent stronger outflow of them, so that it seems to be
regarded as emotion,—not play, but earnest in the exercise of the
Imagination. Hence it is incompatible with [physical] charm; and
as the mind is not merely attracted by the object but is ever being
alternately repelled, the satisfaction in the sublime does not so
much involve a positive pleasure as admiration or respect, which
rather deserves to be called negative pleasure.

But the inner and most important distinction between the

Sublime and Beautiful is, certainly, as follows.... Natural beauty (which is independent) brings with it a purposiveness in its form by which the object seems to be, as it were, pre-adapted to our Judgment, and thus constitutes in itself an object of satisfaction. On the other hand, that which excites in us, without any reasoning about it, but in the mere apprehension of it, the feeling of the sublime may appear as regards its form to violate purpose in respect of the Judgment, to be unsuited to our presentative faculty, and, as it were, to do violence to the Imagination; and yet it is judged to be only the more sublime.

Now we may see from this that in general we express ourselves incorrectly if we call any *object of nature* sublime, although we can quite correctly call many objects of nature beautiful. For how can that be marked by an expression of approval, which is apprehended in itself as being a violation of purpose? All that we can say is that the object is fit for the presentation of a sublimity which can be found in the mind; for no sensible form can contain the sublime properly so-called. This concerns only Ideas of the Reason,[24] which, although no adequate presentation is possible for them, by this inadequateness that admits of sensible presentation, are aroused and summoned into the mind. Thus the wide ocean, disturbed by the storm, cannot be called sublime. Its aspect is horrible; and the mind must be already filled with manifold Ideas if it is to be determined by such an intuition to a feeling itself sublime, as it is incited to abandon sensibility and to busy itself with Ideas that involve higher purposiveness....

We call that *sublime* which is *absolutely great*. But to be great, and to be a great something are quite different concepts (*magnitudo* and *quantitas*). In like manner to *say simply* (*simpliciter*) that anything is *great* is quite different from saying that it is *absolutely great* (*absolute, non comparative magnum*). *The latter is what is great beyond all comparison....*

In a judgment by which anything is designated simply as great, it is not merely meant that the object has a magnitude, but that this magnitude is superior to that of many other objects of the same kind, without, however, any exact determinations of this superiority. Thus there is always at the basis of our judgment a standard which we assume as the same for everyone; this, however is not available for any logical (mathematically definite) judging of magnitude, but only for aesthetical judging of the same, because it is a merely subjective standard lying at the basis of the reflective judgment upon magnitude....

But if we call anything not only great, but absolutely great in every point of view (great beyond all comparison), i.e. sublime, we soon see that it is not permissible to seek for an adequate standard of this outside itself, but merely in itself. It is a magnitude which is like itself alone. It follows hence that the sublime is not to be sought in the things of nature, but only in our Ideas. . . .

The foregoing explanation can be thus expressed: *the sublime is that in comparison with which everything else is small.* Here we easily see that nothing can be given in nature, however great it is judged by us to be, which could not if considered in another relation be reduced to the infinitely small; and conversely there is nothing so small, which does not admit of extension by our Imagination to the greatness of a world, if compared with still smaller standards. Telescopes have furnished us with abundant material for making the first remark, microscopes for the second. Nothing, therefore, which can be an object of the senses is, considered on this basis, to be called sublime. But because there is in our Imagination a striving toward infinite progress, and in our Reason a claim for absolute totality, regarded as a real Idea, therefore this very inadequateness for that Idea in our faculty for estimating the magnitude of things of sense, excites in us the feeling of a supersensible faculty. And it is not the object of sense, but the use which the Judgment naturally makes of certain objects on behalf of this latter feeling, that is absolutely great; and in comparison every other use is small. Consequently it is the state of mind produced by a certain representation with which the reflective Judgment is occupied, and not the Object, that is to be called sublime.

We can therefore append to the preceding formulas explaining the sublime this other: *the sublime is that, the mere ability to think which, shows a faculty of the mind surpassing every standard of Sense.*[25] . . .

7. *According to Kant, there are two different kinds of the sublime: the mathematically sublime and the dynamically sublime. After explaining in detail how the experience of the mathematically sublime arises in us through our attempts to apprehend and comprehend increasingly extensive magnitudes, and finally the infinite itself, Kant reiterates his belief that the very capacity for thinking the infinite, the absolutely great, implies a supersensible faculty.*

Now for the mathematical estimation of magnitude there is, indeed, no maximum (for the power of numbers extends to infinity); but for its aesthetical estimation there is always a maximum, and of this I say that if it is judged as the absolute measure than which no greater is possible subjectively (for the judging subject), it brings with it the Idea of the sublime and produces that emotion which no mathematical estimation of its magnitude by means of numbers can bring about (except so far as that aesthetical fundamental measure remains vividly in the Imagination). For the former only presents relative magnitude by means of comparison with others of the same kind; but the latter presents magnitude absolutely, so far as the mind can grasp it in an intuition.

In receiving a quantum into the Imagination by intuition, in order to be able to use it for a measure or as a unit for the estimation of magnitude by means of numbers, there are two operations of the Imagination involved: *apprehension (apprehensio)* and *comprehension (comprehensio aesthetica)*. As to apprehension there is no difficulty, for it can go on *ad infinitum*; but comprehension becomes harder the further apprehension advances, and soon attains to its maximum, viz. the greatest possible aesthetical fundamental measure for the estimation of magnitude. For when apprehension has gone so far that the partial representations of sensuous intuition at first apprehended begin to vanish in the Imagination, whilst this ever proceeds to the apprehension of others, then it loses as much on the one side as it gains on the other; and in comprehension there is a maximum beyond which it cannot go.

Hence can be explained what Savary[26] remarks in his account of Egypt, viz., that we must keep from going very near the Pyramids just as much as we keep from going too far from them, in order to get the full emotional effect from their size. For if we are too far away, the parts to be apprehended (the stones lying one over the other) are only obscurely represented, and the representation of them produces no effect upon the aesthetical judgment of the subject. But if we are very near, the eye requires some time to complete the apprehension of the tiers from the bottom up to the apex; and then the first tiers are always partly forgotten before the Imagination has taken in the last, and so the comprehension of them is never complete. The same thing may sufficiently explain the bewilderment or, as it were, perplexity, which, it is said, seizes the spectator on his first entrance into St. Peter's at Rome. For there is here a feeling of the inadequacy of his Imagination for presenting the Ideas of a whole, wherein the Imagination reaches its maximum, and, in striving to surpass it, sinks back into itself, by which, however, a kind of emotional satisfaction is produced. . . .

But the infinite is absolutely (not merely comparatively) great. Compared with it everything else (of the same kind of magnitudes) is small. And what is most important is that to be able to think it as *a whole* indicates a faculty of mind which surpasses every standard of Sense. For [to represent it sensibly] would require a comprehension having for unit a standard bearing a definite relation, expressible in numbers, to the infinite, which is impossible. Nevertheless, *the bare capability of thinking* this infinite without contradiction requires in the human mind a faculty itself supersensible. . . .

Nature is therefore sublime in those of its phenomena whose intuition brings with it the Idea of its infinity. . . .

Examples of the mathematically Sublime in nature in mere intuition are all the cases in which we are given, not so much a larger numerical concept, as a large unit for the measure of the Imagination (for shortening the numerical series). A tree, [the height of] which we estimate with reference to the height of a man, at all events gives a standard for a mountain; and if this were a mile high, it would serve as unit for the number expressive of the earth's diameter, so that the latter might be made intuitible. The earth's diameter [would supply a unit] for the known planetary system; this again for the Milky Way; and the immeasurable number of Milky Way systems called nebulae,—which presumably constitute a system of the same kind among themselves—lets us expect no bounds here. Now the Sublime in the aesthetical judging of an immeasurable whole like this lies not so much in the greatness of the number [of units], as in the fact that in our progress we ever arrive at yet greater units. To this the systematic division of the universe contributes, which represents every magnitude in nature as small in its turn; and represents our Imagination with its entire freedom from bounds, and with it Nature, as a mere nothing in comparison with the Ideas of Reason, if it is sought to furnish a presentation which shall be adequate to them.[27]

8. *The dynamically sublime is, according to Kant, aroused in us when we are confronted with powerful natural forces which could easily overwhelm us, yet we recognize our superiority as conscious, supersensible moral agents over the external forces threatening us. The feeling of the sublime, like the feeling of moral obligation is, for Kant, an intimation of the Divine Nature within us and beyond.*

Might is that which is superior to great hindrances. It is called *dominion* if it is superior to the resistance of that which itself possesses might. Nature, considered in an aesthetical judgment as might that has no dominion over us, is *dynamically sublime*.

If nature is to be judged by us as dynamically sublime, it must be represented as exciting fear (although it is not true conversely that every object which excites fear is regarded in our aesthetical judgment as sublime). For in aesthetical judgments (without the aid of concepts) superiority to hindrances can only be judged according to the greatness of the resistance. Now that which we are driven to resist is an evil, and, if we do not find our faculties a match for it, is an object of fear. Hence nature can be regarded by the aesthetical Judgment as might, and consequently as dynamically sublime, only so far as it is considered an object of fear.

But we can regard an object as *fearful*, without being afraid *of* it, viz. if we judge of it in such a way that we merely *think* a case in which we would wish to resist it, and yet in which all resistance would be altogether vain. Thus the virtuous man fears God without being afraid of Him, because to wish to resist Him and His commandments, he thinks is a case that *he* need not apprehend. But in every such case that he thinks as not impossible, he cognizes Him as fearful.

He who fears can form no judgment about the Sublime in nature; just as he who is seduced by inclination and appetite can form no judgment about the Beautiful. The former flies from the sight of an object which inspires him with awe; and it is impossible to find satisfaction in a terror that is seriously felt. Hence the pleasurableness arising from the cessation of an uneasiness is *a state of joy*. But this, on account of the deliverance from danger [which is involved], is a state of joy when conjoined with the resolve that we shall no more be exposed to the danger; we cannot willingly look back upon our sensations [of danger], much less seek the occasion for them again.

Bold, overhanging, and as it were threatening rocks; clouds piled up in the sky, moving with lightning flashes and thunder peals; volcanoes in all their violence of destruction; hurricanes with their track of devastation; the boundless ocean in a state of tumult; the lofty waterfall of a mighty river, and such like; these exhibit our faculty of resistance as insignificantly small in comparison with their might. But the sight of them is the more attractive, the more fearful it is, provided only that we are in security; and we willingly call these objects sublime, because they raise the energies of the soul above their accustomed height, and discover in us a faculty of resistance of a quite different kind, which gives us courage to measure ourselves against the apparent almightiness of nature.

Now, in the immensity of nature, and in the insufficiency of our faculties to take in a standard proportionate to the aesthetical estimation of the magnitude of its *realm*, we find our own limitation; although at the same time in our rational faculty we find a different, non-sensuous standard, which has that infinity itself under it as a unity, in comparison with which everything in nature is small, and thus in our mind we find a superiority to nature even in its immensity. And so also the irresistibility of its might, while making us recognize our own [physical*] impotence, considered as beings of nature, discloses to us a faculty of judging independently of, and a superiority over, nature; on which is based a kind of self-preservation, entirely different from that which can be attacked and brought into danger by external nature. Thus, humanity in our person remains unhumiliated, though the individual might have to submit to this dominion. In this way nature is not judged to be sublime in our aesthetical judgments, in so far as it excites fear; but because it calls up that power in us (which is not nature) of regarding as small the things about which we are solicitous (goods, health, and life), and of regarding its might (to which we are no doubt subjected in respect of these things), as nevertheless without any dominion over us and our personality to which we must bow where our highest fundamental propositions, and their assertion or abandonment, are concerned. Therefore nature is here called sublime merely because it elevates the Imagination to a presentation of those cases in which the mind can make felt the proper sublimity of its destination, in comparison with nature itself.

This estimation of ourselves loses nothing through the fact that we must regard ourselves as safe in order to feel this inspiriting satisfaction; and that hence, as there is no seriousness in the danger, there might be also (as might seem to be the case) just a little seriousness in the sublimity of our spiritual faculty. For the satisfaction here concerns only the *destination* of our faculty which discloses itself in such a case, so far as the tendency to this destination lies in our nature, whilst its development and exercise remain incumbent and obligatory. And in this there is truth [and reality], however conscious the man may be of his present actual powerlessness, when he turns his reflection to it. . . .

Sublimity, therefore, does not reside in anything in nature, but only in our mind, in so far as we can become conscious that we are superior to nature within, and therefore also to nature without us (so far as it influences us). Everything that excites this feeling in us, e.g., the *might* of nature which calls forth our forces, is called then (although improperly) sublime. Only by supposing this Idea in ourselves, and in reference to it, are we capable of attaining to the Idea of the sublimity of that Being, which produces respect in us, not merely by the might that it displays in nature, but rather by means of the faculty which resides in us of judging it fearlessly and of regarding our destination as sublime in respect of it.[28]

NOTES

1. This work, Kant's "pre-Critical" treatment of aesthetic problems, has a grace, a simplicity, and, in places, a naiveté, quite uncharacteristic of his later, more extensive treatment in the *Critique of Judgment* in which he brought to bear on the same problems the heavy dialectical equipment he had forged while thinking out and writing his *Critique of Pure Reason*. There are

still some things of interest and merit in the earlier work, however, aside from the light it sheds on Kant's thinking prior to his being "smitten" with the transcendental. See the new translation of the *Observations* by John T. Goldthwait listed in our "Guide to Supplementary Reading."

2. But the originality of Kant's contribution to aesthetics has often been questioned by scholars. Armand Nivelle, in one of the most recent studies in the development of German aesthetics, *Les Théories Esthétiques en Allemagne de Baumgarten à Kant* (Paris, 1955), holds that Kant certainly could never lay claim to having initiated a "Copernican revolution" in aesthetics. For the central problem discussed in his *Critique of Judgment* (1790), namely, the problem of placing beauty in the order of values and of explaining the mental faculty which apprehends it, had been under consideration since Baumgarten's *Aesthetica* (1750). Nivelle shows how great was Kant's intellectual debt to his predecessors—to Baumgarten, Meier, Sulzer, Mendelssohn, Lessing, and Herder—but also how great was his own contribution in synthesizing materials and in resolving problems from the vantage point of his philosophical genius.

3. There are translations of the *Critique of Pure Reason* by J. M. D. Meiklejohn and by Norman Kemp-Smith, and of the *Critique of Practical Reason* by T. K. Abbott and by L. W. Beck. Translations of the *Critique of Judgment* are listed in our "Guide to Supplementary Reading."

4. *Critique of Pure Reason*, translated by J. M. D. Meiklejohn, revised edition (New York, Colonial Press, 1899), Preface, ix, xi.

5. *Critique of Pure Reason* (Meiklejohn translation), p. 45.

6. *Kant's Kritik of Judgment*, translated by J. H. Bernard (London, Macmillan & Co., 1892), p. 41. (Bernard used "Kritik" in the title of the first edition of his translation, but in the second edition substituted "Critique." Although we cite his first edition, we shall hereafter do so as *Critique of Judgment.*)

7. *Critique of Judgment* (Bernard translation), p. 38.

8. *Critique of Judgment* (Bernard translation), p. 16.

9. But to understand the place and meaning of Kant's discussion of aesthetic problems in his system of critical philosophy it would be of course impossible to separate the two parts of the *Critique of Judgment*, especially since, as Armand Nivelle (*op. cit.*) has shown, Kant was more concerned in this work with completing his system, with solving philosophical problems relating to natural

purpose, than he was with presenting a new theory of beauty. The student who desires an over-view can find it in the excellent, coherent account of Kant's entire philosophic undertaking given by Frederick Copleston, S.J., in his *History of Philosophy*, Vol. 6 (Modern Philosophy), Part II (Kant), (Garden City, N.Y., Image Books, 1964). Chapter 15 deals with Kant's aesthetics and teleology.

10. *Critique of Judgment* (Bernard translation), p. 183 (Sec. 43). For Kant's treatment of art in general, see Secs. 43–44; on the classification and comparison of arts, see Secs. 51–53.

11. "And by an aesthetical Idea I understand that representation of the Imagination which occasions much thought, without, however, any definite thought, i.e., any *concept*, being capable of being adequate to it; it consequently cannot be completely compassed and made intelligible by language." *Critique of Judgment* (Bernard translation), p. 197 (Sec. 49).

12. On Kant's treatment of music, see an article by Herbert M. Schneller, "Immanuel Kant and the Aesthetics of Music," *Journal of Aesthetics and Art Criticism*, XIV (December, 1955), 218–247.

13. *Critique of Judgment* (Bernard translation), p. 223 (Sec. 54).

14. Ibid., p. 188 (Sec. 46).

15. According to Kant, we can learn to do physics by reading Newton, but we can never learn to write poetry by reading Homer. See *Critique of Judgment* (Bernard translation), pp. 190–192 (Sec. 47).

16. On Kant's own artistic preferences, see Rudolph H. Weingartner's "A Note on Kant's Artistic Interests," *JAAC*, XVI (December, 1957), 261–262.

17. Kant's discussion of the logical functions of judgment is in the *Critique of Pure Reason*, "Transcendental Doctrine of Elements," Part II (Transcendental Logic), First Division (Transcendental Analytic), Bk. I, Chap. I, Sec. II.

18. Passages bracketed and marked with asterisks are those which were added in Kant's second edition of the *Critique of Judgment*. Other bracketed passages are Bernard's emendations.

19. *Critique of Judgment* (Bernard translation), pp. 46–48 (Sec. 2); pp. 50–51 (Sec. 4); pp. 53–55 (Sec. 5).

20. Ibid., pp. 57–58 (Sec. 7); p. 62 (Sec. 8); pp. 63–65 (Sec. 9).

21. *Critique of Judgment* (Bernard translation), pp. 67–69 (Sec. 10); pp. 69–70 (Sec. 11).

22. Ibid., pp. 81–84 (Sec. 16); p. 90 (Sec. 17). Kant adds the following footnote at this point: "It might be objected to this explanation that there are things, in which we see a purposive form without cognising any [definite] purpose in them, like the stone implements often got from old sepulchral tumuli with a hole in them as if for a handle. These, although they plainly indicate by their shape a purposiveness of which we do not know the purpose, are nevertheless not described as beautiful. But if we regard a thing as a work of art, that is enough to make us admit that its shape has reference to some design and definite purpose. And hence there is no immediate satisfaction in the contemplation of it. On the other hand a flower, e.g. a tulip, is regarded as beautiful; because in perceiving it we find a certain purposiveness which, in our judgment, is referred to no purpose at all."

23. *Critique of Judgment* (Bernard translation), pp. 91–96 (Secs. 18–22).

24. The Ideas of Reason are discussed in the *Critique of Pure Reason*, "Transcendental Doctrine of Elements," Part II (Transcendental Logic), Second Division (Transcendental Dialectic); Bk. I, Sec. II. "I understand by idea," Kant writes, "a necessary conception of reason, to which no corresponding object can be discovered in the world of sense. Accordingly, the pure conceptions of reason at present under consideration are *transcendental ideas*. They are conceptions of pure reason, for they regard all empirical cognition as determined by means of an absolute totality of conditions. They are not mere fictions, but natural and necessary products of reason, and have hence a necessary relation to the whole sphere of the exercise of the understanding. And finally, they are transcendent, and overstep the limits of all experience, in which, consequently, no object can ever be presented that would be perfectly adequate to a transcendental idea." (Meiklejohn translation, p. 205.)

25. Ibid., pp. 101–103 (Sec. 23); pp. 106–110 (Sec. 25).

26. [*Lettres sur l'Egypte,* par M. Savary, Amsterdam, 1787.]

27. *Critique of Judgment* (Bernard translation), pp. 111–112 (Sec. 26); pp. 115–116 (Sec. 26); pp. 118–119 (Sec. 26).

28. Ibid., pp. 123–126 (Sec. 28); p. 129 (Sec. 28). The reader may be interested in Kant's view of Burke's earlier treatment of the problems he has been discussing. Kant regards Burke as the most important of those thinkers who have attempted to give an empirical and physiological explanation of the sublime and the beautiful. But while he is appreciative of Burke's efforts, he

considers the empirical approach to be only "a beginning of a collection of material for a higher investigation," which is precisely what Kant considers his own "transcendental exposition" to be. See *Critique of Judgment*, Sec. 29.

QUESTIONS AND TOPICS FOR FURTHER STUDY

1. Explain how Kant distinguishes the beautiful from the pleasant and the good. How can a satisfaction be entirely disinterested?

2. Why does Kant believe that "if we judge objects merely according to concepts, then all representation of beauty is lost"?

3. What would be Kant's answer to the view that "there is no arguing about tastes"?

4. How are the various mental faculties involved and affected by aesthetic contemplation, according to Kant?

5. Explain what Kant means by "purposiveness without purpose" and how this is related to aesthetic contemplation.

6. What are the two kinds of beauty mentioned by Kant? Give several examples to illustrate the differences between them.

7. What does Kant mean by "common sense"? Why does he believe that this must be presupposed in order to explain the necessity of judgments of taste?

8. Point out the similarities and differences in the beautiful and the sublime, according to Kant.

9. What are the two kinds of sublimity distinguished by Kant? Give examples of each.

10. Topics for further study: (a) Kant's pre-critical views on the beautiful and the sublime; (b) Kant's view of the fine arts; (c) the relationship between the moral and the aesthetic spheres in Kant; (d) the influence of Edmund Burke on Kant's view of the sublime; (e) Kant's view of artistic genius.

GUIDE TO SUPPLEMENTARY READING

(Works marked with asterisks are available in paperbound editions.)

I. PRIMARY SOURCES

Kant, Immanuel, *Observations on the Feeling of the Beautiful and the Sublime,* translated by John T. Goldthwait (Berkeley and Los Angeles, University of California Press, 1960).

———*Critique of Judgment,* translated with an introduction by J. H. Bernard (New York, Hafner Publishing Company, 1951).

———*Kant's Critique of Aesthetic Judgment,* translated with introductory essays by J. C. Meredith (Oxford, Clarendon Press, 1911).

———*Analytic of the Beautiful from The Critique of Judgment with excerpts from Anthropology from a Pragmatic Viewpoint, Second Book,* translated with an introduction, comments, and notes by Walter Cerf (Indianapolis and New York, Bobbs-Merrill Company, 1963).

II. SECONDARY WORKS

Bosanquet, Bernard, *A History of Aesthetic (New York, Meredian Books, 1957) (reprint), Chap. X.

Carritt, E. F., *The Theory of Beauty* (New York, Barnes and Noble, n.d.), Chap. V.

Cassirer, H. W., *A Commentary on Kant's Critique of Judgment* (London, Methuen and Company, Ltd., 1938).

Gilbert, Katharine, and Helmut Kuhn, *A History of Esthetics,* revised edition (Bloomington, Indiana University Press, 1953), Chap. XI.

Knox, Israel, *The Aesthetic Theories of Kant, Hegel and Schopenhauer* (New York, Humanities Press, 1958).

Kroner, S., *Kant* (Baltimore, Maryland, Penguin Books, 1955), Chap. 8.

Macmillan, Robert A. C., *The Crowning Phase of the Critical Philosophy: A Study in Kant's Critique of Judgment* (London, Macmillan & Co., 1912).

Whitney, G. T., and D. F. Bowers (editors), *The Heritage of Kant* (Princeton, Princeton University Press, 1939).

Zimmerman, Robert L., "Kant: The Aesthetic Judgment," *Journal of Aesthetics and Art Criticism*, XXI (Spring, 1963), pp. 333–44.

CHAPTER 5

Art and the Absolute Spirit

HEGEL

Born in Stuttgart, educated in that city's schools and later in the Protestant seminary of the University of Tübingen, Georg Wilhelm Friedrich Hegel (1770–1831) developed into the greatest German philosopher and the most influential teacher of philosophy in the entire nineteenth century. But before he reached the high point of his productivity and influence as professor of philosophy at the University of Berlin (1818–1831), Hegel served as private tutor in Bern and in Frankfurt, headed a school and edited a newspaper in Bavaria, and taught philosophy in the Universities of Jena and Heidelberg. Although in his youth he had been a romantic liberal and an ardent supporter of the French Revolution, in his maturity he became a staunch conservative, a stringent critic of democratic and liberal movements, and the favored and decorated philosopher of Prussian monarchy. Despite his heavy professional and family responsibilities, Hegel still found time to travel—he went to Switzerland, the Low Countries, France, and Austria—in order to widen his experience and to expand his acquaintance with the fine arts. During his lifetime he set forth his idealistic system of philosophy in four major works: *The Phenomenology of Spirit* (1807); *The Science of Logic* (1812–1816); *The Encyclopedia of the Philosophical Sciences* (1817); and *The Philosophy of Right* (1821). His Berlin lectures on philosophy of history, philosophy of religion, history of philosophy, and philosophy of fine art were edited and published by others after Hegel's sudden death from cholera.

Hegel's greatest ambition as a philosopher was to construct an all-encompassing system of thought that would be capable of explaining everything that is, "reality as such," in all its concreteness. He sought total comprehension, coherent knowledge, absolute truth. Central to his whole philosophic enterprise was his assumption (contrary to Kant's) that reality *is* rational and can be known as it actually is through rational thought. For in knowing reality, mind knows its own; reality *is* Mind or Spirit or Absolute Idea. The ultimate task of philosophy is to get to know completely this Absolute Idea, or, rather, to let the Absolute Idea get to know itself comprehensively as pure thought. As logic, philosophy gets to know the Idea "as it is in and for itself" through the abstract medium of thought, through the categories by which it is defined or determined—basically the categories of Being, Essence, and Notion. As philosophy of nature, philosophy studies the Absolute Idea as it is externalized in the physical world or as it exists "in its otherness" through the sciences of Mechanics, Physics, and Organics. Finally, as philosophy of Spirit, philosophy knows the Idea "as it returns to itself from its otherness" or as it reveals itself in the psychological sphere (Subjective Spirit), the moral and social spheres (Objective Spirit), and in the spheres of art, religion, and philosophy (Absolute Spirit).

In order to understand the progressive stages of thought and the increasingly complex manifestations of reality or spirit, Hegel thinks that it is necessary to grasp the dialectical principle inherent in the development of reality and thought. A concept or thesis is no sooner posited than it produces the opposite concept which negates it; and when these two concepts (or forces or events) are cancelled out, reconciled, and transmuted, a higher and richer concept, their synthesis, results. This synthesis in turn becomes a thesis, and the dialectical, triadic, dynamic development continues. For example, the attempt of thought to comprehend the category of Being, the lowest logical category, produces the category opposite to Being, Nothing; and these two categories, when synthesized, produce the category of Becoming. Through the use of his dialectical method Hegel deduces a vast system of categories which taken as a whole defines the Absolute Idea or Divine Reason. The reality that is thereby defined is, for him, a dynamic rather than a static substance. He sometimes refers to it as "Infinite Power," "the Infinite Energy of the Universe," and "the Sovereign of the World." Its very essence is, he insists, its activity. Spirit enters into the world in order to realize what it is potentially; it seeks in each of its successive phases, or "progressive embodiments," an adequate expression of its unitary nature as "a self-comprehending totality." In philosophy it attains at last the goal to which it has always aspired, the complete consciousness of its perfect freedom or of its "self-contained existence."

Such, in brief,[1] is the philosophical system within which Hegel presents his perspective in aesthetics. As he develops his philosophy of art, he tries to avoid two extreme approaches, that of formulating an abstract philosophy of beauty which would have little or no relevance to actual art objects and to art history, and that of limiting attention to the purely empirical study and classification of particular works of art. The first approach, he believes, would lead to a "metaphysical universality" without concrete content, just as the second, to a "determinate particularity" without rational, coherent form. Hegel tries to combine "metaphysical universality with the determinateness of real particularity."[2] Appreciating, on the one hand, the value of art scholarship and, on the other, metaphysical efforts, such as Plato's, to grasp the idea of beauty, he seeks to give art history a metaphysical basis and, at the same time, to provide metaphysical aesthetics with a concrete content. In doing this, Hegel acknowledges his debt to his predecessors, especially to Plato, whose metaphysics he finds too abstract but whose work nonetheless he accepts "as foundation and as guide," and to Kant, whose critical philosophy forms "the starting point for the true conception of artistic beauty."[3]

At the very outset of his *Philosophy of Fine Art*, Hegel makes it clear that he is limiting the range of his aesthetic theory to the beautiful in fine art, excluding from its range the beauty of nature. Why? First of all, because he believes that when an aesthetician tries to deal with natural beauty he invariably becomes vague; he has no rational criterion for judging such beauty; he cannot speak of it with the same authority he can speak of consciously created beauty, the kind of beauty found only in works intentionally produced by human beings. Furthermore, Hegel believes that artistic beauty is on a higher, quite different level of significance from natural beauty, which is, in his view, only beauty "born again" in and through mind's comprehension. Natural beauty is only a reflection of the spiritual beauty inherent in mind. Works of art can exemplify human interests and manifest spiritual values in a way completely impossible to natural forms. And, as Hegel puts it, "no existence in nature is able, like art, to represent divine ideals." [4] He also reminds us of the relative permanence of works of art in contrast to "transient, vanishing, and mutable" living things. But the main reason for Hegel's exclusion of natural beauty from the domain of aesthetic inquiry is his conviction that the Absolute Idea or God is "more honored by what mind does or makes than by the productions or formations of nature." [5] Hegel sounds like Plotinus when he writes that "the divine element as it makes itself known in the work of art has attained, as being generated out of the mind, an adequate thoroughfare for its existence." [6]

Aesthetics, as the science of the beautiful in fine art, is therefore a subject of the most serious importance to Hegel. He is determined to defend aesthetics against its critics and art against its denigrators. He is opposed to those who would dismiss art lightly as a mere pleasurable diversion unworthy of serious philosophical scrutiny, as well as to those who contemn art because they find its representations deceptive and its world a world of mere appearances or semblances. He is equally opposed to those who would make art a handmaiden of morality or of religion and to those who claim that art is too fragile and precious a thing to survive intensive philosophical analysis and investigation. To be sure, art can be a pleasurable diversion, he admits, but this is not its highest, truest purpose. And certainly art is an appearance or semblance, but is not appearance essential to all phenomenal existence? And is not the external world more of an appearance, even more of a deception, than is art, which can express, far better than any natural form, the inner significance of appearance and can reveal in its own unique way a higher reality, a spiritual content, in a sensuous form? "The hard rind of nature and the common world," Hegel believes, "give the mind more trouble in breaking through to the idea than do the products of art." [7] In answering those who subsume art under morality or under religion, he points out that such a procedure makes the value of art depend on something outside itself, whereas art itself is in fact an autonomous activity, having its purpose in itself, namely, the purpose of representing or revealing spiritual truth. And, finally, Hegel reminds those who fear that "to dissect is to kill" that since art is a product of mind, it would seem appropriate, indeed quite natural, for its works to be submitted to the analysis and comprehension of mind in its widest range, in philosophical investigation; "in works of art, mind has to do with its own." [8]

Hegel is especially firm in his rejection of the view that the aim of art is to imitate, or to copy exactly, the forms of nature. No matter how the principle of imitation is interpreted, it remains, he claims, a purely formal principle which gives no criterion of objective beauty. If imitation were the true aim of art, art would be only a "superfluous labor," "a presumptuous sport." Certainly art must have a higher end than that of deceiving monkeys or pigeons or people by its verisimilitude, its "looks-just-likeness." A trick is not, in Hegel's view, a work of art. Besides, if art were to dedicate itself completely to imitating nature it would always fall far short of nature in its products; art's perspectives would of necessity be quite limited, for despite its outer show it would remain only a "one-sided deception," inwardly completely unlike a natural thing. Art would parody life instead of expressing anything genuine or vital about it. "As a matter of mere imitation," Hegel writes, "art cannot maintain a rivalry with nature, and if it tries, must look like a worm crawling after an elephant." [9] Although an artist must observe, shape, and represent in and through an external world, he is never content, if he is a real artist, to merely copy. For he will not expect to find in nature the rules of his art nor will he judge the success of his works by their resemblances to something external to them. The delight a man may derive from mimicking is far more limited and certainly far less becoming to him as a spiritual being, than the delight he may achieve by creating something original out of himself. The copier is never the creator, Hegel insists, and his productions never become works of art precisely because they have not, like all genuine works of art, been generated "by spiritually productive activity" and received "the baptism of the spiritual".[10]

Art and the Absolute Spirit

1. *Hegel thinks that art is deserving of the most serious philosophical consideration. In his view, art is not merely a means to an end, be that end pleasure or moral improvement; art is, along with religion and philosophy, a free activity capable of revealing the nature of ultimate reality. Because art can express spiritual truth in sensuous form, it is an important stage in the development of Absolute Spirit.*

. . . In the first place, as regards the worthiness of art to be scientifically considered, it is no doubt the case that art can be employed as a fleeting pastime, to serve the ends of pleasure and entertainment, to decorate our surroundings, to import pleasantness to the external conditions of our life, and to emphasize other objects by means of ornament. In this mode of employment art is indeed not independent, not free, but servile. But what we mean to consider, is the art which is free in its end as in its means.

That art is in the abstract capable of serving other aims, and of being a mere pastime, is moreover a relation which it shares with thought. For, on the one hand, science, in the shape of the subservient understanding, submits to be used for finite purposes, and as an accidental means, and in that case is not self-determined, but determined by alien objects and relations; but, on the other hand, science liberates itself from this service to rise in free independence to the attainment of truth, in which medium, free from all interference, it fulfils itself in conformity with its proper aims.

Fine art is not real art till it is in this sense free, and only achieves its highest task when it has taken its place in the same sphere with religion and philosophy, and has become simply a mode of revealing to consciousness and bringing to utterance the Divine Nature, the deepest interests of humanity, and the most comprehensive truths of the mind. It is in works of art that nations have deposited the profoundest intuitions and ideas of their hearts; and fine art is frequently the key—with many nations there is no other—to the understanding of their wisdom and of their religion.

This is an attribute which art shares with religion and philosophy, only in this peculiar mode, that it represents even the highest ideas in sensuous forms, thereby bringing them nearer to the character of natural phenomena, to the senses, and to feeling. The world, into whose depths thought penetrates, is a suprasensuous world, which is thus, to begin with, erected as a *beyond* over against immediate consciousness and present sensation: the power which thus rescues itself from the *here*, that consists in the actuality and finiteness of sense, is the freedom of thought in cognition. But the mind is able to heal this schism which its advance creates: it generates out of itself the works of fine art as the first middle term of reconciliation between pure thought and what is external, sensuous, and transitory, between nature with its finite actuality and the infinite freedom of the reason that comprehends.[11]

2. *According to Hegel, art originates in man's essentially rational nature. Being rational, man seeks to attain to complete self-consciousness and ultimate spiritual freedom. By creating works of art, by making explicit what is implicit, man realizes in concrete form his conscious, creative powers; he gets to know himself better and feels more at home among objects which he himself has made and which express his own nature as a free and productive agent.*

The universal and absolute need out of which art, on its formal side,[12] arises has its source in the fact that man is a thinking consciousness, i.e. that he draws out of himself, and makes explicit for himself, that which is, and, generally, whatever is. The things of nature are only immediate and single, but man as mind redupli-cates himself, inasmuch as *prima facie* he *is* like the things of nature, but in the second place just as really is *for* himself, per-ceives himself, has ideas of himself, thinks himself, and only thus is active self-realizedness. This consciousness of himself man obtains in a twofold way: in the first place theoretically, in as far as he has inwardly to bring himself into his own consciousness, with all that moves in the human breast, all that stirs and works therein, and, generally, to observe and form an idea of himself, to fix before himself what thought ascertains to be his real being, and, in what is summoned out of his inner self as in what is received from without, to recognize only himself. Secondly, man is realized for himself by practical activity, inas-much as he has the impulse, in the medium which is directly given to him, and externally presented before him, to produce himself, and therein at the same time to recognize himself. This purpose he achieves by the modification of external things upon which he impresses the seal of his inner being, and then finds repeated in them his own characteristics. Man does this in order as a free subject to strip the outer world of its stubborn foreign-ness, and to enjoy in the shape and fashion of things a mere external reality of himself.[13] Even the child's first impulse involves this practical modification of external things. A boy throws stones into the river, and then stands admiring the circles that trace themselves on the water, as an effect in which he attains the sight of something that is his own doing. This need traverses the most manifold phenomena, up to the mode of self-production in the medium of external things as it is known to us in the work of art. And it is not only external things that man treats in this way, but himself no less, i.e. his own natural form, which he does not leave as he finds it, but alters of set purpose. This is the cause of all ornament and decoration, though it may be as barbarous, as tasteless, as utterly disfiguring or even destructive as crushing Chinese ladies' feet, or as slitting the ears and lips. It is only among cultivated men that change of the figure,[14] of behaviour, and of every kind and mode of self-utterance emanates from spiritual education.

The universal need for expression in art lies, therefore, in man's rational impulse to exalt the inner and outer world into a spiritual consciousness for himself, as an object in which he recognizes his own self. He satisfies the need of this spiritual freedom when he makes all that exists explicit for himself *within*, and in a corresponding way realizes thus his explicit self *without*, evoking thereby, in this reduplication of himself, what is in him into vision and into knowledge for his own mind and for that of others. This is the free rationality of man, in which, as all action and knowledge, so also art has its ground and necessary origin.[15]

3. *When we contemplate a work of art, Hegel asserts, we do not want to understand its nature scientifically, nor do we desire to put it to some practical use; rather we are interested in the work's individual, immediate appearance. This appearance must contain sensuous elements, of course, in order to be perceptible at all, but, Hegel argues, it can never be merely sensuous if it is to satisfy the higher demands of the human spirit. A work of art, in his view, must be a semblance of the sensuous, in which sensuous elements are spiritualized, if genuine aesthetic satisfaction is to be provided.*

. . . Artistic contemplation accepts the work of art just as it displays itself *qua* external object, in immediate determinateness and sensuous individuality clothed in colour, figure, and sound, or as a single isolated perception, etc., and does not go so far beyond the immediate appearance of objectivity which is presented before it, as to aim, like science, at apprehending the notion of such an objective appearance as a universal notion.

Thus, the interest of art distinguishes itself from the practical interest of desire by the fact that it permits its object to subsist freely and in independence, while desire utilizes it in its own service by its destruction. On the other hand, artistic contemplation differs from theoretical consideration by the scientific intelligence, in cherishing interest for the object as an individual existence, and not setting to work to transmute it into its universal thought and notion.

It follows, then, from the above, that though the sensuous must be present in a work of art, yet it must only appear as surface and *semblance* of the sensuous. For, in the sensuous aspect of a work of art, the mind seeks neither the concrete framework of matter, that empirically thorough completeness and development of the organism which desire demands, nor the universal and merely ideal thought. What it requires is sensuous presence, which, while not ceasing to be sensuous, is to be liberated from the apparatus of its merely material nature. And thus the sensuous in works of art is exalted to the rank of a mere *semblance* in comparison with the immediate existence of things in nature, and the work of art occupies the mean between what is immediately sensuous and ideal thought. This semblance of the sensuous presents itself to the mind externally as the shape, the visible look, and the sonorous vibration of things—supposing that the mind leaves the objects uninterfered with (physically), but yet does not descend into their inner essence (by abstract thought), for if it did so, it would entirely destroy their external existence as separate individuals *for it*. For this reason the sensuous aspect of art only refers to the two theoretical senses of sight and hearing, while smell, taste, and feeling remain excluded from being sources of artistic enjoyment. For smell, taste, and feeling have to do with matter as such, and with its immediate sensuous qualities; smell with material volatilization in air, taste with the material dissolution of substance,[16] and feeling with warmth, coldness, smoothness, etc. On this account these senses cannot have to do with the objects of art, which are destined to maintain themselves in their actual independent existence, and admit of no purely sensuous relation. The pleasant for these latter senses is not the beautiful in art. Thus art on its sensuous side purposely produces no more than a shadow-world of shapes, sounds, and imaginable ideas; and it is absolutely out of the question to maintain that it is owing to simple powerlessness and to the limitations on his actions that man, when evoking worlds of art into existence, fails to present more than the mere surface of the sensuous, than mere *schemata*.[17] In art, these sensuous shapes and sounds present themselves, not simply for their own sake and for that of their immediate structure, but with the purpose of affording in that shape satisfaction to higher spiritual interests, seeing that they are powerful to call forth a response and echo in the mind from all the depths of consciousness. It is thus that, in art, the sensuous is *spiritualized*, i.e. the spiritual appears in sensuous shape.[18]

4. *In Hegel's view, the aim of art is to give outer sensuous shape to inner spiritual content; to inform, or to render perceptible, the Absolute Idea, Infinite Spirit. In striving to attain this aim, art passes through three stages, which represent, for Hegel, the three possible relations of the Idea to its embodiment: the symbolic, the classical, and the romantic. In the first and most primitive of these, the symbolic, the form is only externally related to its content. Sublime aspiration toward the Infinite, rather than adequate expression of it, is the result of symbolic art.*

But inasmuch as the task of art is to represent the idea to direct perception in sensuous shape, and not in the form of thought or of pure spirituality as such, and seeing that this work of representation has its value and dignity in the correspondence and the unity of the two sides, i.e. of the Idea and its plastic embodiment, it follows that the level and excellency of art in attaining a realization adequate to its idea, must depend upon the grade of inwardness and unity with which Idea and Shape display themselves as fused into one.

Thus the higher truth is spiritual being that has attained a shape adequate to the conception of spirit. This is what furnishes the principle of division for the science of art. For before the mind can attain the true notion of its absolute essence, it has to traverse a course of stages whose ground is in this idea itself; and to this evolution of the content with which it supplies itself, there corresponds an evolution, immediately connected therewith, of the plastic forms of art, under the shape of which the mind as artist presents to itself the consciousness of itself. . . .

We have here to consider three relations of the Idea to its outward shaping.

First, the Idea gives rise to the beginning of Art when, being itself still in its indistinctness and obscurity, or in vicious untrue determinateness, it is made the import of artistic creations. As indeterminate it does not yet possess in itself that individuality which the Ideal demands; its abstractness and one-sidedness leave its shape to be outwardly bizarre and defective. The first form of art is therefore rather a mere search after plastic portrayal than a capacity of genuine representation. The Idea has not yet found the true form even within itself, and therefore continues to be merely the struggle and aspiration thereafter. In general terms we may call this form the Symbolic form of art. In it the abstract Idea has its outward shape external to itself [19] in natural sensuous matter, with which the process of shaping begins, and from which, *qua* outward expression, it is inseparable. . . .

These aspects may be pronounced in general terms to constitute the character of the primitive artistic pantheism of the East, which either charges even the meanest objects with the absolute import, or again coerces nature with violence into the expression of its view. By this means it becomes bizarre, grotesque, and tasteless, or turns the infinite but abstract freedom of the substantive Idea disdainfully against all phenomenal being as null and evanescent. By such means the import cannot be completely embodied in the expression, and in spite of all aspiration and endeavour the reciprocal inadequacy of shape and Idea remain insuperable. This may be taken as the first form of art,—Symbolic art with its aspiration, its disquiet, its mystery and its sublimity.[20]

5. *In order to overcome the defects inherent in symbolic art, a second stage of art, one providing a freer, more adequate, more completely realized fusion of form and content, is required. This is classical art, which finds in the shape of the human body the individual form most appropriate for expressing the concrete spiritual meaning.*

In the second form of art, which we propose to call "Classical," the double defect of symbolic art is cancelled. The plastic shape of symbolic art is imperfect, because, in the first place, the Idea in it only enters into consciousness in *abstract* determinateness or indeterminateness, and, in the second place, this must always make the conformity of shape to import defective, and in its turn merely abstract. The classical form of art is the solution of this double difficulty; it is the free and adequate embodiment of the Idea in the shape that, according to its conception, is peculiarly appropriate to the Idea itself. With it, therefore, the Idea is capable of entering into free and complete accord. Hence, the classical type of art is the first to afford the production and intuition of the completed Ideal, and to establish it as a realized fact.

The conformity, however, of notion and reality in classical art must not be taken in the purely *formal* sense of the agreement of a content with the external shape given to it, any more than this could be the case with the Ideal itself. Otherwise every copy from nature, and every type of countenance, every landscape, flower, or scene, etc., which forms the purport of any representation, would be at once made classical by the agreement which it displays between form and content. On the contrary, in classical art the peculiarity of the content consists in being itself concrete idea, and, as such, the concrete spiritual; for only the spiritual is the truly inner self. To suit such a content, then, we must search out that in Nature which on its own merits belongs to the essence and actuality of the mind. It must be the absolute notion that invented the shape appropriate to concrete mind, so that the subjective notion—in this case the spirit of art—has merely found it, and brought it, as an existence possessing natural shape, into accord with free individual spirituality.[21] This shape, with which the Idea as spiritual—as individually determinate spirituality—invests itself when manifested as a temporal phenomenon, is the human form. . . . The human form is employed in the classical type of art not as mere sensuous existence, but exclusively as the existence and physical form corresponding to mind, and is therefore exempt from all the deficiencies of what is merely sensuous, and from the contingent finiteness of phenomenal existence. The outer shape must be thus purified in order to express in itself a content adequate to itself; and again, if the conformity of import and content is to be complete, the spiritual meaning which is the content must be of a particular kind. It must, that is to say, be qualified to express itself completely in the physical form of man, without projecting into another world beyond the scope of such an expression in sensuous and bodily terms. This condition has the effect that Mind is by it at once specified as a particular case of mind, as human mind, and not as simply absolute and eternal, inasmuch as mind in this latter sense is incapable of proclaiming and expressing itself otherwise than as intellectual being.

Out of this latter point arises, in its turn, the defect which brings about the dissolution of classical art, and demands a transition into a third and higher form, viz. into the romantic form of art.[22]

6. *As classical art fails to give final and adequate expression in sensuous form to the free, ever developing inner activity of infinite mind, it is supplanted by a higher form, romantic art. Romantic art turns away from the world known through the senses to the inner spiritual world, there achieving its synthesis of form and content.*

The romantic form of art destroys the completed union of the Idea and its reality, and recurs, though in a higher phase, to that difference and antagonism of two aspects which was left unvanquished by symbolic art. The classical type attained the highest excellence, of which the sensuous embodiment of art is capable; and if it is in any way defective, the defect is in art as a whole, i.e. in the limitation of its sphere. This limitation consists in the fact that art as such takes for its object Mind—the conception of which is infinite concrete universality—in the shape of sensuous concreteness, and in the classical phase sets up the perfect amalgamation of spiritual and sensuous existence as a Conformity of the two. Now, as a matter of fact, in such an amalgamation Mind cannot be represented according to its true notion. For Mind is the infinite subjectivity of the Idea, which, as absolute inwardness,[23] is not capable of finding free expansion in its true nature on condition of remaining transposed into a bodily medium as the existence appropriate to it.

As an escape from such a condition the romantic form of art in its turn dissolves the inseparable unity of the classical phase, because it has won a significance which goes beyond the classical form of art and its mode of expression. . . .

Therefore, in short, we may abide by the statement that in this third stage the object (of art) is free, concrete intellectual being, which has the function of revealing itself as spiritual existence for the inward [24] world of spirit. In conformity with such an object-matter, art cannot work for sensuous perception. It must address itself to the inward mind, which coalesces with its object simply and as though this were itself,[25] to the subjective inwardness, to the heart, the feeling, which, being spiritual, aspires to freedom within itself, and seeks and finds its reconciliation only in the spirit within. It is this inner world that forms the content of the romantic, and must therefore find its representation as such inward feeling, and in the show or presentation of such feeling. The world of inwardness celebrates its triumph over the outer world, and actually in the sphere of the outer and in its medium manifests this its victory, owing to which the sensuous appearance sinks into worthlessness. . . .

This we may take as in the abstract the character of the symbolic, classical, and romantic forms of art, which represent the three relations of the Idea to its embodiment in the sphere of art. They consist in the aspiration after, and the attainment and transcendence of the Ideal as the true Idea of Beauty.[26] . . .

7. *Having treated generally the characteristics of the three universal stages through which art develops, Hegel turns his attention to the various arts, beginning with architecture. He explains why he considers architecture to be fundamentally a symbolic art; sculpture, a classical art; and painting, music, and poetry, romantic arts.*

The first of the particular arts with which, according to their fundamental principle, we have to begin, is architecture considered as a fine art. Its task lies in so manipulating external inorganic nature that it becomes cognate to mind, as an artistic outer world. The material of architecture is matter itself in its immediate externality as a heavy mass subject to mechanical laws, and its forms do not depart from the forms of inorganic nature, but are merely set in order in conformity with relations of the abstract understanding, i.e. with relations of symmetry. In this material and in such forms, the ideal as concrete spirituality does not admit of being realized. Hence the reality which is represented in them remains contrasted with the Idea, as something external which it has not penetrated, or has penetrated only to establish an abstract relation. For these reasons, the fundamental type of the fine art of building is the symbolical form of art. It is architecture that pioneers the way for the adequate realization of the God, and in this its service bestows hard toil upon existing nature, in order to disentangle it from the jungle of finitude and the abortiveness of chance. By this means it levels a space for the God, gives form to his external surroundings, and builds him his temple as a fit place for concentration of spirit, and for its direction to the mind's absolute objects. . . .

Architecture, however, as we have seen, has purified the external world, and endowed it with symmetrical order and with affinity to mind; and the temple of the God, the house of his community, stands ready. Into this temple, then, in the second place, the God enters in the lightning-flash of individuality, which strikes and permeates the inert mass, while the infinite[27] and no longer merely symmetrical form belonging to mind itself concentrates and gives shape to the corresponding bodily existence. This is the task of Sculpture. In as far as in this art the spiritual inward being which architecture can but indicate makes itself at home in the sensuous shape and its external matter, and in as far as these two sides are so adapted to one another that neither is predominant, sculpture must be assigned the classical form of art as its fundamental type. For this reason the sensuous element itself has here no expression which could not be that of the spiritual element, just as, conversely, sculpture can represent no spiritual content which does not admit throughout of being adequately presented to perception in bodily form. Sculpture should place the spirit before us in its bodily form and in immediate unity therewith at rest and in peace; and the form should be animated by the content of spiritual individuality. And so the external sensuous matter is here no longer manipulated, either in conformity with its mechanical quality alone, as a mass possessing weight, nor in shapes belonging to the inorganic world, nor as indifferent to colour, etc.; but it is wrought in ideal forms of the human figure, and, it must be remarked, in all three spatial dimensions. . . .

Now, after architecture has erected the temple, and the hand of sculpture has supplied it with the statue of the God, then, in the third place, this god present to sense is confronted in the spacious halls of his house by the community. The community is the spiritual reflection into itself of such sensuous existence, and is the animating subjectivity and inner life which brings about the result that the determining principle for the content of art, as well as for the medium which represents it in outward form, comes to the particularization [dispersion into various shapes, attributes, incidents, etc.], individualization, and the subjectivity which they require. The solid unity which the God has in sculpture breaks up into the multitudinous inner lives of individuals, whose unity is not sensuous, but purely ideal.[28]

It is only in this stage that God Himself comes to be really and truly spirit—the spirit in His (God's) community; for He here begins to be a to-and-fro, an alternation between His unity within himself and his realization in the individual's knowledge and in its separate being, as also in the common nature and union of the multitude. In the community, God is released from the abstractness of unexpanded self-identity, as well as from the simple absorption in a bodily medium, by which sculpture represents Him. And He is thus exalted into spiritual existence and into knowledge, into the reflected appearance which essentially displays itself as inward and as subjectivity. Therefore the higher content is now the spiritual nature, and that in its absolute shape. But the dispersion of which we have spoken reveals this at the same time as particular spiritual being, and as individual character. Now, what manifests itself in this phase as the main thing is not the serene quiescence of the God in Himself, but appearance as such, being which is *for* another, self-manifestation. And hence, in the phase we have reached, all the most manifold subjectivity in its living movement and operation—as human passion, action, and incident, and, in general, the wide realm of human feeling, will, and its negation,—is for its own sake the object of artistic representation. In conformity with this content, the sensuous element of art has at once to show itself as made particular in itself and as adapted to subjective inwardness. Media that fulfil this requirement we have in colour, in musical sound, and finally in sound as the mere indication of inward perceptions and ideas; and as modes of realizing the import in question by help of these media we obtain painting, music, and poetry. In this region the sensuous medium displays itself as subdivided in its own being and universally set down as ideal. Thus it has the highest degree of conformity with the content of art, which, as such, is spiritual, and the connection of intelligible import and sensuous medium develops into closer intimacy than was possible in the case of architecture and sculpture. The unity attained, however, is a more inward unity, the weight of which is thrown wholly on the subjective side, and which, in as far as form and content are compelled to particularize themselves and give themselves merely ideal existence, can only come to pass at the expense of the objective universality of the content and also of its amalgamation with the immediately sensuous element.

The arts, then, of which form and content exalt themselves to ideality, abandon the character of symbolic architecture and the classical ideal of sculpture, and therefore borrow their type from the romantic form of art, whose mode of plasticity they are most adequately adapted to express. And they constitute a totality of arts, because the romantic type is the most concrete in itself.[29] . . .

8. *At the apex of romantic art, Hegel places poetry. For poetry is, he holds, the most inwardly directed, the freest, and the most spiritual of all the arts.*

As regards the third and most spiritual mode of representation of the romantic art-type, we must look for it in poetry. Its characteristic peculiarity lies in the power with which it subjects to the mind and to its ideas the sensuous element from which music and painting in their degree began to liberate art. For sound, the only external matter which poetry retains, is in it no longer the feeling of the sonorous itself, but is a sign, which by itself is void of import. And it is a sign of the idea which has become concrete in itself, and not merely of indefinite feeling and of its nuances and grades. This is how sound develops into the *Word*, as voice articulate in itself, whose import it is to indicate ideas and notions. The merely negative point up to which music had developed now makes its appearance as the completely concrete point, the point which is mind, the self-conscious individual, which, producing out of itself the infinite space of its ideas, unites it with the temporal character of sound. Yet this sensuous element, which in music was still immediately one with inward feeling, is in poetry separated from the content of consciousness. In poetry the mind determines this content for its own sake, and apart from all else, into the shape of ideas, and though it employs sound to express them, yet treats it solely as a symbol without value or import. Thus considered, sound may just as well be reduced to a mere letter, for the audible, like the visible, is thus depressed into a mere indication of mind. For this reason the proper medium of poetical representation is the poetical imagination and intellectual portrayal itself. And as this element is common to all types of art, it follows that poetry runs through them all and develops itself independently in each. Poetry is the universal art of the mind which has become free in its own nature, and which is not tied to find its realization in external sensuous matter, but expatiates exclusively in the inner space and inner time of the ideas and feelings. Yet just in this its highest phase art ends by transcending itself, inasmuch as it abandons the medium of a harmonious embodiment of mind in sensuous form, and passes from the poetry of imagination into the prose of thought.[30]

9. *In his philosophy of art, Hegel gives extensive attention to dramatic poetry, particularly tragedy. According to Hegel, tragedy presents in dramatic form the conflict and collision of the universal moral forces which rule mankind—for example love, honor, duty to the state, religious obligation, and family interest. The demands and claims which these forces make on individuals are sometimes excessive as well as incompatible one with another. But tragedy must do more than represent the collision of these powers; it must also point the way to their ultimate reconciliation by denying their exclusive claims over the individual, without, however, denying their fundamental justification. The death of one or more of the contending individuals exemplifying moral powers is sometimes but not always necessary in a tragedy in order to achieve the spiritual reconciliation.*

The final result, then, of the development of tragedy conducts us to this issue and only this, namely, that the twofold vindication of the mutually conflicting aspects is no doubt retained, but the *one-sided* mode is cancelled, and the undisturbed ideal harmony brings back again that condition of the chorus, which attributes without reserve equal honour to all the gods. The true course of dramatic development consists in the annulment of *contradictions* viewed as such, in the reconciliation of the forces of human action, which alternately strive to negate each other in their conflict. Only so far is misfortune and suffering not the final issue, but rather the satisfaction of spirit, as for the first time, in virtue of such a conclusion, the necessity of all that particular individual's experience, is able to appear in complete accord with reason, and our emotional attitude is tranquillized on a true ethical basis; rudely shaken by the calamitous result to the heroes, but reconciled in the substantial facts. And it is only in so far as we retain such a view securely that we shall be in a position to understand ancient tragedy. We have to guard ourselves therefore from concluding that a *dénouement* of this type is merely a moral issue conformably to which evil is punished and virtue rewarded, as indicated by the proverb that "when crime turns to vomit, virtue sits down at table." We have nothing to do here with this wholly personal aspect of a self-reflecting personality and its conception of good and evil, but are concerned with the appearance of the affirmative reconciliation and the equal validity of both powers engaged in conflict, if the collision is complete. To as little extent is the necessity of the issue a blind destiny, or in other words a purely irrational, unintelligible fate, identified with the classical world by many; rather it is the rationality of destiny, albeit it does not as yet appear as self-conscious Providence, the divine final end of which in conjunction with the world and individuals appears on its own account and for others, depending as it does on just this fact that the highest Power paramount over particular gods and mankind cannot suffer this, namely, that the forces, which affirm their self-subsistence in modes that are abstract or incomplete, and thereby overstep the boundary of their warrant, no less than the conflicts which result from them, should retain their self-stability. Fate drives personality back upon its limits, and shatters it, when it has grown overweening. An irrational compulsion, however, an innocence of suffering would rather only excite indignation in the soul of the spectator than ethical tranquility. ... The higher conception of reconciliation in tragedy is on the contrary related to the resolution of specific ethical and substantive facts from their contradiction into their true harmony. The way in which such an accord is established is asserted under very different modes; I propose therefore merely to direct attention to the fundamental features of the actual process herein involved.

First, we have particularly to emphasize the fact, that if it is the one-sidedness of the pathos which constitutes the real basis of collisions this merely amounts to the statement that it is asserted in the action of life, and therewith has become the unique pathos of a particular individual. If this one-sidedness is to be abrogated then it is this individual which, to the extent that his action is exclusively identified with this isolated pathos, must perforce be stripped and sacrificed. For the individual here is merely this single life, and, if this unity is not secured in its stability on its own account, the individual is shattered.

The most complete form of this development is possible when the individuals engaged in conflict relatively to their concrete or objective life appear in each case essentially involved in one whole, so that they stand fundamentally under the power of that against which they battle, and consequently infringe that, which, conformably to their own essential life, they ought to respect. Antigone, for example, lives under the political authority of Creon; she is herself the daughter of a king and the affianced of Haemon, so that her obedience to the royal prerogative is an obligation. But Creon also, who is on his part father and husband, is under obligation to respect the sacred ties of relationship, and only by breach of this can give an order that is in conflict with such a sense. In consequence of this we find immanent in the life of both that which each respectively combats, and they are seized and broken by that very bond which is rooted in the compass of their own social existence. Antigone is put to death before she can enjoy what she looks forward to as a bride, and Creon too is punished in the fatal end of his son and wife, who commit suicide, the former on account of Antigone's death, and the latter owing to Haemon's. Among all the fine creations of the ancient and the modern world—and I am acquainted with pretty nearly everything in such a class, and one ought to know it, and it is quite possible— the "Antigone" of Sophocles is from this point of view in my judgment the most excellent and satisfying work of art.

The tragic issue does not, however, require in every case, as a means of removing both over-emphasized aspects and the equal honour which they respectively claim, the downfall of the contestant parties. The "Eumenides" ends, as we all know, not with the death of Orestes, or the destruction of the Eumenides, these avenging spirits of matricide and filial affection, as opposed to Apollo, who seeks to protect unimpaired the worth of and reverence for the family chief and king, who prompted Orestes to slay Clytemnestra, but with Orestes released from the punishment and honour bestowed on both divinities. At the same time we cannot fail to see in this adjusted conclusion the nature of the authority which the Greeks attached to their gods when they presented them as mere individuals contending with each other. They appear, in short, to the Athenian of everyday life merely as definite aspects of ethical experience which the principles of morality viewed in their complete and harmonious coherence bind together. The votes of the Areopagus are equal on either side. It is Athene, the goddess, the life of Athens, that is, imagined in its essential unity, who adds the white pebble, who frees Orestes, and at the same time promises altars and a cult to the Eumenides no less than Apollo. As a contrast to this type of objective reconciliation the settlement may be, *secondly*, of a more personal character. In other words, the individual concerned in the action may in the last instance surrender his one-sided point of view. In this betrayal of personality of its essential pathos, however, it cannot fail to appear destitute of character; and this contradicts the masculine integrity of such plastic figures. The individual, therefore, can only submit to a higher Power and its counsel or command, to the effect that while on his own account he adheres to such a pathos, the will is nevertheless broken in its bare obstinacy by a god's authority. In such a case the knot is not loosened, but, as in the case of Philoctetes, it is severed by a *deus ex machina*.

But as a ... final class, and one more beautiful than the above rather external mode of resolution, we have the reconciliation more properly of the soul itself, in which respect there is, in virtue of the personal significance, a real approach to our modern point of view. The most perfect example of this in ancient drama is found in the ever admirable "Oedipus at Colonos" of Sophocles. The protagonist here has unwittingly slain his father, secured the sceptre of Thebes, and the bridal bed of his own mother. He is not rendered unhappy by these unwitting crimes; but the power of divination he has of old possessed makes him realize, despite himself, the darkness of the experience that confronts him, and he becomes fearfully, if indistinctly, aware of what his position is. In this resolution of the riddle in himself he resembles Adam, losing his happiness when he obtains the knowledge of good and evil. What he then does, the seer, is to blind himself, then abdicate the throne and depart from Thebes, very much as Adam and Eve are driven from Paradise. From henceforward he wanders about a helpless old man. Finally a god calls the terribly afflicted man to himself, the man, that is, who refusing the request of his sons that he should return to Thebes, prefers to associate with the Erinyes; the man, in short, who extinguishes all the disruption in himself and who purifies himself in his own soul. His blind eyes are made clear and bright, his limbs are healed, and become a treasure of the city which received him as a free guest. And this illumination in death is for ourselves no less than for him the more truly visible reconciliation which is worked out both in and for himself as individual man, in and through, that is, his essential character. Critics have endeavoured to discover here the temper of the Christian life; we are told we have here the picture of a sinner, whom God receives into His grace; and the fateful misfortunes which expire in their infinite condition, are made good with the seal of blessedness in death. The reconciliation of the Christian religion, however, is an illumination of the soul, which, bathed in the everlasting waters of salvation, is raised above mortal life and its deeds. Here it is the heart itself, for in such a view the spiritual life can effect this, which buries that life and its deed in the grave of the heart itself, counting the recriminations of earthly guilt as part and parcel of its own earthly individuality; and which, in the full assuredness of the eternally pure and spiritual condition of blessedness, holds itself in itself calm and steadfast against such impeachment. The illumination of Oedipus, on the contrary, remains throughout, in consonance with ancient ideas, the restoration of conscious life from the strife of ethical powers and violations to the renewed and harmonious unity of this *ethical content itself*.[31]

10. *From Hegel's discussion of tragedy we return now to his general treatment of the various arts. He is convinced that his proposed scheme of classifying arts is more adequate than others in that it is based on a recognition of a higher rational principle; having grasped this principle and the universal types of development it entails, for the first time it has been possible to trace the "self-unfolding Idea of beauty."*

Such we may take to be the articulated totality of the particular arts, viz., the external art of architecture, the objective art of sculpture, and the subjective art of painting, music and poetry.

Many other classifications have been attempted, for a work of art presents so many aspects, that, as has often been the case, first one and then another is made the basis of classification. For instance, one might take the sensuous medium. Thus architecture is treated as crystallization; sculpture, as the organic modelling of the material in its sensuous and spatial totality; painting, as the coloured surface and line, while in music, space, as such, passes into the point of time possessed of content within itself, until finally the external medium is in poetry depressed into complete insignificance. Or, again, these differences have been considered with reference to their purely abstract attributes of space and time. Such abstract peculiarities of works of art may, like their material medium, be consistently explored in their characteristic traits; but they cannot be worked out as the ultimate and fundamental law, because any such aspect itself derives its origin from a higher principle, and must therefore be subordinate thereto.

This higher principle we have found in the types of art—symbolic, classical, and romantic—which are the universal stages or elements of the Idea of beauty itself. For symbolic art attains its most adequate reality and most complete application in architecture, in which it holds sway in the full import of its notion, and is not yet degraded to be, as it were, the inorganic nature dealt with by another art. The classical type of art, on the other hand, finds adequate realization in sculpture, while it treats architecture only as furnishing an enclosure in which it is to operate, and has not acquired the power of developing painting and music as absolute[32] forms for its content. The romantic type of art, finally, takes possession of painting and music, and in like manner of poetic representation, as substantive and unconditionally adequate modes of utterance. Poetry, however, is conformable to all types of the beautiful, and extends over them all, because the artistic imagination is its proper medium, and imagination is essential to every product that belongs to the beautiful, whatever its type may be.

And, therefore, what the particular arts realize in individual works of art, are according to their abstract conception simply the universal types which constitute the self-unfolding Idea of beauty. It is as the external realization of this Idea that the wide Pantheon of art is being erected, whose architect and builder is the spirit of beauty as it awakens to self-knowledge, and to complete which the history of the world will need the evolution of ages.[33]

11. *Although Hegel gives to art a high place in his system, he gives a higher place still to religion and philosophy. For even in its highest manifestation, in poetry, art points beyond itself to a still higher realm, passing, as Hegel says, "from the poetry of imagination to the prose of thought." Art can no longer satisfy the deepest spiritual needs and aspirations of mankind, Hegel believes. It is, therefore, a thing of the past, a subject for intellectual consideration, not just a source of aesthetic appreciation.*

But if, on the one side, we assign this high position to art, we must no less bear in mind, on the other hand, that art is not, either in content or in form, the supreme and absolute mode of bringing the mind's genuine interests into consciousness. The form of art is enough to limit it to a restricted content. Only a certain circle and grade of truth is capable of being represented in the medium of art. Such truth must have in its own nature the capacity to go forth into sensuous form and be adequate to itself therein, if it is to be a genuinely artistic content, as in the case with the gods of Greece. There is, however, a deeper form of truth, in which it is no longer so closely akin and so friendly to sense as to be adequately embraced and expressed by that medium. Of such a kind is the Christian conception of truth; and more especially the spirit of our modern world, or, to come closer, of our religion and our intellectual culture, reveals itself as beyond the stage at which art is the highest mode assumed by man's consciousness of the absolute. The peculiar mode to which artistic production and works of art belong no longer satisfies our supreme need. We are above the level at which works of art can be venerated as divine, and actually worshipped; the impression which they make is of a more considerate kind, and the feelings which they stir within us require a higher test and a further confirmation. Thought and reflection have taken their flight above fine art....

The reflective culture of our life of to-day, makes it a necessity for us, in respect of our will no less than of our judgment, to adhere to general points of view, and to regulate particular matters according to them, so that general forms, laws, duties, rights, maxims are what have validity as grounds of determination and are the chief regulative force. But what is required for artistic interest as for artistic production is, speaking generally, a living creation, in which the universal is not present as law and maxim, but acts as if one with the mood and the feelings, just as, in the imagination, the universal and rational is contained only as brought into unity with a concrete sensuous phenomenon. Therefore, our present in its universal condition is not favourable to art. As regards the artist itself, it is not merely that the reflection which finds utterance all round him, and the universal habit of having an opinion and passing judgment about art infect him, and mislead him into putting more abstract thought into his works themselves; but also the whole spiritual culture of the age is of such a kind that he himself stands within this reflective world and its conditions, and it is impossible for him to abstract from it by will and resolve, or to contrive for himself and bring to pass, by means of peculiar education or removal from the relations of life, a peculiar solitude that would replace all that is lost.

In all these respects art is, and remains for us, on the side of its highest destiny, a thing of the past.[34] Herein it has further lost for us its genuine truth and life, and rather is transferred into our *ideas* than asserts its former necessity, or assumes its former place, in reality. What is now aroused in us by works of art is over and above our immediate enjoyment, and together with it, our judgment; inasmuch as we subject the content and the means of representation of the work of art and the suitability or unsuitability of the two to our intellectual consideration. Therefore, the *science* of art is a much more pressing need in our day, than in times in which art, simply as art, was enough to furnish a full satisfaction. Art invites us to consideration of it by means of thought, not to the end of stimulating art production, but in order to ascertain scientifically what art is.[35]

NOTES

1. The student should be warned, however, that any summary statement of Hegel's philosophy is bound to do injustice to the complexity, profundity, and (at times) obscurity of his work.

W. T. Stace's *Philosophy of Hegel*, listed in our "Guide to Supplementary Reading," is a useful and lucidly written guidebook to the entire Hegelian system.

2. *The Introduction to Hegel's Philosophy of Fine Art*, translated by Bernard Bosanquet (London, Kegan Paul, Trench & Co., 1886), p. 41. Subsequently this work in this edition will be cited as "Hegel, *Introduction* (B. B.)." Some of Bosanquet's explanatory notes are included below and are initialed "B. B." in order to distinguish them from the present editor's notes.

3. According to Hegel, Kant attempted, but failed to achieve, "the higher grasp of the true unity of necessity and freedom, of the particular and the universal, of the sensuous and the rational," which Hegel thinks he himself has achieved through his conception of the Absolute Idea. See Hegel, *Introduction* (B. B.), pp. 151–152.

4. Hegel, *Introduction* (B. B.), p. 55.

5. Ibid., p. 56.

6. Ibid., p. 57.

7. Hegel, *Introduction* (B. B.), p. 16.

8. Ibid., p. 22.

9. Ibid., p. 82.

10. Ibid., p. 55.

11. Ibid., pp. 11–13.

12. I.e. considered generally, apart from the wishes and, perhaps, selfish aims of individual artists. B. B., p. 58.

13. Reality derivative from his own reality. B. B., p. 59.

14. He means as in attitude, bearing, gentle movement, etc. B. B., p. 60.

15. Hegel, *Introduction* (B. B.), pp. 58–60.

16. Nothing can be tasted which is not dissolved in a liquid. B. B., p. 73.

17. Abstract forms, which are to reality as a diagram to a picture. B. B., p. 73.

18. Hegel, *Introduction* (B. B.), pp. 71–74.

19. I.e. not in a separate ideal shape devoted to it.... B. B., p. 145.

20. Hegel, *Introduction* (B. B.), pp. 138–139; pp. 145–147.

21. I.e. God or the Universe *invented* man to be the expression of mind; art *finds* him, and adapts his shape to the artistic embodiment of mind as concentrated in individual instances. B. B., p. 149.

22. Hegel, *Introduction* (B. B.), pp. 148–149; pp. 150–151.

23. It is the essence of mind or thought to have its parts outside one another. The so-called terms of a judgment are a good instance of parts in thought which are inward to each other. B. B., p. 152.

24. "Inward," again, does not mean merely inside our heads, but having the character of spirit in that its parts are not external to one another. A judgment is thus inward. B. B., p. 154.

25. I.e. does not keep up a distinction between percipient and object, as between things in space. Goodness, nobleness, etc., are not felt to be other than or outside the mind. B. B., p. 155.

26. Hegel, *Introduction* (B. B.), pp. 151–152; pp. 154–155; pp. 156–157.

27. In the sense "self-complete," "not primarily regarded as explained by anything outside,...." B. B., p. 162.

28. The unity of the individuals forming a church or nation is not visible, but exists in common sentiments, purposes, etc., and in the recognition of their community. B. B., p. 164.

29. Hegel, *Introduction* (B. B.), pp. 160–161; pp. 162–163; pp. 164–167.

30. Hegel, *Introduction* (B. B.), pp. 171–173.

31. *Hegel's Philosophy of Fine Art*, translated by F. P. B. Osmaston (London, G. Bell & Sons, Ltd., 1920), Vol. IV, pp. 321–326. In the preceding passages, Hegel has been mainly concerned with Greek tragedy; he does, however, also discuss modern (especially Shakespearean) tragedy elsewhere. For an excellent compilation of his writings on tragedy, including his full treatment of dramatic action, character, motivation, language, etc., see *Hegel on Tragedy*, edited by Anne and Henry Paolucci, listed in our "Guide to Supplementary Reading."

32. Adequate, and so of permanent value. B. B., *Introduction*, p. 174.

33. Hegel, *Introduction* (B. B.), pp. 173–175.

34. Benedetto Croce calls Hegel's aesthetics "a funeral oration." For his evaluation of Hegel's views on art, see Part II ("History

of Aesthetic") of Croce's *Aesthetic as Science of Expression and General Linguistic,* translated by Douglas Ainslie (New York, Noonday Press, 1953), Chap. IX, pp. 297–303.

35. Hegel, *Introduction* (B. B.), pp. 16–17; pp. 18–20.

QUESTIONS AND TOPICS FOR FURTHER STUDY

1. Why should art be of particular concern to the philosopher, according to Hegel? What does he mean by "free art"?

2. Explain how art originates, according to Hegel. Why is he opposed to hedonistic interpretations of the origin of art?

3. What does Hegel mean by "aesthetic semblance"? How, in his view, does art succeed in "spiritualizing" the sensuous?

4. What does Hegel consider to be the aim of art? Explain the various stages through which art passes in seeking to attain this end. Why must art ultimately fail to achieve its end?

5. Taking as examples a Hindu temple, a Greek statue, and a German symphony, explain how Hegel might interpret these according to his philosophy of art.

6. Why does Hegel consider the use of the human form to be the appropriate exemplification of classical art?

7. Why does Hegel consider architecture to be primarily a symbolic art; sculpture, a classical art; and painting, music, and poetry, romantic arts?

8. Explain why Hegel believes poetry to be the freest and most spiritual of all the arts. Give some examples of poems which might support his claim.

9. Summarize Hegel's view of the nature of tragedy. Why does he consider Sophocles' *Antigone* to be a superb tragedy?

10. Topics for further study: (a) Hegel's view of Aristotle's theory of tragedy; (b) Hegel on the art of painting; (c) the influence of Kant on Hegel's aesthetics; (d) the relationship of art and religion in Hegel's philosophy; (e) Hegel's view of the art of his contemporaries.

GUIDE TO SUPPLEMENTARY READING

(Works marked with asterisks are available in paperbound editions.)

I. PRIMARY SOURCES

Hegel, G. W. R., *The Introduction to Hegel's Philosophy of Fine Art*, translated from the German with notes and prefatory essay by Bernard Bosanquet (London, Kegan Paul, Trench & Co., 1886).

———*The Philosophy of Fine Art*, translated by F. P. B. Osmaston, four volumes (London, G. Bell and Sons, Ltd., 1920).

———**Hegel on Tragedy*, edited with an introduction by Anne and Henry Paolucci (Garden City, N.Y., Anchor Books, Doubleday and Co., Inc., 1962).

———*Encyclopedia of Philosophy*, translated and annotated by Gustav Emil Mueller (New York, Philosophical Library, 1959).

II. SECONDARY WORKS

Bosanquet, Bernard, **A History of Aesthetic* (New York, Meredian Books, 1957), (reprint), Chap. XII; Appendix I.

Bradley, A. C., "Hegel's Theory of Tragedy" in *Oxford Lectures in Poetry* (London, Macmillan and Co., Ltd., 1950). (Also reprinted in **Hegel on Tragedy*, listed above.)

Carritt, E. F., *The Theory of Beauty* (New York, Barnes and Noble, Inc., n.d.), (reprint), Chap. VII.

Gilbert, Katharine, and Helmut Kuhn, *A History of Esthetics*, revised edition (Bloomington, Indiana University Press, 1953), Chap. XIV.

Kaminsky, Jack, *Hegel on Art, An Interpretation of Hegel's Aesthetics* (New York, State University of New York, 1962).

Kedney, John Steinfort, *Hegel's Aesthetics, A Critical Exposition* (Chicago, S. C. Griggs and Co., 1885).

Knox, Israel, *The Aesthetic Theories of Kant, Hegel and Schopenhauer* (New York, The Humanities Press, 1958).

Mueller, Gustav E., "The Functions of Aesthetics in Hegel's Philosophy," *Journal of Aesthetics and Art Criticism*, V (Spring, 1946), 49–53.

Stace, Walter T., **The Philosophy of Hegel, A Systematic Exposition* (New York, Dover Publications, 1955).

CHAPTER 6

Art, Will, and Idea

SCHOPENHAUER

The life of the world's greatest pessimist, Arthur Schopenhauer (1788–1860), was not a happy one—until it was almost over.[1] As a sensitive and brilliant boy, Arthur was dominated by his strong-willed German father, who was determined that his son should become a prosperous businessman like himself. Later, when young Schopenhauer pleaded for a college education, his father (whom he idolized) prevailed against such "impractical ideas" and took his son on extensive travels, then sent him to school in France and England so that he could learn other languages for trading purposes, and, finally, entered him into a merchant's office in Hamburg for further training. His father's death (possibly a suicide) in 1805 gave the seventeen-year-old merchant's apprentice a chance to reconsider his life plans. Consequently, after getting the consent of his mother—a popular novelist of the day who cared little for her gloomy offspring—Schopenhauer undertook a program of studies in classics, philosophy, and science at Gotha, Göttingen, and Berlin. In a few years, he had become thoroughly acquainted with the philosophies of Kant and Plato, the philosophers who most influenced his own views, and had learned what he could from the chief philosophers of his day, including Fichte, Schleiermacher, Schelling, and Hegel, all of whom he grew to detest. Throughout this time, Schopenhauer was laying the groundwork for his new system of idealistic-voluntaristic pessimism.

After completing his dissertation (*On the Fourfold Root of the Principle of Sufficient Reason*) in 1813, Schopenhauer received his Ph.D. from the University of Jena and went for a while to live in Weimar with his mother. But a bitter quarrel between the two eventually occurred, resulting in a permanent estrangement. The next few years Schopenhauer spent in Dresden where he did research and writing. In 1819, when he was only thirty, his chief work, *The World as Will and Representation* was published, but at that time the work brought him no recognition whatsoever. He was further disappointed when he failed to gain attention through lecturing at the University of Berlin. (He is said to have arranged his lecture hour so as to coincide with that of the day's idol, Hegel.) Since money from his father's estate made it possible for him to live without working, he decided to give up academic ambitions, and after traveling for a while he finally settled down in Frankfurt am Main, where he remained for the rest of his life. His bachelor daily routine became fixed, he resigned himself to neglect and loneliness, and a series of poodles were his chosen companions. Although he published a few shorter works during this period, they, like his major work, created little stir.[2]

Then at last, in the final decade of his life, fame unexpectedly came to him through the publication of his essays, *Parerga and Paralipomena* (1851), a work which appealed to the new intellectual and cultural climate. The last few years of Schopenhauer's life were therefore the happiest. He rejoiced in his long-delayed recognition and welcomed the adoration of new-found disciples. He fully desired and expected to live to be a hundred, but death overtook him suddenly, when he was seventy-two years old.

Schopenhauer's philosophy of art can be understood only in the context of his metaphysics—his explanation of ultimate reality or of reality as a whole. With Plato, he believes that ultimate reality is not what appears to be real but is what lies above and beyond sensuous knowledge. With Kant, he believes that the intellect always stands between us and things, thus making it impossible for us to know things as they are in themselves, apart from our knowing selves. We have to begin with what is given, with the world as representation, the world as it exists for, and is conditioned by, the subject. Time, space, and causality are *a priori* forms of representation through which the understanding molds sensations into perceptions. Since the phenomena we know appear to be related coherently, we assume that they all have a reason for being; we assume, that is, what Schopenhauer calls the *principle of sufficient reason:* "Nothing is without a reason for its being."[3]

This *a priori* principle is the basis of all science, whether it be logic, physics, mathematics, or psychology; it is the inexorable law of *becoming*, of *knowing*, of *being*, and of *motivation*. Without presupposing the principle of sufficient reason, we would be unable to draw the simplest logical conclusion, to distinguish between cause and effect, to grasp relations of succession and position, or to act consistently. This explains why the order of the perceived world, the world as representation, appears intelligible; it is the result of synthesizing mental activity.

But the world is more, Schopenhauer continues, than a subject's idea or representation. This mental world is not the ultimately real world; it is only the world as it appears and exists. To get at another aspect of the world—at the "kernel of reality"—the thinker must probe deeply into himself as an individual, himself as more than a purely knowing subject. As an individual with a body, he exists in space and time, which compose, according to Schopenhauer, "the principle of individuation" *(principium individuationis)*. His body, like everything else that appears, can be known as phenomenon, as representation, as an object among other objects, but it can also be known inwardly and immediately in terms of its dynamic qualities which are basically manifestations of its true nature, its nature as will. "My body and my will are one," says Schopenhauer. Or, as he also puts it, "the action of the body is nothing but the act of the will objectified, i.e., passed into perception."[4]

Leaving behind the world of representation Schopenhauer now proceeds to explore the world of will; from the phenomenon he turns to the noumenon, the thing-in-itself. He sees the manifestations of will everywhere—in natural forces, in organic and inorganic matter, in animal instincts, and in human appetites and passions. But he believes that the will in itself (i.e. apart from its manifestations) is unknowable, since as a unitary cosmic principle independent of space and time its ultimate nature can never be grasped. We can know it only as it objectifies itself, becomes visible, in its different grades with their innumerable exemplifications. These grades of the will's objectification Schopenhauer calls "Platonic Ideas." They are "the eternal forms of things," "the patterns or prototypes" of the species which exist in nature. The Ideas are multiplied into individual phenomena through space and time, but in their ultimate nature they remain eternal subsisting forms which are completely independent of space, time, and causality.[5]

The will can reach progressively higher grades of objectification or of Idea only through perpetual conflict and strife. Hungering for existence, its various forms fight "for the matter, the space, and the time of the others."[6] This is why we find in nature an endless striving and a universal conflict; the will-to-live maintains its existence by preying upon itself. This conflict is especially evident, and especially revolting, at the human level, where "*homo homini lupus*."[7] Moreover, in order to preserve and propagate itself at the highest levels of objectification, the will creates for itself higher powers of perception and, finally, a refined instrument for furthering its ends, namely, the human intellect. But because the will is always at variance with itself, because its insatiable appetites can never be satisfied and its blind, powerful urges brought to stable fulfillment, man—the tragic victim of the will— finds himself far from being a completely rational animal. Instead, he is always striving, desiring, and failing; inevitably he is either frustrated, when he does not get what he wants, or bored, when he does. In the long run the human being gets infinitely more pain than he does enjoyment. For pain, which for Schopenhauer is positive, always outweighs pleasure, which is only a temporary negation of pain. Suffering, then, rather than satisfaction, is man's lot in his tragi-comic existence; an individual is as likely to find happiness, permanently lasting pleasure, as he is to find the pot of gold at the end of the rainbow.

Schopenhauer's conclusion is that there is no hope for man as long as he persists in affirming the will-to-live. But, even so, he does not advocate suicide as a way out of suffering. For if one destroys one's body, and with it one's consciousness, one does not thereby destroy one's deeper self; the individual phenomenal self is removed, but not the noumenal self, the one will which is present in all phenomena, the cosmic will.[8] Renouncing suicide as a way out of life's sorrows, the wise man lives on, resigned to the fact that the suffering he experiences is universal to all creatures of will. His heart is filled with compassion for all those who suffer, and he attempts to alleviate their suffering in so far as it lies in his power to do so. If he eventually becomes strong and good enough, if he learns to renounce voluntarily selfish egoism and seeks through a life of strict asceticism to break and to mortify the will deliberately, he may at last attain that rare but precious deliverance from willing which to the Christian is the Kingdom of Grace and to the Buddhist, Nirvana.

In the meantime, life offers us at least one consolation which can make pain easier to endure if not to accept. This consolation, which temporarily quiets the will in us and lifts us to momentary bliss, is art. For in aesthetic contemplation of works of art we can rise above the level of particular things and contemplate their forms; we can know their Ideas which transcend the principle of sufficient reason and all relations to will. Such contemplation requires that we fix our attention on the object presented, on *what* it is, not on where it came from, why it exists, or how it can be put to use.[9] We must contemplate the object not so much as an individual thing but as an Idea, an external archetype, a pure representation totally detached from will. By doing this we can lose our own individuality; we and the object become one. The aesthetic perceiver becomes "pure will-less, painless, timeless subject of knowledge."[10] Like the artistic genius, the aesthetic perceiver can be "lost in the work" in so far as he gives rapt yet objective attention to the universals in particulars, seeing things independently of the principle of sufficient reason. We should be grateful to the artistic genius for lending us his eyes, for embodying his aesthetic imaginative vision of things in art forms that manifest the various grades, the ideal stages, of the will's objectification. A temple, a fountain, a landscaped garden, a painting, a statue, and a poetic tragedy are concrete examples of the increasingly higher stages through which the will's objectification can be depicted visibly, beautifully, and painlessly in aesthetic form. And music can copy the will itself in such a way that its inner turmoils are given powerful and painless expression.

But all the arts provide only temporary deliverance from the will, and we are deluded, Schopenhauer believes, if we expect more from them than a momentary emancipation from our passions and desires. Salvation is to be sought and found ultimately by following the way of the ascetic rather than the way of the artist.[11]

Art, Will, and Idea

1. *In approaching the problem of aesthetic experience, Schopenhauer first distinguishes aesthetic knowing from other kinds of knowing. Whereas scientific knowing, for example, is concerned*

with attaining concepts and tracing relationships, aesthetic know-
ing is concerned with eternal objects, Platonic Ideas, which
transcend rational concepts and relationships. The task of genius
is to know these Ideas through the use of pure contemplation and
to give them material embodiment in works of art.

But what kind of knowledge is concerned with that which is
outside and independent of all relations, that which alone is really
essential to the world, the true content of its phenomena, that
which is subject to no change, and therefore is known with equal
truth for all time, in a word, the *Ideas*, which are the direct and
adequate objectively of the thing-in-itself, the will? We answer,
Art, the work of genius. It repeats or reproduces the eternal Ideas
grasped through pure contemplation, the essential and abiding in
all the phenomena of the world; and according to what the
material is in which it reproduces, it is sculpture or painting,
poetry or music. Its one source is the knowledge of Ideas; its one
aim the communication of this knowledge. While science, following the unresting and inconstant stream of the fourfold forms of
reason and consequent, with each end attained sees further, and
can never reach a final goal nor attain full satisfaction, any more
than by running we can reach the place where the clouds touch
the horizon; art, on the contrary, is everywhere at its goal. For it
plucks the object of its contemplation out of the stream of the
world's course, and has it isolated before it. And this particular
thing, which in that stream was a small perishing part, becomes
to art the representative of the whole, an equivalent of the endless
multitude in space and time. It therefore pauses at this particular
thing; the course of time stops; the relations vanish for it; only
the essential, the Idea, is its object. We may, therefore, accurately
define it as the *way of viewing things independent of the principle*
of sufficient reason, in opposition to the way of viewing them
which proceeds in accordance with that principle, and which is
the method of experience and of science. This last method of
considering things may be compared to a line infinitely extended
in a horizontal direction, and the former to a vertical line which
cuts it at any point. The method of viewing things which proceeds
in accordance with the principle of sufficient reason is the rational
method, and it alone is valid and of use in practical life and in
science. The method which looks away from the content of this

principle is the method of genius, which is only valid and of use in art. The first is the method of Aristotle; the second is, on the whole, that of Plato. The first is like the mighty storm, that rushes along without beginning and without aim, bending, agitating, and carrying away everything before it; the second is like the silent sunbeam, that pierces through the storm quite unaffected by it. The first is like the innumerable showering drops of the waterfall, which, constantly changing, never rest for an instant; the second is like the rainbow, quietly resting on this raging torrent. Only through the pure contemplation described above, which ends entirely in the object, can Ideas be comprehended; and the nature of *genius* consists in pre-eminent capacity for such contemplation.[12]

2. *Schopenhauer contrasts the practical cognition of ordinary men with the imaginative cognition of the artistic genius. Such a genius "sees" objects in a different light than his commonplace relatives. His imagination ranges at a higher level, aims at knowledge of real objects, Platonic Ideas, rather than of mere useful ones.*

Imagination has rightly been recognised as an essential element of genius; it has sometimes even been regarded as identical with it; but this is a mistake. As the objects of genius are the eternal Ideas, the permanent, essential forms of the world and all its phenomena, and as the knowledge of the Idea is necessarily knowledge through perception, is not abstract, the knowledge of the genius would be limited to the Ideas of the objects actually present to his person, and dependent upon the chain of circumstances that brought these objects to him, if his imagination did not extend his horizon far beyond the limits of his actual personal existence, and thus enable him to construct the whole out of the little that comes into his own actual apperception, and so to let almost all possible scenes of life pass before him in his own consciousness. Further, the actual objects are almost always very imperfect copies of the Ideas expressed in them; therefore the man of genius requires imagination in order to see in things, not that which Nature has actually made, but that which she endeavoured to make, yet could not because of that conflict of her forms among themselves.... We shall return to this farther on in treating of sculpture. The imagination then extends the intellectual horizon of the man of genius beyond the objects which actually present themselves to him, both as regards quality and quantity. Therefore extraordinary strength of imagination accompanies, and is indeed a necessary condition of genius. . . .

The common mortal, that manufacture of Nature which she produces by the thousand every day, is, as we have said, not capable, at least not continuously so, of observation that in every sense is wholly disinterested, as sensuous contemplation, strictly so called, is. He can turn his attention to things only so far as they have some relation to his will, however indirect it may be. Since in this respect, which never demands anything but the knowledge of relations, the abstract conception of the thing is sufficient, and for the most part even better adapted for use; the ordinary man does not linger long over the mere perception, does not fix his attention long on one object, but in all that is presented to him hastily seeks merely the concept under which it is to be brought, as the lazy man seeks a chair, and then it interests him no further. This is why he is so soon done with everything, with works of art, objects of natural beauty, and indeed everywhere with the truly significant contemplation of all the scenes of life. He does not linger; only seeks to know his own way in life, together with all that might at any time become his way. Thus he makes topographical notes in the widest sense; over the consideration of life itself as such he wastes no time. The man of genius, on the other hand, whose excessive power of knowledge frees it at all times from the service of will, dwells on the consideration of life itself, strives to comprehend the Idea of each thing, not its relations to other things; and in doing this he often forgets to consider his own path in life, and therefore for the most part pursues it awkwardly enough. While to the ordinary man his faculty of knowledge is a lamp to lighten his path, to the man of genius it is the sun which reveals the world.[13] . . .

3. *The difference between the genius's aesthetic experience and that of the ordinary mortal is, Schopenhauer recognizes, one of degree rather than kind, otherwise, aesthetic enjoyment of art and nature would not be so widespread. The artistic genius lends us his eyes that we might see the beauty he has seen and which he shares with us through his creations.*

Genius, then, consists, according to our explanation, in the capacity for knowing, independently of the principle of sufficient reason, not individual things, which have their existence only in their relations, but the Ideas of such things, and of being oneself the correlative of the Idea, and thus no longer an individual, but the pure subject of knowledge. Yet this faculty must exist in all men in a smaller and different degree; for if not, they would be just as incapable of enjoying works of art as of producing them; they would have no susceptibility for the beautiful or the sublime; indeed, these words could have no meaning for them. We must therefore assume that there exists in all men this power of knowing the Ideas in things, and consequently of transcending their personality for the moment, unless indeed there are some men who are capable of no aesthetic pleasure at all. The man of genius excels ordinary men only by possessing this kind of knowledge in a far higher degree and more continuously. Thus, while under its influence he retains the presence of mind which is necessary to enable him to repeat in a voluntary and intentional work what he has learned in this manner; and this repetition is the work of art. Through this he communicates to others the Idea he has grasped. This Idea remains unchanged and the same, so that aesthetic pleasure is one and the same whether it is called forth by a work of art or directly by the contemplation of nature and life. The work of art is only a means of facilitating the knowledge in which this pleasure consists. That the Idea comes to us more easily from the work of art than directly from nature and the real world, arises from the fact that the artist, who knew only the Idea, no longer the actual, has reproduced in his work the pure Idea, has abstracted it from the actual, omitting all disturbing accidents. The artist lets us see the world through his eyes. That he has these eyes, that he knows the inner nature of things apart from all their relations, is the gift of genius, is inborn; but that he is able to lend us this gift, to let us see with his eyes, is acquired, and is the technical side of art.[14] ...

4. *Having analyzed aesthetic experience into two distinct parts: (1) the objective, i.e. knowledge of the Idea and (2) the subjective, i.e. knowledge of the self as a will-less subject of knowledge, Schopenhauer proceeds to show how pleasure arises from these two constituent parts. First, the subjective part. As long as a man is*

*a creature that wills, he is inevitably a dissatisfied, suffering,
frustrated creature. But when he ceases to will, he is disinterested
and objective in his standpoint; he achieves at last peace of mind,
freedom from pain and frustration. Through aesthetic contemplation, he can achieve such a will-less state and thus experience the
purest of pleasures, that which comes from knowing a truth
independent of all relations.*

In the aesthetical mode of contemplation we have found *two
inseparable constituent parts*—the knowledge of the object, not as
individual thing but as Platonic Idea, that is, as the enduring form
of this whole species of things; and the self-consciousness of the
knowing person, not as individual, but as *pure will-less subject of
knowledge.* The condition under which both these constituent
parts appear always united was found to be the abandonment of
the method of knowing which is bound to the principle of
sufficient reason, and which, on the other hand, is the only kind
of knowledge that is of value for the service of the will and also
for science. Moreover, we shall see that the pleasure which is
produced by the contemplation of the beautiful arises from these
two constituent parts, sometimes more from the one, sometimes
more from the other, according to what the object of the aesthetical contemplation may be.

All *willing* arises from want, therefore from deficiency, and
therefore from suffering. The satisfaction of a wish ends it; yet
for one wish that is satisfied there remains at least ten which are
denied. Further, the desire lasts long, the demands are infinite; the
satisfaction is short and scantily measured out. But even the final
satisfaction is itself only apparent; every satisfied wish at once
makes room for a new one; both are illusions; the one is known
to be so, the other not yet. No attained object of desire can give
lasting satisfaction, but merely a fleeting gratification; it is like the
alms thrown to the beggar, that keeps him alive to-day that his
misery may be prolonged till the morrow. Therefore, so long as
our consciousness is filled by our will, so long as we are given up
to the throng of desires with their constant hopes and fears, so
long as we are the subject of willing, we can never have lasting
happiness nor peace. It is essentially all the same whether we
pursue or flee, fear injury or seek enjoyment; the care for the
constant demands of the will, in whatever form it may be, con-

tinually occupies and sways the consciousness; but without peace no true well-being is possible. The subject of willing is thus constantly stretched on the revolving wheel of Ixion, pours water into the sieve of the Danaids, is the ever-longing Tantalus.

But when some external cause or inward disposition lifts us suddenly out of the endless stream of willing, delivers knowledge from the slavery of the will, the attention is no longer directed to the motives of willing, but comprehends things free from their relation to the will, and thus observes them without personal interest, without subjectivity, purely objectively, gives itself entirely up to them so far as they are ideas, but not in so far as they are motives. Then all at once the peace which we were always seeking, but which always fled from us on the former path of the desires, comes to us of its own accord, and it is well with us. It is the painless state which Epicurus prized as the highest good and as the state of the gods; for we are for the moment set free from the miserable striving of the will; we keep the Sabbath of the penal servitude of willing; the wheel of Ixion stands still.

But this is just the state which I described above as necessary for the knowledge of the Idea, as pure contemplation, as sinking oneself in perception, losing oneself in the object, forgetting all individuality, surrendering that kind of knowledge which follows the principle of sufficient reason, and comprehends only relations; the state by means of which at once and inseparably the perceived particular thing is raised to the Idea of its whole species, and the knowing individual to the pure subject of will-less knowledge, and as such they are both taken out of the stream of time and all other relations. It is then all one whether we see the sun set from the prison or from the palace.[15]

5. *In exploring further the subjective part of aesthetic pleasure, Schopenhauer finds an explanation of the feeling of the sublime. This feeling is essentially the same as the feeling of the beautiful in that it too is aroused when one attains pure, will-less knowing in contemplating the Platonic Idea in nature and art; however, the sublime has a feature distinguishing it from the feeling of the beautiful. This feature is a sense of exaltation derived from the awareness of the superiority of forces hostile to the will.*

All these reflections are intended to bring out the subjective part of aesthetic pleasure; that is to say, that pleasure so far as it consists simply of delight in perceptive knowledge as such, in opposition to will. And as directly connected with this, there naturally follows the explanation of that disposition or frame of mind which has been called the sense of the *sublime*.

We have already remarked above that the transition to the state of pure perception takes place most easily when the objects bend themselves to it, that is, when by their manifold and yet definite and distinct form they easily become representatives of their Ideas, in which beauty, in the objective sense, consists. This quality belongs pre-eminently to natural beauty, which thus affords even to the most insensible at least a fleeting aesthetic satisfaction: indeed it is so remarkable how especially the vegetable world invites aesthetic observation, and, as it were, presses itself upon it, that one might say, that these advances are connected with the fact that these organisms, unlike the bodies of animals, are not themselves immediate objects of knowledge, and therefore require the assistance of a foreign intelligent individual in order to rise out of the world of blind will and enter the world of idea, and that thus they long, as it were, for this entrance, that they may attain at least indirectly what is denied them directly. But I leave this suggestion which I have hazarded, and which borders perhaps upon extravagance, entirely undecided, for only a very intimate and devoted consideration of nature can raise or justify it. As long as that which raises us from the knowledge of mere relations subject to the will, to aesthetic contemplation, and thereby exalts us to the position of the subject of knowledge free from will, is this fittingness of nature, this significance and distinctness of its forms, on account of which the Ideas individualised in them readily present themselves to us; so long is it merely *beauty* that affects us and the sense of the *beautiful* that is excited. But if these very objects whose significant forms invite us to pure contemplation, have a hostile relation to the human will in general, as it exhibits itself in its objectivity, the human body, if they are opposed to it, so that it is menaced by the irresistible predominance of their power, or sinks into insignificance before their immeasurable greatness; if, nevertheless, the beholder does not direct his attention to this eminently hostile relation to his will, but, although perceiving and recognising it, turns consciously away from it, forcibly detaches himself from his will and its relations, and, giving himself up entirely to knowledge, quietly contemplates those very objects that are so terrible to the will, comprehends only their Idea, which is foreign to all relation, so that he lingers gladly over its contemplation, and is thereby raised above himself, his person, his will, and all will:—in that case he is filled with the sense of the *sublime,* he is in the state of spiritual exaltation, and therefore the object producing such a state called *sublime.* Thus what distinguishes the sense of the sublime from that of the beautiful is this: in the case of the beautiful, pure knowledge has gained the upper hand without a struggle, for the beauty of the object, *i.e.* that property which facilitates the knowledge of its Idea, has removed from consciousness without resistance, and therefore imperceptibly, the will and the knowledge of relations which is subject to it, so that what is left is the pure subject of knowledge without even a remembrance of will. On the other hand, in the case of the sublime that state of pure knowledge is only attained by a conscious and forcible breaking away from the relations of the same object to the will, which are recognised as unfavourable, by a free and conscious transcending of the will and the knowledge related to it.

This exaltation must not only be consciously won, but also consciously retained, and it is therefore accompanied by a constant remembrance of will; yet not of a single particular volition, such as fear or desire, but of human volition in general, so far as it is universally expressed in its objectivity the human body. If a single real act of will were to come into consciousness, through actual personal pressure and danger from the object, then the individual will thus actually influenced would at once gain the upper hand, the peace of contemplation would become impossible, the impression of the sublime would be lost, because it yields to the anxiety, in which the effort of the individual to right itself has sunk every other thought. A few examples will help very much to elucidate this theory of the aesthetic sublime and remove all doubt with regard to it; at the same time they will bring out the different degrees of this sense of the sublime. It is in the main identical with that of the beautiful, with pure will-less knowing, and the knowledge, that necessarily accompanies it of Ideas out of all relation determined by the principle of sufficient reason, and it is distinguished from the sense of the beautiful only by the additional quality that it rises above the known hostile relation of the object contemplated to the will in general.[16] ...

6. *Schopenhauer gives many examples of things that might evoke in us the feeling of the sublime. Among these are:*

Nature convulsed by a storm; the sky darkened by black threatening thunder-clouds; stupendous, naked, over-hanging cliffs, completely shutting out the view; rushing, foaming torrents; absolute desert; the wail of the wind sweeping through the clefts of the rocks. Our dependence, our strife with hostile nature, our will broken in the conflict, now appears visibly before our eyes. Yet, so long as the personal pressure does not gain the upper hand, but we continue in aesthetic contemplation, the pure subject of knowing gazes unshaken and unconcerned through that strife of nature, through that picture of the broken will, and quietly comprehends the Ideas even of those objects which are threatening and terrible to the will. In this contrast lies the sense of the sublime.

But the impression becomes still stronger, if, when we have before our eyes, on a large scale, the battle of the raging elements, in such a sense we are prevented from hearing the sound of our own voice by the noise of a falling stream; or, if we are abroad in the storm of tempestuous seas, where the mountainous waves rise and fall, dash themselves furiously against steep cliffs, and toss their spray high into the air; the storm howls, the sea boils, the lightning flashes from black clouds, and the peals of thunder drown the voice of storm and sea. Then, in the undismayed beholder, the two-fold nature of his consciousness reaches the highest degree of distinctness. He perceives himself, on the one hand, as an individual, as the frail phenomenon of will, which the slightest touch of these forces can utterly destroy, helpless against powerful nature, dependent, the victim of chance, a vanishing nothing in the presence of stupendous might; and, on the other hand, as the eternal, peaceful, knowing subject, the condition of the object, and, therefore, the supporter of this whole world; the terrific strife of nature only his idea; the subject itself free and apart from all desires and necessities, in the quiet comprehension of the Ideas. This is the complete impression of the sublime. Here he obtains a glimpse of a power beyond all comparison superior to the individual, threatening it with annihilation.[17]

7. So far, Schopenhauer has been mainly concerned with the subjective part of aesthetic experience, with that part derived from the subject's pleasurable awareness of himself as a pure, will-less knower. Now he turns his attention to the objective part of aesthetic experience, particularly in relation to the nature of the beautiful. An object is beautiful only if (1) it makes us objective, i.e. aware of ourselves not as individuals but as universal knowing subjects, and (2) we recognize in the object not the individual object but the universal Idea, the species objectified. These two aspects of aesthetic experience are beyond all human willing as well as beyond all rational spatial and temporal relations.

The course of the discussion has made it necessary to insert at this point the treatment of the sublime, though we have only half done with the beautiful, as we have considered its subjective side only. For it was merely a special modification of this subjective side that distinguished the beautiful from the sublime. This difference was found to depend upon whether the state of pure will-less knowing, which is presupposed and demanded by all aesthetic contemplation, was reached without opposition, by the mere disappearance of the will from consciousness, because the object invited and drew us towards it; or whether it was only attained through the free, conscious transcending of the will, to which the object contemplated had an unfavourable and even hostile relation, which would destroy contemplation altogether, if we were to give ourselves up to it. This is the distinction between the beautiful and the sublime. In the object they are not essentially different, for in every case the object of aesthetical contemplation is not the individual thing, but the Idea in it which is striving to reveal itself; that is to say, adequate objectivity of will at a particular grade. Its necessary correlative, independent, like itself of the principle of sufficient reason, is the pure subject of knowing; just as the correlative of the particular thing is the knowing individual, both of which lie within the province of the principle of sufficient reason.

When we say that a thing is *beautiful*, we thereby assert that it is an object of our aesthetic contemplation, and this has a double meaning; on the one hand it means that the sight of the thing makes us *objective*, that is to say, that in contemplating it we are no longer conscious of ourselves as individuals, but as pure will-less subjects of knowledge; and on the other hand it means that we recognise in the object, not the particular thing, but an Idea; and this can only happen, so far as our contemplation of it is not subordinated to the principle of sufficient reason, does not follow the relation of the object to anything outside it (which is always ultimately connected with relations to our own will), but rests in the object itself. For the Idea and the pure subject of knowledge always appear at once in consciousness as necessary correlatives, and on their appearance all distinction of time vanishes, for they are both entirely foreign to the principle of sufficient reason in all its forms, and lie outside the relations which are imposed by it; they may be compared to the rainbow and the sun, which have no part in the constant movement and succession of the falling drops. Therefore, if, for example, I contemplate a tree aesthetically, i.e., with artistic eyes, and thus recognise, not it, but its Idea, it becomes at once of no consequence whether it is this tree or its predecessor which flourished a thousand years ago, and whether the observer is this individual or any other that lived anywhere and at any time; the particular thing and the knowing individual are abolished with the principle of sufficient reason, and there remains nothing but the Idea and the pure subject of knowing, which together constitute the adequate objectivity of will at this grade. And the Idea dispenses not only with time, but also with space, for the Idea proper is not this special form which appears before me but its expression, its pure significance, its inner being, which discloses itself to me and appeals to me, and which may be quite the same though the spatial relations of its form be very different.[18]

8. *From Schopenhauer's perspective, all things are to some extent beautiful. For all things may be observed aesthetically, i.e. objectively; and, all things represent varying grades of the objectification of Ideas by will. Things are to be judged more or less beautiful according to the extent to which they facilitate objective comprehension by the purity and completeness of their expression of the Ideas.*

Since, on the one hand, every given thing may be observed in a purely objective manner and apart from all relations; and since, on the other hand, the will manifests itself in everything at some grade of its objectivity, so that everything is the expression of an Idea; it follows that everything is also *beautiful*. That even the most insignificant things admit of pure objective and will-less contemplation, and thus prove that they are beautiful, is shown by what was said above in this reference about the Dutch pictures of still-life (§38). But one thing is more beautiful than another, because it makes this pure objective contemplation easier, it lends itself to it, and, so to speak, even compels it, and then we call it very beautiful. This is the case sometimes because, as an individual thing, it expresses in its purity the Idea of its species by the very distinct, clearly defined, and significant relation of its parts, and also fully reveals that Idea through the completeness of all the possible expressions of its species united in it, so that it makes the transition from the individual thing to the Idea, and therefore also the condition of pure contemplation, very easy for the beholder. Sometimes this possession of special beauty in an object lies in the fact that the Idea itself which appeals to us in it is a high grade of the objectivity of will, and therefore very significant and expressive. Therefore it is that man is more beautiful than all other objects, and the revelation of his nature is the highest aim of art. Human form and expression are the most important objects of plastic art, and human action the most important object of poetry. Yet each thing has its own peculiar beauty, not only every organism which expresses itself in the unity of an individual being, but also everything unorganised and formless, and even every manufactured article. For all these reveal the Ideas through which the will objectifies itself at its lowest grades; they give, as it were, the deepest resounding bass-notes of nature. Gravity, rigidity, fluidity, light, and so forth, are the Ideas which express themselves in rocks, in buildings, in waters. Landscape-gardening or architecture can do no more than assist them to unfold their qualities distinctly, fully, and variously; they can only give them the opportunity of expressing themselves purely, so that they lend themselves to aesthetic contemplation and make it easier. . . .

The knowledge of the beautiful always supposes at once and inseparably the pure knowing subject and the known Idea as object. Yet the source of aesthetic satisfaction will sometimes lie more in the comprehension of the known Idea, sometimes more in the blessedness and spiritual peace of the pure knowing subject freed from all willing, and therefore from all individuality, and the pain that proceeds from it. And, indeed, this predominance of one or the other constituent part of aesthetic feeling will depend upon whether the intuitively grasped Idea is a higher or a lower grade of the objectivity of will.[19] . . .

9. *Schopenhauer proceeds to discuss the various arts, ranking them in order of their increasingly higher objectification of Idea by will. Here we will consider three of the art forms discussed in detail by Schopenhauer: (1) architecture, which expresses as the lowest objectification of will the conflict between gravity and rigidity, (2) poetic tragedy, which as the highest objectification of will expresses the conflict of the will with itself, and (3) music, which is placed by Schopenhauer in a class by itself above all the other art forms because it gives a direct objectification of the will itself. First, architecture:*

If now we consider *architecture* simply as a fine art and apart from its application to useful ends, in which it serves the will and not pure knowledge, and therefore ceases to be art in our sense; we can assign to it no other aim than that of bringing to greater distinctness some of those ideas, which are the lowest grades of the objectivity of will; such as gravity, cohesion, rigidity, hardness, those universal qualities of stone, those first, simplest, most inarticulate manifestations of will; the bass notes of nature; and after these light, which in many respects is their opposite. Even at these low grades of the objectivity of will we see its nature revealing itself in discord; for properly speaking the conflict between gravity and rigidity is the sole aesthetic material of architecture; its problem is to make this conflict appear with perfect distinctness in a multitude of different ways. It solves it by depriving these indestructible forces of the shortest way to their satisfaction, and conducting them to it by a circuitous route, so that the conflict is lengthened and the inexhaustible efforts of both forces become visible in many different ways. The whole mass of the building, if left to its original tendency, would exhibit a mere heap or clump, bound as closely as possible to the earth, to which gravity, the form in which the will appears here, continually presses, while rigidity, also objectivity of will, resists. But this very tendency, this effort, is hindered by architecture from obtaining direct satisfaction, and only allowed to reach it indirectly and by roundabout ways. The roof, for example, can only press the earth through columns, the arch must support itself, and can only satisfy its tendency towards the earth through the medium of the pillars, and so forth. But just by these enforced digressions, just by these restrictions, the forces which reside in the crude mass of stone unfold themselves in the most distinct and multi-

farious ways; and the purely aesthetic aim of architecture can go
no further than this. Therefore the beauty, at any rate, of a
building lies in the obvious adaptation of every part, not to the
outward arbitrary end of man (so far the work belongs to
practical architecture), but directly to the stability of the whole,
to which the position, dimensions, and form of every part must
have so necessary a relation that, where it is possible, if any one
part were taken away, the whole would fall to pieces. For just
because each part bears just as much as it conveniently can, and
each is supported just where it requires to be and just to the
necessary extent, this opposition unfolds itself, this conflict
between rigidity and gravity, which constitutes the life, the manifestation of will, in the stone, becomes completely visible, and
these lowest grades of the objectivity of will reveal themselves distinctly. . . .

Now, because the Ideas which architecture brings to clear perception, are the lowest grades of the objectivity of will, and consequently their objective significance, which architecture reveals
to us, is comparatively small; the aesthetic pleasure of looking at
a beautiful building in a good light will lie, not so much in the
comprehension of the Idea, as in the subjective correlative which
accompanies this comprehension; it will consist pre-eminently in
the fact that the beholder, set free from the kind of knowledge
that belongs to the individual, and which serves the will and
follows the principle of sufficient reason, is raised to that of the
pure subject of knowing free from will. It will consist then principally in pure contemplation itself, free from all the suffering of
will and of individuality. In this respect the opposite of architecture, and the other extreme of the series of the fine arts, is the
drama, which brings to knowledge the most significant Ideas.
Therefore in the aesthetic pleasure afforded by the drama the
objective side is throughout predominant.

Architecture has this distinction from plastic art and poetry: it
does not give us a copy but the thing itself. It does not repeat, as
they do, the known Idea, so that the artist lends his eyes to the
beholder, but in it the artist merely presents the object to the
beholder, and facilitates for him the comprehension of the Idea
by bringing the actual, individual object to a distinct and complete
expression of its nature.[20]

10. *If architecture is the lowest of the arts in terms of the*

objectification of will, poetry is the highest, revealing as it does, the Idea of mankind, the highest grade of the objectification of will. In its most objective forms, epic and drama, poetry accomplishes its end by the presentation of significant characters in situations in which they reveal themselves and mankind. Tragedy, the highest poetic art, represents for Schopenhauer a confirmation of his pessimistic appraisal of life and suggests the way of salvation: resignation to suffering and denial of the very will-to-live itself.

If now, with the exposition which has been given of art in general, we turn from plastic and pictorial art to poetry, we shall have no doubt that its aim also is the revelation of the Ideas, the grades of the objectification of will, and the communication of them to the hearer with the distinctness and vividness with which the poetical sense comprehends them. Ideas are essentially perceptible; if, therefore, in poetry only abstract conceptions are directly communicated through words, it is yet clearly the intention to make the hearer perceive the Ideas of life in the representatives of these conceptions, and this can only take place through the assistance of his own imagination. But in order to set the imagination to work for the accomplishment of this end, the abstract conceptions, which are the immediate material of poetry as of dry prose, must be so arranged that their spheres intersect each other in such a way that none of them can remain in its abstract universality; but, instead of it, a perceptible representative appears to the imagination; and this is always further modified by the words of the poet according to what his intention may be. As the chemist obtains solid precipitates by combining perfectly clear and transparent fluids; the poet understands how to precipitate, as it were, the concrete, the individual, the perceptible idea, out of the abstract and transparent universality of the concepts by the manner in which he combines them. For the Idea can only be known by perception; and knowledge of the Idea is the end of art. The skill of a master, in poetry as in chemistry, enables us always to obtain the precise precipitate we intended. This end is assisted by the numerous epithets in poetry, by means of which the universality of every concept is narrowed more and more till we reach the perceptible. . . .

From the general nature of the material, that is, the concepts, which poetry uses to communicate the Ideas, the extent of its province is very great. The whole of nature, the Ideas of all grades, can be represented by means of it, for it proceeds according to the Idea it has to impart, so that its representations are sometimes descriptive, sometimes narrative, and sometimes directly dramatic. If, in the representation of the lower grades of the objectivity of will, plastic and pictorial art generally surpass it, because lifeless nature, and even brute nature, reveals almost its whole being in a single well-chosen moment; man, on the contrary, so far as he does not express himself by the mere form and expression of his person, but through a series of actions and the accompanying thoughts and emotions, is the principal object of poetry, in which no other art can compete with it, for here the progress or movement which cannot be represented in plastic or pictorial art just suits its purpose.

The revelation of the Idea, which is the highest grade of the objectivity of will, the representation of man in the connected series of his efforts and actions, is thus the great problem of poetry....

In the more objective kinds of poetry, especially in the romance, the epic, and the drama, the end, the revelation of the Idea of man, is principally attained by two means, by true and profound representation of significant characters, and by the invention of pregnant situations in which they disclose themselves. . . . Unfolding and rendering distinct the Idea expressing itself in the object of every art, the Idea of the will which objectifies itself at each grade, is the common end of all the arts. The life of man, as it shows itself for the most part in the real world, is like the water, as it is generally seen in the pond and the river; but in the epic, the romance, the tragedy, selected characters are placed in those circumstances in which all their special qualities unfold themselves, the depths of the human heart are revealed, and become visible in extraordinary and very significant actions. Thus poetry objectifies the Idea of man, an Idea which has the peculiarity of expressing itself in highly individual characters.

Tragedy is to be regarded, and is recognized as the summit of poetical art, both on account of the greatness of its effect and the difficulty of its achievement. It is very significant for our whole system, and well worthy of observation, that the end of this highest poetical achievement is the representation of the terrible side of life. The unspeakable pain, the wail of humanity, the triumph of evil, the scornful mastery of chance, and the irretrievable fall of the just and innocent, is here presented to us; and in this lies a significant hint of the nature of the world and of existence. It is the strife of will with itself, which here, completely unfolded at the highest grade of its objectivity, comes into fearful prominence. It becomes visible in the suffering of men, which is now introduced, partly through chance and error, which appear as the rulers of the world, personified as fate, on account of their insidiousness, which even reaches the appearance of design; partly it proceeds from man himself, through the self-mortifying efforts of a few, through the wickedness and perversity of most. It is one and the same will that lives and appears in them all, but whose phenomena fight against each other and destroy each other. In one individual it appears powerfully, in another more weakly; in one more subject to reason, and softened by the light of knowledge, in another less so, till at last, in some single case, this knowledge, purified and heightened by suffering itself, reaches the point at which the phenomenon, the veil of Maya, no longer deceives it. It sees through the form of the phenomenon, the *principium individuationis*. The egoism which rests on this perishes with it, so that now the *motives* that were so powerful before have lost their might, and instead of them the complete knowledge of the nature of the world, which has a *quieting* effect on the will, produces resignation, the surrender not merely of life, but of the very will to live. Thus we see in tragedies the noblest men, after long conflict and suffering, at last renounce the ends they have so keenly followed, and all the pleasures of life for ever, or else freely and joyfully surrender life itself.[21] ...

11. *For music Schopenhauer reserves a special place in his treatment of the arts. Unlike other arts, which objectify will indirectly by means of Ideas, music directly copies or expresses the will itself. It therefore has an immediacy, a power, a penetration superior to all the other arts. However, since it is the same will that objectifies itself both in the Ideas and in music, Schopenhauer thinks it is possible to draw analogies between the various grades of the objectification of will by Ideas and music. While he considers such analogies to be suggestive and significant, they should not mislead us, he points out, into thinking of music as an expression of the phenomenon (i.e. the visible appearance of things);*

for music expresses the inner nature of every phenomenon, the will itself. This explains why music can be the universal language of feelings.

The (Platonic) Ideas are the adequate objectification of will. To excite or suggest the knowledge of these by means of the representation of particular things (for works of art themselves are always representations of particular things) is the end of all the other arts, which can only be attained by a corresponding change in the knowing subject. Thus all these arts objectify the will indirectly only by means of the Ideas; and since our world is nothing but the manifestation of the Ideas in multiplicity, through their entrance into the *principium individuationis* (the form of the knowledge possible for the individual as such), music also, since it passes over the Ideas, is entirely independent of the phenomenal world, ignores it altogether, could to a certain extent exist if there was no world at all, which cannot be said of the other arts. Music is as *direct* an objectification and copy of the whole *will* as the world itself, nay, even as the Ideas, whose multiplied manifestation constitutes the world of individual things. Music is thus by no means like the other arts, the copy of the Ideas, but the *copy of the will itself*, whose objectivity the Ideas are. This is why the effect of music is so much more powerful and penetrating than that of the other arts, for they speak only of shadows, but it speaks of the thing itself. Since, however, it is the same will which objectifies itself both in the Ideas and in music, though in quite different ways, there must be, not indeed a direct likeness, but yet a parallel, an analogy, between music and the Ideas whose manifestation in multiplicity and incompleteness is the visible world. The establishing of this analogy will facilitate, as an illustration, the understanding of this exposition, which is so difficult on account of the obscurity of the subject.

I recognise in the deepest tones of harmony, in the bass, the lowest grades of the objectification of will, unorganised nature, the mass of the planet. . . . There is a limit of depth, below which no sound is audible. This corresponds to the fact that no matter can be perceived without form and quality, i.e., without the manifestation of a force which cannot be further explained, in which an idea expresses itself, and, more generally, that no matter can be entirely without will. Thus, as a certain pitch is inseparable from the note as such, so a certain grade of the manifestation of will is inseparable from matter. Bass is thus, for us, in harmony what unorganised nature, the crudest mass, upon which all rests, and from which everything originates and develops, is in the world. Now, further, in the whole of the complemental parts which make up the harmony between the bass and the leading voice singing the melody, I recognise the whole gradation of the Ideas in which the will objectifies itself. Those nearer to the bass are the lower of these grades, the still unorganised, but yet manifold phenomenal things; the higher represent to me the world of plants and beasts. . . . Lastly, in the *melody*, in the high, singing, principal voice leading the whole and progressing with unrestrained freedom, in the unbroken significant connection of *one* thought from beginning to end representing a whole, I recognise the highest grade of the objectification of will, the intellectual life and effort of man. As he alone, because endowed with reason, constantly looks before and after on the path of his actual life and its innumerable possibilities, and so achieves a course of life which is intellectual, and therefore connected as a whole; corresponding to this, I say, the *melody* has significant intentional connection from beginning to end. It records, therefore, the history of the intellectually enlightened will. This will expresses itself in the actual world as the series of its deeds; but melody says more, it records the most secret history of this intellectually-enlightened will, pictures every excitement, every effort, every movement of it, all that which the reason collects under the wide and negative concept of feeling, and which it cannot apprehend further through its abstract concepts. Therefore it has always been said that music is the language of feeling and of passion, as words are the language of reason. . . .

But it must never be forgotten, in the investigation of all these analogies I have pointed out, that music has no direct, but merely an indirect relation to them, for it never expresses the phenomenon, but only the inner nature, the in-itself of all phenomena, the will itself. It does not therefore express this or that particular and definite joy, this or that sorrow, or pain, or horror, or delight, or merriment, or peace of mind; but joy, sorrow, pain, horror, delight, merriment, peace of mind *themselves*, to a certain extent in the abstract, their essential nature, without accessories, and therefore without their motives. Yet we completely understand them in this extracted quintessence. Hence it arises that our imagination is so easily excited by music, and now seeks to give form to that invisible yet actively moved spirit-world which speaks to us directly, and clothe it with flesh and blood, i.e., to embody it in an analogous example. This is the origin of the song with words, and finally of the opera, the text of which should therefore never forsake that subordinate position in order to make itself the chief thing and the music a mere means of expressing it, which is a great misconception and a piece of utter perversity; for music always expresses only the quintessence of life and its events, never these themselves, and therefore their differences do not always affect it. It is precisely this universality, which belongs exclusively to it, together with the greatest determinateness, that gives music the high worth which it has at the panacea for all our woes. Thus, if music is too closely united to the words, and tries to form itself according to the events, it is striving to speak a language which is not its own. . . .

According to all this, we may regard the phenomenal world, or nature, and music as two different expressions of the same thing, which is therefore itself the only medium of their analogy, so that a knowledge of it is demanded in order to understand that analogy. Music, therefore, if regarded as an expression of the world, is in the highest degree a universal language, which is related indeed to the universality of concepts, much as they are related to the particular things. . . .

The unutterable depth of all music by virtue of which it floats through our consciousness as the vision of a paradise firmly believed in yet ever distant from us, and by which also it is so fully understood and yet so inexplicable, rests on the fact that it restores to us all the emotions of our inmost nature, but entirely without reality and far removed from their pain. So also the seriousness which is essential to it, which excludes the absurd from its direct and peculiar province, is to be explained by the fact that its object is not the idea, with reference to which alone deception and absurdity are possible; but its object is directly the will, and this is essentially the most serious of all things, for it is that on which all depends.[22] . . .

12. *Schopenhauer now summarizes his views on the value of art and of aesthetic experience in a world of will and representation.*

Though more a way of consolation than a way of salvation, art can lift us temporarily to a plane above willing and bring us moments of delight in the course of life's inevitable sufferings.

For if, according to our view, the whole visible world is just the objectification, the mirror, of the will, conducting it to knowledge of itself, and, indeed, as we shall soon see, to the possibility of its deliverance; and if, at the same time, the world as idea, if we regard it in isolation, and, freeing ourselves from all volition, allow it alone to take possession of our consciousness, is the most joy-giving and the only innocent side of life; we must regard art as the higher ascent, the more complete development of all this, for it achieves essentially just what is achieved by the visible world itself, only with greater concentration, more perfectly, with intention and intelligence, and therefore may be called, in the full significance of the word, the flower of life. If the whole world as idea is only the visibility of will, the work of art is to render this visibility more distinct. It is the *camera obscura* which shows the objects more purely, and enables us to survey them and comprehend them better. It is the play within the play, the stage upon the stage in "Hamlet."

The pleasure we receive from all beauty, the consolation which art affords, the enthusiasm of the artist, which enables him to forget the cares of life,—the latter an advantage of the man of genius over other men, which alone repays him for the suffering that increases in proportion to the clearness of consciousness, and for the desert·loneliness among men of a different race,—all this rests on the fact that the in-itself of life, the will, existence itself, is, as we shall see farther on, a constant sorrow, partly miserable, partly terrible; while, on the contrary, as idea alone, purely contemplated, or copied by art, free from pain, it presents to us a drama full of significance. This purely knowable side of the world, and the copy of it in any art, is the element of the artist. He is chained to the contemplation of the play, the objectification of will; he remains beside it, does not get tired of contemplating it and representing it in copies; and meanwhile he bears himself the cost of the production of the play, i.e., he himself is the will which objectifies itself, and remains in constant suffering. That pure, true, and deep knowledge of the inner nature of the world

becomes now for him an end in itself: he stops there. Therefore
it does not become to him a quieter of the will, as, we shall see
in the next book, it does in the case of the saint who has attained
to resignation; it does not deliver him for ever from life, but only
at moments, and is therefore not for him a path out of life, but
only an occasional consolation in it, till his power, increased by
this contemplation and at last tired of the play, lays hold on
the real.[23] . . .

NOTES

1. On the life of Schopenhauer, see William Wallace, *Life of
Schopenhauer* (London, Walter Scott, 1890) and Helen Zimmern,
Schopenhauer, His Life and Philosophy, revised edition (London,
George Allen & Unwin, 1932).

2. These shorter works were *On the Will in Nature* (1836)
and *The Two Fundamental Problems of Ethics* (1841). The two
essays composing the latter work have been recently re-translated
and issued in paper editions in "The Library of Liberal Arts."
They are: *Essay on the Freedom of the Will*, translated by Konstantin Kolenda (New York, Liberal Arts Press, 1960) and *On the
Basis of Morality*, translated by E. F. J. Payne (New York,
Bobbs-Merrill Co., 1965).

3. Schopenhauer explains in detail how this principle operates
in *On the Fourfold Root of the Principle of Sufficient Reason*,
translated by Madame Karl Hillebrand (London, George Bell &
Sons, 1897). He claims that no one can really understand his
philosophical system without first studying this work.

4. Arthur Schopenhauer, *The World as Will and Idea*, translated by R. B. Haldane and J. Kemp (London, Trübner & Co.,
1883), Vol. I, p. 130. All subsequent quotations and selections will
be taken from this edition, which will be cited henceforth as
W. W. I. (Haldane & Kemp). There is another translation of
Schopenhauer's major work by E. F. J. Payne, published under the
title *The World as Will and Representation* (Indian Hills,
Colorado, The Falcon Wing's Press, 1958), 2 vols.

5. Schopenhauer explains in detail his conception of Platonic Idea in Book 3 of Vol. I of *The World as Will and Idea*. See also the supplements to this book in Vol. III of Haldane and Kemp's translation (or Vol. II of Payne's translation, cited above).

6. Schopenhauer, W. W. I. (Haldane & Kemp), Vol. I, p. 191.

7. Ibid., p. 192. "Man is a wolf to man."

8. See W. W. I. (Haldane & Kemp), Vol. I, pp. 514–520 (Sec. 69).

9. Schopenhauer, W. W. I. (Haldane & Kemp), Vol. I, p. 231.

10. Ibid.

11. The Fourth and final Book of Schopenhauer's *World as Will and Idea* is concerned with the ways in which the will may be affirmed and denied.

12. Schopenhauer, W. W. I. (Haldane & Kemp), Vol. I, pp. 238–240 (Sec. 36).

13. Schopenhauer, W. W. I. (Haldane & Kemp), Vol. I, pp. 241–243 (Sec. 36).

14. Ibid., Vol. I, pp. 251–252 (Sec. 37).

15. Ibid., Vol. I, pp. 253–255 (Sec. 38).

16. Ibid., Vol. I, pp. 259–262 (Sec. 39).

17. Ibid., Vol. I, pp. 264–265 (Sec. 39).

18. Ibid., Vol. I, pp. 270–271 (Sec. 41).

19. Ibid., Vol. I, pp. 271–272 (Sec. 41); pp. 274–275 (Sec. 42).

20. Ibid., Vol. I, pp. 276–278 (Sec. 43); p. 280 (Sec. 43).

21. Ibid., Vol. I, pp. 313–315 (Sec. 51); p. 324 (Sec. 51); pp. 326–327 (Sec. 51).

22. Ibid., Vol. I, pp. 332–336 (Sec. 52); pp. 338–339 (Sec. 52); p. 341 (Sec. 52).

23. Ibid., pp. 345–346 (Sec. 52).

QUESTIONS AND TOPICS FOR
FURTHER STUDY

1. How does aesthetic knowing differ from other kinds of knowing, according to Schopenhauer? Does he consider what the artist knows to be more worth knowing than what the scientist knows?

2. In what respects is the aesthetic experience of an artistic genius different from that of an ordinary man, in Schopenhauer's view? Of what use is the genius to the ordinary man?

3. Explain what Schopenhauer means by: (1) will, (2) idea or representation, (3) Platonic Idea. How are these related in his aesthetics?

4. Explain the two distinct parts of aesthetic experience, as analyzed by Schopenhauer. Illustrate how the two parts might be distinguished in an experience of a specific art work with which you are familiar.

5. What features distinguish the sublime from the beautiful, according to Schopenhauer? What aesthetic elements do they have in common? Explain why Schopenhauer considers all things to be to some extent beautiful.

6. According to what standard does Schopenhauer classify the various arts? Why does he place architecture lowest, and poetry highest among the art forms?

7. What is Schopenhauer's view of tragedy? Why does he regard it as "the summit of poetical art"?

8. Why does music get special consideration in Schopenhauer's discussion of the arts? In what sense does he consider it to be a universal language?

9. What is the function of art in life, according to Schopenhauer? Why does he place the saint above the artist in achievement and worth?

10. Topics for further study: (a) Platonic and Kantian elements in Schopenhauer's aesthetic theory; (b) the relationship of Schopenhauer's aesthetics to his ethics; (c) Kant and Schopenhauer on the sublime; (d) Schopenhauer's theory of the ludicrous; (e) the influence of Schopenhauer's theory of music on Richard Wagner.

GUIDE TO SUPPLEMENTARY READING

(Works marked with asterisks are available in paperbound editions.)

I. PRIMARY SOURCES

Schopenhauer, Arthur, *The World as Will and Representation*, translated by E. F. J. Payne (Indian Hills, Colorado, The Falcon's Wing Press, 1958). Two volumes.

——*The World as Will and Idea*, translated by R. B. Haldane and J. Kemp (Garden City, N.Y., Dolphin Books, Doubleday and Company, 1961).

——*Essays*, translated by T. Bailey Saunders (London, Allen & Unwin, 1951).

II. SECONDARY WORKS

Caldwell, William, *Schopenhauer's System in its Philosophical Significance* (Edinburgh and London, William Blackwood & Sons, 1896).

Copleston, Frederick, S.J., *Arthur Schopenhauer: Philosopher of Pessimism*, (London, Burns, Oates and Washbourne, Ltd., 1946).

Dehnert, Edmund J., "*Parsifal* as Will and Idea," *Journal of Aesthetics and Art Criticism*, XVIII (June, 1960), 511–520.

Gardiner, Patrick, *Schopenhauer* (Baltimore, Md., Penguin Books, 1963). Chap. 5.

Gilbert, Katharine, and Helmut Kuhn, *A History of Esthetics*, revised edition (Bloomington, Indiana University Press, 1953). Chap. XV.

Green, L. D., "Schopenhauer and Music," *Musical Quarterly*, XVI (1930), 199–206.

Knox, Israel, *The Aesthetic Theories of Kant, Hegel, and Schopenhauer* (New York, Humanities Press, 1958).

Osborne, Harold, "Revelatory Theories of Art," *British Journal of Aesthetics*, IV (October, 1964), 332–347.

Whittaker, Thomas, *Schopenhauer* (London, A. Constable, 1909).

CHAPTER 7

Aesthetics Humanized

VÉRON AND GUYAU

An observer at a recent International Congress on Aesthetics remarked (half facetiously) that to the Germans aesthetics is a subject to be pursued academically; to the English, it is an interesting topic to be discussed leisurely; to the Americans and Russians, it is a challenging problem to be solved pragmatically; and to the Italians and French, an issue of life and death to be disputed passionately. Vitalistic spirit and passionate disputation have certainly been characteristic of French thinkers, especially those of the nineteenth century. Although during that century France gave to the history of aesthetics its fair share of metaphysical dreamers such as Victor Cousin, sterile academicians such as Charles Lévêque, pragmatic reformers such as P. J. Proudhon, cerebral critics such as Charles Baudelaire, religious idealists such as F. R. Lamennais, and scientifically oriented rationalists such as Paul Souriau, it also produced a number of thinkers who disputed the traditional approaches to aesthetic theory and who promoted an awareness of the vitality inherent in art.[1] Two of the most important of these were Eugène Véron and Jean Marie Guyau.

One of the initiators of the expressionist theory of art, Véron fought strongly against the pseudo-Platonism of many of his contemporaries, with its rules for defining and achieving ideal beauty.[2] As a humanist, he called for a renewal of genuine artistic inspiration and for more personalized forms of artistic creation. This renewal could be achieved, he believed, only when artists gave up searching for eternal essences and returned to the facts of human existence in order to express the truth about these facts in terms of individual feelings rather than in terms of universal ideas. "Art for Man," not

"Art for the Academy" was Véron's motto; human personality, not divine beauty should become the artist's and the aesthetician's paramount concern. His contemporary, Guyau, sometimes called "the father of sociological aesthetics," also protested against the trivialization and dehumanization of art which, he claimed, resulted from fallacious aesthetic beliefs.[3] To Guyau aesthetic experience was not to be valued, as some evolutionists claimed, simply because it burned up energy not needed in the struggle for existence or, as some intellectualists claimed, because it offered a purely disinterested pleasure quite unrelated and unaffected by the urgent demands of everyday life. From the perspective of his poetic vitalism, Guyau reinterpreted the entire aesthetic domain, showing how at every point humanity is projected into it. Attempts to dehumanize art or to divorce it from its human and social connections could lead, he taught, only to its destruction. Although they differed in basic philosophical presuppositions, Véron and Guyau shared in the convictions that art is in vital continuity with life; that the creative spirit is sterilized when it is deprived of sincere, spontaneous feeling and a desire to communicate this feeling to others; and, finally, that the aesthetician should immerse himself in life itself instead of in metaphysical doctrine if he expects to say anything relevant about art. Like their American contemporaries Santayana and Dewey, these two French thinkers proposed to naturalize and to humanize aesthetics.

VÉRON

Born and brought up in Paris, Eugène Véron (1825–1889) attended the École Normale there, and having completed a program in liberal arts, became a teacher of rhetoric in the University of Paris. An ardent republican, he left the university in 1852 when Napoleon III established the Second French Empire. After teaching privately for a while, he turned to journalism for a career, becoming a successful newspaper writer and editor, first in Paris and later in Lyons. But Véron's talents and interests were far from exhausted by journalism. His preoccupation with the arts and their relation to life was reflected in a little book published in 1862, on the role various arts play in promoting intellectual progress.[4] A few years later, his interest in economic problems led him to make a comparative study of workers' associations in France, England, and Germany; he also found time to pursue historical research in order to write a history of Prussia, which he revised in the seventies to take into account changes resulting from the Franco-Prussian War. As a culmination of his continuing interest in the arts, he completed and published the definitive statement of his aesthetics in 1878, seeing this work, L'Esthétique, translated into English during the following year. In the last decade of his life, he produced works on ethics and on the natural history of religions;[5] also during this period he served as general inspector of provincial museums under the Third French Republic and became director of a well-known periodical, L'Art, from the press of which he issued his last book, Delacroix (1887), two years before his death. A man of remarkable talent and versatility though not of genius, Véron expressed his personality strikingly in his books. He was a fearless and independent thinker, an avowed enemy of academicism and cant in all fields, a firm believer in progress through science and education, a true humanist, and, above all, a passionate lover of the free and spontaneous spirit.[6]

"No science has suffered more from metaphysical dreaming than that of aesthetics," Véron states in the first sentence of his Aesthetics. Such dreaming is inevitable, he holds, so long as philosophers persist in the error of defining aesthetics as "the science of the beautiful" and use the term "beauty" to refer to a vaguely defined ideal or an obscure metaphysical entity which has little if any relation to material reality. Furthermore, the error is compounded when these same philosophers use the adjective "beautiful" to embrace the whole range of "admirative impressions" which we derive from art. There is a great deal more to art, Véron believes, than is ever dreamed of in the typical academician's philosophy of beauty. "Art, in truth," he writes, "addresses all the feelings without exception; hope or fear, joy or grief, love or hatred. It interprets every emotion that agitates the human heart, and never troubles itself with its relation to visible or ideal perfection. It even expresses what is ugly or horrible without ceasing to be art and worthy of admiration."[7]

Véron also holds that the imitation theory of art is incapable of explaining the power and significance of art. He argues that in admiring a work of art what we really admire is not its verisimilitude but its manifestation of the genius who created it, the man who had the sensitivity to perceive intensely, the emotional capacity to feel deeply, and the strength of intelligence to concentrate his impressions powerfully, then to render them in visible or audible form so that they may be communicated to a spectator or an auditor. The worth of a work of art comes, in Véron's view, not from the beauty of its representational qualities, but from the worth of the artist's personality. Aesthetics, then, in his view, should be defined not as "the science of beauty," but as "the science whose object is the study and elucidation of the manifestations of artistic genius."[8]

In accord with his definition of aesthetics, Véron undertakes to explain the nature of artistic genius and the process by which it can be manifested in works of art. Like Plato, he holds that inspiration is at the heart of artistic creation, but unlike Plato he does not consider inspiration, or possession by a dominant idea or feeling, to be an abnormal phenomenon or a potential threat to moral stability. To be sure, inspiration sometimes takes the artist far beyond the range of rational calculation, but, Véron insists, this is the very power without which he could never be an artist. For the artistic genius sees things not as unrelated bits and pieces, but in their relations one to another; he grasps or intuits these relations as an *ensemble*, fusing them imaginatively into a harmonious whole which expresses perfectly the effect he intends and which he will take infinite pains to perfect. The artist of genius, as he proceeds with his creative undertaking, transforms his material into his own image; he "personalizes" it; and finally succeeds in leaving upon his finished work that indelible imprint of his individuality, his unique style. Moreover, Véron holds, genius or spontaneous creativity is always innate; it may be perfected and transformed, but it can never be acquired by effort or produced by training. The artistic genius is born with superior imaginative, conative, and intellectual capacities, and as he develops he will reveal a peculiar aptitude for estimating aesthetic values, as well as an intense desire to manifest externally in artistic form his spontaneous and intense feelings. "In order to become an artist, it is necessary at first to start by being one," writes Véron in his book on *Delacroix*.[9]

Although he sees a place for the kind of art that aims at the creation of beauty—this he calls decorative art—Véron is primarily interested in the kind of art that expresses the personality of its creator. By expression he refers to "the manifestation by attitude and physiognomy of the habitual sentiment or accidental emotion of the soul; that is, of the dispositions or passions which constitute the moral life."[10] In creating an expressive work of art, an artist must envisage and maintain the reciprocal relation between what Véron considers to be the two terms of all expression, the sign (i.e. the external artistic manifestation) and the thing signified (i.e. the imaginative vision or the intended total effect). Only in this way can his work be truly expressive, capable of giving rise to "the idea of a personal and subjective creation—that is to say, of an intelligence manifesting, under visible and material form, an individual sentiment or idea suggested by the object or spectacle represented."[11]

In his *Delacroix*, Véron explains why he considers artistic expression to be basically artistic composition.[12] In the art of painting, composition is, he points out, the ability to arrange the relations of lines and colors in such a way that they condense and manifest the feeling and thought of the artist, his vision of the aesthetic significance of his subject, in the most communicable, contagious form. An expressionist painter such as Delacroix must have a strong emotional response to his subject before he can compose and communicate it. His painting is the "living reconstitution," the "vibrant synthesis" of the artist's personal emotion presented to the view of spectators; it is the result of a "sort of internal fermentation" and of "an incubation more or less long" during which the artist transformed through his labors the impressions he had experienced. In his work, "everything is penetrated by the colors of his own personality." Véron praises Delacroix for possessing what he considers to be that artist's, and every expressionist artist's most striking characteristics: universality of artistic genius and exceptional power of concentrating and making evident the mood or psychological expressiveness of subject matter.

Art as Emotional Expression

1. *Véron uses what he considers to be an anti-metaphysical approach to aesthetics. He begins not with a priori definitions of beauty or of art, but with observations on the nature of art as a spontaneous human activity which originated in the pleasure human beings derived from their immediate sense experiences and developed further as their modes of self-expression became more complex.*

Aesthetics being, as has been said, the science of the beautiful in the arts, it would seem but natural to begin by explaining what beauty and art are respectively.

We shall not, however, do so, because we distrust *a priori* definitions, and because it seems to us more reasonable and scientific to search among facts, to see whether they are not able of themselves to afford us the definitions we want. Facts always come before theories; and we are convinced that only by going back to the first beginnings and following the development of things through the procession of time, can we arrive at an idea of them, at once fair, exact, and complete.

This somewhat slow method may be less favourable to eloquence; it lends itself reluctantly to the brilliant amplifications of which metaphysicians are so fond, when, with a stroke of their wings, they transport themselves to the ethereal regions where their imaginations love to soar. But to us it seems all the more necessary to use it in our inquiry, as, perhaps in the whole range of metaphysics, there is no subject the literature of which can show so great an abuse of fine words, resounding periods, and, above all, crude definitions.

When once we have discovered the origin of art among men, and have examined its method throughout the series of its various manifestations, we shall find it easy, first, to comprehend its exact role, its function and its aim; secondly, to draw up a definition, of which the whole subject of Aesthetics shall be no more than the development. . . .

Art, far from being the artificial result of a fortuitous combination of circumstances, which might never have happened at all, is a spontaneous product, the immediate and necessary outcome of human activity. It is an indication of a want of comprehension of its great importance, to attempt to refer it to a special manifestation of some particular and more or less restricted faculty. In reality it is nothing less than the direct expression of man's nature in its most simple and human aspect. Art, we may truly say, came before thought itself. Before he ever attempted to understand or explain the conditions of the world in which he lived, man, open to pleasure through his eyes and ears, sought in combinations of forms, sounds, movements, shadow and light, for certain special enjoyments. Traces of these early aspirations are extant in the recently discovered works of a time when his intellectual activity must have been confined within very narrow scope.

It is a very remarkable fact that, from the first day of his existence, mere imitation did not satisfy him. Side by side with the dead bones upon which we can to this day recognize figures of animals more or less rudely imitated, have been found bracelets, necklets, and other ornaments, the design of which proves voluntary and personal search after imaginary forms. Weapons of stone, to be used either in warfare or the chase, exhibit a variety of forms, and occasionally an elegance of shape and decoration, which, adding nothing to their utility for attack or defence, must have proceeded from a purely Aesthetic motive.

The art of the cave-dwellers, then, was already personal, and, though they made use of imitation, they were no slaves to it. The fact is very important, and it would, in all probability, be confirmed by the other artistic manifestations of the same epoch, could we acquire information as to the contemporary forms of dancing, music, and poetry.

When man, by the exercise of his cerebral faculties, became capable of thought, and transferred to a new purpose the means of expression, that so far had only served him to make known his animal feelings and his natural wants, the role of art did not become less important. On the contrary, such a duplication of human activity gave it a new impulse, creating in it, as the effect of opposition, a more precise knowledge of the constituent elements of art, and of each of the arts separately. Primitive confusion gave place to a series of distinct creations, which sprang equally from personal emotion, and from the necessity of affording it gratification by some ever spontaneous expression, more or less immediate, according to the intrinsic character of the emotion and the greater or less complexity and exteriority of its means of making itself known.

Singing and dancing reduced to cry and gesture, are but the interpretation of joy, triumph, and similar emotions. Expression by means of sculpture and painting is less direct, because the process is exterior and more complex; the emotions, too, which these interpret are much less simple. Dances and songs themselves become very complicated, when to the indication of natural emotion is added, or substituted, artistic refinement of movement or attitude, or the portrayal of any complex idea. The skilful diversity of our opera ballets, the development of passion or character in epic and dramatic poetry, although contained in embryo in the cry or gesture by which a child can express its feelings, evidently result from a series of combinations for which it would be absurd to search among the products of prehistoric arts. They imply a development which is only rendered possible by the intervention of the spirit of analysis and reflection.

That which is true of dancing and singing—which include music and poetry—applies still more strongly to sculpture, architecture, and painting. The mere existence of these arts, even in their simplest forms, is enough to prove that in every age man has found peculiar pleasure in certain combinations of line and colour. But in what state would these arts have been today, had not the development of our purely intellectual faculties enlarged, in every sense, the field of our activity and multiplied to infinity the source of our emotions?

We shall not consider in detail all the arguments which we could adduce to support our contention. What we have said is enough to make it understood that, from the beginning, all arts, even those which seem slaves to mere imitation, were essentially manifestations of the personality of man, spontaneous effects of the instinct that drives all living things to express their emotions by exterior signs, and to seek the augmentation of their pleasures— the instinct which, in man particularly, finds gratification through the inexhaustible faculty of combination and appropriation, whose infinite multiplicity constitutes his superiority over all other animals.[13]

2. *Véron's aesthetics is founded upon a materialistic theory of sense perception. Pleasures come from the excitation and stimulation by impressions of sense organs. When we experience aesthetic pleasure there is an intensity, variety, and concord of vibrations or sensory reverberations. The most completely satisfying aesthetic pleasures come not from smell, taste, and touch, but from sight and hearing because these senses have a wider extension and are intimately related to aesthetic sentiments, for example, the feeling of sympathy. Upon this basis, Véron develops his view that aesthetic pleasure is essentially admirative: what we really enjoy in a work of art is not its fidelity to nature but its manifestation of human nature, that is, the power of artistic genius or the unique personality objectified in the work of art.*

We may say then that the pleasures of the ear and of the eye consist, like every other pleasure, in a momentary exaggeration of cerebral activity, caused by an accelerated vibration of the nerve fibres. Such acceleration is the result of a variety of conditions a certain number of which we have noticed.

It is of some importance, however, that we should call express attention to certain differences which distinguish these pleasures from those of smell, taste, and touch.

The principle governing the differences is the fact that, in most cases, the enjoyments of the palate, of smell or of touch, are closely confined within themselves. Whenever they are accompanied by sentiments and ideas, it is because they are connected by the power of memory to anterior impressions of some other kind.

On the other hand, the sensations of hearing and sight are intimately connected with, and spring spontaneously from, the centres where sentiments and ideas are elaborated. It is this particular character of the organs of the eye and ear that has constituted them, by speech and writing, the indispensable aids to human development, and the depositaries of its successive acquisitions. But, though it has been possible so to use this property of these two organs, as to conventionally extend their domain over nearly all the manifestations of the cerebral activity of man, it is not the less true that there are certain sensations and ideas that are their peculiar province, which may be called the aesthetic sentiments. Notions of order, harmony, proportion, fitness, variety, unity, spirit, rise spontaneously from the sensations which we owe to the eye and the ear. And if later, these notions are more or less unconsciously transformed into ideas that become, in their turn, rules of artistic production, it is entirely due to the work of analysis, which discovers and distinguishes these abstract elements in the complexity of primitive impressions.

Now these are precisely the elements that constitute aesthetic sensation, and it is because they are contained in it that that sensation gives us so great pleasure. When they are wanting we experience nothing but suffering.

Every work that produces in us an impression in which these elements are found, seems beautiful to us; and that, in proportion to the extent of their co-existence. Should they all exist in one work, in complete measure and with the greatest imaginable harmony, that work would be perfect. Under such conditions the pleasure created for us by its beauty would be duplicated by that other sentiment which is, more properly speaking, aesthetic pleasure; namely sympathetic admiration of the superior faculties that enable an artist to carry out such a work.

It is the spontaneous intervention of the artist's personality in the complex multiplicity of sentiments of which aesthetic enjoyment is composed which makes so many people believe that its source is to be found in imitation. Because the majority of poetic works breathe the spirit of reality, people imagine that the admiration they feel is due to the fidelity of the imagination; whereas it is in fact the artistic power of the imitator that strikes and attracts them. Suppose we take the trouble to analyse the remarks and criticisms of the crowds who visit the museums on holidays—we must acknowledge that in spite of the style of their observations, what they at bottom admire or censure, is not the greater or less accuracy of reproduction, but the degree of talent which they are led to attribute to the authors of the works before them. They challenge the work indeed, but behind it they see perhaps unconsciously the worker. The picture or statue is but the starting point and first cause of their emotion. If the expression of their feeling goes no farther, it is because they do not know how to analyse their impressions; and besides, they are governed by the habits and language of superficial criticism. But still it is the personality of the artist that is at stake; by it they are affected; their admiration may be always summarised in the words "What genius it must have required to execute such a work as this!"

The influence of this personality is so predominant that it sometimes takes the place of everything else. Thus a work full of carelessness and other faults often extorts our admiration solely by the personality of its author which shines through it with powerful originality, and by the energy with which it manifests the character and constitution of an individual impression. While, on the other hand, we have nothing but contemptuous deference to offer to those honest but mediocre works, where correctness of drawing, skilful composition, and exact harmony of colour replace the absent personality. We must feel the hand and individual genius of the artist. In art, retiring modesty is too often synonymous with imbecility. The artist, who feels acutely, expresses his emotion in the vivid colours in which it is painted in his imagination. This seal of origin, strange though it may appear, is always the most powerful recommendation to connoisseurs. They find in the impression that results from it, a peculiar and penetrating zest to which they are curiously sensible.

In one word, aesthetic pleasure is admirative. Its enjoyment results from that stimulation of cerebral energy and activity produced in us by intensity or multiplicity of impressions or harmonious impulses, which carry us ever nearer to what we conceive to be the ideal limit of possible perfection, in the category in which any particular work of art under consideration may be placed.

This sentiment of admiration is partly explained by the approximation to a perfection which must ever remain for us an ideal; but, above all, by the sympathetic surprise that we feel at the evidence of various merit given by the artist whose personality is reflected in his work. The more numerous, varied, intense, and harmonious our impressions are, the more complete and profound will be the enjoyment derived from them.[14]

3. *After reminding us again of the emotional and moral needs which art satisfies, Véron finally gives his general definition of art, a definition which takes into account, he believes, the human basis of art, its emotional content, and its function in enhancing human experience.*

We have seen that art, far from being the blossom and fruit of civilization, is rather, its germ. It began to give evidence of its existence so soon as man became self-conscious, and is to be found clearly defined in his very earliest works.

By its psychologic origin it is bound up with the constituent principles of humanity. The salient and essential characteristic of man is his incessant cerebral activity, which is propagated and developed by countless acts and works of varied kind. The aim and rule of this activity is the search after *the best*; that is to say, the more and more complete satisfaction of physical and moral wants. This instinct, common to all animals, is seconded in man by an exceptionally well-developed faculty to adapt the means to the end.

The effort to satisfy physical wants has given birth to all the industries that defend, preserve, and smooth the path of life; the effort to satisfy the moral wants—of which one of the most important is the gratification of our cerebral activity itself—has created the arts, long before it could give them power sufficient for the conscious elaboration of ideas. The life of sentiment preceded the manifestations of intellectual life by many centuries.

The gratification, *in esse* or *in posse*, of either real or imaginary wants, is the cause of happiness, joy, pleasure, and of all the feelings connected with them; the contrary is marked by grief, sadness, fear, etc.: but in both cases there is emotion, whether grave or gay, and it is the nature of such emotion to give more or less lively evidence of its existence by means of exterior signs. When expressed by gesture and rhythmic movement, such motion produces the dance; when by rhythmic notes, music; when by rhythmic words, poetry.

As in another aspect man is essentially sympathetic and his joy or pain is often caused as much by the good or evil fortunes of others as by his own; as, besides, he possesses in a very high degree the faculty of combining series of fictitious facts, and of representing them in colours even more lively than those of reality: it results that the domain of art is of infinite extent for him. For the causes of emotion are multiplied for every man—not only by the number of similar beings who live around him and are attached to him by the more or less closely knit bonds of affection, alliance, similitude of situation or community of ideas and interests; but, also, by the never-ending multiude of beings and events that are able to originate or direct the imaginings of poets.

To these elements of emotion and moral enjoyment, must be added the combinations of lines, of forms and of colours, the dispositions and opposition of light and shade, etc. The instinctive search after this kind of emotion or pleasure, the special organ of which is the eye, has given birth to what are called the arts of design—sculpture, painting, and architecture.

We may say then, by way of general definition, that art is the manifestation of emotion, obtaining external interpretation, now by expressive arrangements of line, form or colour, now by a series of gestures, sounds, or words governed by particular rhythmical cadence.

If our definition is exact, we must conclude, from it, that the merit of a work of art, whatever it may be, can be finally measured by the power with which it manifests or interprets the emotion that was its determining cause, and that, for a like reason, must constitute its innermost and supreme unity.[15] ...

4. *Having given his definition of art, Véron now proceeds to discuss its relevance to the various arts—poetry, music, painting, sculpture, and architecture. Recognizing the many points of connection among the different arts, Véron hesitates to give any strict classification of the arts. In another part of his work he does suggest, however, that the arts divide themselves naturally into two major groups: (1) the arts of the eye: architecture, sculpture, and painting, which have as their common feature development in space at a single point of time and are regulated by the laws of proportion; and (2) the arts of the ear: dancing, music, and poetry, which have as their common feature development in time through successive movements and are regulated by the laws of rhythm. Véron considers the art listed first in each of the two series to be the least expressive of that series, however, he asserts that all of the arts of the second group are superior to the entire first group in that they are more expressive of "the inner essence of life" and of the personality of the artist.*

The domain of poetry is almost without limits, because it embraces all the feelings without exception, and because most ideas are equally accessible to it. Moreover, thanks to the peculiar constitution of man's imagination, it is enabled in a certain measure to exercise the functions of each and every art. Not only can it communicate to us impressions of line, form, and colour, in describing a spectacle or object with sufficient relief to create almost optical illusion; but, by variety of rhythm and intonation, by choice, arrangement, and harmony of the words employed, it possesses sufficient musical power to charm the ear, apart from the thought or feeling expressed.

Nor is this all. By arrangement and proportion of parts, by relief, by intonation and expression of verses, by variety and precision in phrase, and by contrasting images, it is possible to excite in an auditor general impressions only to be described by terms borrowed from the arts which appeal to the eye. Truly we may say of a great poem, that its versification recalls architecture by making a similar impression upon the intellect; that in strength and vigour of contour it may be compared to sculpture; while in colour it equals the works of the greatest painters.

The power of music, being mainly concerned with the concord between rhythm and sound and the auditory fibres which they put in motion, is also bound up with the other arts by singular analogies, whose nature science is now just beginning to understand. Thanks, then, to the mutual relations of the numbers which constitute notes, which have at last been accurately determined, music may be called an architecture of sound, in the same sense in which architecture may be said to be the music of space—and in both an equal respect for necessary proportion and harmony must be observed. Again, it is by the connection between sonorous and luminous vibrations that we account for the resemblance that exists between sensations of sound and color. Language had long established and consecrated these resemblances, before science had explained their cause....

Notes are the raw material of musicians, as stones, of architects, or colors, of painters. Melody, which is caused by the succession alone of notes, arranges these materials as after a design, easily recognised and determined by the intellect to which it appeals; and harmony, which consists of the concord between notes or groups of notes, imparts a sensation similar to that resulting from the coloring of a picture.

The visual arts confine themselves less strictly to the sensations produced on the eye by combinations of form, line, and color. Doubtless such impressions remain the dominant ones, as is but natural, seeing that they are the *raison d'être* of the said arts. Any sculptor, architect, or painter, who would despise proportion, correctness, or harmony, would cease to deserve the name of artist; just as would a poet who wrote verse that would not scan, or a musician who neglected the laws of harmony. The antecedent condition of these arts is an eye peculiarly sensitive to the pleasures which spring from the mere sight of things. The next condition is, a special faculty to give to these visible appearances all the eloquence of which they are capable, and thus outwardly to manifest the impressions that they have caused upon the soul of the artist.

The painter is, before all, a man who, having received from nature the gift of extraordinary sensibility in his optic nerves, enjoys life mainly through the eye; just as the pleasures of the gourmet all arise from the exceptional irritability or development of his nerve tufts and buccal papillae. He finds a charm in combinations of line, form, and color, which nothing else can give in equal degree. This attraction determines his vocation, and is the source of all his emotions. To obey his unconquerable desire for the external manifestation of his feelings, he applies himself to the reproduction, in ideal or realistic form, of the combinations of shape and color which entrance his soul.

To the fundamental note, resulting from the vibration of the optic nerves, must, however, as in other cases, be added the *cortège* of accompanying harmonics. The direct impression received by the eye is combined with a crowd of secondary impressions, the more or less simultaneous appearance of which is to be explained by the constitution of the human brain; their number and importance increasing in direct proportion with its intellectual power and development. There is, between the purely artistic faculties, and those which cannot be so considered, a scarcely conceivable multitude of harmonies or discords, constituting a corresponding multitude of actual and potential artists of different degrees of merit. Thus sculpture, painting, and architecture, afford an illimitable power for the expression or suggestion of a more or less considerable number of feelings, or even of ideas. The domain of sculpture, without being so narrow and confined as the exclusive admirers of classic art would have it, cannot be made to embrace so much as that of architecture; which is more varied in its methods, and able to press all beautiful shapes into its service. Still less can its scope be compared to that of painting; which is, by far, the most expressive of the arts which appeal to the eye.

We see, then, how difficult it is to make good any absolute wall of division between the different arts. Notwithstanding their varied modes of procedure, they are for ever making little raids upon each other, because each have the same point of departure and ultimate aim—man, the common centre round which they all revolve, and whose complex nature is to some extent reflected in everything that emanates from him.[16]

5. While he does not push his division of the arts too far, Véron does insist that art generally is of two quite different kinds: decorative art, which has as its object beauty, and expressive art. Because previous aestheticians have tried to make the conception of beauty and the conception of art "co-terminous," the field of aesthetics has been confused and obscured, Véron claims. He holds that whereas the beautiful does not encompass the whole range of art, art, properly defined, encompasses the beautiful as well as the expressive.

To sum up—there are two distinct kinds of art. The one, decorative art, we understand to be that whose main object is the gratification of the eye and ear, and whose chief means to perfection of form are harmony and grace of contour, diction or sound. Such art rests upon the desire for beauty, and has nothing in view beyond the peculiar delight caused by the sight of beautiful objects. It has produced admirable works in the past, and may produce them again now or in the future, on condition that its inspiration be sought in actual and existing life, and not in the imitation of works sanctified by time. We must recognize, however, that modern art has no tendency in this latter direction. Beauty no longer suffices for us. Indeed, for the last two thousand years something more has been required; for even among the *chefs d'oeuvre* of the Greeks not a few owe their creation to a different sentiment. . . .

The chief characteristic of modern art—of art, that is, left to follow its own inspiration free from academic patronage—is power of expression. Through form this, the second kind of art, traces the moral life, and endeavours to occupy men, body and soul, but with no thought of sacrificing the one to the other. It is ever becoming more imbued with the quite modern idea that the whole being is *one*, metaphysicians notwithstanding, and that its aim can only be complete by refusing to separate the organ from its function. The moral life is but the general result of the conditions of the physical. The one is bound to the other by necessary connections which cannot be broken without destroying both. The first care of the artist should be to seek out and grasp the methods of manifestation so as to comprehend and master their unity.

Art, thus understood, demands from its votary an ensemble of intellectual faculties higher and more robust than if founded solely upon an ideal of beauty. Art founded upon the latter notion would be sufficiently served by one possessing an acute sense of the beautiful—the degree of his sensibility being indicated by the plastic perfection of his work. But expressive art demands the power to penetrate beneath outward appearances and to seize a hidden thought, the power to grasp either the permanent characteristic or the particular and momentary emotion; in a word, it demands that complete eloquence of representation which art might have dispensed with while it confined itself to the investigation or delineation of a single expression, but which became absolutely indispensable from the moment that the interpretation of the entire man became its avowed object.

We may say, too, that modern art is doubly expressive; because, while the artist is indicating by form and sound the sentiments and ideas of the personages whom he introduces, he is also by the power and manner of such manifestation giving an unerring measure of his own sensibility, imagination, and intelligence.

Expressive art is in no way hostile to beauty; it makes use of it as one element in the subjects which require it, but its domain is not enclosed within the narrow bounds of such a conception. It is by no means indifferent to the pleasures of sight and hearing, but it sees something beyond them. Its worth must not be measured only by perfection of form, but also and chiefly, by the double power of expression which we have pointed out, and, as we must not omit to add, by the value of the sentiments and ideas expressed.[17] ...

GUYAU

The son of a female author of books on education, Jean Marie Guyau (1854–1888) was born in Laval, France, and was educated at home by his mother's second husband, the Platonic scholar and philosopher, Alfred Fouillée.[18] The brilliant but sickly youth made rapid progress in literature and philosophy; by the time he was twenty he had written an essay on the development of utilitarian ethics which won him recognition by the Academy of Moral Sciences in Paris. The following year (1874) he began to teach philosophy at the Lycée Condorcet, but his tuberculous condition soon became worse and he was forced to give up all hopes of an academic career. During the rest of his short life, he resided mainly on the French Riviera, where he continued his omnivorous reading and wrote prolifically even though he knew he was living under the shadow of impending death. He translated the *Manual* of Epictetus the Stoic; wrote treatises on the ethics of Epicurus and on contemporary English moral philosophy; composed essays on a variety of philosophical and educational topics; produced a book of poetry;[19] and completed his three major works, *The Problems of Contemporary Aesthetics* (1884), *The Non-Religion of the Future* (1887), and *Art from the Sociological Viewpoint* (published posthumously, 1889, with an introduction by his devoted stepfather). When death finally came to him at the age of thirty-three, he faced it with Epicurean detachment and Stoical calm. For, as he said, he had "fought bravely."[20]

One of the major tasks which Guyau set for his aesthetic theorizing was to demonstrate the serious and vital importance of art to life, in opposition to those who, following Kant, Schiller, and Herbert Spencer, viewed art as primarily a disinterested activity, a form of play.[21] Characteristics of play are indeed found in artistic activity, Guyau admits, and from one point of view art is a sort of "gymnastics of the mind" which permits us to use up the surplus energy unconsumed in our workaday existence, but this does not mean that art's value is to be justified by its mere useful uselessness. Guyau refuses to draw a sharp distinction between the beautiful and the useful or between the beautiful and the agreeable, nor is he willing to characterize aesthetic experience as experience totally disinterested and independent of desire and passion. For he believes that the most fundamental human needs —those of breathing, moving, eating, and reproducing—can take on aesthetic quality in the very process of finding their fullest satisfaction. Beauty, in his view, grows out of the soil of the agreeable and the desirable.

Guyau is opposed, then, to intellectualizing or compartmentalizing aesthetic experience. He wants, to the contrary, to widen the aesthetic domain so that it can include sensation and activity as well as intellect and can ultimately encompass the whole of life. Art, he teaches, involves activity as much as it does passivity; it is an effort to create, not just a desire to enjoy. Its true goal is fuller and richer life, more completely vitalized reality. If art is an imitation, it is always, as Aristotle points out, an imitation of action, which succeeds in accomplishing its purpose, Guyau believes, to the extent that it takes on the vitality of real life.

Under certain conditions, Guyau continues, almost all of the movements, sensations, and feelings of life can become beautiful. Movements become beautiful when they have strength, harmony, rhythm, order, and grace, and are expressive of an admirable inner life. The movements of men working, using their bodies in order to achieve rational ends, can be equally as beautiful as men playing, using their bodies without useful ends in mind. Sensations become beautiful when they are agreeable and acquire a maximum degree of intensity compatible with a maximum degree of extension or of diffusion throughout the whole nervous system. Guyau, like his contemporary Santayana, is far more appreciative than previous aestheticians of the role that tactile, gustatory, and olfactory sensations play in aesthetic experience. He holds that some textures tastes, and smells can rightly be called beautiful. Feelings become beautiful, as do movements, when they are strong, harmonious and graceful; that is to say, when they are the expression of a will which is harmoniously related to the world and to other wills. Aesthetic and moral feelings thus turn out to be essentially identical, Guyau believes, but he does not believe that art should be identified with morality in any narrow sense. He rejects both "art for art's sake" and "art for morality's sake," and proposes to put in their place, "art for life's sake."

Having set forth these views in his *Problems of Contemporary Aesthetics*, Guyau defines beauty as consisting in "a perception or an action which stimulates simultaneously the three forms of life in us—sensibility, intelligence, and will—and produces pleasure by the rapid consciousness of this general stimulation."[22] No one psychological element is sufficient to account for the aesthetic experience. Our whole being must be involved in this experience; our whole life must be at once intensified and expanded. The greatest artist, therefore, is, according to Guyau, the one who does not try to appeal to just one aspect of the self, but who elicits the interests of the whole person, as a creature who feels, thinks, and acts. Such an artist is able to make the most elevated idea concretely sensuous, as well as to transform the purely sensuous into something expressive of the ideal. Because he responds with exquisite sensitivity to life, he can interpret life with sensitivity in his art, thereby making art alive and life artistic.

But, finally, neither art nor life can be understood in isolation; both are, in Guyau's view, basically social phenomena. The emotions which are transmitted through art have a social character; they arise and are dependent upon sympathy, a sense of social solidarity. In his second work on aesthetics, *Art from the Sociological Viewpoint*,[23] from which our selections are taken, Guyau undertakes a detailed examination of the universal sympathy which is, he holds, the principle according to which the most complex aesthetic emotion and artistic expression can be explained. Without the power of social sympathy, he contends, great artistic achievement would be impossible since the artist's social imagination would be severely limited and the extent of his feelings drastically curtailed; good art criticism would be nonexistent since the critic could neither understand his subject's work nor communicate his insights into it in an intelligible and interesting manner; nature would appear dead and unrelated to us; and whatever art remained would be either coldly formalistic or boringly trivial. Guyau's aim, then, is to show how living society creates and sustains art, and art in turn socializes and humanizes man and nature.

Art and Social Solidarity

1. Guyau believes that the basis of aesthetic pleasure is an in-
wardly felt harmony among the various constituents of the self,
a sense of organic solidarity and sociability within the psyche.
Aesthetic emotion is essentially a state of being in sympathy with
oneself, not as an isolated but as a social being whose very nature
is to relate emotionally or sympathetically to one's environment
and to one's fellow men. Were it not for our feeling of social
solidarity, our capacity to feel sympathy for the whole dynamic
social life of which we are a part, Guyau believes, we could never
appreciate beauty in its simplest or in its most complex form. But
because we can project on to inanimate objects our own feelings
and because we share this anthropomorphizing capacity with other
human beings, reality can seem alive, sociable, and aesthetically
pleasing.

If we rise from the rudiments of beauty to its highest development, its social side progressively increases until it ends up
dominating everything. It seems to us that the first degree of
aesthetic emotion consists of the solidarity and sympathy between
the various parts of the inner self; we will consider social solidarity
and universal sympathy as the most complex and elevated principle
of aesthetic emotion.

In the first place, there can be no aesthetic emotion without
sympathetic emotion, and no sympathetic emotion without an
object with which we communicate in one way or another, to
which we attribute a personality, and which we endow with a
certain unity and life. Thus there is no aesthetic emotion outside
of an act of intelligence by which we more or less anthropo-
morphize things by making animate beings out of them, and
conceiving these animated beings in the human image.

Even abstractions must assume a semblance of life in order to
become beautiful. It has been said that a sequence of abstract
arguments is aesthetic in itself. This may be so, as it already constitutes a harmony; but it is above all the human and sympathetic
side of that harmony which renders it uniquely aesthetic. For

instance, let us take a series of abstract arguments on abstract subjects, such as a sequence of algebraic theorems. What we admire in it will not be a strictly cold and bare intelligence, but an intelligence which follows a direction, which sets itself a goal, and, thrusting obstacles aside, makes an effort to reach that goal; in other words, a will, and what is more, a human will with which we sympathize and whose struggle, efforts, and triumph we love. There is something *impassioned* and *impassioning* in a sequence of arguments that leads to the discovery of a truth, and it is that that makes it aesthetic. A purely abstract exercise of the intelligence without a corresponding awakening of desire and of all inner forces, could not have made Pascal forget a toothache so easily. Our very imagination, just as our will and sensibility, is involved in the most abstract reasoning, and this is shown by the fact that we always *picture* the reasoning: we see a veritable construction rising up before us, sometimes a ladder we climb either up or down, and sometimes a skillful arrangement of concentric lines of convolution. To reason is to move, to climb, to conquer. Reasoning can be abstract in reference to things without being in the least abstract in reference to our personality, to ourselves; we can put our whole being into a theorem, and let us add that in doing so we put something of the concrete world into it, or even the whole world we carry within us.

The so-called inanimate objects are considerably more alive than the abstractions of science, and that is why they interest us, move us, arouse our sympathy toward them and by that very act arouse aesthetic emotions. A simple ray of sunlight or moonlight touches us when it evokes in our mind the smiling images of those two familiar celestial bodies.

Let us take a landscape as an example: it will appear to us as an association between man and the creatures of nature.

1. To appreciate a landscape, we must be in tune with it. To understand the sunbeam, we must vibrate with it; we must quiver with the moonbeam in the evening darkness; and we must sparkle with the blue or golden stars; to understand the night we must feel the shudder of dark spaces, of that vague and unknown vastness passing through us. To feel spring we must have in our hearts some of the lightness of a butterfly's wings, the fine dust of which we breathe as it is widely scattered through the vernal air.

2. To understand a landscape, we must bring it in tune with

ourselves, in other words we must humanize it. We must *animate* nature, or else it means nothing to us. Our eye has its own light and sees only what it illuminates.

3. For this very reason we must introduce an objective harmony into a landscape, trace certain broad lines in it, relate it to a few central points, in short, systematize it. Real landscapes exist within as well as outside us: we contribute to them, we draw them, so to speak, for a second time and work out the vague thought of nature more clearly in our minds. Poetic feeling does not stem from nature, it is rather nature itself that emerges from it somewhat transformed. The living and sentient being endows things with his own feelings and life. To love nature one must already have the soul of a poet: the tears of things, *lacrymae rerum,* are our own tears. It has been said that a landscape is a "state of soul." That is not enough, however; to express this sympathetic communication and this type of association between ourselves and the soul of things we must put it in the plural and say: a landscape is a state of souls.[24]

2. *Guyau now briefly compares the moral and the aesthetic emotion. Both emotions, he holds, are basically social; both seek permanent value; but aesthetic emotion, unlike moral emotion, finds in its object an achieved, rather than a willed harmony and perfection.*

If the feeling for nature already is a social emotion, all the aesthetic feelings evoked by our fellow men will be all the more sociable in character. As the feeling of beauty evolves, it becomes more and more impersonal.

The highest moral emotion is also a social emotion, but it differs from aesthetic emotion by the goal it pursues and imposes upon the will: namely, to achieve the most social and universal conditions of life within the individual and society. Moral sentiment is fundamentally active and, as Kant says, *teleological.* Without entirely excluding activity or even purposiveness from aesthetic emotion, we have nevertheless recognized that this emotion is the feeling of an already existing solidarity—whether in its beginning stage or full development—and not of a solidarity yet to be established: it is a harmony felt and not a harmony willed and painfully sought; it is a social sympathy already ruling our hearts, the echo in us of collective, universal life. One might say that beauty is the good already realized, and that moral good is beauty to be realized in the individual or in society. Moral good, to use a theological phrase, is the reign of law; beauty is either the reign of nature or the reign of grace, for nature is already true solidarity, albeit imperfect. Grace is both real and perfect solidarity, either between the various parts of the same being or between the various beings: all in one, one in all. That is why pleasures in which there is nothing impersonal are neither lasting nor beautiful: on the other hand, pleasure completely universal in character would be eternal, and being love, it would be grace. It is in the negation of egoism—a negation compatible with life itself—that aesthetics, in the same way as ethics, must look for the imperishable.[25]

3. *So far Guyau has been concerned with aesthetic emotion, the kind of emotion evoked by impersonal natural beauty. Now he turns to artistic emotion, which is evoked by consciously pre-arranged means for stimulating the sense of beauty. Although he does not think we should slight the lesser, "inorganic" arts which aim merely at pleasing the senses—e.g. the art of cooking—Guyau considers the arts which represent life in its manifold forms to be much more significant. He points out several factors which account for our finding artistic imitations of life pleasing. All of these factors are related to the individual and social sympathy awakened in the perceiver by works of art.*

We have seen that the aesthetic emotion evoked by beauty amounts in us to a general, and, so to speak, a collective stimulation of life in all its conscious forms—sensibility, intelligence, will. How shall we now define the artistic emotion which is evoked by art?

Art is a series of means methodically arranged so as to produce the general and harmonious stimulation of conscious life that constitutes the feeling of beauty. To that end art can make use only of sensations which it arranges more or less ingeniously, such as flavors, scents, or colors. These are the very elementary arts of which Plato speaks in the *Gorgias*, namely, the art of perfumery, and also of polychromy. These arts do not seek to create life or to give the impression of creating it; they limit themselves to taking products manufactured by nature and modifying them but slightly, without subjecting them to a thorough reorganization. They are the *inorganic* arts, so to speak, that express life as little as possible. Besides, let us not forget that to be entirely without expression, a sensation must be isolated and detached in the mind; such sensations do not exist and the very art of cooking can acquire some representational value by association: an appetizing salad is a little garden plot on the table, an epitome of country life; the taste of an oyster brings us a drop of ocean water, a fragment of life in the sea.

The arts that really deserve their name proceed in an entirely different fashion: to them, pure and simple sensation is not the goal; it is rather a means of establishing contact and intercourse between the sentient being and a life similar to his own; it is therefore essentially representative not only of life, but of collective life as well.

Let us analyze the pleasure that we derive from this essential element in art, namely the imitation of life.

The first element is the intellectual pleasure of recognizing objects through memory. We compare the image which art gives us with that which our memory supplies; we approve or we criticize. This pleasure, reduced to its most intellectual quality, is present even in the contemplation of a map. But as a rule it is mixed with many other pleasures of a more sensitive nature: indeed, the inner image furnished by memory is revived by the contact with the image confronting us, and before each work of art we relive a part of our lives. In every imitation by a human being of what he has felt and perceived like us, we rediscover a fragment of our own sensations and feelings and inner self. In some way a work of art is always a portrait and if we look carefully, we will recognize something of ourselves in that portrait. That is the "egotistical" part of sensitive pleasure, as Comte calls it.

The second element is the pleasure of sympathizing with the author of the work of art, with the work he put into it, his intentions crowned with success, and his skill. We also have the correlative pleasure of feeling and criticizing his failings. Art is one of the most remarkable displays of human activity; it is the most difficult form of work and one in which we put most of ourselves; hence it above all deserves to awaken our interest and sympathy. Thus it is that we rarely forget the artist as we contemplate a work of art. Moreover, the admiration we still have today for difficulties overcome was greater when art was in its infancy. Indeed, the first work of human art was the tool, be it the axe or the stone knife, and what was first admired about the tool was the skill of the craftsman which, through difficulties overcome, resulted in the creation of something useful. Having thus been the primitive art of man, industry became more and more subtle; it was applied to less and less coarse materials from the wood and flint which had been handled by the primitive craftsman to the colors mixed on the painter's palette or the phrases shaped by the poet and writer of today. Nevertheless, manual skill is always more or less in evidence in every work of art and in periods of decadence it becomes almost the only merit. At such times the public, blasé and cool, sympathizes less with the characters created by the author of a work than with the author himself; this is a kind of perversity which nevertheless enables us to see in exaggerated form the usual phenomenon of sympathy or antipathy for the artist which is inseparable from all judgment of art.

The third element is the pleasure of sympathizing with the beings represented by the artist. In art there is also an element of pleasure derived from an antipathy that is sometimes mixed with a slight fear and that is compensated for by the feeling of illusion. This type of pleasure derived from works of art can be experienced even by monkeys, who grimace with satisfaction or affection before pictures representing their own kind, and who get angry or frightened by those of other animals. Let us remember that the primitive arts, poetry as well as drawing and sculpturing, always started with representations of animate beings; only much later did they apply themselves to picturing the inanimate environment in which these beings move. Even today it is still man or the human side of nature that affects us in any literary description or work of art.[26]

4. *Guyau thinks that he has now shown that the artistic emotion, like the aesthetic emotion, is basically social. He offers an analogy here which he believes will make his meaning clearer and will suggest how an artist succeeds in transmitting his emotion to others through his work. This analogy shows that Guyau, like Véron and Tolstoy, recognizes how important it is for the artist to respond sympathetically to his subject in order to communicate it effectively and contagiously to his public. The analogy also shows that he is equally aware that the aesthetic appreciator must,*

*in turn, be capable of sharing in the "spiritual companionship" with
the artist and his subject. Guyau concludes with some reflections
on how the different arts express a sense of vital movement and
promote the life more abundant.*

In the final analysis, therefore, the artistic emotion we experience in the presence of a life similar to our own and brought
close to us by the artist is a social emotion; to the direct pleasure
of agreeable sensations (rhythm of sounds or harmony of colors)
is added all the pleasure we derive from the fact that our own
lives in society are sympathetically stimulated by the imaginary
beings evoked by the artist. Let us take as an example a wire that
has to be electrified; the physicist cannot enter into direct contact
with it; how will he set about it? There is a way of sending a
current through it in the desired direction; it is done by bringing
it near another wire which carries an electric current; the first
wire will immediately become electrified through induction. This
wire that we have to magnetize without any outside contact and
through which we must succeed in sending vibrations from afar
and in a direction known in advance, can be compared to the
different individuals that make up the public of an artist. The
task of the poet or artist is to stimulate life by bringing it near
to another with which it can sympathize: it is an indirect stimulation, brought about by induction. Assuming you do not know the
meaning of love, the artist will force you to experience all the
emotions of love. How? By showing you a being that loves. You
will look, you will listen, and as far as possible you yourself will
love. Basically all arts are but various ways of condensing the
individual emotion so as to make it instantly transferable to others
and thus to some extent sociable. I am moved by the sight of grief
as in the painting "The Soldier's Widow" precisely because that
perfect representation shows me that a soul has been understood
and penetrated by another soul, that in spite of physical barriers
a human and moral bond has been established between the human
spirit and the sorrow with which it sympathizes. In other words,
I behold a union, a living bond of spiritual companionship which
beckons me to join it and I do indeed join it with all my mind and
heart. The interest we take in a work of art is the result of an
association that is established between ourselves, the artist, and the
characters in the work; it is a new society whose affections,
pleasures, and pains, in fact, whose whole lot we espouse.

Finally, invention is added to expression in order to extend *ad infinitum* the contagious power of emotions and thoughts. This invention used by the arts gives us access not only to all the sufferings and joys of real beings living around us, but also to those of all other possible beings. Our sensitivity is increased by the entire world created by poetry. Thus art plays a considerable role in the growing permeability of consciousness that marks each progressive stage in evolution. There thus comes into being a moral and spiritual environment in which we are continuously immersed and which mingles with our own lives: in this environment, reciprocal induction multiplies the intensity of all emotions and thoughts, as is often the case in meetings where a large group of people share the same feelings and thoughts.

Movement is the outward sign of life in the same way as action —that is to say deliberate movement—is its inward sign; moreover, it is the greatest means of communication between beings. Thus all arts can be reduced to the art of producing or simulating movement and action, and thereby evoking in us sympathetic movements or seeds of actions. Music is movement made sensible to the ear, a vibration of life propagated from one body to another. The most primitive rhythm, the simple beat of our fingers or of the drum, is also movement and life, for rhythm represents a walking or a running, a dancing or the beating of a heart. The aim of sculpture and painting—as Socrates noted long ago—is to represent the modifications of form through movement. Moreover, as Fechner points out, colors have a symbolic value that expresses life and feelings, and hence the movements themselves. Architecture is the art of introducing movement into inert material; to build is to animate. In the first place, architecture organizes materials and arranges them; in the second place, it subjects them to a kind of combined action which in one single movement lifts the building above the ground and through a harmony of lines and a continuous ascending movement makes light what once was heavy, and causes that which tends to sag and collapse to rise and hold steady in an attitude of life. Sully-Prudhomme is right when he says that architectural beauty goes hand in hand with a certain lightening of the material; by the same token architecture is ugly when it is oppressive and heavy, when it is both unorganized and inert.

My last observation is that since architecture is designed to contain life, the movements and the life it shelters within its walls will, as it were, penetrate and pierce through the materials. A building that is meant to hold life is itself a kind of living body with its various openings onto the outside world; its windows are like eyes, its doors are like mouths, and everything tells of the coming and going of animate beings. The first edifice of the animal was its shell which was practically one with its body; later came the nest whose image blended with that of its family. Even now architecture contains a social or familial element; our very temples remain houses of mystery adapted to a superhuman life, ready to receive their God and enter into communion with Him, now reaching for the sky with all the surge of their bells, now sinking themselves into the earth with all the depth of their crypts, as if to show the way to the unknown visitor.

In short, through the medium of feeling, art is an extension of society to all creatures of nature and even to beings believed to be beyond nature, or to fictitious beings created by human imagination. Artistic emotion is therefore basically social; it widens individual life by merging it with a greater and more universal life. *The highest aim of art is to produce an aesthetic emotion of a social nature.*[27]

NOTES

1. Unfortunately, several major historians of aesthetics have underestimated the importance of French contributions to the field. Bosanquet ignored them, Croce minimized them, and Gilbert and Kuhn treated them rather sketchily. As one might expect, the best accounts are found in French. See T. M. Mustoxydis' *Histoire de l'esthétique française, 1700–1900* (Paris, Champion, 1920) which contains an excellent general bibliography covering French aesthetics from its origins to 1914. On later developments in French aesthetics, see Valentin Feldman's *L'Esthétique française contemporaine* (Paris, Felix Alcan, 1936). The late Raymond Bayer covered the whole field in his *Histoire de l'esthétique* (Paris, Armand Colin, 1961).

2. Véron devotes an appendix in his *L'Esthétique* (Paris, Reinwald, 1878) to a critical exposition of "The Aesthetics of Plato" which really should be entitled "The Aesthetics of Pseudo-Platonists." "Under the authority of the 'Platonic Ideal' they [official and academic critics] have successively anathematized all the efforts that have been made to rescue art from routine." (p. 392).

3. He states his criticisms of the aesthetic theories of his day in the First Book of *Les problèmes de l'esthétique contemporaine* (Paris, Felix Alcan, 1884).

4. This work, which has never been translated, was entitled *Le progrès intellectuel dans l'humanité: supériorité des arts modernes sur les arts anciens: poésie, sculpture, peinture, musique* (Paris, Guillaumin, 1862).

5. *La Morale* (Paris, Reinwald, 1884) and *Histoire naturelle de religions* (Paris, Doin, 1885). There is a brief discussion of art in *La Morale*, Part III, Chap. IX, 204–210.

6. It has been difficult to find material on his life and works (other than his *Aesthetics*) in either English or French. The bare facts of his life are recorded in the *Larousse Grande Dictionnaire universel du XIXe Siecle,* Vol. 15, p. 922, and in the second *Supplement* (Vol. 17, p. 1980) of this work. However, the reader can glean a good deal about the man from his works, which is perhaps after all what Véron himself would have preferred.

7. *Aesthetics,* translated by W. H. Armstrong (London, Chapman & Hall, 1879), p. 97. All further quotations and selections are from this edition.

8. *Aesthetics,* p. 109.

9. *Eugène Delacroix* (Paris, Librairie de l'Art, 1887), p. 132 (translation by editor).

10. *Aesthetics,* p. 121.

11. *Aesthetics,* p. 120.

12. *Delacroix,* p. 128 ff.

13. *Aesthetics,* pp. 1–2; pp. 29–32.

14. *Aesthetics,* pp. 51–54.

15. *Aesthetics,* pp. 88–90.

16. *Aesthetics,* pp. 90–91; pp. 93–94. On the classification of the arts see pp. 28–29 and pp. 152–156.

17. *Aesthetics*, pp. 126–127. Our selections have been drawn entirely from Part I of Véron's work. In Part II, he devotes separate chapters to architecture, sculpture, painting, dance, music, and poetry.

18. One of the best sources of information about Guyau's life and thought is Alfred Fouillée's *La morale, l'art et la religion d'apres M. Guyau* (Paris, Felix Alcan, 1889).

19. Guyau's book of poetry is entitled *Vers d'un philosophe* (6e ed., Paris, Felix Alcan, 1908). It contains poems on philosophical reflection, love, nature and humanity, and on art. On the last topic, some of the titles are "L'art et le monde," "Sur les groupes de Michel-Ange au tombeau des Medicis," "Le mal du poet," and "Mes vers d'hier soir." In his *Non-Religion of the Future* (translation, Henry Holt, 1897), Guyau called metaphysics "the poetry of pure reason" and poetry "the metaphysics of the senses and of the heart." Both the metaphysician and the poet celebrate "the projection of humanity into all things" (p. 413).

20. In light of Guyau's own "existential predicament," the reader may be interested in his refutation of pessimism in Part III, Chap. IV, Sec. II of *The Non-Religion of the Future* and his treatment of death and immorality in Part III, Chap. V, Sec. IV of that same work. The sentence with which *The Non-Religion of the Future* concludes is characteristic of the man: "Man's last agony and his last pulse of curiosity is one" (translation, op. cit., p. 538).

21. The following account of Guyau's aesthetic views is based on Book I of his *Les problèmes de l'esthétique contemporaine*. For a translation see our "Guide to Supplementary Reading."

22. Guyau, *Les problèmes de l'esthétique contemporaine*, p. 77 (translation by editor).

23. Although the title is here given in English, to our knowledge *L'Art au point de vue sociologique* has never been translated into English. Portions have been translated by Ilona Ricardo especially for inclusion in the present volume.

24. *L'Art au point de vue sociologique* by Jean Marie Guyau, (Paris, Felix Alcan, 1889), pp. 13–15 (translation by Ilona Ricardo). All subsequent selections are from this work in this edition, which will henceforth be cited as *L'Art* . . . .

25. *L'Art* . . . , pp. 15–16 (translation by Ilona Ricardo).

26. *L'Art* . . . , pp. 16–18 (translation by Ilona Ricardo).

27. *L'Art* . . . , pp. 19–21 (translation by Ilona Ricardo). Now

considering its importance and rich contents, it is surprising that an English translation of Guyau's major work on aesthetics has never been made. For the benefit of readers who may not have access to the original work or who cannot read French, a résumé of its table of contents may be of interest. Chap. I deals with social solidarity as the central principle in explaining the most complex artistic emotion; Chap. II, with genius "as power of sociability and as creation of an new social milieu" (including a discussion of Taine's and Hennequin's theories); Chap. III, with "Sympathy and sociability in criticism"; Chap. IV, "Expression of individual and social life in art" (containing criticisms of formalism, a discussion of Flaubert, etc.); Chap. V, Idealism, Realism, and Trivialism; Chap. VI, "The psychological and sociological novel"; Chaps. VII–IX, "The introduction of philosophical and social ideas into poetry (Lamartine, Vigny, Alfred de Musset, Hugo, Sully-Prudhomme, Leconte de Lisle, and including a parody of philosophical poetry, *Les Blasphèmes*); Chap. X, On style as a means of expression and as an instrument of sympathy (including discussions of the principle of the economy of force and the principle of poetic suggestion, the image, rhythm, poetical evolution of contemporary prose, etc.); Chap. XI, "The Literature of the Decades and of the *Déséquilibrés:* their general unsociable character."

QUESTIONS AND TOPICS FOR FURTHER STUDY

1. How does Véron's approach to aesthetics differ from the approaches of his predecessors? What is his explanation of the origin of the various arts?

2. Explain Véron's view that aesthetic pleasure is essentially admirative. How do we get to know an artist's personality through his works of art?

3. Do you think that communication of artistic emotion is implicit in Véron's definition of art? Why or why not? How does he propose to judge the merits of a given work of art?

4. What are some of the similarities and differences among poetry, music, painting, and architecture, according to Véron? Do you find any evidence of the influence of Lessing on his views?

5. Explain and illustrate Véron's distinction between decorative and expressive art.

6. What is the difference between "aesthetic emotion" and "artistic emotion" according to Guyau? Why do you suppose he makes this distinction?

7. How does Guyau explain our aesthetic appreciation of inanimate objects and of natural phenomena? Give some examples of such appreciation.

8. What does Guyau mean by the statement that "aesthetics, in the same way as ethics, must look for the imperishable"?

9. According to what criteria does Guyau rank some arts higher than others? How does his explanation of our enjoyment of artistic imitation resemble and differ from Aristotle's?

10. Topics for further study: (a) Véron's criticisms of the "aesthetics of the Academy"; (b) Véron's views on artistic taste; (c) Véron and Guyau on artistic expression; (d) Guyau's interpretation of the "aesthetics of religion"; (e) Guyau's criticisms of "aesthetic disinterestedness."

GUIDE TO SUPPLEMENTARY READING

(Works marked with asterisks are available in paperbound editions.)

VÉRON

I. PRIMARY SOURCE

Véron, Eugène, *Aesthetics*, translated by W. H. Armstrong (London, Chapman and Hall, 1879).

II. SECONDARY WORKS

Blanshard, Frances B., *Retreat from Likeness in the Theory of Painting* (New York, Columbia University Press, 1949), Chap. 4.

Ducasse, Curt J., *The Philosophy of Art* (New York, Dial Press, 1929), Chap. II.

Stolnitz, Jerome, *Aesthetics and Philosophy of Art Criticism: A Critical Introduction* (Boston, Houghton Mifflin Co., 1960), Chap. 7.

G U Y A U

I. PRIMARY SOURCES

Guyau, Jean Marie, *The Problems of Contemporary Aesthetics, Book I,* translated by Helen L. Mathews (Los Angeles, De Vorss & Co., 1947).

———*The Non-Religion of the Future: A Sociological Study,* introduction by Nahum N. Glatzer (New York, Schocken Books, 1962), Part IV, Chap. II, 411–423.

II. SECONDARY WORKS

Gilbert, Katherine E., and Helmut Kuhn, *A History of Esthetics,* revised edition (Bloomington, Indiana University Press, 1953), Chap. XVI.

Kallen, Horace M., *Art and Freedom,* 2 vols. (New York, Duell, Sloan and Pearce, 1942), Vol. I., Chap. XIII, Sec. 73, 597–603.

Knight, William, *The Philosophy of the Beautiful, Being Outlines of the History of Aesthetics,* 2 vols. (New York, Charles Scribner's Sons, 1905), Vol. I, Chap. IX, Sec. 9, 138–141.

CHAPTER 8

Art as Emotional Communication

TOLSTOY

Leo Tolstoy (1828–1910) aspired in one lifetime to attain not only the highest level of artistic accomplishment but also the highest level of spiritual development.[1] He was born of noble parents at a country estate in Yasnaya Polyana, a village in the Tula province of Czarist Russia, and, although his parents died when he was still quite young, his childhood and youth were, on the whole, happy and secure under the supervision of female relatives. In his early manhood the carefree young count moved in the high society of Kazan and Moscow, leading a rather dissolute existence. After an unsuccessful period of study at Kazan University, he entered the army and served first in the Caucasus and later in the Crimea. He was present at the siege of Sevastapol in 1854. His literary career began with the publication of *Childhood* in 1852; later he drew on his military adventures for further stories, and before long he was well-known as one of Russia's most promising young writers. Two visits to Europe expanded further his literary and cultural horizon, but he was always drawn back to his childhood home, Yasnaya Polyana, where he was involved in efforts to educate the peasants on his family estate. When he was thirty-four, he married a doctor's teen-age daughter, Sonya Bers, with whom he lived happily for many years and who, besides bearing him thirteen children, assisted him in preparing for publication his greatest novels, *War and Peace* (1865–66) and *Anna Karenina* (1875–77).

A major turning point in Tolstoy's emotional life, an experience which profoundly affected both his interpersonal relations and his art, occurred during the late eighteen-seventies when he underwent an agonizing self-examination, the result of which was religious conversion. Prefaced by a period of deepest pessimism, this conversion caused him to renounce religious orthodoxy—he was finally excommunicated from the Greek Orthodox Church in 1901—and to embrace fervently what he conceived to be the essential teachings of Jesus as expressed in the Gospels. From that time on, Tolstoy's art became a handmaiden to his religion, a simplified form of Christianity based on the profoundest love of God and man with nonresistance to evil its chief doctrine.[2] To this later period of Tolstoy's creativity belong such works as his autobiographical *Confession,* his short stories *The Death of Ivan Ilyich* and *Master and Man,* his play *Power of Darkness,* his novel *Resurrection,* and his work on aesthetics *What Is Art?* all of which reveal a new Tolstoy, still the consummate artist but now, above all, the moralist promulgating the message of Jesus. His fame as religious sage for a time overshadowed his fame as writer; his home became a place for pilgrimage, a focal point for the hopes of millions of restless pre-revolutionary Russians.

After his religious conversion, Tolstoy's relations with his wife, who was sixteen years his junior, became increasingly estranged. Finally, after a long series of marital crises had made life at Yasnaya Polyana unbearable, he fled secretly with his daughter, Alexandra, to an undetermined destination.[3] Illness struck the eighty-two-year-old refugee while traveling, and he died at a railway station at Astapovo.

In *What Is Art?* (1897), Tolstoy records his maturest views on a subject which had occupied his thoughts off and on for a period of fifteen years. During this period, he had made several preliminary attempts, none of which satisfied him, to formulate and record his views on art.[4] In an early essay, *On Art* (written before, but published after *What Is Art?*), he stresses three characteristics of every genuine work of art: (1) it contains a new idea of vital importance to mankind; (2) this idea is so clearly expressed that all can understand it; and (3) the work is the result of an artist's effort to satisfy an inner need. A work having all of these characteristics cannot be otherwise than moral in content, beautiful in form, and true in feeling.[5] Although the essay *On Art* reveals the direction of Tolstoy's thinking and contains several of the basic ideas that he later was to articulate more fully, it lacks the conviction, the brilliance, the emotional import of his final, definitive work on art.

What Is Art? is not a carefully reasoned, cooly objective treatise on aesthetics. On the contrary, it is a virulent attack on what Tolstoy considers to be counterfeit art; an impassioned plea for art for morality's sake rather than art for art's sake; a powerful statement of the view that art is communication of religious perception; and a stringent moral judgment on all art, including Tolstoy's own, that does not measure up to his standards. *What Is Art?* is also intended by Tolstoy to be a devastating critique of aesthetics, a pseudoscience in his view, concerned with the impossible (and pernicious) task of defining the nature of beauty. An examination of the history of modern aesthetic speculation convinced Tolstoy that it is only so much bunkum, manufactured by obscurantists for the consumption of the indolent upper classes.[6] Aesthetic theory, he claims, rests upon the basic mistake of supposing that the concept of beauty, not the concept of art, is its paramount concern; it has never made any progress because it has supposed that one, beauty, has something to do with the definition of the other, art. But to interpret art in terms of beauty, Tolstoy argues, is to ground it in nothing more substantial than mere personal preference. A fresh start, then, is absolutely necessary if art's existence is to be justified. This Tolstoy sets as his own major task.

The definition of art given by Tolstoy in *What Is Art?* is close to, if not derived from, that given previously by Eugène Véron. Véron's definition, as summarized by Tolstoy, is that "art is the external manifestation by means of lines, colors, movements, sounds, or words, of emotions felt by man." [7] While finding this definition superior to metaphysical definitions, Tolstoy considers it to be inexact "because a man may express his emotions by means of lines, colors, sounds, or words, and yet may not act on others by such expression, and then the manifestation of his emotions is not art." [8] The artist must do more than express his emotions; he must also communicate them to others. Emotional "infection" is essential to art.

Throughout his presentation, Tolstoy's focus is always on the moral function of art in the life of all men. He is convinced that failure to realize the highest function of art—the communication of religious perception—leads to irreparable harm to the artist, to the aesthetic consumer, and to society at large. Art itself is perverted when its purpose becomes mere pleasurable sensation, and the results of "art for art's sake" are everywhere to be seen in the impoverishment of subject matter, the obscurity of form, and the insincere and unnatural manner in the kind of art it inspires. Tolstoy lays the blame for bad art on several factors: on the increasing commercialization of art, on art criticism, and on schools of art; all of these destroy the creative imagination and spoil the taste of students and public alike. Tolstoy is without compunction, therefore, in rejecting as spurious works that do not measure up to his moral and aesthetic criteria of good art. Thus he rejects the works of the Greek dramatists, the works of Dante, Milton, and Shakespeare, the paintings of Raphael and Michelangelo, the music of Bach and Beethoven, and most of the works of his contemporaries. He especially holds up for ridicule and condemnation the operas of Wagner and the poetry of the French Symbolists and Decadents.

Consistent with his convictions, Tolstoy also condemns as bad art his own early works, which sprang, he says regretfully, from perverted taste due to false training, with the exception of two short stories, God Sees the Truth and The Prisoner of the Caucasus.[9] Among the examples he gives of good literary art, good because they express and can communicate love of God and man, are Les Misérables, The Tale of Two Cities, Uncle Tom's Cabin, and Adam Bede.[10] He also approves of the works of Homer, the Hebrew prophets, the Psalms, the Gospel parables, and the hyms of the Vedas, since these, he holds, express universal feelings of high moral quality and thus accord with the moral purpose of art.

While readers of What Is Art? may find Tolstoy's definition of art admirable, they may, at the same time, be amazed or even outraged by his blindness to the aesthetic values of some of the greatest artistic achievements of Western civilization. They may suspect that it was his later rather than his earlier taste that was perverted, but they may still be at a loss to explain how Tolstoy could be led to such distorted evaluations and absurd conclusions in his discussion of works of art. The explanation can be only briefly suggested here. Tolstoy's idealization of the peasant and his denigration of the connoisseur, his exaltation of the spiritual at the expense of the sensuous, his unwillingness to admit a wide range of worthy goals for artistic creativity, and his inability to comprehend that an artist is often most genuinely moral when he least appears to be so—these are some of the factors that contributed to the peculiar distortion in Tolstoy's perspective in aesthetics. But despite this distortion and the absurdities resulting from it, there can be no doubt of Tolstoy's complete sincerity in undertaking a task which is by no means absurd, namely, the task of relating art to the basic needs and the highest aspirations of mankind. Like Plato, who at times he resembles strikingly, Tolstoy insists that art should not be taken lightly or at its face value; and also like Plato, he envisages an ideal social order in which art, science, and religion will cooperate in promoting the welfare of the whole and in perfecting human nature.

Art as Emotional Communication

1. *Tolstoy begins his discussion of art by scrutinizing those activities usually called artistic. Using a metholological naiveté, he insists on a fresh, unprejudiced examination and evaluation of all such activities by raising such questions as: "What is the meaning of these so-called artistic activities?" "Of what value are they and for whom?" "Do they really merit the name art?" and "Is art activity producing beauty?"*

And therefore it is necessary for a society in which works of art arise and are supported, to find out whether all that professes to be art is really art; whether (as is presupposed in our society) all that which is art is good; and whether it is important and worth those sacrifices which it necessitates. It is still more necessary for every conscientious artist to know this, that he may be sure that all he does has a valid meaning; that it is not merely an infatuation of the small circle of people among whom he lives which excites in him the false assurance that he is doing a good work; and that what he takes from others for the support of his often very luxurious life, will be compensated for by those productions at which he works. And that is why answers to the above questions are especially important in our time.

What is this art, which is considered so important and necessary for humanity that for its sake these sacrifices of labor, of human life, and even of goodness may be made?

"What is art? What a question! Art is architecture, sculpture, painting, music, and poetry in all its forms," usually replies the ordinary man, the art amateur, or even the artist himself, imagining the matter about which he is talking to be perfectly clear, and uniformly understood by everybody. But in architecture, one inquires further, are there not simple buildings which are not objects of art, and buildings with artistic pretensions which are unsuccessful and ugly and therefore cannot be considered as works of art? Wherein lies the characteristic sign of a work of art?

It is the same in sculpture, in music, and in poetry. Art, in all its forms, is bounded on one side by the practically useful, and on the other by unsuccessful attempts at art. How is art to be marked off from each of these? The ordinary educated man of our circle, and even the artist who has not occupied himself especially with aesthetics, will not hesitate at this question either. He thinks the solution has been found long ago, and is well known to every one.

"Art is such activity as produces beauty," says such a man. . . .

What is this strange conception "beauty," which seems so simple to those who talk without thinking, but in defining which all the philosophers of various tendencies and different nationalities can come to no agreement during a century and a half? What is this conception of beauty, on which the dominant doctrine of art rests? [11] . . .

2. *A review of the history of aesthetics should convince anyone, Tolstoy believes, that the question "What is beauty?" has never been satisfactorily answered. The definitions and theories of beauty of modern European aestheticians can be classified as (1) objectivistic (i.e. the object of beauty exists independently of the observer), and (2) subjectivistic (i.e. the object of beauty is beautiful in so far as it pleases the beholder.) Both kinds of theory can be reduced, Tolstoy argues, to a common denominator: pleasure.*

To what do these definitions of beauty amount? Not reckoning the thoroughly inaccurate definitions of beauty which fail to cover the conception of art, and which suppose beauty to consist either in utility, or in adjustment to a purpose, or in symmetry, or in order, or in proportion, or in smoothness, or in harmony of the parts, or in unity amid variety, or in various combinations of these—not reckoning these unsatisfactory attempts at objective definition, all the aesthetic definitions of beauty lead to two fundamental conceptions. The first is that beauty is something having an independent existence (existing in itself), that it is one of the manifestations of the absolutely Perfect, of the Idea, of the Spirit, or Will, or of God; the other is that beauty is a kind of pleasure received by us, not having personal advantage for its object.

The first of these definitions was accepted by Fichte, Schelling, Hegel, Schopenhauer, and the philosophizing Frenchmen, Cousin, Jouffroy, Ravaisson, and others, not to enumerate the second-rate aesthetic philosophers. And this same objective-mystical definition of beauty is held by a majority of the educated people of our day. It is a conception very widely spread, especially among the elder generation.

The second view, that beauty is a certain kind of pleasure received by us, not having personal advantage for its aim, finds favor chiefly among the English aesthetic writers, and is shared by the other part of our society, principally by the younger generation.

So there are (and it could not be otherwise) only two definitions of beauty: the one objective, mystical, merging this conception into that of the highest perfection, God—a fantastic definition, founded on nothing; the other, on the contrary, a very simple and intelligible subjective one, which considers beauty to be that which pleases (I do not add to the word "pleases" the words "without the aim of advantage," because "pleases" naturally presupposes the absence of the idea of profit).

On the one hand, beauty is viewed as something mystical and very elevated, but unfortunately at the same time very indefinite, and consequently embracing philosophy, religion, and life itself (as in the theories of Schelling and Hegel, and their German and French followers); or, on the other hand (as necessarily follows from the definition of Kant and his adherents), beauty is simply a certain kind of disinterested pleasure received by us. And this conception of beauty, although it seems very clear is, unfortunately, again inexact; for it widens out on the other side, i.e. it includes the pleasure derived from drink, from food, from touching a delicate skin, etc., as is acknowledged by Guyau, Kralik, and others.

It is true that, following the development of the aesthetic doctrines on beauty, we may notice that, though at first (in the times when the foundations of the science of aesthetics were being laid) the metaphysical definition of beauty prevailed, yet the nearer we get to our own times the more does an experimental definition (recently assuming a physiological form) come to the front, so that at last we even meet with such aestheticians as Véron and Sully, who try to escape entirely from the conception of beauty. But such aestheticians have very little success, and with the majority of the public, as well as of artists and the learned, a conception of beauty is firmly held which agrees with the definitions contained in most of the aesthetic treatises, i.e. which regards beauty either as something mystical or metaphysical, or as a special kind of enjoyment.

What, then, is this conception of beauty, so stubbornly held to by people of our circle and day as furnishing a definition of art.

In the subjective aspect, we call beauty that which supplies us with a particular kind of pleasure.

In the objective aspect, we call beauty something absolutely perfect, and we acknowledge it to be so only because we receive, from the manifestation of this absolute perfection, a certain kind of pleasure; so that this objective definition is nothing but the subjective conception differently expressed. In reality both conceptions of beauty amount to one and the same thing; namely, the reception by us of a certain kind of pleasure; i.e. we call "beauty" that which pleases us without evoking in us desire.[12]

---

3. *The conclusion Tolstoy draws from his investigation into the theory of beauty is that there can be no objective definition of beauty since pleasurable sensation is relative to the beholder. But what is considered beautiful to a certain group, i.e. what pleases them, is not necessarily art. To understand the meaning of art is to understand, first of all, that its aim is not to be identified with the creation of beauty.*

There is no objective definition of beauty. The existing definitions (both the metaphysical and the experimental) amount only to one and the same subjective definition, which (strange as it seems to say so) is, that art is that which makes beauty manifest, and beauty is that which pleases (without exciting desire). . . . There is and can be no explanation of why one thing pleases one man and displeases another, or *vice versa*. So that the whole existing science of aesthetics fails to do what we might expect from it, being a mental activity calling itself a science; namely, it does not define the qualities and laws of art, or of the beautiful (if that be the content of art), or the nature of taste (if taste decides the question of art and its merit), and then, on the basis of such definitions, acknowledge as art those productions which correspond to these laws, and reject those which do not come under them. But this science of aesthetics consists in first acknowledging a certain set of productions to be art (because they please us), and then framing such a theory of art that all those productions which please a certain circle of people should fit into it. . . .

All the existing aesthetic standards are built on this plan. Instead of giving a definition of true art, and then deciding what is and what is not good art by judging whether a work conforms or does not conform to the definition, a certain class of works, which for some reason please a certain circle of people, is accepted as being art, and a definition of art is then devised to cover all these productions. . . . No matter what insanities appear in art, when once they find acceptance among the upper classes of our society, a theory is quickly invented to explain and sanction them; just as if there had never been periods in history when certain special circles of people recognized and approved false, deformed, and insensate art which subsequently left no trace and has been utterly forgotten. And to what lengths the insanity and deformity of art may go, especially when, as in our days, it knows that it is considered infallible, may be seen by what is being done in the art of our circle today.

So that the theory of art, founded on beauty, expounded by aesthetics, and, in dim outline, professed by the public, is nothing but the setting up as good of that which has pleased and pleases us, i.e. pleases a certain class of people.

In order to define any human activity, it is necessary to understand its sense and importance. And, in order to do that, it is primarily necessary to examine that activity in itself, in its dependence on its causes, and in connection with its efforts, and not merely in relation to the pleasure we can get from it. . . .

To see the aim and purpose of art in the pleasure we get from it, is like assuming (as is done by people of the lowest moral development, e.g. by savages) that the purpose and aim of food is the pleasure derived when consuming it.

Just as people who conceive the aim and purpose of food to be pleasure cannot recognize the real meaning of eating, so people who consider the aim of art to be pleasure cannot realize its true meaning and purpose, because they attribute to an activity, the meaning of which lies in its connection with other phenomena of life, the false and exceptional aim of pleasure. People come to understand that the meaning of eating lies in the nourishment of the body only when they cease to consider that the object of that activity is pleasure. People will come to understand the meaning of art only when they cease to consider that the aim of that activity is beauty, i.e. pleasure. . . .

To the question, What is this art, to which is offered up the labor of millions, the very lives of men, and even morality itself? we have extracted replies from the existing aesthetics, which all amount to this: that the aim of art is beauty, that beauty is recognized by the enjoyment it gives, and that artistic enjoyment is a good and important thing, because it *is* enjoyment. In a word, that enjoyment is good because it is enjoyment. Thus, what is considered the definition of art is no definition at all, but only a shuffle to justify existing art. Therefore, however strange it may seem to say so, in spite of the mountains of books written about art, no exact definition of art has been constructed. And the reason of this is that the conception of art has been based on the conception of beauty.[13]

4. *Having completed his negative task—the task of showing that art cannot be understood as mere pleasurable sensation—Tolstoy is now ready to approach his positive task of defining art in its genuine sense. In defining art as the communication of feelings, Tolstoy stresses three aspects of artistic communication: (1) the internal: the evocation of experienced feeling within the artist; (2) the external: the objectification of the artist's feeling through an artistic medium; and (3) the interpersonal: the transmission of this feeling through the medium to others who thereby experience the artist's feeling.*

In order correctly to define art, it is necessary, first of all, to cease to consider it as a means to pleasure, and to consider it as one of the conditions of human life. Viewing it in this way, we cannot fail to observe that art is one of the means of intercourse between man and man.

Every work of art causes the receiver to enter into a certain kind of relationship both with him who produced, or is producing, the art, and with all those who, simultaneously, previously, or subsequently, receive the same artistic impression.

Speech, transmitting the thoughts and experiences of men, serves as a means of union among them, and art acts in a similar manner. The peculiarity of this latter means of intercourse, distinguishing it from intercourse by means of words, consists in this, that whereas by words a man transmits his thoughts to another, by means of art he transmits his feelings.

The activity of art is based on the fact that a man, receiving through his sense of hearing or sight another man's expression of feeling, is capable of experiencing the emotion which moved the man who expressed it. To take the simplest example: one man laughs, and another, who hears, becomes merry; or a man weeps, and another, who hears, feels sorrow. A man is excited or irritated, and another man, seeing him, comes to a similar state of mind. By his movements, or by the sounds of his voice, a man expresses courage and determination, or sadness and calmness, and this state of mind passes on to others. A man suffers, expressing his sufferings by groans and spasms, and this suffering transmits itself to other people; a man expresses his feeling of admiration, devotion, fear, respect, or love to certain objects, persons, or phenomena, and others are infected by the same feelings of admiration, devotion, fear, respect, or love to the same objects, persons, and phenomena.

And it is on this capacity of man to receive another man's expression of feeling, and experience those feelings himself, that the activity of art is based.

If a man infects another or others, directly, immediately, by his appearance, or by the sounds he gives vent to at the very time he experiences the feeling; if he causes another man to yawn when he himself cannot help yawning, or to laugh or cry when he himself is obliged to laugh or cry, or to suffer when he himself is suffering—that does not amount to art.

Art begins when one person, with the object of joining another or others to himself in one and the same feeling, expresses that feeling by certain external indications. To take the simplest example: a boy, having experienced, let us say, fear on encountering a wolf, relates that encounter; and, in order to evoke in others the feeling he has experienced, describes himself, his condition before the encounter, the surroundings, the wood, his own light-heartedness, and then the wolf's appearance, its movements, the distance between himself and the wolf, etc. All this, if only the boy, when telling the story, again experiences the feelings he has lived through and infects the hearers and compels them to feel what the narrator had experienced, is art. If even the boy had not seen a wolf but had frequently been afraid of one, and if, wishing to evoke in others the fear he had felt, he invented an encounter with a wolf, and recounted it so as to make his hearers share the feelings he experienced when he feared the wolf, that also would be art. And just in the same way it is art if a man, having experienced either the fear of suffering or the attraction of enjoyment (whether in reality or in imagination), expresses these feelings on canvas or in marble so that others are infected by them. And it is also art if a man feels or imagines to himself feelings of delight, gladness, sorrow, despair, courage, or despondency, and the transition from one to another of these feelings, and expresses these feelings by sounds, so that the hearers are infected by them, and experience them as they were experienced by the composer.

The feelings with which the artist infects others may be most various,—very strong or very weak, very important or very insignificant, very bad or very good: feelings of love for native land, self-devotion and submission to fate or to God expressed in a drama, raptures of lovers described in a novel, feelings of voluptuousness expressed in a picture, courage expressed in a triumphal march, merriment evoked by a dance, humor evoked by a funny story, the feeling of quietness transmitted by an evening landscape or by a lullaby, or the feeling of admiration evoked by a beautiful arabesque—it is all art.

If only the spectators or auditors are infected by the feelings which the author has felt, it is art.

To evoke in oneself a feeling one has once experienced, and having evoked it in oneself, then, by means of movements, lines, colors, sounds, or forms expressed in words, so to transmit that feeling that others may experience the same feeling—this is the activity of art.

Art is a human activity, consisting in this, that one man consciously, by means of certain external signs, hands on to others feelings he has lived through, and that other people are infected by these feelings, and also experience them.

Art is not, as the metaphysicians say, the manifestation of some mysterious Idea of beauty, or God; it is not, as the aesthetical physiologists say, a game in which man lets off his excess of stored-up energy; it is not the expression of man's emotions by external signs; it is not the production of pleasing objects; and, above all, it is not pleasure; but it is a means of union among men, joining them together in the same feelings, and indispensable for the life and progress toward well-being of individuals and of humanity.[14]

5. How is one to distinguish real art from counterfeit art? Tolstoy thinks infectious quality is the chief sign of all genuine art. Furthermore, the more intense the infectious quality, the better the work of art (considered independently of its subject matter). Tolstoy finds three conditions govern the degree of infectiousness in a work of art: (1) individuality of feeling; (2) clarity of feeling; and (3) sincerity of feeling. He explains why he considers sincerity to be the most important among the three.

Art, in our society, has been so perverted that not only has bad art come to be considered good, but even the very perception of what art really is has been lost. In order to be able to speak about the art of our society, it is, therefore, first of all necessary to distinguish art from counterfeit art.

There is one indubitable indication distinguishing real art from its counterfeit, namely, the infectiousness of art. If a man, without exercising effort and without altering his standpoint, on reading, hearing, or seeing another man's work, experiences a mental condition which unites him with that man and with other people who also partake of that work of art, then the object evoking that condition is a work of art. And however poetical, realistic, effectful, or interesting a work may be, it is not a work of art if it does not evoke that feeling (quite distinct from all other feelings) of joy, and of spiritual union with another (the author) and with others (those who are also infected by it). . . .

The chief peculiarity of this feeling is that the receiver of a true artistic impression is so united to the artist that he feels as if the work were his own and not some one else's,—as if what it expresses were just what he had long been wishing to express. A real work of art destroys, in the consciousness of the receiver, the separation between himself and the artist; nor that alone, but also between himself and all whose minds receive this work of art. In this freeing of our personality from its separation and isolation, in this uniting of it with others, lies the chief characteristic and the great attractive force of art.

If a man is infected by the author's condition of soul, if he feels this emotion and this union with others, then the object which has effected this is art; but if there be no such infection, if there be not this union with the author and with others who are moved by the same work—then it is not art. And not only is infection a sure sign of art, but the degree of infectiousness is also the sole measure of excellence in art.

The stronger the infection the better is the art; as art, speaking now apart from its subject-matter, i.e. not considering the quality of the feelings it transmits.

And the degree of the infectiousness of art depends on three conditions:—

(1) On the greater or lesser individuality of the feeling transmitted; (2) on the greater or lesser clearness with which the feeling is transmitted; (3) on the sincerity of the artist, i.e. on the greater or lesser force with which the artist himself feels the emotion he transmits.

The more individual the feeling transmitted the more strongly does it act on the receiver; the more individual the state of soul into which he is transferred the more pleasure does the receiver obtain, and therefore the more readily and strongly does he join in it.

The clearness of expression assists infection, because the receiver, who mingles in consciousness with the author, is the better satisfied the more clearly the feeling is transmitted, which, as it seems to him, he has long known and felt, and for which he has only now found expression.

But most of all is the degree of infectiousness of art increased by the degree of sincerity in the artist. As soon as the spectator, hearer, or reader feels that the artist is infected by his own production, and writes, sings, or plays for himself, and not merely to act on others, this mental condition of the artist infects the receiver; and, contrariwise, as soon as the spectator, reader, or hearer feels that the author is not writing, singing, or playing for his own satisfaction,—does not himself feel what he wishes to express,—but is doing it for him, the receiver, a resistance immediately springs up, and the most individual and the newest feelings and the cleverest technique not only fail to produce any infection, but actually repel.

I have mentioned three conditions of contagiousness in art, but they may be all summed up into one, the last, sincerity, i.e. that the artist should be impelled by an inner need to express his feeling. That condition includes the first; for if the artist is sincere he will express the feeling as he experienced it. And as each man is different from every one else, his feeling will be individual for every one else; and the more individual it is,—the more the artist has drawn it from the depths of his nature,—the more sympathetic and sincere will it be. And this same sincerity will impel the artist to find a clear expression of the feeling which he wishes to transmit.

Therefore this third condition—sincerity—is the most important of the three. It is always complied with in peasant art, and this explains why such art always acts so powerfully; but it is a condition almost entirely absent from our upper-class art, which is continually produced by artists actuated by personal aims of covetousness or vanity.

Such are the three conditions which divide art from its counterfeits, and which also decide the quality of every work of art apart from its subject-matter.[15]

6. *Tolstoy now turns his attention to the subject matter of art. What feelings are to be evoked, objectified, and communicated by art? Generally, the feelings appropriate to art, Tolstoy answers, are those of the religious perception of the age in which the artist lives; specifically, in our age, the feelings are those revealed by the Christian religion: (1) the feelings related to the fatherhood of God and the brotherhood of man; and (2) the universal feelings common to all men. Both of these kinds of feelings are approved by Tolstoy since they foster the loving union of man with man.*

How in art are we to decide what is good and what is bad in subject-matter?

Art, like speech, is a means of communication, and therefore of progress, i.e. of the movement of humanity forward toward perfection. Speech renders accessible to men of the latest generation all the knowledge discovered by the experience and reflection, both of preceding generations and of the best and foremost men of their own times; art renders accessible to men of the latest generations all the feelings experienced by their predecessors, and those also which are being felt by their best and foremost contemporaries. And as the evolution of knowledge proceeds by truer and more necessary knowledge dislodging and replacing what is mistaken and unnecessary, so the evolution of feeling proceeds through art,—feelings less kind and less needful for the well-being of mankind are replaced by others kinder and more needful for that end. That is the purpose of art. And, speaking now of its subject-matter, the more art fulfils that purpose the better the art, and the less it fulfils it the worse the art.

And the appraisement of feelings (i.e. the acknowledgment of these or those feelings as being more or less good, more or less necessary for the well-being of mankind) is made by the religious perception of the age. . . .

If humanity progresses, i.e. moves forward, there must inevitably be a guide to the direction of that movement. And religions have always furnished that guide. All history shows that the progress of humanity is accomplished not otherwise than under the guidance of religion. But if the race cannot progress without the guidance of religion,—and progress is always going on, and consequently also in our own times,—then there must be a religion of our times. So that, whether it pleases or displeases the so-called cultured people of today, they must admit the existence of religion,—not of a religious cult, Catholic, Protestant, or another, but of religious perception,—which, even in our times, is the guide always present where there is any progress. And if a religious perception exists amongst us, then our art should be appraised on the basis of that religious perception; and, as has always and everywhere been the case, art transmitting feelings flowing from the religious perception of our time should be chosen from all the indifferent art, should be acknowledged, highly esteemed, and encouraged; while art running counter to that perception should be condemned and despised, and all the remaining indifferent art should neither be distinguished nor encouraged.

The religious perception of our time, in its widest and most practical application, is the consciousness that our well-being, both material and spiritual, individual and collective, temporal and eternal, lies in the growth of brotherhood among all men—in their loving harmony with one another. . . .

The essence of the Christian perception consists in the recognition by every man of his sonship to God, and of the consequent union of men with God and with one another, as is said in the gospel (John xvii.21). Therefore the subject-matter of Christian art is such feeling as can unite men with God and with one another.

The expression *unite men with God and with one another* may seem obscure to people accustomed to the misuse of these words which is so customary, but the words have a perfectly clear meaning nevertheless. They indicate that the Christian union of man (in contradiction to the partial, exclusive union of only some men) is that which unites all without exception. . . .

Christian art, i.e. the art of our time, should be catholic in the original meaning of the word, i.e. universal, and therefore it should unite all men. And only two kinds of feeling do unite all men: first, feelings flowing from the perception of our sonship to God and of the brotherhood of man; and next, the simplest feelings of common life, accessible to every one without exception—such as the feeling of merriment, of pity, of cheerfulness, of tranquillity, etc. Only these two kinds of feelings can now supply material for art good in its subject-matter. . . .

Christian art either evokes in men those feelings which, through love of God and of one's neighbor, draw them to greater and ever greater union, and make them ready for and capable of such union; or evokes in them those feelings which show them that they are already united in the joys and sorrows of life. And therefore the Christian art of our time can be and is of two kinds: (1) art transmitting feelings flowing from a religious perception of man's position in the world in relation to God and to his neighbor—religious art in the limited meaning of the term; and (2) art transmitting the simplest feelings of common life, but such, always, as are accessible to all men in the whole world—the art of common life—the art of a people—universal art. Only these two kinds of art can be considered good art in our time.

The first, religious art,—transmitting both positive feelings of

love to God and one's neighbor, and negative feelings of indignation and horror at the violation of love,—manifests itself chiefly
in the form of words, and to some extent also in painting and
sculpture; the second kind (universal art), transmitting feelings
accessible to all, manifests itself in words, in painting, in sculpture,
in dances, in architecture, and, most of all, in music.[16]

*7. Conceiving of art as an indestructible spiritual organ of human
life, Tolstoy condemns those so-called artists who fail to communicate the highest religious perception of their time and praises
those true artists who attempt to transmit feelings fostering the
unity of mankind.*

Art is a spiritual organ of human life which cannot be destroyed, and therefore, notwithstanding all the efforts made by
people of the upper classes to conceal the religious ideal by which
humanity lives, that ideal is more and more clearly recognized by
man, and even in our perverted society is more and more often
partially expressed by science and art. During the present century
works of the higher kind of religious art have appeared more and
more frequently, both in literature and in painting, permeated by
a truly Christian spirit, as also works of the universal art of
common life, accessible to all. So that even art knows the true
ideal of our times, and tends toward it. On the one hand, the
best works of art of our times transmit religious feelings urging
toward the union and the brotherhood of man (such are the
works of Dickens, Hugo, Dostoievsky; and in painting, of Millet,
Bastien Lepage, Jules Breton, L'Hermitte, and others); on the
other hand, they strive toward the transmission, not of feelings
which are natural to people of the upper classes only, but of such
feelings as may unite every one without exception. There are as
yet few such works, but the need of them is already acknowledged.
In recent times we also meet more and more frequently with
attempts at publications, pictures, concerts, and theatres for the
people. All this is still very far from accomplishing what should
be done, but already the direction in which good art instinctively
presses forward to regain the path natural to it can be discerned.
The religious perception of our time—which consists in
acknowledging that the aim of life (both collective and individual) is the union of mankind—is already sufficiently distinct

that people have now only to reject the false theory of beauty, according to which enjoyment is considered to be the purpose of art, and religious perception will naturally take its place as the guide of the art of our time.

And as soon as the religious perception, which already unconsciously directs the life of man, is consciously acknowledged, then immediately and naturally the division of art, into art for the lower and art for the upper classes, will disappear. There will be one common, brotherly, universal art; and first, that art will naturally be rejected which transmits feelings incompatible with the religious perception of our time,—feelings which do not unite, but divide men,—and then that insignificant, exclusive art will be rejected to which an importance is now attached to which it has no right.

And as soon as this occurs, art will immediately cease to be what it has been in recent times,—a means of making people coarser and more vicious; and it will become, what it always used to be and should be, a means by which humanity progresses toward unity and blessedness.[17]

8. *Tolstoy believes there can and should be a close relationship between science and art in furthering the development of the spiritual life of mankind. While recognizing the emergence of science as a dominant force in molding the life of our time, Tolstoy objects as strenuously to "science for science's sake" as he does to "art for art's sake." Both science and art should be subservient to the moral end of the betterment of mankind.*

Science and art are as closely bound together as the lungs and the heart, so that if one organ is vitiated the other cannot act rightly.

True science investigates and brings to human perception such truths and such knowledge as the people of a given time and society consider most important. Art transmits these truths from the region of perception to the region of emotion. Therefore, if the path chosen by science be false, so also will be the path taken by art. Science and art are like a certain kind of barge with kedge-anchors which used to ply on our rivers. Science, like the boats which took the anchors up-stream and made them secure, gives directions to the forward movement; while art, like the windlass worked on the barge to draw it toward the anchor, causes the actual progression.

And thus a false activity of science inevitably causes a correspondingly false activity of art.

As art in general is the transmission of every kind of feeling, but in the limited sense of the word we only call that art which transmits feelings acknowledged by us to be important, so also science in general is the transmission of all possible knowledge; but in the limited sense of the word we call science that which transmits knowledge acknowledged by us to be important.

And the degree of importance, both of the feelings transmitted by art and of the information transmitted by science, is decided by the religious perception of the given time and society, i.e. by the common understanding of the purpose of their lives possessed by the people of that time or society....

As by the theory of art for art's sake, it appears that occupation with all those things that please us—is art, so, by the theory of science for science's sake, the study of that which interests us—is science.

So that one side of science, instead of studying how people should live in order to fulfil their mission in life, demonstrates the righteousness and immutability of the bad and false arrangements of life which exist around us; while the other part, experimental science, occupies itself with the questions of simple curiosity or with technical improvements.

The first of these divisions of science is harmful, not only because it confuses people's perceptions and gives false decisions, but also because it exists, and occupies the ground which should belong to true science. It does this harm, that each man, in order to approach the study of the most important questions of life, must first refute these erections of lies which have during ages been piled around each of the most essential questions of human life, and which are propped up by all the strength of human ingenuity.

The second division—the one of which modern science is so particularly proud, and which is considered by many people to be the only real science—is harmful in that it diverts attention from the really important subjects to insignificant subjects, and is also directly harmful in that, under the evil system of society which the first division of science justifies and supports, a great part of the technical gains of science are turned, not to the advantage, but to the injury of mankind....

It is to be hoped that the work I have tried to perform concerning art will be performed also for science—that the falseness of the theory of science for science's sake will be demonstrated; that the necessity of acknowledging Christian teaching in its true meaning will be clearly shown, that on the basis of that teaching a reappraisement will be made of the knowledge we possess, and of which we are so proud; that the secondariness and insignificance of experimental science, and the primacy and importance of religious, moral, and social knowledge will be established; and that such knowledge will not, as now, be left to the guidance of the upper classes only, but will form a chief interest of all free, truth-loving men, such as those who, not in agreement with the upper classes, but in their despite, have always forwarded the real science of life.

Astronomical, physical, chemical, and biological science, as also technical and medical science, will be studied only in so far as they can help to free mankind from religious, juridical, or social deceptions, or can serve to promote the well-being of all men, and not any single class.

Only then will science cease to be what it is now—on the one hand a system of sophistries, needed for the maintenance of the existing worn-out order of society, and, on the other hand, a shapeless mass of miscellaneous knowledge, for the most part good for little or nothing,—and become a shapely and organic whole, having a definite and reasonable purpose comprehensible to all men; namely, the purpose of bringing to the consciousness of men the truths that flow from the religious perception of our times.

And only then will art, which is always dependent on science, be what it might and should be, an organ co-equally important with science for the life and progress of mankind.[18]

9. *Speculating on the art of the future, Tolstoy envisages an art that will be truly universal in its sources and ends by drawing on the creative potentialities of common men and aiming at the integration of mankind through common feelings and ideals.*

Art of the future, that is to say, such part of art as will be chosen from among all the art diffused among mankind, will consist, not in transmitting feelings accessible only to members of the rich classes, as is the case today, but in transmitting such feelings as embody the highest religious perception of our times. Only those productions will be considered art which transmit feelings drawing men together in brotherly union, or such universal feelings as can unite all men. . . .

And the artists producing art will also not be, as now, merely a few people selected from a small section of the nation, members of the upper classes or their hangers-on, but will consist of all those gifted members of the whole people who prove capable of, and are inclined toward, artistic activity.

Artistic activity will then be accessible to all men. It will become accessible to the whole people, because, in the first place, in the art of the future, not only will that complex technique, which deforms the productions of the art of today and requires so great an effort and expenditure of time, not be demanded, but, on the contrary, the demand will be for clearness, simplicity, and brevity—conditions mastered, not by mechanical exercises, but by the education of taste. And secondly, artistic activity will become accessible to all men of the people because, instead of the present professional schools which only some can enter, all will learn music and depictive art (singing and drawing) equally with letters in the elementary schools, and in such a way that every man, having received the first principles of drawing and music, and feeling a capacity for, and a call to, one or other of the arts, will be able to perfect himself in it. . . .

The art of the future will thus be completely distinct, both in subject-matter and in form, from what is now called art. The only subject-matter of the art of the future will be either feelings drawing men toward union, or such as already unite them; and the forms of art will be such as will be open to every one. And therefore, the ideal of excellence in the future will not be the exclusiveness of feeling, accessible only to some, but, on the contrary, its universality. And not bulkiness, obscurity, and complexity of form, as is now esteemed, but, on the contrary, brevity, clearness, and simplicity of expression. Only when art has attained to that, will art neither divert nor deprave men as it does now, calling on them to expend their best strength on it, but be what it should be,— a vehicle wherewith to transmit religious, Christian perception from the realm of reason and intellect into that of feeling, and really drawing people in actual life nearer to that perfection and unity indicated to them by their religious perception.[19]

10. *Tolstoy concludes that the social significance of art is enormous. Under the guidance of religious perception, art, aided by science, can bring about a new era of peace and goodwill among all men, establishing eventually a kingdom of God on earth.*

Art is not a pleasure, a solace, or an amusement; art is a great matter. Art is an organ of human life, transmitting man's reasonable perception into feeling. In our age the common religious perception of men is the consciousness of the brotherhood of man—we know that the well-being of man lies in union with his fellowmen. True science should indicate the various methods of applying this consciousness to life. Art should transform this perception into feeling.

The task of art is enormous. Through the influence of real art, aided by science guided by religion, that peaceful coöperation of man which is now obtained by external means—by our law-courts, police, charitable institutions, factory inspection, etc.—should be obtained by man's free and joyous activity. Art should cause violence to be set aside.

And it is only art that can accomplish this.

All that now, independently of the fear of violence and punishment, makes the social life of man possible (and already now this is an enormous part of the order of our lives)—all this has been brought about by art. If by art it has been inculcated how people should treat religious objects, their parents, their children, their wives, their relations, strangers, foreigners; how to conduct themselves to their elders, their superiors, to those who suffer, to their enemies, and to animals; and if this has been obeyed through generations by millions of people, not only unenforced by any violence, but so that the force of such customs can be shaken in no way but by means of art—then, by the same art, other customs, more in accord with the religious perception of our time, may be evoked. If art has been able to convey the sentiment of reverence for images, for the eucharist, and for the king's person; of shame at betraying a comrade, devotion to a flag, the necessity of revenge for an insult, the need to sacrifice one's labor for the erection and adornment of churches, the duty of defending one's honor or the glory of one's native land—then that same art can also evoke reverence for the dignity of every man and for the life of every animal; can make men ashamed of luxury, of violence, of revenge, or of using for their pleasure that of which others are in need; can compel people freely, gladly, and without noticing it, to sacrifice themselves in the service of man.

The task for art to accomplish is to make that feeling of brotherhood and love of one's neighbor, now attained only by the best members of society, the customary feeling and the instinct of all men. By evoking, under imaginary conditions, the feeling of brotherhood and love, religious art will train men to experience those same feelings under similar circumstances in actual life; it will lay in the souls of men the rails along which the actions of those whom art thus educates will naturally pass. And universal art, by uniting the most different people in one common feeling, by destroying separation, will educate people to union, will show them, not by reason, but by life itself, the joy of universal union reaching beyond the bounds set by life.

The destiny of art in our time is to transmit from the realm of reason to the realm of feeling the truth that well-being for men consists in being united together, and to set up, in place of the existing reign of force, that kingdom of God, i.e. of love, which we all recognize to be the highest aim of human life.

Possibly, in the future, science may reveal to art yet newer and higher ideals, which art may realize; but, in our time, the destiny of art is clear and definite. The task for Christian art is to establish brotherly union among men.[20]

NOTES

1. On the life of Tolstoy, see Aylmer Maude, *Leo Tolstoy* (New York, Dodd, Mead & Co., 1918) and Ernest J. Simmons, *Leo Tolstoy* (Boston, Little, Brown & Co., 1946).

2. For Tolstoy's views on religion, see Stanley R. Hopper (ed.), *Life Up Your Eyes: The Religious Writings of Leo Tolstoy* (New York, Julian Press, 1960).

3. The story of his battles with his wife and his melodramatic flight from her is recounted in Tikhon I. Polner's *Tolstoy and His Wife* (New York, W. W. Norton, 1945).

4. Some of Tolstoy's early writings on art, including the important essay "On Art" (c. 1895), are collected in Aylmer Maude (ed.), *Tolstoy on Art* (London, Humphrey Milford, 1924). This volume also contains Tolstoy's essay "Shakespeare and the Drama" (1906). In addition, it contains a number of illustrations of paintings mentioned by Tolstoy in *What Is Art?*

5. Aylmer Maude (ed.), *Tolstoy on Art*, cited above, pp. 82–84.

6. Tolstoy's brief survey of philosophies of beauty may be found in Chap. III of *What Is Art?*

7. Leo N. Tolstoy, *What Is Art?*, translated by Aylmer Maude (New York, Thomas Y. Crowell & Co., 1899), p. 39. All subsequent quotations and selections will be taken from this edition.

8. Tolstoy, *What Is Art?* (Maude translation), p. 40.

9. Tolstoy, *What Is Art?* (Maude translation), pp. 148–149.

10. Ibid., p. 145.

11. Ibid., pp. 8–9; p. 13.

12. Ibid., pp. 32–34.

13. Ibid., pp. 35–39.

14. Ibid., pp. 40–43.

15. Ibid., pp. 132–135.

16. Ibid., pp. 135–136; pp. 138–139; pp. 142–145.

17. Ibid., pp. 164–165.

18. Ibid., pp. 174–176; p. 182.

19. Tolstoy, *What Is Art?* (Maude translation), pp. 167–168; p. 173.

20. Ibid., pp. 183–184.

QUESTIONS AND TOPICS FOR
FURTHER STUDY

1. Why does Tolstoy object to defining art in terms of beauty? Does he see any basic difference in subjectivistic and objectivistic theories of beauty?

2. Upon what assumptions does Tolstoy proceed in defining art? What is his definition? What advantages does he think it has over previous definitions?

3. What does Tolstoy mean by the "infectious quality" of a work of art? What three conditions govern the degree of infectiousness? Which of these does he consider most important? Why?

4. Explain what Tolstoy means by the religious perception of an age. How does he think religious perception can be embodied in works of art?

5. Discuss some of the examples Tolstoy gives of good and bad art, and explain why, in light of his theory, he considers them to be good or bad. Do you agree with his judgments? Why or why not?

6. Explain the relationship of art to science, according to Tolstoy. Why does he object to "science for science's sake" and to "art for art's sake"?

7. What will be the characteristics of the art of the future, according to Tolstoy? Were he living today do you think he would find the art of our time closer to his ideals? Explain why or why not.

8. In what respects do Tolstoy's views on art resemble those of Plato, Véron, and Guyau? In what respects do they differ?

9. Explain why Tolstoy considers art to be "an indestructible spiritual organ of life." What objections can you raise to his theory of art?

10. Topics for further study: (a) the evolution of Tolstoy's theory of art; (b) the relationship of Tolstoy's aesthetics to his philosophy of religion; (c) Tolstoy's theory of tragedy and his play *Power of Darkness;* (d) Tolstoy's criticisms of Shakespeare; (e) Tolstoy's later short stories as illustrative of his theory of art.

GUIDE TO SUPPLEMENTARY READING

(Works marked with asterisks are available in paperbound editions.)

I. PRIMARY SOURCES

Tolstoy, Leo N., *What Is Art?*, translated by Aylmer Maude, with an introduction by Vincent Tomas (New York, Liberal Arts Press, 1960).

——*What Is Art? and Essays On Art*, translated by Aylmer Maude (New York, Oxford University Press, 1962).

II. SECONDARY WORKS

Garrod, Heathcote W., *Tolstoi's Theory of Art* (Oxford, The Clarendon Press, 1935).

Geiger, Don, "Tolstoy as a Defender of 'Pure Art' that Unwraps Something," *Journal of Aesthetics and Art Criticism*, XX (Fall, 1961), 81–89.

Knight, G. Wilson, *The Wheel of Fire; Interpretations of Shakespeare's Tragedy* (New York, Meridian Books, 1957). Chap. XIV ("Tolstoy's Attack on Shakespeare").

Knox, Israel, "Tolstoi's Esthetic Definition of Art," *Journal of Philosophy*, 27 (1930), 65–70.

Lavrin, Janko, *Tolstoy: An Approach* (New York, Macmillan Company, 1946).

Maude, Aylmer, *Tolstoy on Art* (London, Humphrey Milford, 1924).

Redpath, Theodore, *Leo Tolstoi* (London, Bowes and Bowes, 1960).

Simmons, Ernest J., *Leo Tolstoy* (Boston, Little, Brown and Company, 1946). Part IV, Chap. XXXI.

Stolnitz, Jerome, *Aesthetics and Philosophy of Art Criticism* (Boston, Houghton Mifflin Company, 1960), pp. 166–182.

Symons, Arthur, *Studies in Prose and Verse* (London, J. M. Dent and Company, 1904) ("Tolstoi on Art").

CHAPTER 9

Aesthetics Turns to Science

TAINE, FECHNER, LEE, AND DESSOIR

The astonishing development of the physical and biological sciences during the nineteenth century not only increased man's knowledge of nature, making possible new inventions and technology which radically transformed his world, it also decreased his reliance on metaphysical systems and challenged his faith in theological beliefs. As science advanced it seemed to make metaphysics superfluous and theology obsolete. For truth was being rapidly attained, not through speculation and revelation, but through observation and experimentation. The belief became widespread that the answers to all human problems, when they came, would come not "from above"—from a Plato, a Thomas Aquinas, a Hegel, but "from below"—from a Claude Bernard, a Pasteur, a Faraday. Scientists were carrying on experiments in order to investigate the phenomena of heat, light, sound, and electricity; to discover the constitution of matter; and to determine the functions of the nervous system and the causes of disease. The physiological effects of music were being scrutinized by Hermann Helmholtz,[1] and new forms of construction for the architecture of the future were being tested by Gustave Eiffel. Even fiction, in the hands of Zola, and painting, under the impressionists, were becoming experimental. One of the most dazzling intellectual achievements of the century, Charles Darwin's theory of evolution, seemed to signal the triumph of the empirical spirit of careful observation, cautious induction, and thorough experimentation over hasty generalization, careless deduction, and wishful thinking. In the last quarter of the century, modest, fact-loving Darwin was lauded (at least by his admirers) as "the Newton of biology," a living proof that the scientist could unravel confused thought, throw light on the mystery of man's origin, and explain empirically man's noblest achievements as well as his most primitive acts.

It is not surprising that in this century aestheticians too became scientifically oriented and experimental in approach.[2] They began to hope that through the use of scientific methods they could discover the origins of art, trace artistic creativity to its hereditary and environmental sources, study statistically the elements entering into the composition of individual and social aesthetic preferences, and investigate empirically the various components of works of art. Form, color, and tone became subjects for scientific curiosity rather than for inspired speculation. By the end of the century, German thinkers had "invented" "psychometric" aesthetics and had set up a "science of art"; English thinkers had developed "evolutionary," "physiological," and "anthropomorphic" aesthetics; and a French thinker, Charles Henry,[3] had even defined the "science of art" as "a psychobiological physics."

In France, Auguste Comte had, early in the century, preached positivism as the only true system of philosophy and had discussed art as a purely empirical phenomenon, eschewing all transcendental interpretations of it. Before the middle of the century, M. E. Chevreul,[4] an important precursor of experimental aesthetics, had investigated color phenomena scientifically, thus paving the way to impressionism. Hippolyte Taine, from the sixties on, advocated the application of scientific methods to the understanding and interpretation of art; he saw no reason why aesthetics could not become as scientific as botany. In the last quarter of the century, the French philosopher and psychologist Paul Souriau[5] analyzed the aesthetics of movement in scientific terms and called for the replacement of all-inclusive metaphysical tomes on beauty by detailed scientific monographs on particular aesthetic topics. It was not long before the monographists had overtaken and passed the metaphysicians.

In England, where the ground for empirical aesthetics had been broken long before by Burke's *Enquiry*, Herbert Spencer, in the context of his ambitious "Synthetic Philosophy," gave an interpretation of art as the overflow in play of superfluous impulses which he thought accorded very well with his own, pre-Darwinian evolutionary theory.[6] Later, Alexander Bain, James Sully, and Grant Allen developed elaborate psychological and physiological approaches to aesthetics. Allen, following in the Spencerian tradition, defined the aesthetic impulse as "the subjective concomitant of the normal amount of activity, not directly connected with life-serving function, in the peripheral end-organs of the cerebro-spinal nervous system."[7] The beautiful was, in his view, "that which affords the maximum of stimulation with the minimum of fatigue and waste."[8] Before the end of the century, Vernon Lee and C. Anstruther-Thomson were attempting to solve aesthetic problems on the basis of the very latest theory of emotion formulated by the psychologists William James and Carl Lange. For a time it seemed as though no "advanced" thinker was any longer interested in "doing" aesthetics from a strictly metaphysical standpoint.

But it was in Germany, the spawning ground of aesthetic theories since the days of Baumgarten, that experimental aesthetics, under the aegis of the new science of psychology, received its strongest impetus and reached its highest development in the nineteenth century. The German psychologist Wilhelm Wundt, who opened the world's first psychological laboratory in Leipzig in 1879, was to some extent concerned with investigating aesthetic phenomena, but it was above all another German psychologist, Gustav Fechner, who provided the guiding hand as aesthetics turned from metaphysics to science, from the philosopher's study to the scientist's laboratory, from abstract conceptions of beauty to specific verifiable propositions about a certain type of highly pleasurable experience. Later, other German thinkers—Theodor Lipps, Karl Groos, and Max Dessoir—directed aesthetic inquiry along new paths,[9] sometimes more fruitful if less adventurous than those first explored by Fechner, but not before he had received international recognition as "the founder of experimental aesthetics" and had earned the right to be called "the Newton of aesthetics."

In this chapter, Taine, Fechner, Lee, and Dessoir have been chosen to represent the movement by which aesthetics turned to science in hope of discovering solutions to its problems. Although the solutions were not always found and the high expectations of experimental aesthetics had later to be modified, through the efforts of thinkers such as these aesthetics entered at last into "the age of science."

TAINE

The son of a rural French lawyer, Hippolyte Taine (1828–1893) went to Paris when he was seventeen to study at Bourbon College. Later he transferred to the École Normale, where as a student of philosophy he quickly distinguished himself for his remarkable intellect and his insatiable thirst for learning. Of the young Hippolyte one of his professors correctly predicted that his life-time motto would be Spinoza's "Live to think." Taine's own naturalistic philosophy was developed during these formative years; and it was as much influenced by his critical reading of Spinoza, Descartes, Condillac, and Hegel as by the scientific advances in medicine, biology, chemistry, and psychology being made during his century.[10] The history of his life after he received his doctorate in 1853 is mainly the history of his continuing intellectual labors, his publications and his ever widening influence. Among his major works were *The History of English Literature* (1863), *The Philosophy of Art* (1865–1869),[11] *On Intelligence* (1870), and *The Origins of Contemporary France* (1876–1893). He also found time to marry; to visit Italy, England, the Low Countries, and Germany; to teach—he was professor of aesthetics and history of art at the Ecole des Beaux-Arts in Paris when he delivered his famous lectures on the philosophy of art—and to associate with most of the great French literary figures of his day. The brilliance of his style, his amazing erudition, the simplicity and fecundity of his ideas, and his ability to embody in his criticism the scientific aspirations of his generation made Taine a literary institution during his lifetime and a source of never-ending influence after his death.

Taine's approach to art purports to be empirical, analytical, and mechanistic. He wants to establish his conclusions on experience; to analyze complex phenomena into their simple constitutive elements; and to explain the dynamic interaction of the parts of a whole. His ambition is to apply to works of art the methods which have already been used successfully by natural scientists to probe the mysteries of nature. Works of art, he believes, can be understood in terms of the simple causes acting in unison to produce complex effects. To divide in order to conquer, to analyze in order to comprehend—these are Taine's rules for the direction of his critical project. He believes that what is true of the origin of morality is also true of the origin of art: "Vice and virtue are products, like vitrol; and every complex phenomena has its springs from other more simple phenomena on which it hangs."[12]

The soil in which works of art grow are moral dispositions, Taine teaches, and moral dispositions themselves are the inevitable result of certain determining factors, namely, *race, milieu, moment*, and *faculté maîtresse* or master faculty. By *race*, he refers to "the innate and hereditary dispositions which man brings with him to the light, and which, as a rule, are united with the marked differences in the temperament and structure of the body";[13] by *milieu* he refers to the environment or "given surroundings," including the climatic conditions, political circumstances, and social conditions within which the work is created; by *moment* he means the time, the epoch, "the acquired momentum"; and by *faculté maîtresse* or master faculty, he refers to the dominant internal aptitude or disposition characteristic of a given artist, for example, imagination, sensibility, or sensuality. These forces acting in unison produce a moral disposition or combination of moral dispositions which are the direct causes of all human products from pots and pans to poetry. "The cause given," Taine believes, "they appear; the cause withdrawn, they vanish."[14] While Taine does not claim that we have as yet attained the same degree of exactness, the same ability to predict occurrences in the aesthetic sphere as we have in the sphere of nature—at present we must be content with approximations or "literary impressions"—he is absolutely convinced that the same determining laws govern all phenomena, be they material or spiritual.

But the method which Taine proposes to follow is far more in accord with the scientific spirit of his time than is his own application of it. He proceeds to give a definition of art which, he claims, corresponds with the "positive facts open to observation," i.e. "works of art arranged by families in galleries and libraries, like plants in an herbarium and animals in a museum,"[15] and which, he further claims, is the result of his having discovered "by numerous comparisons and progressive eliminations, traits common to all works of art"[16] and traits which distinguish these works from all other human productions. But there is nothing really new in the definition which Taine finally so proudly exhibits, for it is only a reformulation of the "imitation of essences" theory derived from Aristotle by English thinkers in the eighteenth century. The aim of art, according to this theory, is not exact or selective imitation of objects and beings, but rather the imitation of their essential or predominant characters.[17] The essential character of a lion, to give one of Taine's examples, is the lion's carnivorousness, from which all the beast's other affiliated qualities are derived.[18] The artist can make this essential character not just dominant, as it is in nature, but, by grasping and modifying relationships, predominant.[19] Like Aristotle, Taine holds that art can accomplish what nature attempts but fails to do. In fact, art was invented, he believes, precisely in order to make up for the deficiencies in nature's imperfect productions, for art can "manifest some essential, salient character, consequently some important idea, clearer and more completely than is attainable from real objects."[20]

In our selection from Taine, we shall present only his method rather than his application (or misapplication) of it.

The Empirical Method in Aesthetics

Taine considers his method to be empirical, open-minded, and exhaustive; it is, he believes, completely scientific. He proposes to start not with formulas of beauty, but with aesthetic facts in order to determine the nature of art. In the following introduction to his philosophy of art, he delineates three sociological spheres within which the work of art must be placed in order to be understood. Starting with the placement of the work in the context of its creator's other works, in its immediate family, so to speak, we must proceed outward until we see the work in its most inclusive sociological context, the cultural milieu within which it was created and the imprint of which it bears.

The basis of the method herein set forth consists in recognizing that a work of art is not an isolated production, and that it is necessary to study the conditions out of which it proceeds and by which it is explained.

The first step is not a difficult one. A work of art—a picture, a tragedy, or a statue—evidently belongs to a group *(ensemble)* composed of all the works of the artist producing it. This is an elementary step. It is well known that the different works of an artist bear a family likeness, like the children of one parent; that is to say, all possess marked resemblances. We know that every artist has his own style, a style recognizable throughout his productions. If he is a painter, he has his own coloring, rich or impoverished; his favorite conceptions, vulgar or refined; his attitudes and rules of composition, even processes of execution; his favorite pigments, tints, models, and manner of working. If he is a writer, he has his own characters, calm or passionate; his own plots, simple or complex; his own dénouements, comic or tragic, and even a special vocabulary. This is so true, that a connoisseur placed before an original work not signed by any prominent master, will be able to inform you with nearly absolute certainty by whom the work is executed, and, if sufficiently experienced and delicate in his perceptions, the period of the artist's life, and the particular stage of his development to which the work belongs.

Such is the first consideration necessary to bestow upon a work of art. And here is the second. The artist himself, considered in connection with his productions, is not isolated; he also belongs to a group *(ensemble)*, one greater than himself, comprising the school or family of artists of the time and country to which he belongs. For example, around Shakespeare, who, at the first glance, seems to be a marvelous celestial gift coming like an aerolite from heaven, we find several dramatists of high order—Webster, Ford, Massinger, Marlowe, Ben Jonson, Beaumont, and Fletcher—all of whom wrote in the same style and in the same spirit. There are the same characters in their dramas as in Shakespeare's, the same terrible types of passion, the same bloody unforeseen catastrophes, the same sudden and violent outbursts, the same irregular, capricious, overflowing, magnificent style, the same exquisite poetic feeling for rural life and landscape, and the same delicate, tender, affectionate ideals of woman. . . .

This being the second step, there now remains the third. This family of artists is itself comprehended in another group *(ensemble)*, yet more vast, which consists of the society around it, a society possessing tastes and sympathies conformable with its own. The social and intellectual condition of a community is the standard of that of artists; they do not live in it isolated men; we listen only to their voices beyond the gulf of ages, but, along with their sonorous tones vibrating in our ears, comes a low, deep reverberation, which is the grand, infinite, and united voice of the people singing in harmony with them. Artists have become great, solely through this accord. And it is well that it should be so. Phidias and Ictinus, the constructors of the Parthenon and of the Olympian Jupiter, were, like other Athenians, pagans and free citizens, brought up in the palaestra, exercising and wrestling naked, and accustomed to deliberate and vote in the public assemblies; possessing the same habits, the same interests, the same ideas, the same faith; men of the same race, the same education, the same language; so that in all the important acts of their life they recognized themselves as part of the multitude of which their audience was composed. . . .

Everywhere may be found similar examples of the alliance, the intimate harmony existing between an artist and his contemporaries; and we may rest assured, that if we desire to comprehend the taste or the genius of an artist, the reasons leading him to choose a particular style of painting or drama, to prefer this or that character or coloring, and to represent particular sentiments, we must seek for them in the social and intellectual conditions of the community in the midst of which he lived.

We have accordingly to state this law: that, in order to comprehend a work of art, an artist or a group of artists, we must clearly comprehend the general social and intellectual condition of the times to which they belong.[21] Herein is to be found the final explanation; herein resides the primitive cause determining all that follows it. This truth . . . is confirmed by experience. If we pass in review the principal epochs of the history of art, we find the arts appearing and disappearing along with certain accompanying social and intellectual conditions. For example, Greek tragedy, that of Aeschylus, Sophocles, and Euripides, appears at the time when the Greeks were victorious over the Persians; in the heroic era of small republican cities, when they conquered their independence and established their ascendency in the civilized world; and we see it disappearing along with this independence and this vigor, when a degeneracy of character and the Macedonian conquest delivered the Greeks over to strangers. . . .

Allow me to use a comparison, in order to impress more strongly on your minds the effect of an intellectual and social *milieu* on the Fine Arts. Suppose you are leaving the land of the south for that of the north; you perceive on entering a certain zone, a particular mode of cultivation and a particular species of plant; first come the aloe and the orange; a little later, the vine and the olive; after these, the oak and the chestnut; a little further on, oats and the pine, and finally, mosses and lichens. Each zone has its own mode of cultivation and peculiar vegetation; both begin at the commencement, and both finish at the end of the zone; both are attached to it. The zone is the condition of their existence; by its presence or its absence is determined what shall appear and what shall disappear. Now, what is this zone but a certain temperature; in other words, a certain degree of heat and moisture; in short, a certain number of governing circumstances analogous to what we have just entitled the general social, and intellectual state of a community? Just as there is a physical temperature, which by its variations determines the appearance of this or that species of plant, so is there a moral temperature, which by its variations determines the appearance of this or that species of art. And as we study the physical temperature in order to comprehend various species of plants, whether maize or oats, the orange or the pine, so it is necessary to study the moral temperature in order to comprehend the appearance of various phases of art, whether pagan sculpture or realistic painting, mystic architecture or classic literature, voluptuous music or ideal poetry. The productions of the human mind, like those of animated nature, can only be explained by their *milieu*. . . .

Ancient aesthetic systems put forth definitions of beauty, declaring, for instance, that the beautiful is the expression of the moral ideal, or the expression of the invisible, or, again, the expression of human passions; then starting from these, as if from the articles of a code, they absolved, condemned, admonished, and directed. . . . The modern method, which I strive to pursue, and which is beginning to be introduced in all moral sciences, consists in considering human productions, and particularly works of art, as facts and productions of which it is essential to mark the characteristics and seek the causes; and nothing beyond this. Thus understood, science neither pardons nor proscribes; she states facts and explains them. She does not say to you, despise Dutch art because it is vulgar, and confine yourself to Italian art; nor despise Gothic art because it is morbid, and confine yourself to Greek art. She leaves every one free to follow their own predilections, to prefer what is conformable to personal temperament, and to study attentively that which best corresponds to the development of one's own intellect. As to aesthetic science, she has sympathies for every form of art, and for every school—even for those the most opposed to each other. She accepts them as so many manifestations of human intelligence, judging that the more numerous they are, and the more contradictory, the more they display the new and numerous phases of man's genius. Aesthetic science is like botany, in which the orange, the laurel, the pine, and the birch, are of equal interest; it is a kind of botanical method, applied not to plants, but to the works of man. . . .

I wish to apply this method at once to the first and the principal question, meeting one at the threshold of a course on aesthetics, namely, a definition of art. What is art, and in what does its nature consist? Instead of dictating a formula, I shall appeal to you with facts, for facts exist here as elsewhere—positive facts open to observation; I mean *works* of *art* arranged by families in galleries and libraries, like plants in an herbarium, and animals in a museum. Analysis may be applied to one as well as to the other. It is as allowable to investigate a work of art as it is to investigate a plant or an animal. There is no more need of discarding experience in the first class than in the second; the entire process consists in discovering, by numerous comparisons and progressive eliminations, traits common to all works of art, and, at the same time, distinctive traits, by which works of art are separated from other productions of the human intellect.[22] . . .

FECHNER

A Lutheran pastor's son, Gustav Theodor Fechner (1801–1887) studied at the University of Leipzig, where he immersed himself in philosophical and scientific studies and completed a program in medicine. Instead of practicing medicine after his graduation in 1822, however, he became a lecturer on experimental physics. During the next eighteen years he gained some reputation through his experimental work on chemical, electrical, and color phenomena as well as through a series of satirical articles on medicine and natural philosophy which were published under the pseudonym of "Dr. Mises." A turning point in his life came in 1840 when he was stricken by a strange malady which for several years made him blind and mentally deranged. Fortunately, he eventually made a recovery, emerging from his illness feeling as though he had been born again. Now a physicist transformed into a philosopher, Fechner was determined to solve the fundamental problems of life and death. Although he returned to his teaching, research, and writing, and attained eventually world renown for his pioneering contributions to experimental psychology and aesthetics, his chief preoccupation for the rest of his life was with the formulation of a spiritualistic *Weltanschauung*, Panpsychism, which allowed him to explain satisfactorily for the first time the true relationship of mind and matter as two aspects of the same Cosmic Reality. Today he is remembered not so much for his abstruse metaphysical system, but mainly as an important contributor to experimental psychology and aesthetics, the author of *Elements of Psychophysics* (1861) and *Introduction to Aesthetics* (1876).[23]

Although Fechner's interest in art went back to his early youth, his experimental work in aesthetics was first stimulated by an attempt to determine the validity of Adolf Zeising's view that the golden section ratio was the basis of beauty in visual forms.[24] After initially raising some doubts as to Zeising's findings as they applied to specific works of art, Fechner undertook a series of experiments in which he had various observers express their preferences to a series of simple geometrical forms of varying dimensions, some of which were constructed according to the golden section ratio. Later he also allowed the subjects to adjust or construct figures in order to make them as aesthetically pleasing as possible. Finally, he examined the measurements of hundreds of existing objects—playing cards, calling cards, books, grave-crosses, picture frames, etc.—which might conceivably embody the proportions most pleasing to aesthetic contemplation. Through these procedures, Fechner was developing and applying three elementary methods of experimental aesthetics: the method of choice or selection, the method of adjustment or construction, and the method of application or use.

In his *Introduction to Aesthetics,* Fechner describes many of his experiments, interprets their outcome, and propagandizes for an empirical, hedonistic approach to aesthetics, an "aesthetics from below" which he hopes will eventually give a substantial inductive basis for the deductive approach, an "aesthetics from above." He also presents in this work a large number of aesthetic principles or laws which he has found necessary in explaining the pleasure felt in aesthetic experience. Six of these he holds to be especially important. According to the first law, the principle of aesthetic threshold, sensations must be intense enough to cross the level of aesthetic awareness before they can be fully perceived and appreciated. The second law, the principle of aesthetic assistance or intensification, draws attention to the fact that weak aesthetic effects which might have little significance working independently may, by coalescing, succeed in crossing the threshold of aesthetic consciousness and become aesthetically pleasing. The third law, the principle of the binding of the manifold into a unity, stresses the importance of composition, of the interrelatedness of various elements into a whole which can be aesthetically comprehended. According to the fourth and fifth laws, the organization of an object must be such that (a) it has a unanimity, a truthfulness, a lack of contradiction, and (b) it manifests itself to consciousness with clarity.[25]

The sixth law, the principle of aesthetic association, is Fechner's best known law, though it did not really originate with him.[26] According to this law, our aesthetic experience of an object depends not just on direct sensory stimulation but also on whatever associations we bring from memory to the experience of the particular object. Whatever we have heard, seen, read, thought, felt, or learned about the object, or objects like it, can affect our response to it. The nexus of associated memories is as directly related to the object as is its very name. Even shape and color are, so to speak, "visible colors." When we see a table, according to Fechner, we don't just see what literally presents itself to perception as a mere four-cornered phenomenon, but we "see" everything a table can be used for—sitting, eating, working, etc.

We see it not with a literal, but with a "spiritual eye," and our "vision" gives us one dominant unitary impression which is the thing's "spiritual color." The memory ingredients, that is to say, have been amalgamated into a single impression which can be changed, however, when a minute sensuous distinction brings about a different set of associations. An orange, a yellow bowling ball, a harvest moon, and a golden sphere may all appear to have the same shape and color to a perceiver, but they arouse quite different aesthetic responses due to their different associated meanings. One has only to think of the difference between a woman's response to a diamond she knows to be real and one which she knows to be a fake or a man's aesthetic response to a withered old woman who happens to be a beggar and a withered old woman who happens to be his mother, to see why Fechner holds the principle of association to be so crucial in aesthetic enjoyment.

Despite the rather primitive and elementary nature of the instruments Fechner used in his early investigations of aesthetic phenomena and despite the fact that in the constructive part of his system of aesthetics he often indulged himself in ungrounded "aesthetics from above," his efforts undoubtably marked the beginning of a new direction in modern aesthetics. The first chapter of his great *Vorschule der Aesthetik (Introduction to Aesthetics)*, from which our selections below are taken, is a kind of manifesto of modern scientific aesthetics.

Aesthetics "From Above" and "From Below"

Fechner begins his major work on aesthetics by distinguishing between two different but related approaches to the field. The first, "aesthetics from above," is rationalistic and deductive; the second, "aesthetics from below" is empirical and inductive. Although he does not think that the two approaches are mutually contradictory—to the contrary, they are mutually complementary—he thinks that each apart from the other has defects as well as merits. Furthermore, he holds that a satisfactory "aesthetics from above" has not yet been achieved, nor is it as present possible, although it has often been aimed at and missed, resulting in aesthetic systems which, because they lack an empirical basis, seem to him to be "giants with feet of clay." In order for a generally valid aesthetic system to be achieved, the whole aesthetic domain, with all of its particular fields, will have to be mastered and a coherent order imposed upon all of them. But Fechner sees no reason why a general philosophical aesthetics cannot some day exist. Just as an adequate philosophy of nature would be able to explain the assumptions and implications of the various natural sciences without affecting their empirical content, so would a general theory of aesthetics explain the basis of the various fields of empirical aesthetics without replacing them. Prerequisite to the establishment of an adequate "aesthetics from above," however, is a great deal more progress in creating an "aesthetics from below." Fechner claims that since the way "from above" is so unclear at present, he himself will be content to follow strictly the way "from below," hoping, as he proceeds, to contribute his "little splinter of knowledge" toward the eventual construction of a general aesthetics.

The dual way in which human knowledge tries to find a basis and to develop itself is applicable also in aesthetics, the theory of pleasure and displeasure or, as others call it, the theory of beauty. To put it briefly, aesthetics is approached either *from above*, in that one goes from the most general ideas and concepts to the specific, and *from below*, in that one goes from the specific to the general. In the first case, one merely divides and subdivides the domain of aesthetic experience according to an ideally constructed framework seen from above; in the second case, one constructs the whole of aesthetics from the ground up on the basis of aesthetical facts and laws. In the former, aesthetics is first and foremost a matter of ideas and concepts of beauty, art, and style, and of their position in the system of the most general concepts, especially their relation to the True and the Good; and thus one rises easily as far as the Absolute, the Divine, the Divine Ideas, and the Divine Creativity. From the pure heights of such generalities one then descends into the earthly empirical region—of the specific, temporal, and spatial beauty—and measures all particulars according to the yardstick of the general. In the latter, one starts out from experiences of what pleases and displeases, basing on these experiences all the concepts and laws

which must have a place in aesthetics, and then tries to generalize
them more and more with reference to the general laws of what
ought to be *(Sollens)* to which the laws of pleasure must always
remain subordinate, and thus to arrive at a system comprising the
most general possible concepts and laws.

The two ways can also be differentiated as the philosophical
and the empirical way. In themselves they do not contradict each
other in so far as a correct and complete knowledge of the
highest principles of being, of divine and human things, must
also include the principles of a correct consideration of aesthetic
relationships, and, on the other hand, must include a correct
generalization of the empirical facts and laws of the aesthetic
domain. Both ways traverse the same territory, but in opposite
directions, and everywhere the possibility of motion in one direction is completed through motion in the opposite direction.
Both ways, however, have their special advantages, difficulties,
and dangers.

The first way puts us, so to speak, right from the start at the
goal toward which we would be only striving if we were using
the second way. We do perceive from that point the most
general view, the highest perspectives, but in this way one does
not come very readily to a clear orientation about the bases of
pleasure and displeasure in the particular, which after all must
also be our concern. We never get beyond vaguely defined
concepts, which in their generality do not make the particular
stand out very clearly. In order for this way to guide us correctly
we must moreover presuppose a correct point of departure, which
basically we could find only in a completely philosophical or
even theological system, neither of which we possess as yet. We
have only many attempts at such systems, and also many attempts
to put aesthetics into relation with them, all of which so far leave
much to be desired in satisfying our need of the most general
and highest viewpoints. But even though they do not completely
satisfy this need, they still at least keep it active and alive. These
disadvantages and advantages have also been evident more or less
in all of the numerous presentations of aesthetics and ways of
dealing with aesthetical questions which, stemming from Schelling,
Hegel, and even Kant, have up until now taken the direction
from above.

On the other hand, the second way, the way from below,
perceives or promises, at least initially, a clear orientation not

only in the domain of the concepts which govern the domain of pleasure and displeasure but also about the principles governing pleasure and displeasure in the particular and matters related thereto. But by this way one does not, however, come very readily to the most general viewpoints and ideas; one remains easily deluded in particularity, onesidedness, viewpoints of secondary range and importance, as we see especially in the Englishmen such as Hutcheson, Hogarth, Burke, Hay, and others, who have preferred to take the way from below.

According to the preceding, the attempts which have since been made in the treatment of aesthetics in the first manner will satisfy more the one whose main interest lies in the disposition of things under the most general concepts or ideas and who finds satisfaction in some kind of organization of these without placing excessive demands on their clarity and matter-of-factness; whereas an attempt to treat aesthetics in the second manner is more apt to satisfy the one who values above all an easy and clear orientation towards what is nearest at hand and who, for his part, does not demand a higher level and generality than that which has been achieved. In general, we can say that from the start higher claims are made for aesthetics from above, but aesthetics from below satisfies more easily the smaller claims made for it. . . .

One can raise the question whether the merits and advantages of both ways cannot be unified through illuminating the way from below with ideas from above or by directing it to principles from above. This certainly sounds fine, and it is true that recently the way from below has repeatedly been followed and the way from above even understood in this manner. Now the most general formal principles of the thought and investigation involved in aesthetics from below as well as from above will remain those common to all domains of research; but in other respects, here it might be the same with aesthetics as with physics, which has been confused and misled by every light through which natural philosophy has tried to clarify and lead it. He who first of all seeks light—and the way from below is a way of seeking it—cannot wish to illuminate this way with an already existing light.

The essential tasks of a general aesthetics can be summed up, in my opinion, as follows: a clarification of the concepts to which the aesthetical facts and relationships are subordinate and a definition of the laws—laws of which the precepts of art contain the most important applications—which govern these facts and relationships. Treatments of aesthetics from above, however, have rather envisaged only the first task, in that they have tried to replace rather than to complete the explanation of aesthetic facts through laws by an explanation through concepts or ideas.

Indeed, if one looks at most of our textbooks and general treatises on aesthetics—and most of them follow the way from above—one will find that the main content of their presentations consists of arguments and disputes about the correct definition of beauty, the sublime, ugliness, the pleasant or agreeable, the graceful, the comic, the tragic, the ridiculous, humor, style, manner, art, beauty of art and beauty of nature, subdivisions of the particulars under these concepts, and classifications of the total aesthetic domain from the viewpoint of these. But there is more to the task of aesthetics than just this, for in everything that concerns us aesthetically the question will not just be under which concepts does it belong and where does it stand in the system of our concepts, even though one does have to ask these things since they are necessary to a clear orientation in our domain of knowledge. The most crucial question, however, will always remain the following: Why does something please or displease, and to what extent does it rightly please or displease? This question can only be answered by means of the laws of pleasure and displeasure and with the aid of the laws of what ought to be; just as the question why a body moves in a certain way or to what point we have to move it can only be answered not with the concept and classification of the various ways of motion but only with laws of motion and consideration of the ends to be reached. And as long as the conceptual explanations of aesthetics can not be given through an explanation by laws they will remain a hollow framework.[27] . . .

VERNON LEE

Violet Paget (1856–1935), who is known by her pseudonym "Vernon Lee," was born in France of English parents and spent her formative years traveling on the Continent and receiving her education from a series of governesses.[28] A precocious but rather ugly girl, Violet early decided upon a literary career which she began at the age of fourteen with a literary piece in an Italian newspaper. In the early eighteen-seventies she settled with her parents and invalid half-brother in Florence where she resided—except for several extended visits to England—for the rest of her life. She first won recognition as an author with her *Eighteenth Century Studies* (1880), a work which revealed her intimate knowledge of that period of Italian culture. Later, she wrote a novel satirizing aestheticism, *Miss Brown* (1884), and in the years that followed she produced a large number of critical studies, essays, philosophical dialogues, novels, and short stories. The work which first brought her fame as an aesthetician was an article, "Beauty and Ugliness" (1897),[29] on which she had collaborated with her "very dear friend," Clementina Anstruther-Thomson, the "C.A.T." so often referred to in her later writings.[30] Aside from her continuing interest in aesthetics and literature, Vernon Lee was also very much interested in social problems. During the First World War, while she was living in England, she was, like Bertrand Russell at the time, an ardent pacifist and an outspoken critic of international affairs. After the war, she returned to her beloved villa in Florence, where she quietly continued her writing. Of her later works on aesthetics, the most important were *Laurus Nobilis* (1909), *Beauty and Ugliness* (1912), *The Beautiful* (1913), *The Handling of Words* (1923),[31] and *Music and Its Lovers* (1932).[32] In 1924, she was pleased to accept an honorary degree of Doctor of Letters from the University of Durham in England. Among her many friends were Walter Pater, Henry James (whom she offended by satirizing in a novel), Bernard Berenson (who accused her and "C.A.T." of plagiarizing from him),[33] H. G. Wells (whose extra-marital relations she condemned), Desmond MacCarthy, and John Singer Sargent (who painted portraits of her and "C.A.T."). But even with her many friends, her wealth, and her fame, Vernon Lee, as an aged spinster, never felt fulfilled as a woman or satisfied with her reception as an aesthetician. She was a highly complex, lonely individual for whom keenness of intellect, brilliance of style, and enthusiasm of spirit were compensations for what life never brought her, complete personal fulfillment. At the age of seventy-eight she died of a heart condition in Florence.

Vernon Lee's aesthetic views evolved as her experience with art and life expanded and as she came under the influence of new knowledge and strong personalities. Prior to meeting Clementina Anstruther-Thomson in 1887, her aesthetic views seem to reflect the influence of her friend, the critic Walter Pater.[34] The power of beauty, in her early aesthetics, lies in its capacity to make one live more fully and intensely. She considers the beautiful object to have value because it can impose upon feelings an order, a rhythm, and a harmony intrinsically satisfying.[35] Then, in the late eighteen-eighties, when she became acquainted with Miss Anstruther-Thomson, who seemed to her to be one of the most sensitive and responsive aesthetic perceivers who ever lived, Vernon Lee's interests in aesthetic experience became more empirical and scientific as she attempted to fathom the psychological processes involved in the apprehension and appreciation of form. Assisted by Miss Anstruther-Thomson's highly developed intuition, she began to explore the "mimetic connection" between perception of form and motion, and after exhaustive and exhausting investigation—"C.A.T." had a nervous breakdown as a result— she reached the conclusion that "it is we, the beholders, who, so to speak, *make form exist* in ourselves by alternation of our respiratory and equilibratory processes, and by imitated movements of various parts of the body." [36]

Not long after the publication of "Beauty and Ugliness," coauthored with Miss Anstruther-Thomson, Vernon Lee became acquainted with the writings of other thinkers who had been investigating aesthetic phenomena from a purely psychological standpoint and who had reached conclusions quite similar to hers and "C.A.T.'s." Particularly relevant were the works of the German psychologist Theodor Lipps,[37] in which the theory of *Einfühlung* ("feeling into") or empathy was fully set forth. Lipps conceived empathy to be basically "the inward side of imitation." Objects were enjoyed aesthetically when individuals objectified their own egoes in the objects. He held that aesthetic pleasure was only "objectified self-enjoyment" which is "dependent upon the attribution of life, of soul" to an object. Having profited from Lipps' profound and extensive psychological investigations, which confirmed and clarified her own views, Vernon Lee revised her theory and discarded its previous psychological basis, the James-Lange theory of emotions.[38] In her revisions, she also took into account the work of another German psychologist, Karl

Groos,[39] who had interpreted empathy as a sort of "inner mimicry" or "aesthetic sympathy" and who had discussed the "motor phenomena of an imitative character" which, he believed, accompany aesthetic enjoyment in some individuals, characterized as "motor types" (e.g. Miss Anstruther-Thomson).

Vernon Lee, the former proponent of Paterian aesthetics, had now become an enthusiastic proponent of what she called "a new science of aesthetics,"[40] an aesthetics which she believed to be founded on empirical observation, reliant on scientific method, and capable of empirical verification. Although she realized that in her day this science was still only in its formative stage, she was convinced that its central discovery, the discovery of empathy, had already been made and that it was only a matter of time before the major problems of aesthetics would finally be solved. She looked forward to that day when, at long last, a reconciliation of art and life would be achieved.

In her later explanations of empathy,[41] Vernon Lee points out what she now considers to be misinterpretations of the phenomenon of empathy and warns against oversimplifying the complexities involved in the empathic process. Because in German "*sich einfühlen*" means "to feel *oneself* into," it is easy to make the mistake of holding that empathy somehow involves a projection of the ego of the observer into what is experienced. But in an empathic experience, she contends, we are not conscious of an ego projecting itself into an object; rather we are conscious of the object itself which appears to have the dynamic attributes projected into it. The mountain, not we, appears to do the rising. Furthermore, she insists, empathy should not be confused with sympathy or with an inner "feeling with" an object. To empathize is not to mimic inwardly, although such mimicry may occur as a result of empathy. When we say "the mountain rises" the action of rising is thought of because we have to raise our head, direct our glance upward, and bend our neck to "take in" the shape of the mountain, but as we do so, we forget about our actions despite the fact that we could never without them experience the shape before us and attribute the rising to it. We tend to merge our activities with the qualities of the object we perceive. But to do this involves more than the mere attribution of our immediate activities to the particular object before us. What Fechner called "the principle of aesthetic association" complicates and enrichens our empathic experiences.[42] For in experiencing the rising of a particular mountain, all our past experiences of activities involving and related to rising, as well as thoughts of future such activities, form a "general idea of rising" or of "upward movement" which enters into our present experience. Thus, according to Vernon Lee, a great deal more than seeing or hearing is involved in animating the inanimate, in investing with life the inert, in experiencing empathy.

Aesthetics and Empathy

1. *Vernon Lee believes that during the latter part of the nineteenth century a "new science of aesthetics," empirical and pluralistic in its methods, had been gradually developing through important but so far uncorrelated studies made by psychologists, biologists, anthropologists, connoisseurs, and others. The new science is, she admits, still in its rudimentary stages, but its boundaries can now be roughly fixed, its progress assessed, and its further tasks set. She thinks that a great deal of confusion can be avoided if first of all the artistic sphere and the aesthetic sphere are clearly defined and kept separate. She proposes that the word "aesthetic" be used henceforth to refer only to "that which has to do with the beautiful" (or with the ugly) and "artistic" to refer to "that which has to do with art." This does not mean that the two spheres are unrelated; indeed, a full exploration of the aesthetic sphere, the sphere of the beautiful, will reveal, she believes, the very sources of artistic creation and appreciation. The psychological aesthetician seeks to discover "the facts of consciousness" and to understand the physiological processes which account for, or at least accompany, our experience of the forms considered beautiful or ugly. To do this, it is necessary, she thinks, to keep in mind that there is often a marked difference between our response to the form seen and to the object (or subject) suggested by it, between, that is, our really seeing it and our merely recognizing it. The aesthetic seeing of form is not an immediate and passive experience; it involves a certain kind of activity on our part, a projection of our own experiences and activities into it. Since aesthetics has recently discovered and begun to explore this phenomenon of Einfühlung ("feeling into") or empathy, a new, scientific, and "anthropomorphic aesthetics" has at last been made possible.*

One of the most valuable negative results of modern aesthetics—a result to which the various students, connoisseurs, archeologists, historians, psychologists have cooperated without fully appreciating its importance—is the distinction between the qualities of a visible figure, pattern, or, more summarily, "form," and the qualities suggested by the identification of this form as representing a given object. For each of these sets of qualities can affect us independently, even sometimes contradictorily; and the manner of perceiving them is not similar. Thus it is possible that a given form, that is, a given arrangement of lines, planes, and colours, may affect us as being what we call ugly, although the object represented, that is, the thing which we are made to think of, affects us as being what we call beautiful.

Take, for instance, certain painted or carved garlands: they give us the pleasure of thinking of the beauty, freshness, sweetness, etc., of flowers and the pleasantness of concomitant circumstances; yet they give us, at the same time, the displeasure of their broken lines and irregular bulgings, of confusion and lack of harmony; the flowers suggested were delightful, but the pattern suggesting them was wretched. Or take a portrait, say by Van Eyck or Rembrandt. It may strike us as ugly when we recognise it as the face of a human being, and endow it with its associated peculiarities of disagreeable texture, poor health, and bad temper or sensuality. But it may at the same time strike us as beautiful if we attend to its intrinsic peculiarities as a visible form, the manner in which it fills up space, the movement of lines and surfaces, the total harmony of its appearance.

This difference between the thing seen and the thing suggested explains why crowds will be interested by pictures which lovers of art reject utterly; and why, on the other hand, aesthetic persons will be fascinated by patterns on stuffs and shapes of utensils which the man bent on practical or literary interest passes by without a glance; and, similarly, why so many "works of art," illustrations to books or portraits for instance, will be thrown aside as eyesores after a moment's keen interest; whereas quite unobstrusive things, barely commented on at first, a cornice, a chair, a table, a pot, may work their way into our affections and cause positive distress by their defacement.

This difference between what is commonly designated as form and subject (though it were clearer to say "form and object") corresponds with that between seeing and recognizing. When a sportsman sees a hare previous to firing at it, he does not, he cannot, see the whole shape of the animal; but he notices, he detects, some peculiarity which, given the surroundings, suggests the notion of a hare. Neither more nor less than the notion of a hare, that is to say, a synthesis of various qualities, is suggested to his dog by a certain scent. What are wrongly called optical delusions, by which we misjudge sizes, directions, and shapes, and occasionally take one thing for another, a flat surface for a bossy one, smoke for water, a bush for a man, are a proof that the supposed act of seeing is, nine times out of ten, the mental construction of an object upon one or two visual indications.

This abbreviated way of seeing is usual whenever we have to decide what a fact of sight probably represents in order to adapt our action or to pass on to some other similar interpretation; it is the way of seeing characterising either rapid change in the world around us or rapid shifting of our attention. But the thorough and, so to say, *real seeing,* the perception of the visible form in its detail and its whole, takes place whenever we are brought long or frequently before the same external things, and have occasion to grow familiar with their aspect: it is in this manner that we see the rooms we inhabit, the country we live in, the clothes we wear, the tools we handle, the persons we take interest in; the characteristic of this seeing, as distinguished from recognising, being the survival, in our memory, of an image, more or less vivid, of that thing's visible presence. Therefore, as already hinted, we may tolerate ugliness when we merely recognise, that is, detect a characteristic and follow a train of suggestion; but we demand beauty whenever our attention recurs to a form, lingers on its details, or is confronted steadily with its image in memory. And conversely, we avoid and forget the ugly facts of reality, while we seek to see once more, or to remember, all sights which have affected us as being beautiful. And whereas, of course, attractiveness of suggestion is the extrinsic quality of works of art, and the quality liable to change and to wearing out; their enduring fascination, their intrinsic merit, consists in the attractiveness, which we call beauty, of their form.

Now, the thorough seeing of form, the dwelling of our attention upon its intrinsic peculiarities, the realisation, in fact, of form as such, implies upon our part a special activity which, according to the case, is accompanied by satisfaction or dissatisfaction. This special activity is the interpretation of form according to the facts of our own inner experience, the attribution to form of modes of being, moving, and feeling similar to our own; and this projection of our own life into what we see is pleasant or unpleasant because it facilitates or hampers our own vitality.

The discovery of this projection of our inner experience into the forms which we see and realise is the central discovery of modern aesthetics.[43] . . .

2. *The discovery of the phenomenon of empathy, Vernon Lee holds, is the central truth of the new science of aesthetics. She realizes, however, that no one person can be credited with its discovery. Poets such as Wordsworth and Coleridge had recognized its existence, critics (e.g. Lord Kames) had taken notice of it, and certain German philosophers—Lotze and Vischer—had actually discussed it earlier in the nineteenth century. But no one before the German psychologist, Theodor Lipps—"a new Darwin" to Vernon Lee—had set forth the theory of empathy so clearly, fully, and convincingly. Lipps and Karl Groos in Germany had been studying the phenomenon of empathy at the same time as Vernon Lee and C. Anstruther-Thomson were studying it in England, although without any knowledge of the others' work. In the following selection, Vernon Lee sets forth her theory as she and C. Anstruther-Thomson originally formulated it upon the basis of the James–Lange theory of emotion. She afterwards restates it so that it takes into account Lipps' and Groos' contributions as well as her own further investigations.*

In an essay on *Beauty and Ugliness*, published in the *Contemporary Review* (October–November, 1897), the aesthetic seeing, the "realisation," of form, was connected by C. Anstruther-Thomson and the present writer with bodily conditions and motor phenomena of a most complex and important kind. It was claimed by one of these writers that a long course of special training had magnified not only her powers of self-observation, but also most probably the normally minute, nay, so to speak, microscopic and imperceptible bodily sensations accompanying the action of eye and attention in the realisation of visible form. Among these habitually disregarded or completely fused sensations there could be distinguished, with certain individuals at least, not merely the "muscular strains," already noticed by Lotze and Fechner, and the vaguer organic perturbations referred to by Groos, but definite "sensations of direction" (tensions corresponding to *up*, *down*, *through*, *alongside*, similar to those remarked upon by William James in his *Psychology*) and sensations of modification in the highly subtle apparatus for equilibrium; and finally, sensations of altered respiration and circulation sufficient to account for massive conditions of organic well-being and the reverse.

These observations, whether they deal with mere individual idiosyncrasy, with peculiarities (as Professor Groos suggests) of the "motor type," [44] or whether they prove of more general character, were welded into a theory of aesthetic pleasure and pain by the perhaps hasty acceptance of what is known in recent psychology as the "Lange–James Hypothesis." [45] Professors Lange and William James had, it should be explained, independently of one another, suggested that the conditions of bodily change, e.g. the reddening and shrinking of shame, the constriction, turning cold and white, the semi-paralysis of fear, which had hitherto been accepted as after-effects of various emotions, were, on the contrary, the contents of that "feeling"; in fact, constituted, together with the idea of the feeling's objective cause, the whole of that feeling, say of shame or of fear. By an obvious analogy, the feeling of the various muscular strains, changes of equilibrium and respiratory and circulatory changes, might be considered as constituting the special aesthetic emotion, varying with every form contemplated, and agreeable or disagreeable according as these changes were or were not favourable to life as a whole. The hypothesis advanced in the *Contemporary Review* sinned first by building upon the Lange–James theory, of which itself would be one of the strongest proofs; and secondly, by misapprehending the still most difficult problem whether pleasure and pain are separate emotions or merely modalities of all emotion. But, despite these and many other faults, the essay on *Beauty and Ugliness* has an undeniable importance—that of originating not in psychological speculations, but in study of the individual work of art and its individual effects; and thereby attacking the central problem of aesthetics, and arriving at the fact of *Einfühlung* or *Empathy* from sides other than those whence Lipps, Groos and their followers have started.

If the authors of that essay were to restate their views after study of contemporary German aestheticians, and after additional observation and meditation on their own part, the result might be summed up, and the theory of *Einfühlung* (or *Empathy*) rounded off as follows: All visual perception is accompanied by interpretation of the seen shapes in terms of previous experience. When attention shifts rapidly for the sake of practical adaptation or expression, the shape is seen in the most summary and partial manner, barely sufficient to awaken the idea of peculiarities which may be associated with it, as texture, weight, temperature, position, smell, taste, use, etc., and to initiate, in most cases, some series of movements by which we adapt ourselves to these peculiarities. This process is that of recognizing, naming; and it becomes an ever-shortened and more automatic act of guessing from a minimum of data at the real nature of the seen object and at our proper reactions towards its presence. Such is visual perception considered as recognition. But when, instead of such perfunctory shifting, the attention deals long or frequently (in actual present fact or in memory) with any visible shape, there sets in another kind of interpretation; and other data of experience become fused with those of sight. There come to be attributed to that shape not objective qualities with which it has previously been found accompanied, but modes of activity of our own evoked in the realisation of the relations of that shape's constituent elements; and, instead of adjusting into movements destined to react upon the seen object, our motor activities rehearse the tensions, pressures, thrusts, resistances, efforts, and volition, in fact, the life, with its accompanying emotions, which we project into the form and attribute to it. . . .

After thus analyzing the presumable nature of the aesthetic phenomenon, it is perhaps well to remind the reader that, by the very constitution thereof, such analytical knowledge of it is normally denied us during its duration. For, in the first place, the dynamic conditions generated by constant repetition, and therefore bearing no sort of "local signs," are, by the act of *Empathy (Einfühlung)* projected out of ourselves and attributed to the seen shapes, much in the same way as changes in the eye and optic nerve are not localized in them, but projected, as the attribute colour, into the objects originally producing them. And, in the second place, the accompanying organic changes are also divested of definite "local signs," and fused into a complex emotional quality (well-being, *malaise*, high or low spirits) which must be disintegrated before its components can be picked out. Hence, whatever the processes into which the aesthetic phenomenon be analyzed by methods of special introspection or reasoning, the phenomenon as such remains a dualism expressible only as follows: "This form is beautiful"; and "I like seeing this form." Moreover, as both Professor Lipps and the authors of the essay on *Beauty and Ugliness* insist, the aesthetic phenomenon is individual and varies with every single individual form; and, since it consists in the attribution of an individual and varying complexus of dynamic (and perhaps organic) conditions, it must always, in real experience, bear the character of the individual form by which it is elicited. There is, in reality, no such thing as "the Beautiful." There are only separate and different beautiful forms.[46]

DESSOIR

Max Dessoir (1867–1947) was born in Berlin and was educated at the University of Berlin, where he received a Ph.D. in 1889, and at the University of Würzberg, where he received an M.D. three years later. From 1897 until 1933 he was professor of philosophy at the University of Berlin. Along with his philosophical investigations, he pursued research in psychology, parapsychology, and history of art. His major work, *Aesthetics and the General Science of Art,* appeared in 1906,[47] the year in which he also founded a journal with the same name. A few years later, as a result of his continuous efforts and his contagious enthusiasm, a Society for Aesthetics and General Science of Art was founded under his leadership. From then on, until the Nazis curtailed his activities, Dessoir was the guiding figure in German aesthetics and art criticism, stimulating and directing research on problems relating to art, organizing congresses on aesthetics—the first international congress on aesthetics was held under his direction in Berlin in 1913—and writing books and articles. During the Hitler regime, Dessoir, a Jew, was removed from his post as editor of his beloved journal and was not allowed to attend the Second International Congress on Aesthetics held in Paris in 1937. He managed to survive the Nazi debacle, however, and lived on to rejoice in the news, which he received after the war ended, that aesthetics had, in the meantime, found a new home in America where a journal and a society not unlike his own had been founded. Today Dessoir

is gratefully remembered by scholars here and abroad for his penetrating critical intellect, his broad and deep interest in art, and
for his service in organizing and promoting the cause of aesthetics
and science of art for several decades.[48]

Two of the characteristic features of Dessoir's approach to
aesthetics are his keenly critical but relatively unbiased appraisal
of competing aesthetic theories and his nondogmatic presentation
of his own tentative conclusions. After critically weighing the
defects and merits of various theories, objectivist and subjectivist,
he holds that while each one may be relatively justified, no one
is justifiable absolutely. To believe in an "all-explaining formula"
is to be deluded. The aesthetician should explore the richness of
the reality of art and not be led astray by a search for a general
formula which by explaining everything really explains nothing.[49]
To be systematic and methodical in his approach, the aesthetician
does not have to adhere to some absolutist system or rely solely
on a single method in studying artistic phenomena. "System and
method signify for us: to be free from *one* system and *one*
method."[50] The aesthetician must always be on his guard against
"aestheticizing" or "historicizing" art; for to do either is to anes-
thetize its living spirit.

Both the historical and the theoretical approach are useful,
Dessoir believes, in the study of art.[51] But while both approaches
are of value, neither should lose sight of the original character of
art. An approach to art, such as Taine's, which attempts to explain
art primarily in sociological terms usually overlooks the important
formal or structural features of works of art without which they
would be nonexistent. A history of art is, after all, a "biography
of a historical subject," namely Art, which man has consciously
and freely created. The historian of art should always keep in
mind that, having been created through intelligence, art forms
develop according to their own "inner logic" according to which
they solve their problems and attain their ends. When the historian
sees art as an expression of an epoch, or of a race or of a milieu, he
inevitably distorts and damages the reality and vitality of art.

The opposite approach, which is systematic and theoretical, also
has liabilities as well as assets. Although the Hegelian method with
its all-encompassing Absolute Idea is no longer popular, some
theorists tend to universalize theoretic conceptions useful in one
field and to extend them to the field of art. However, the

methodology and principles valid for the natural sciences have not proven to be valid and valuable for the cultural sciences, nor have the methodology and principles of either of these two types of sciences proven to be applicable or sufficient in explaining art. The theorist of art, as easily as the historian, can overlook the uniqueness of art.

In discussing the uniqueness of art, Dessoir, like Véron, calls attention to the importance of personality to the creation and contemplation of works of art. But even though a specific work seems to be permeated by the unique personality of the artist, Dessoir believes, contrary to Véron, that we must be able to separate the work from its creator if we are to understand its objective characteristics. For only by doing this can we relate it to other works of the same artist, to works by other artists of the same period or of the same school, and to other works of the same type. Art history itself would be impossible otherwise. Still, we should not forget that we cannot and should not eliminate completely the "living experience" which the work of art expresses; the subjective content, "the core of personality," evident in the work of art must always be respected and appreciated. Not only can we grasp and analyze the objective characteristics of a work of art, but we can also feel through it the living genius of its creator.

In understanding art more fully, Dessoir believes, then, that neither "theoretical constructions" nor "historical data" can be neglected. One of the major tasks of the General Science of Art is to discover the "system of relations" which will give a logical coherence to the historical data available, thereby harmonizing and strengthening the theoretical and the historical approaches. Just as the history of art imposes certain limits on the theory of art by providing it with facts without which it would be empty, so does the theory of art impose limits on art history by providing it with the unifying conceptions without which it would be blind.

Although Dessoir is no proponent of "art for art's sake," he continually urges that the autonomy of art—its original, unique character—be recognized and respected. In an individual work of art the specific content is of paramount importance because that is what is given form. Form and content, like body and soul, are essentially different, yet interdependent. The appreciation of a work of art is not a process which involves the mere passive enjoyment of a complex stimulus, pleasurable though it may be;

rather it involves an effort, an active involvement on the part of the spectator or auditor. He must learn to speak its language—a language of gestures, tones, words, forms, and images—before he can grasp its structure and feel its texture. Dessoir is strongly opposed to what he calls "aesthetic narcissism;" art can never be understood by those who look at a work as they would look into a mirror, projecting onto it their own dreams and fantasies. The work of art must be allowed to be itself—namely, an object which demands of us an acceptance, a participation, and even a self-transcendence in order to be understood and conquered.[52]

Aesthetics and the General Science of Art

1. *Dessoir begins his discussion of the fundamental questions of contemporary aesthetics by raising objections to the traditional unitary approach to aesthetic problems which has depended upon a supposed identity of the spheres of beauty, art, and aesthetic value. Nature as well as art can be beautiful, and beauty itself is not the only aim of art. Moreover, art cannot be understood fully without going beyond the aesthetic sphere to consider art's place in the whole cultural life. In light of these and other considerations, Dessoir thinks it is wise not to try to keep the various spheres united, but to clearly differentiate them so that both the discipline of aesthetics and the General Science of Art, which is far wider in its scope than aesthetics, can perform their separate but interrelated functions in attaining reliable knowledge.*

In the development which our science has undergone, from its inception up to the present day, one thought has held central place—that aesthetic enjoyment and production, beauty and art, are inseparably allied. The subject-matter of this science is held to be, though varied, of a unitary character. Art is considered as the representation of the beautiful, which comes to pass out of an aesthetic state or condition, and is experienced in a similar attitude; the science which deals with art in its varieties is, inasmuch as it constitutes a unity, designated by the single name of aesthetics.

The critical thought of the present day is, however, beginning to question whether the beautiful, the aesthetic, and art stand to one another in a relation that can be termed almost an identity. The undivided sway of the beautiful has already been assailed. Since art includes the tragic and the comic, the graceful and the sublime, and even the ugly, and since aesthetic pleasure can attach itself to all these categories, it is clear that by "the beautiful" something narrower must be meant than the artistically and aesthetically valuable. Yet beauty might still constitute the end and aim and central point of art, and it might be that the other categories but denote the way to beauty—beauty in a state of becoming, as it were.

But even this view, which sees in beauty the real content of art, and the central object of aesthetic experiences, is open to serious question. It is confronted with the fact, above all, that the beauty enjoyed in life and that enjoyed in art are not the same. The artist's copy of the beauty of nature takes on a quite new character. Solid objects in space become in painting flat pictures, the existent is in poetry transformed into matter of speech; and in every realm is a like metamorphosis. The subjective impression might indeed be supposed to remain the same, in spite of objective differentiations. But even that is not the case. Living human beauty—an acknowledged passport for its possessor—speaks to all our senses; it often stirs sex-feeling in however delicate and scarce conscious a way; it involuntarily influences our actions. On the other hand, there hangs about the marble statue of a naked human being an atmosphere of coolness in which we do not consider whether we are looking upon man or woman: even the most beauteous body is enjoyed as sexless shape, like the beauty of a landscape or a melody. To the aesthetic impression of the forest belongs its aromatic fragrance, to the impression of tropical vegetation its glowing heat, while from the enjoyment of art the sensations of the lower senses are barred. In return for what is lost, as it were, art-enjoyment involves pleasure in the personality of the artist, and in his power to overcome difficulties, and in the same way many other elements of pleasure, which are never produced by natural beauty. Accordingly, what we call beautiful in art must be distinguished from what goes by that name in life, both as regards the object and the subjective impression.

Another point, too, appears from our examples. Assuming that we may call the pure, pleasurable contemplation of actual things and events aesthetic—and what reason against it could be adduced from common usage?—it is thus clear that the circle of the aesthetic is wider than the field of art. Our admiring and adoring self-abandonment to nature-beauties bears all the marks of the aesthetic attitude, and needs for all that no connection with art. Further: in all intellectual and social spheres a part of the productive energy expresses itself in aesthetic forms; these products, which are not works of art, are yet aesthetically enjoyed. As numberless facts of daily experience show us that taste can develop and become effective independently of art, we must then concede to the sphere of the aesthetic a wider circumference than that of art.

This is not to maintain that the circle of art is a narrow section of a large field. On the contrary, the aesthetic principle does not by any means exhaust the content and purpose of that realm of human production which taken together we call "art." Every true work of art is extraordinarily complex in its motives and its effects; it arises not alone from the free play of aesthetic impulse, and aims at more than pure beauty—at more than aesthetic pleasure. The desires and energies in which art is grounded are in no way fulfilled by the serene satisfaction which is the traditional criterion of the aesthetic impression, as of the aesthetic object. In reality the arts have a function in intellectual and social life, through which they are closely bound up with all our knowing and willing.

It is, therefore, the duty of a general science of art to take account of the broad facts of art in all its relations. Aesthetics is not capable of this task, if it is to have a determined, self-complete, and clearly bounded content. We may no longer obliterate the differences between the two disciplines, but must rather so sharply separate them by ever finer distinctions that the really existent connections become clear. The first step thereto has been taken by Hugo Spitzer.[53] The relation of earlier to current views is comparable to that between materialism and positivism. While materialism ventured on a pretty crude resolution of the spiritual into the corporeal, positivism set up a hierarchy of forces of nature, whose order was determined by the relation of dependence. Thus mechanical forces, physico-chemical processes, the biological and the social-historical groups of facts, are not traced back each to the preceding by an inner connection, but are so linked that the higher orders appear as dependent on the lower. In the same way it is now sought to link art methodologically with the aesthetic. Perhaps even more closely, indeed, since already aesthetics and the science of art often play into each other's hands, like the tunnel-workers who pierce a mountain from opposite points, to meet at its center.

Often it so happens, but not invariably. In many cases research is carried to an end, quite irrespectively of what is going on in other quarters. The field is too great, and the interests are too various. Artists recount their experiences in the process of creation, connoisseurs enlighten us as to the technique of the special arts; sociologists investigate the social function, ethnologists the origin, of art; psychologists explore the aesthetic impression, partly by experiment, partly through conceptual analysis; philosophers expound aesthetic methods and principles; the historians of literature, music, and pictorial art have collected a vast deal of material—and the sum total of these scientific inquiries constitutes the most substantial though not the greatest part of the published discussions, which, written from every possible point of view, abound in newspapers and magazines. "There is left, then, for the serious student, naught but to resolve to fix a central point somewhere, and thence to find out a way to deal with all the rest as outlying territory" (Goethe).

Only by the mutual setting of bounds can a united effect be possible from the busy whirl of efforts. Contradictory and heterogeneous facts are still very numerous. He who should undertake to construct thereof a clear intelligible unity of concepts, would destroy the energy which now proves itself in the encounters, crossing of swords, and lively controversies of scholars, and would mutilate the fullness of experience which now expresses itself in the manifold special researches. System and method signify for us: to be free from *one* system and *one* method.[54]

2. *Dessoir now surveys some of the problems which fall within the domain of the General Science of Art. How did art originate? What are the sources of artistic creation? How are the various arts to be related and differentiated from one another? What are the relations of art to morality and to society as a whole? These are some of the questions which, he thinks, can best be dealt with by the General Science of Art, leaving aesthetics free to deal primarily with the problem of the beautiful and with other, more limited (but nonetheless important) questions pertaining to aesthetic*

*value. After taking a brief glance at some of the contributions
made to the General Science of Art, Dessoir concludes that a great
deal more investigation and research will be necessary before the
problems related to the complex phenomenon of art can be satisfactorily solved.*

From a period more or less remote there have existed poetics,
musical theory, and the science of art. To examine the pre-
suppositious methods and aims of these disciplines from the
epistemological point of view, and to sum up and compare their
most important results, is the task of a general science of art;
this has besides, in the problems of artistic creation and the origin
of art, and of the classification of the arts[55] and their social
function, certain fields of inquiry that would otherwise have no
definite place. They are worked, indeed, with remarkable diligence
and productiveness. Most to be regretted, on the other hand, is
that so little energy is applied to laying the epistemological
foundation.

The theory of the development of art deals with it both in its
individual and its generally human aspect. Concerning the genesis
of the child's understanding of art and impulse to produce it, we
learn most from the studies of his drawings at an early age. Here
are to be noted well-established results of observation even though
as yet they are few in number. On the other hand, the unfolding
of primitive feeling (and of the aesthetic sensibility in general)
during the historical period can be only approximately reconstructed. The case is somewhat more favorable for our information
in regard to the beginnings of art, especially since it has been
systematically assembled by Ernst Grosse, and Yrjö Hirn.[56] If the
conditions of the most primitive of the races now living in a state
of nature can be taken as identical with those at the beginnings
of civilization, the entire vast material of ethnology can be made
use of. We gather therefrom how close-linked with the useful and
the necessary beauty is, and see clearly that primitive art is
thoroughly penetrated by the purpose of a common enjoyment,
and is effective in a social way; but beyond such general principles
one can go only with hesitation, inasmuch as it seems scarcely
possible to us, creatures of civilization, to fix the boundaries of
what is really art there.

There are three conjectures as to objective origin of art. It may
be that the separate arts have developed through variation from

one embryonic state. Or the main arts may have been separate from the very first, having arisen independently of each other. Finally, there are middle views, like that of [Herbert] Spencer, according to which poetry, music, and the dance on the one hand, and writing, painting, and sculpture on the other, have a common root; Möbius[57] recognizes three primitive arts, to which the others are to be traced back. The solution of this question would be especially important, could one hope to find Darwin's maxim for all aetiological investigations valid for our field also—that is, the dictum: What is of like origin is of like character.

As psychological conditions, from which the artistic activity is likely first to have arisen, the following functions have been suggested and maintained—the play-instinct, imitation, the need for expression and communication, the sense for order and arrangement, the impulse to attract others and the opposed impulse to startle others. Each of these theories of conditions must clearly connect itself with one or the other of the just-named theories of art's origin; for had music, taken in our sense and independently, existed as the original art, one could hardly regard imitation as the psychological root of art. All in all, art and the play-instinct seem most closley linked; that is also true, moreover, of its development with the child.

I come now to the fundamental problems of artistic creation. It is they which present the most obstinate difficulties to a thorough and exact investigation, for experiment and the questionnaire—which aims at least at objectivity—are but crude means to the end in view. At the present day, as earlier, there is no lack of very refined, penetrating—nay, brilliant analyses. They have a very superior value; but this has no special significance for the present status of the science of aesthetics, and for this reason our survey may omit much which yet has an interest for individuals.

The influence of heredity and environment on the artist's talent offers rich material for research. It is conceded, though, that how the most material and the most spiritual of influences, inherited disposition and fortune, the chances of descent and of intercourse with one's fellows—how all this is fused into a unified personality, can be established only in individual cases by the biographer. A second very productive source of material in this field has appeared in Lombroso's[58] teaching. The days of the most violent controversies lie behind us. It is the general view that genius and madness are near allied in their expression, that greatness often breaks forth

in questionable forms; yet the majority perceive an essential difference; the genius points onward, the mind diseased harks back; the
one has purposive significance, the other not. After these more
introductory inquiries, the real work begins. It has to show in
what points every gift for art coincides with generally disseminated
abilities, and just where the specific power sets in, which the
inartistic person lacks. Take, for example, the memory. We retain
this or that fact without, in principle, any selection; the remembrance of the artist, on the contrary, is dissociative—it favors what
is needful for its own ends. The memory of the painter battens on
forms and colors, the consciousness of the musician is filled with
melodies, the fancy of the poet lives in verbal images. Also there
is, especially with the poet, a peculiar understanding for human
experience. In truth, the fanciful products of the imagination are
but the starting-point for the soul-knowledge of the poet. Without
going into details we may say that by such penetrating and
delimiting analyses the superficial theory of inspiration is refuted.
Out of date, too, is the notion that the artist creates by putting
things together; on the contrary his fancy has the whole before the
parts, it gives to the world an organism, within which the members
gradually emerge. Finally, the old theory is no longer held, according to which the work of art is already complete in the inner man,
and afterwards merely brought to light. More definite explanation is given by the doctrine of the way in which the artistic
creation runs its course, which Eduard v. Hartmann[59] has skillfully
portrayed.

The distinction, differentiation, and comparison of the special
arts offers opportunity and material for numberless special studies.
Music is here the least fully represented, since it is only exceptionally that art-philosophers feel a drawing to it. So much the
more, however, are they inclined to the study of poetry. They are
even beginning to make use, for poetics, of the studies in the
modern psychology of language, since it is acknowledged that
language is the essential element, and thus more than the mere
form of expression, of the poetic art. Th. A. Meyer[60] has thrown
an apple of discord into the question whether the poet's words
must, in order to arouse pleasure, also awaken an image. As a
matter of fact, the aesthetic value does not depend on the chance-
aroused sense-images, but on the language itself and the images
which belong to it alone; for the most part the understanding of
the words alone is enough to give the reader pleasure in the poetic

treatment. In the general theory of the visually representative arts there are two opposed doctrines. The one emphasizes the common element, and believes to have found it in the so-called *Fernbild*, or distant image; the other seeks salvation in complete separations—as, for instance, of the so-called *Griffelkunst*, or graphic art, from painting. Only the future can decide between them.

The existence of the total field of art as an essential factor of human endeavors involves difficulties which must be removed partly in the philosophical consideration, partly in law and governmental practice. The last factor must also be taken account of in theory; for so long as we do not live in a ideal world, the state will claim regulation of all activities expressing themselves in it, and so also of art. In first line it is concerned for art's relation to morality. Secondly, the social problems arise: does art bind men together, or part them? does it reconcile or intensify oppositions? is it democratic or aristocratic? is it a necessity or a luxury? does it further or reject patriotic, ethical, pedagogical ends? The artistic education of youth and the race has become a burning question. [John] Ruskin and [William] Morris have developed from art-critics to critics of the social order, and Tolstoi has contracted the democratic point of view to the most extreme degree. With the desire to transform art from the privilege of the few to the possession of all is, finally, bound up the wish that art shall emerge from another seclusion—that it shall not be throned in museums and libraries, in theatres and concert-halls, but shall mingle with our daily domestic life, and direct and color every act of the scholar as of the peasant.

A satisfactory decision can be reached only by him who keeps in view that art presents something extremely complex, and by no means mere aesthetic form; that, on the other hand, the aesthetic life is not banished to the sacred circle of the independent arts. With this conclusion we return to the first words of our reflections herein presented.[61]

NOTES

1. In his work *On the Sensations of Tone as a Physiological Basis for a Theory of Music* (1863).

2. On experimental and psychological aesthetics, see Thomas Munro, *Toward Science in Aesthetics* (New York, Liberal Arts Press, 1956); the same author's article, "The Psychology of Art: Past, Present, Future," *Journal of Aesthetics and Art Criticism*, XXI (Spring, 1953), 263–282; Douglas N. Morgan's "Psychology and Art [1950]: A Summary and Critique," in *Aesthetics Today* (New York, Meridian Books, 1961), pp. 279–298; also the article by H. S. Langfeld, "Experimental Aesthetics," in the *Encyclopaedia Britannica*, 14th edition. For material on specific topics, see Albert R. Chandler and Edward N. Barnhart's *A Bibliography of Psychological and Experimental Aesthetics* (Berkeley, University of California Press, 1938).

3. On Charles Henry, see Horace M. Kallen's *Art and Freedom* (New York, 1942), Vol. II, p. 580.

4. Michel Eugène Chevreul (1786–1889), chemist and color-theorist, wrote *De la loi du contraste simultané des couleurs* (1839), a work which influenced Pisarro and other impressionists.

5. Paul Souriau (1852–1925), *L'Esthétique du Mouvement* (Paris, 1889).

6. See Thomas Munro's account of Spencer's contributions to aesthetics in *Evolution in the Arts* (Cleveland, 1964), Chap. V.

7. Grant Allen (1848–1899), *Physiological Aesthetics* (London, 1877), p. 34.

8. Ibid., p. 39.

9. On the development of other aspects of German aesthetics after Kant, including a succinct discussion of empathy, see Ernest K. Mundt's "Three Aspects of German Aesthetic Theory," *JAAC*, XVII (March, 1959), 287–310.

10. For an account of the formation of Taine's method, see Sholom J. Kahn's *Science and Criticism* (New York, 1953), Chap. II.

11. Published first in five separate volumes: (1) *Philosophie de l'art* (1865); (2) *Philosophie de l'art en Italie* (1866); (3) *De l'ideal*

dans l'art (1867); (4) *Philosophie de l'art dans les Pays-Bas* (1868); (5) *Philosophie de l'art en Grece* (1869). Each of these volumes was translated into English not long after it appeared, and all were later published in a two-volume English edition, *Lectures on Art* (1883–1884).

12. Taine, *History of English Literature,* translated by H. Van Laun (New York, Holt & Williams, 1871), p. 6.

13. Ibid., p. 10.

14. Ibid., p. 18.

15. Taine, *The Philosophy of Art,* translated by J. Durand, (London, H. Bailliere, 1865), p. 22. All subsequent quotations and selections from this work are from this edition.

16. Taine, *Philosophy of Art,* p. 23.

17. Taine defines essential character as "a quality from which all others, or at least most other qualities, derive according to determined affinities *(liaisons fixes)."* *Philosophy of Art,* p. 51.

18. See *Philosophy of Art,* pp. 51–53.

19. *Philosophy of Art,* p. 57.

20. Ibid., p. 64. "Art accomplishes this end," Taine adds, "by employing a group *(ensemble)* of connected parts, the relationships of which she systematically modifies. In the imitative arts of sculpture, painting, and poetry, these groups correspond to real objects" (p. 64). In the nonimitative arts of music and architecture, Taine goes on to explain, the relationships modified are mathematical. See *Philosophy of Art,* Chap. VI.

21. In Part II of *The Philosophy of Art* ("On the Production of the Work of Art"), Taine attempts to prove this law by appealing to empirical and rational considerations.

22. *Philosophy of Art,* Chap. I, pp. 4–6; pp. 8–9; pp. 11–13; pp. 14–16; p. 19; pp. 20–21; Chap. II, pp. 22–23.

23. A fascinating account of Fechner's life and thought is given by the American psychologist G. Stanley Hall in his *Founders of Modern Psychology* (New York, 1912). A brief summary of his philosophy may be found in Erdmann's *History of Philosophy.* (See listings in our "Guide to Supplementary Reading.")

24. Adolf Zeising (1810–1876) was professor of philosophy at the University of Munich and the author of several works on aesthetics, including *Aesthetische Forschungen* (1855) and *Der Goldene Schnitt* (1884, posthumous). Fechner's account of his experiments to test the validity of Zeising's views was given in

Zur experimentalen Aesthetik (Leipzig, Hirzel, 1871). The golden section ratio is a:b : : b:a+b. For example, if one divides a line so that the length of its smaller section (a) is, in relation to its larger section (b), what the length of the larger section is to the whole line (a+b), one has divided the line according to the golden section ratio.

25. These six principles are discussed in the first volume of the *Vorschule der Aesthetik* (Leipzig, Breitkopf and Hartel, 1876). In the latter part of the second volume Fechner presents other principles among which are the principle of aesthetic contrast, the principle of aesthetic summation, the principle of the expression of pleasure and pain, the principle of the aesthetic mean, and the principle of the economic application of means.

26. The principle of association had originated in early British empirical philosophy and was later applied to aesthetics by several British critics (e.g., Archibald Alison) in the eighteenth century. Rudolf Lotze discussed it in his works before the middle of the nineteenth century. Fechner's classic statement of the principle is found in Vol. I, Chap. IX of the *Vorschule*, on which the following account is based.

27. Fechner, *Vorschule der Aesthetik*, Vol. I, Chap. I, pp. 1–6. This translation has been made by Ilona Ricardo especially for the present volume. To our knowledge, there exists no English translation of the *Vorschule*, and this is probably the first time that this much of Fechner's major (and mammoth) work has appeared in English. Anyone who has struggled with Fechner's tortuous prose will understand the difficulties involved in translating it.

28. The following account of Vernon Lee's life is based in part on Peter Gunn's recent biography of her—the first complete biography of her ever published—*Vernon Lee: Violet Paget, 1856–1935* (London, Oxford University Press, 1964). A Harvard thesis by Burdett H. Gardner entitled "Violet Paget; An Essay in Biographical Criticism" was done earlier (1954). Vernon Lee's literary remains are in the Colby College Library (Waterville, Maine).

29. The article was published in *The Contemporary Review*, October–November, 1897, and was later reprinted, along with other articles by Vernon Lee, in the volume *Beauty and Ugliness* (1912). This and her other works are listed fully in our "Guide to Supplementary Reading."

30. After "C.A.T.'s" death, Vernon Lee edited her manuscripts in a volume entitled *Art and Man* (1924), the introduction to which sheds considerable light on their intimate friendship, professional collaboration, and aesthetic theories.

31. *The Handling of Words* is a collection of essays, lectures, and notes by Vernon Lee on topics such as "On Literary Construction," "On Style," "Aesthetics of the Novel," "The Nature of the Writer," "Can Writing be Taught?" and includes brief analyses of the style of various writers, for the most part English. Throughout the work, the recurrent theme is "that the efficacy of all writing depends not more on the Writer than on the Reader, without whose active response, whose output of experience, feeling and imagination, the living phenomenon, the only reality, of Literary Art cannot take place." (vii–viii).

32. *Music and Its Lovers* is a lengthy (579 pp.) work based mainly on about a hundred responses to a questionnaire designed by Vernon Lee to determine individual differences in the experience of the expressive and emotional power of music. In discussing the various responses, the author divides her answerers generally into "listeners"—those who were able to follow musical structure —and "hearers"—those who usually only associated feelings and thoughts with music.

33. The whole sad story of the battle with Berenson is recounted in Peter Gunn's *Vernon Lee*, pp. 151–157.

34. See especially *Laurus Nobilis* for Vernon Lee's early aesthetics.

35. See *Laurus Nobilis*, p. 239.

36. *Beauty and Ugliness*, p. 236.

37. Theodor Lipps (1851–1914), author of *Spatial Aesthetics and Geometrico-optical Illusions* (1897) and *Aesthetics* (1903–1906). Vernon Lee translated selections from his works, including his important article, "Aesthetische Einfühlung," in *Beauty and Ugliness*, pp. 35–44.

38. Vernon Lee explains the James–Lange theory briefly in the selections which are to follow.

39. Karl Groos (1861–1946), author of *Introduction to Aesthetics* (1892) and *The Play of Men* (1899). Vernon Lee refers to him and quotes him frequently in *Beauty and Ugliness*, especially in the chapter "The Central Problem of Aesthetics" which contains also Groos' answers to one of her questionnaires on Inner Mimicry (see pp. 120–122).

40. See *Beauty and Ugliness*, p. 1.

41. In *The Beautiful*, for example, on Chap. IX of which the following account is based.

42. Vernon Lee does not refer to Fechner in this connection although she was quite familiar with his experiments and principles.

43. This selection is taken from *Beauty and Ugliness, and Other Studies in Psychological Aesthetics* by Vernon Lee and Clementina Anstruther-Thomson (London, John Lane, 1912), pp. 14–17.

44. The "motor type" of individual is one who is aware of his or her bodily reactions to visual or auditory stimuli. Groos claimed that this type of individual has superior aesthetic sensitivity and that he and Miss Anstruther-Thomson were definitely of this type.

45. In a footnote at this point (*Beauty and Ugliness*, p. 26), Vernon Lee quotes several passages from William James' *Principles of Psychology* (1890), including the following passages: "Our natural way of thinking about these coarser emotions is that the mental perception of some fact excites the mental affection called the emotion, and that this latter state of mind gives rise to the bodily expression. My theory, on the contrary, is that *the bodily changes follow directly the perception of the exciting fact, and that our feeling of the same changes as they occur is the emotion.*" (Vol. II, p. 449). "I now proceed to urge the vital point of my whole theory, which is this: *If we fancy some strong emotion, and then try to abstract from our consciousness of it all the feelings of its bodily symptoms, we find we have nothing left behind,* no 'mind-stuff' out of which the emotion can be constituted, and that a cold and neutral state of intellectual perception is all that remains." (Vol. II, p. 451).

46. *Beauty and Ugliness*, pp. 25–29; pp. 30–31.

47. Though the title is here given in English, *Aesthetik und allgemeine Kunstwissenschaft in den Grundzugen* (Stuttgart, F. Enke, 1906) has unfortunately never been translated into English. The only one of Dessoir's works available in English is *Outlines of the History of Psychology*, translated by Donald Fisher (New York, Macmillan, 1912).

48. See "In Memory of Max Dessoir" by Kaarle S. Laurilla, *JAAC*, VI (December, 1947), 105–107.

49. See below, pages 308–309.

50. See below, page 309.

51. This paragraph and the three following paragraphs are based on Dessoir's article "Art History and Systematic Theories of Art," *JAAC*, XIX (Summer, 1961), 463–469.

52. See Dessoir's article "The Contemplation of Works of Art," *JAAC*, VI (December, 1947), 108–119, on which this paragraph has been based.

53. Hugo Spitzer (1854–1937), German philologist and author of *Critical Studies of the Aesthetics of the Present* (1897).

54. This selection, and the one which follows, is taken from Dessoir's paper "The Fundamental Questions of Contemporary Aesthetics," translated by Ethel D. Puffer, in *Congress of Arts and Science; Universal Exposition, St. Louis, 1904*, edited by Howard J. Rogers (Boston, Houghton Mifflin, 1905), Vol. I, pp. 434–436.

55. For Dessoir's own system for classifying the arts, see Thomas Munro's *The Arts and Their Interrelations* (New York, Liberal Arts Press, 1951), pp. 192–194.

56. Ernst Grosse (1862–1927), German aesthetician, and Yrjö Hirn (1870–1952), Finnish sociologist and philosopher of art, both published works entitled *The Origins of Art* (Grosse, 1894; Hirn, 1900).

57. Paul Julius Möbius (1853–1907) was a German neurologist and follower of Fechner. He wrote works on the pathological basis of the thought of Rousseau (1889), Schopenhauer (1899), and Nietzsche (1902), as well as general work on art and artists (*Über Kunst und Künstler*, 1901).

58. Cesare Lombroso (1835–1909), Italian psychiatrist and criminologist, wrote *The Man of Genius in Relation to Psychiatry* (1889) and *Genius and Insanity* (1877).

59. Eduard von Hartmann (1842–1906), German aesthetician and philosopher of the Unconscious, wrote two major works which together composed his *Aesthetik: German Aesthetics Since Kant* (1886) and *Philosophy of Beauty* (1887).

60. Theodor Alexander Meyer, German aesthetician, was the author of a work on style in poetry (*Das Stilgesetz der Poesie*, 1901).

61. Max Dessoir, "The Fundamental Questions of Contemporary Aesthetics," op. cit., pp. 439–441.

QUESTIONS AND TOPICS FOR
FURTHER STUDY

1. With special reference to art, explain Taine's view that "the productions of the human mind, like those of animated nature, can be explained by their milieu." Give some of your own examples which might support his view.

2. How does aesthetics resemble botany, according to Taine? Why, in his view, should a study of aesthetics promote a wider range of aesthetic taste?

3. What does Fechner mean by "aesthetics from above" and "aesthetics from below"? Where does he place Hegel and Kant? Where does he place Burke? Why?

4. What specific points of agreement do you find in Fechner's and Taine's approach to aesthetics? What criticisms do you think Fechner might make of Taine's approach?

5. Explain what Vernon Lee means by "seeing" and "recognizing'" an object. Why is this distinction so important to her theory of empathy?

6. Summarize Vernon Lee and C. Anstruther-Thomson's original theory of empathy. What changes does Lee make in her second formulation of the theory? Why does she make these changes?

7. Why does Vernon Lee hold that there is no absolute beauty? Judging by what she has to say about beauty, what would she probably say about ugliness?

8. Explain why Dessoir believes that aesthetics and the General Science of Art should become separate disciplines. What are some of the problems with which each should be concerned? What would they have in common?

9. Do you find any evidence of the influence of Fechner on Dessoir's views? In what respects do they appear to be scientific in their approach to aesthetics?

10. Topics for further study: (a) Taine's criteria of literary excellence; (b) Taine's taste in painting; (c) Fechner's methods of experimental aesthetics; (d) Vernon Lee and C. Anstruther-Thomson's appreciation of Greek sculpture; (e) Vernon Lee's views on musical expressiveness; (f) Dessoir's conception of aesthetic contemplation.

GUIDE TO SUPPLEMENTARY READING

(Works marked with asterisks are available in paperbound editions.)

TAINE

I. PRIMARY SOURCES

Taine, Hippolyte, *Lectures on Art,* two volumes, translated by J. Durand (New York, Henry Holt and Co., 1883–1884).
——*History of English Literature,* translated by H. Van Laun (New York, Holt & Williams, 1871). Introduction.

II. SECONDARY WORKS

Jenkins, Iredell, "Hippolyte Taine and the Background of Modern Aesthetics," *The Modern Schoolman,* Vol. XX (March, 1943), 141–156.

Kahn, Sholom, *Science and Aesthetic Judgment, A Study in Taine's Critical Method* (New York, Columbia University Press, 1953).

Morawski, Stefan, "The Problem of Value and Criteria in Taine's Aesthetics," *Journal of Aesthetics and Art Criticism,* XXI (Summer, 1963), 407–421.

Munro, Thomas, *Evolution in the Arts, and other Theories of Cultural History* (Cleveland, The Cleveland Museum of Art, 1964). Chap. VIII.

Wellek, René, "Hippolyte Taine's Literary Theory and Criticism," *Criticism,* Winter, 1959.

Wolfenstein, Martha, "The Social Background of Taine's Philosophy of Art," *Journal of the History of Ideas,* Vol. V (June, 1944), 332–358.

FECHNER

Bosanquet, Bernard, *A History of Aesthetic* (New York, Meridian Books, 1957), pp. 381–387.

Chandler, Albert Richard, *Beauty and Human Nature: Elements of Psychological Aesthetics* (New York and London, D. Appleton-Century Co., 1934). Chap. 3.

Croce, Benedetto, *Aesthetic as Science of Expression and General Linguistic,* translated by Douglas Ainslie (New York, Noonday Press, 1953), pp. 394–397.

Erdmann, Johann Eduard, *A History of Philosophy,* translated by Williston S. Hough (London, Swan Sonnenschein & Co., 1890), Vol. III, 282–298.

Gilbert, Katharine A., and Helmut Kuhn, *A History of Esthetics,* revised edition (Bloomington, Indiana University Press, 1953), pp. 527–532.

Hall, G. Stanley, *Founders of Modern Psychology* (New York, D. Appleton and Co., 1912).

Kainz, Friedrich, *Aesthetics the Science,* translated by Herbert M. Schueller (Detroit, Wayne State University Press, 1962). (See Index for numerous references to Fechner.)

Kallen, Horace M., *Art and Freedom* (New York, Duell, Sloan & Pearce, 1942), Vol. II, 617–628.

Sully, James, "Fechner's Aesthetics," *Mind,* Vol. II (1877), 102–108.

VERNON LEE

I. PRIMARY SOURCES

Lee, Vernon (Paget, Violet), *Beauty and Ugliness, And Other Studies in Psychological Aesthetics,* with Clementina Anstruther-Thomson (London, John Lane, 1912).

——*The Beautiful: An Introduction to Psychological Aesthetics* (Cambridge, University Press, 1913).

——*The Handling of Words, and Other Studies in Literary Psychology* (London, John Lane, 1923).

——*Laurus Nobilis, Chapters on Art and Life* (London, John Lane, 1909).

——*Music and Its Lovers* (London, George Allen & Unwin, 1932).

——Introduction to C. Anstruther-Thomson, *Art and Man: Essays and Fragments* (New York, E. P. Dutton & Co., 1924).

II. SECONDARY WORKS

Gunn, Peter, *Vernon Lee: Violet Paget, 1856–1935* (London, Oxford University Press, 1964). Chap. 11.

Kainz, Friedrich, *Aesthetics the Science,* translated by Herbert M. Schueller (Detroit, Wayne State University Press, 1962), pp. 144–169.

Langfeld, Herbert S., *The Aesthetic Attitude* (New York, Harcourt, Brace & Howe, 1920).

Listowel, Earl of, *A Critical History of Modern Aesthetics* (London, George Allen & Unwin, 1933). Chap. VII.

Richards, Ivor A., *Principles of Literary Criticism* (New York, Harcourt, Brace, 1925). Chap. II.

Sparshott, F. E., *The Structure of Aesthetics* (Toronto, University of Toronto Press, 1963), pp. 240–244.

DESSOIR

I. PRIMARY SOURCES

Dessoir, Max, "Aesthetics and the Philosophy of Art in Contemporary Germany," *Monist,* Vol. 36 (1926), 299–310.

——"Art History and Systematic Theories of Art," *JAAC,* XIX (Summer, 1961), 463–469.

——"The Contemplation of Works of Art," *JAAC,* VI (December, 1947), 108–119.

——"The Fundamental Questions of Contemporary Aesthetics," in *Congress of Arts and Science, Universal Exposition, St. Louis, 1904,* edited by Howard J. Rogers (Boston, Houghton Mifflin, 1905), Vol. I, 434–437.

II. SECONDARY WORKS

Kainz, Friedrich, *Aesthetics the Science,* translated by Herbert M. Schueller (Detroit, Wayne State University Press, 1962). (See Index for numerous references to Dessoir.)

Listowel, Earl of, *A Critical History of Modern Aesthetics* (London, George Allen & Unwin, 1933). Chap. XI.

Munro, Thomas, *Toward Science in Aesthetics, Selected Essays* (New York, The Liberal Arts Press, 1956), pp. 114–147.

CHAPTER 10

Pleasure and the Sense of Beauty

SANTAYANA

George Santayana (1863–1952), the first great American aesthetician, was Spanish in his origins, Greek in his ideals, English in his habits, and Italian in his tastes.[1] Born in Madrid of Spanish parents, Santayana remained in Spain with his father when his mother, who had been married previously to an American merchant, returned to the United States to educate her first husband's children. At the age of nine, he went to live with his mother in Boston. There he quickly learned English, attended the Brimmer School, and, later, was graduated from Boston Latin School. By the time he entered Harvard College in 1882, he was already developing into a poet and a philosopher. At Harvard, his philosophy teachers included the pragmatist William James and the idealist Josiah Royce, both of whom recognized young Santayana's genius, and encouraged him, after his graduation from Harvard in 1886, to continue his philosophical studies in Germany.

At the University of Berlin, Santayana was captivated by an exposition of Greek ethical theory, in which he found, for the first time, an adequate ideal of rational living and a firm basis for his own views on goodness, truth, and beauty. Returning to Harvard in 1889, he received his Ph.D., and was invited by James to become a member of the philosophy department. Although he was associated with Harvard for the next twenty-three years, he spent his summers, leaves, and other periods of free time, in England or on the Continent, studying, lecturing, traveling, and visiting family and friends. During these years he achieved fame, first as poet, then as author of books on aesthetics and religion, and finally, as profound and original philosopher with the publica-

324

tion of the five volumes of *The Life of Reason* (1905–06). In this work, usually considered his masterpiece, Santayana depicted, in his inimitable poetical style, "the phases of human progress" in common sense, in society, in religion, in art, and in science, and envisaged an ideal rational life, in which impulse and reflection were fused, natural tendencies brought to ideal fullfillment, and harmony achieved between natural conditions and human aspirations.

Santayana never particularly liked being a professor, even though he was an effective and popular one; consequently, when he was at last financially independent (after his mother's death), he resigned from the Harvard faculty, left America, and never returned. The rest of his life was spent in England and in Europe, where he felt freer and happier in pursuing his work. He continued to give expression to "idealistic materialism," the philosophy he lived by, in essays, reviews, articles, soliloquies, dialogues, memoirs, philosophical treatises, and in a novel, *The Last Puritan* (1935). During the First World War he lived in England, the modern nation he most admired. As old age approached, he decided to settle permanently in Rome, where he resided undisturbed throughout the Second World War and afterward. Although he neither practiced nor renounced Catholicism, the religion to which he was born—he considered its dogmas to be "literally false" but "poetically true"—he chose to spend his final years, as a paying guest, in a Catholic hospital, tended by nuns. When he died there, at the age of eighty-eight, he was buried, as he had requested, in neutral ground in a Catholic cemetery in Rome.

Santayana's most important contribution to aesthetics was made early in his academic career, with the publication of *The Sense of Beauty* (1896), a book which had grown out of his lectures on aesthetic history and theory at Harvard. With the appearance of this book, it has sometimes been said, the history of American aesthetics begins.[2] Although one can find in Santayana's work evidence of the influence of various writers on aesthetics—Plotinus, Schopenhauer, Taine, Lotze, Lipps, and Fechner—the traditional materials have been remolded and reinterpreted so as to accord with the author's naturalistic and psychological approach to aesthetic experience. Throughout the book, Santayana attempts to show how, at every point, the sense of beauty rests on human feelings and human interests, reaching its "apotheosis" in a subjective phenomenon: the objectification of pleasure. Santayana considers the prejudice against the subjective to be one of the chief obstacles to the development of an adequate aesthetic theory.[3] Like John Dewey, he holds that an aesthetic theory should not be formulated only on the basis of our aesthetic appreciation of works of art; due attention must be given to other spheres of human appreciations and activities. Also like Dewey, he rejects all approaches to aesthetic theory that distort aesthetic facts to fit metaphysical systems. In Santayana's view, aesthetic speculation, if it is to be theoretically meaningful as well as practically beneficial, must follow closely the facts of feeling. In this way, and in this way only, can theory clarify aesthetic experience, and justify its own existence. In Santayana's words:

> If when a theory is bad it narrows our capacity for observation and makes all appreciation vicarious and formal, when it is good it reacts favourably upon our powers, guides the attention to what is really capable of affording entertainment, and increases, by force of new analogies, the range of our interests. Speculation is an evil if it imposes a foreign organization on our mental life; it is a good if it only brings to light, and makes more perfect by training, the organization already inherent in it.[4]

With this conception of the aim of aesthetic theory in mind, Santayana undertakes, in *The Sense of Beauty*, a sympathetic and detailed study of the elements of human nature involved in aesthetic judgments. Unlike intellectual judgments, which are judgments of facts or of inferred relations, aesthetic judgments are judgments of immediately perceived, positive values. These values cannot be divorced from emotional consciousness: from human appreciating, preferring, evaluating, and desiring. Santayana approvingly quotes Spinoza's maxim: "We desire nothing because it is good, it is good because we desire it." [5] Aesthetics must deal with the irrational, "feeling aspects" of human nature. Although it cannot define beauty with absolute finality, it can, and should, explain the conditions under which aesthetic experience is possible, and what is involved in the *sense* of beauty.[6]

The aesthetic theory presented by Santayana in that stage of his philosophical development represented in *The Sense of Beauty* is simple in its basic tenets, though complex in its subtle ramifications. The beauty we attribute to objects is not *in the objects*, it is *in us*. The sense of beauty is subjective; it has to do primarily not with objects, but with subjects. At its basis is a psychological phenomenon by which we *project* qualities of sensation and emotion into objects. The pleasure we feel in the perception of an object, we mistakenly regard as an objective property of that object. Beauty is "pleasure objectified." [7] To understand fully the sense of beauty we must understand the materials which go into the building up of sensations into perceptions; we must understand, further, how these sensations are synthesized consciously into beauty of form; and, finally, how the perception of an object can evoke in us associated meanings, thus resulting in beauty of expression.

If *The Sense of Beauty* was Santayana's first word on aesthetics—that beauty is pleasure objectified—it was not his last. Having dealt with the general nature of aesthetic experience in his first book, he later discussed various aspects of art in *Reason in Art* (1905), the fourth volume of *The Life of Reason*. In this work, he disclosed the natural basis of art in instinct and inventive genius; explained how auditory and plastic forms acquire ideal values; and defended the view that art is the best instrument of happiness. As his philosophy matured and his interests turned from aesthetic to ontological problems, Santayana tended to modify his early views on aesthetics and to revise his psychological definition of aesthetic experience in light of his later doctrine of essences, introduced in *Scepticism and Animal Faith* (1923) and elaborated in *The Realms of Being* (1927–1940). He had become convinced that aesthetic and moral values were essentially indistinguishable: every aesthetic experience is a moral good, and every experience of a moral good is aesthetic.[8] Both aesthetic and moral values, in his later view, are intuitive experience of the good; both are a "joy in the immediate;" and in both the essential characteristic is the same: felt harmony. Beauty, in his final treatment, is the feeling one experiences when a "vital harmony" is fused with an image, and one is immediately transported into the realm of essence: the infinite and eternal realm of self-sufficient, ideal objects which are universal yet individual, immaterial yet concrete, and are known through immediate intuition as the pure, positive data of consciousness.[9]

The only critic of his views whom Santayana trusted fully,

however, was himself; and while *he* felt free to criticize and reformulate his early views on aesthetics, he never wanted them wholly discredited. If (as he would have us believe), at the time he wrote *The Sense of Beauty*, he had not been philosophically mature, if his categories then had been limited and his language somewhat misleading, still, he assures us, the import of his teachings was sound, the indication "transcendent," and, even then, he had been on the right trail that would lead him eventually from the definition of the sense of beauty to the discovery of the realm of essence.[10]

Pleasure and the Sense of Beauty

1. *The method Santayana uses in developing his aesthetic theory is, he points out, psychological rather than didactic or historical. He believes that to understand beauty one must understand, first of all, the feelings involved in it; one must deal with the inner, subjective realm of human interests, passions, and preferences. Critical of past attempts to define beauty, he gives his own requirements for an adequate definition.*

It would be easy to find a definition of beauty that should give in a few words a telling paraphrase of the word. We know on excellent authority that beauty is truth, that it is the expression of the ideal, the symbol of divine perfection, and the sensible manifestation of the good. A litany of these titles of honour might easily be compiled, and repeated in praise of our divinity. Such phrases stimulate thought and give us a momentary pleasure, but they hardly bring any permanent enlightenment. A definition that should really define must be nothing less than the exposition of the origin, place, and elements of beauty as an object of human experience. We must learn from it, as far as possible, why, when, and how beauty appears, what conditions an object must fulfil to be beautiful, what elements of our nature make us sensible of beauty, and what the relation is between the constitution of the object and the excitement of our susceptibility. Nothing less will really define beauty or make us understand what aesthetic experience is.[11] ...

2. *For Santayana, aesthetics, the theory of beauty, is primarily
concerned with the perception of values. These values, which
are dependent upon emotional consciousness, upon appreciations
and preferences, spring from vital, immediate, and irrational
parts of human nature. Aesthetic judgments, judgments of value,
are not to be confused with intellectual judgments, judgments
of fact or of relation. A judgment of value is, Santayana holds, a
perception of the positive, intrinsic qualities of immediate experience. And, while the essence of aesthetic perception is pleasure,
aesthetic pleasure must be distinguished from physical pleasure.*

... All pleasures are intrinsic and positive values, but all pleasures
are not perceptions of beauty. Pleasure is indeed the essence of
that perception, but there is evidently in this particular pleasure a
complication which is not present in others and which is the
basis of the distinction made by consciousness and language
between it and the rest. It will be instructive to notice the degrees
of this difference.

The bodily pleasures are those least resembling perceptions of
beauty. By bodily pleasures we mean, of course, more than
pleasures with a bodily seat; for that class would include them
all, as well as all forms and elements of consciousness. Aesthetic
pleasures have physical conditions, they depend on the activity
of the eye and the ear, of the memory and the other ideational
functions of the brain. But we do not connect those pleasures
with their seats except in psychological studies; the ideas with
which aesthetic pleasures are associated are not the ideas of their
bodily causes. The pleasures we call physical, and regard as low,
on the contrary, are those which call our attention to some part
of our own body, and which make no object so conspicuous to
us as the organ in which they arise.

There is here, then, a very marked distinction between physical
and aesthetic pleasure; the organs of the latter must be transparent,
they must not intercept our attention, but carry it directly to
some external object. The greater dignity and range of aesthetic
pleasure is thus made very intelligible. The soul is glad, as it
were, to forget its connexion with the body and to fancy that it
can travel over the world with the liberty with which it changes
the objects of its thought. The mind passes from China to Peru
without any conscious change in the local tensions of the body.

This illusion of disembodiment is very exhilarating, while immersion in the flesh and confinement to some organ gives a tone of grossness and selfishness to our consciousness. The generally meaner associations of physical pleasures also help to explain their comparative crudity.[12]

3. *According to Santayana, we cannot distinguish the genuine aesthetic pleasure from other pleasures by defining it as an unselfish, impersonal, and disinterested enjoyment. He points out that even unselfish interests have to be somebody's interests, and that all real pleasures are, perhaps, ultimately disinterested in that they are not sought with ulterior motives, but for their own sake.*

The distinction between pleasure and the sense of beauty has sometimes been said to consist in the unselfishness of aesthetic satisfaction. In other pleasures, it is said, we gratify our senses and passions; in the contemplation of beauty we are raised above ourselves, the passions are silenced and we are happy in the recognition of a good that we do not seek to possess. The painter does not look at a spring of water with the eyes of a thirsty man, nor at a beautiful woman with those of a satyr. The difference lies, it is urged, in the impersonality of the enjoyment. But this distinction is one of intensity and delicacy, not of nature, and it seems satisfactory only to the least aesthetic minds.

In the second place, the supposed disinterestedness of aesthetic delights is not very fundamental. Appreciation of a picture is not identical with the desire to buy it, but it is, or ought to be, closely related and preliminary to that desire. The beauties of nature and of the plastic arts are not consumed by being enjoyed; they retain all the efficacy to impress a second beholder. But this circumstance is accidental, and those aesthetic objects which depend upon change and are exhausted in time, as are all performances, are things the enjoyment of which is an object of rivalry and is coveted as much as any other pleasure. And even plastic beauties can often not be enjoyed except by a few, on account of the necessity of travel or other difficulties of access, and then this aesthetic enjoyment is as selfishly pursued as the rest.

The truth which the theory is trying to state seems rather to be that when we seek aesthetic pleasures we have no further pleasure in mind; that we do not mix up the satisfactions of vanity and proprietorship with the delight of contemplation. This is true, but it is true at bottom of all pursuits and enjoyments. Every real pleasure is in one sense disinterested. It is not sought with ulterior motives, and what fills the mind is no calculation, but the image of an object or event, suffused with emotion. . . . The content of selfishness is a mass of unselfishness. . . .

But as impersonal thoughts are such only in their object, not in their subject or agent, since all thoughts are the thoughts of somebody: so also unselfish interests have to be somebody's interests. If we were not interested in beauty, if it were of no concern to our happiness whether things were beautiful or ugly, we should manifest not the maximum, but the total absence of aesthetic faculty.[13] . . .

4. *Nor does Santayana regard as convincing the doctrine of the universality of the aesthetic judgment. He points to the considerable disagreement on aesthetic matters, and is inclined to explain what agreement there is by the similarity of background and faculties of those agreeing. To say that what is beautiful to one ought to be beautiful to another is, in Santayana's view, absurd.*

The supposed disinterestedness of our love of beauty passes into another characteristic of it often regarded as essential,—its universality. The pleasures of the senses have, it is said, no dogmatism in them; that anything gives me pleasure involves no assertion about its capacity to give pleasure to another. But when I judge a thing to be beautiful, my judgment means that the thing is beautiful in itself, or (what is the same thing more critically expressed) that it should seem so to everybody. The claim to universality is, according to this doctrine, the essence of the aesthetic; what makes the perception of beauty a judgment rather than a sensation. All aesthetic precepts would be impossible, and all criticism arbitrary and subjective, unless we admit a paradoxical universality in our judgment, the philosophical implications of which we may then go on to develop. But we are fortunately not required to enter the labyrinth into which this method leads; there is a much simpler and clearer way of studying such questions, which is to challenge and analyze the assertion before us and seek its basis in human nature. . . .

That the claim of universality is such a natural inaccuracy will not be hard to show. There is notoriously no great agreement upon aesthetic matters; and such agreement as there is, is based upon similarity of origin, nature, and circumstance among men, a similarity which, where it exists, tends to bring about identity in all judgments and feelings. It is unmeaning to say that what is beautiful to one man *ought* to be beautiful to another. If their senses are the same, their associations and dispositions similar, then the same things will certainly be beautiful to both. If their natures are different, the form which to one will be entrancing will be to another even invisible, because his classifications and discriminations in perception will be different, and he may see a hideous detached fragment or a shapeless aggregate of things, in what to another is a perfect whole—so entirely are the unities of objects unities of function and use. It is absurd to say that what is invisible to a given being *ought* to seem beautiful to him. Evidently this obligation of recognizing the same qualities is conditioned by the possession of the same faculties. But no two men have exactly the same faculties, nor can things have for any two exactly the same values. . . .

. . . Nothing has less to do with the real merit of a work of imagination than the capacity of all men to appreciate it; the true test is the degree and kind of satisfaction it can give to him who appreciates it most. The symphony would lose nothing if half mankind had always been deaf, as nine-tenths of them actually are to the intricacies of its harmonies; but it would have lost much if no Beethoven had existed. And more: incapacity to appreciate certain types of beauty may be the condition *sine qua non* for the appreciation of another kind; the greatest capacity both for enjoyment and creation is highly specialized and exclusive, and hence the greatest ages of art have often been strangely intolerant.[14]

5. *The claim to universality in judgments about beauty rests upon the mistaken notion that beauty is an objective property of things, Santayana argues. Beauty, a value, cannot, in his view, exist apart from perception; it is an emotional pleasure regarded as a quality of a thing perceived.*

There is, however, something more in the claim to universality in aesthetic judgments than the desire to generalize our own opinions.

There is the expression of a curious but well-known psychological phenomenon, viz., the transformation of an element of sensation into the quality of a thing. If we say that other men should see the beauties we see, it is because we think those beauties *are in the object*, like its colour, proportion, or size. Our judgment appears to us merely the perception and discovery of an external existence, of the real excellence that is without. But this notion is radically absurd and contradictory. Beauty, as we have seen, is a value; it cannot be conceived as an independent existence which effects our senses and which we consequently perceive. It exists in perception, and cannot exist otherwise. A beauty not perceived is a pleasure not felt, and a contradiction. . . .

. . . Beauty is an emotional element, a pleasure of ours, which nevertheless we regard as a quality of things. . . .

. . . Most of the pleasures which objects cause are easily distinguished and separated from the perception of the object: the object has to be applied to a particular organ, like the palate, or swallowed like wine, or used and operated upon in some way before the pleasure arises. The cohesion is therefore slight between the pleasure and the other associated elements of sense; the pleasure is separated in time from the perception, or it is localized in a different organ, and consequently is at once recognized as an effect and not as a quality of the object. But when the process of perception itself is pleasant, as it may easily be, when the intellectual operation, by which the elements of sense are associated and projected, and the concept of the form and substance of the thing produced, is naturally delightful, then we have a pleasure intimately bound up in the thing, inseparable from its character and constitution, the seat of which in us is the same as the seat of the perception. We naturally fail, under these circumstances, to separate the pleasure from the other objectified feelings. It becomes, like them, a quality of the object, which we distinguish from pleasures not so incorporated in the perception of things, by giving it the name of beauty.[15]

---

6. *Having reached his definition of the sense of beauty, Santayana makes more explicit its meaning and implications and shows how it expresses, in summary form, his entire aesthetic theory.*

We have now reached our definition of beauty, which, in the terms of our successive analysis and narrowing of the conception, is value positive, intrinsic, and objectified. Or, in less technical language, Beauty is pleasure regarded as the quality of a thing.

This definition is intended to sum up a variety of distinctions and identifications which should perhaps be here more explicitly set down. Beauty is a value, that is, it is not a perception of a matter of fact or of a relation: it is an emotion, an affection of our volitional and appreciative nature. An object cannot be beautiful if it can give pleasure to nobody: a beauty to which all men were forever indifferent is a contradiction in terms.

In the second place, this value is positive, it is the sense of the presence of something good, or (in the case of ugliness) of its absence. It is never the perception of a positive evil, it is never a negative value. That we are endowed with the sense of beauty is a pure gain which brings no evil with it. When the ugly ceases to be amusing or merely uninteresting and becomes disgusting, it becomes indeed a positive evil: but a moral and practical, not an aesthetic one. In aesthetics that saying is true—often so disingenuous in ethics—that evil is nothing but the absence of good: for even the tedium and vulgarity of an existence without beauty is not itself ugly so much as lamentable and degrading. The absence of aesthetic goods is a moral evil: the aesthetic evil is merely relative, and means less of aesthetic good than was expected at the place and time. No form in itself gives pain, although some forms give pain by causing a shock of surprise even when they are really beautiful: as if a mother found a fine bull pup in her child's cradle, when her pain would not be aesthetic in its nature.

Further, this pleasure must not be in the consequence of the utility of the object or event, but in its immediate perception; in other words, beauty is an ultimate good, something that gives satisfaction to a natural function, to some fundamental need or capacity of our minds. Beauty is therefore a positive value that is intrinsic; it is a pleasure. These two circumstances sufficiently separate the sphere of aesthetics from that of ethics. Moral values are generally negative, and always remote. Morality has to do with the avoidance of evil and the pursuit of good: aesthetics only with enjoyment.

Finally, the pleasures of sense are distinguished from the perception of beauty, as sensation in general is distinguished from perception; by the objectification of the elements and their appearance as qualities rather of things than of consciousness. The passage from sensation to perception is gradual, and the path may be sometimes retraced: so it is with beauty and the pleasures of sensation. There is no sharp line between them, but it depends upon the degree of objectivity my feeling has attained at the moment whether I say "It pleases me," or "It is beautiful." If I am self-conscious and critical, I shall probably use one phrase; if I am impulsive and susceptible, the other. The more remote, interwoven, and inextricable the pleasure is, the more objective it will appear; and the union of two pleasures often makes one beauty....

... Thus beauty is constituted by the objectification of pleasure. It is pleasure objectified.[16]

7. *Santayana now turns his attention to the materials of beauty, the elements of consciousness which are pleasurably objectified through aesthetic perception. These materials are not derived from the senses only; they are derived, in varying degrees, from all human functions, including vital forces, sexual instincts, and social feelings.*

Our task will now be to pass in review the various elements of our consciousness, and see what each contributes to the beauty of the world. We shall find that they do so whenever they are inextricably associated with the objectifying activity of the understanding. Whenever the golden thread of pleasure enters that web of things which our intelligence is always busily spinning, it lends to the visible world that mysterious and subtle charm which we call beauty.

There is no function of our nature which cannot contribute something to this effect, but one function differs very much from another in the amount and directness of its contribution. The pleasures of the eye and ear, of the imagination and memory, are the most easily objectified and merged in ideas; but it would betray inexcusable haste and slight appreciation of the principle involved, if we called them the only materials of beauty. Our effort will rather be to discover its other sources, which have been more generally ignored, and point out their importance. For the five senses and the three powers of the soul, which play so large a part in traditional psychology, are by no means the only sources or factors of consciousness; they are more or less external divisions of its content, and not even exhaustive of that.

The nature and changes of our life have deeper roots, and are controlled by less obvious processes. . . .

The aesthetic value of vital functions differs according to their physiological concomitants: those that are favourable to ideation are of course more apt to extend something of their intimate warmth to the pleasures of contemplation, and thus to intensify the sense of beauty and the interest of thought. Those, on the other hand, that for physiological reasons tend to inhibit ideation, and to drown the attention in dumb and unrepresentable feelings, are less favourable to aesthetic activity. The double effect of drowsiness and reverie will illustrate this difference. The heaviness of sleep seems to fall first on the outer senses, and of course makes them incapable of acute impressions; but if it goes no further, it leaves the imagination all the freer, and by heightening the colours of fancy, often suggests and reveals beautiful images. . . .

If, however, the lethargy is more complete, or if the cause of it is such that the imagination is retarded while the senses remain awake,—as is the case with an over-fed or over-exercised body,— we have a state of aesthetic insensibility. . . .

Half-way between vital and social functions, lies the sexual instinct. If nature had solved the problem of reproduction without the differentiation of sex, our emotional life would have been radically different. So profound and, especially in woman, so pervasive an influence does this function exert, that we should betray an entirely unreal view of human nature if we did not inquire into the relations of sex with our aesthetic susceptibility. . . .

. . . As a harp, made to vibrate to the fingers, gives some music to every wind, so the nature of man, necessarily susceptible to woman, becomes simultaneously sensitive to other influences, and capable of tenderness toward every object. The capacity to love gives our contemplation that glow without which it might often fail to manifest beauty; and the whole sentimental side of our aesthetic sensibility—without which it would be perceptive and mathematical rather than aesthetic—is due to our sexual organization remotely stirred. . . .

The function of reproduction carries with it not only direct modifications of the body and mind, but a whole set of social institutions, for the existence of which social instincts and habits are necessary in man. These social feelings, the parental, the patriotic, or the merely gregarious, are not of much direct value for aesthetics, although, as is seen in the case of fashions, they are important in determining the duration and prevalence of a taste once formed. Indirectly they are of vast importance and play a great role in arts like poetry, where the effect depends on what is signified more than on what is offered to sense. Any appeal to a human interest rebounds in favour of a work of art in which it is successfully made. That interest, unaesthetic itself, helps to fix the attention and to furnish subject-matter and momentum to arts and modes of appreciation which are aesthetic. Thus comprehension of the passion of love is necessary to the appreciation of numberless songs, plays, and novels, and not a few works of musical and plastic art.[17]

8. *According to Santayana, the senses of touch, taste, and smell are unaesthetic, lower senses only because of their function. Since they are not intrinsically spatial, they cannot represent nature or give an organized basis for the play of sensation. Sounds, however, despite their lack of intrinsic spatial character, have certain objective properties which allow them to be discriminated, measured, and organized into music.*

The senses of touch, taste, and smell, although capable no doubt of a great development, have not served in man for the purposes of intelligence so much as those of sight and hearing. It is natural that they remain normally in the background of consciousness, and furnish the least part of our objectified ideas, the pleasures connected with them should remain also detached, and unused for the purpose of appreciation of nature. They have been called the unaesthetic, as well as the lower, senses; but the property of these epithets, which is undeniable, is due not to any intrinsic sensuality or baseness of these senses, but to the function which they happen to have in our experience. Smell and taste, like hearing, have the great disadvantage of not being intrinsically spatial: they are therefore not fitted to serve for the representation of nature, which allows herself to be accurately conceived only in spatial terms. They have not reached, moreover, the same organization as sounds, and therefore cannot furnish any play of subjective sensation comparable to music in interest. . . .

Sound shares with the lower senses the disadvantage of having no intrinsic spatial character; it, therefore, forms no part of the properly abstracted external world, and the pleasures of the ear cannot become, in the literal sense, qualities of *things*. But there is in sounds such an exquisite and continuous gradation in pitch, and such a measurable relation in length, that an object almost as complex and describable as the visible one can be built out of them. What gives spatial forms their value in description of the environment is the ease with which discriminations and comparisons can be made in spatial objects: they are measurable, while unspatial sensations commonly are not. But sounds are also measurable in their own category: they have comparable pitches and durations, and definite and recognizable combinations of those sensuous elements are as truly *objects* as chairs and tables. Not that a musical composition exists in any mystical way, as a portion of the music of the spheres, which no one is hearing; but that, for a critical philosophy, visible objects are also nothing but possibilities of sensation. The real world is merely the shadow of that assurance of eventual experience which accompanies sanity. This objectivity can accrue to any mental figment that has enough cohesion, content, and individuality to be describable and recognizable, and these qualities belong no less to audible than to spatial ideas.

There is, accordingly, some justification in Schopenhauer's speculative assertion that music repeats the entire world of sense, and is a parallel method of expression of the underlying substance, or will. The world of sound is certainly capable of infinite variety and, were our sense developed, of infinite extensions; and it has as much as the world of matter the power to interest us and to stir our emotions. It was therefore potentially as full of meaning. But it has proved the less serviceable and constant apparition; and, therefore, music, which builds with its materials, while the purest and most impressive of the arts, is the least human and instructive of them.[18]

9. *Sight is considered by Santayana to be perception* par excellence, *not only because through sight we become most easily aware of objects, but also because aesthetic form itself is usually a synthesis of the seen. Without sight, we would never become acquainted with the effects and values of colors, which are so important in our enjoyment of visual art forms.*

. . . Sight is a method of presenting psychically what is practically absent; and as the essence of the *thing* is its existence in
our absence, the *thing* is spontaneously conceived in terms of sight.

Sight is, therefore, perception *par excellence*, since we become
most easily aware of objects through visual agency and in visual
terms. Now, as the values of perception are those we call aesthetic,
and there could be no beauty if there was no conception of independent objects, we may expect to find beauty derived mainly
from the pleasures of sight. And, in fact, form, which is almost
a synonym of beauty, is for us usually something visible: it is a
synthesis of the seen. But prior to the effect of form, which
arises in the constructive imagination, comes the effect of colour;
this is purely sensuous, and no better intrinsically than the effects
of any other sense: but being more involved in the perception
of objects than are the rest, it becomes more readily an element
of beauty.

The values of colours differ appreciably and have analogy to the
differing values of other sensations. As sweet or pungent smells,
as high and low notes, or major and minor chords, differ from
each other by virtue of their different stimulation of the senses,
so also red differs from green, and green from violet. There is a
nervous process for each, and consequently a specific value.
This emotional quality has affinity to the emotional quality of
other sensations; we need not be surprised that the high rate of
vibration which yields a sharp note to the ear should involve
somewhat the same feeling that is produced by the high rate of
vibration which, to the eye, yields a violet colour. These affinities
escape many minds; but it is conceivable that the sense of them
should be improved by accident or training. There are certain
effects of colour which give all men pleasure, and others which
jar, almost like a musical discord. A more general development
of this sensibility would make possible a new abstract art, an art
that should deal with colours as music does with sound.[19]

10. *Having completed his survey of the sensuous materials of
beauty, Santayana reminds us that the ideas which we abstract
from the organs of perception are not separate factors of thought,
but are discriminations in the total content of consciousness;
furthermore, the pleasures accompanying ideation are, in reality,
parts of a unitary, vital continuum of feeling. He concludes this*

portion of his discussion by pointing out that although form may be more important to the total aesthetic effect than material, material is perhaps more fundamental and universal.

We have now gone over those organs of perception that give us the materials out of which we construct objects, and mentioned the most conspicuous pleasures which, as they arise from those organs, are easily merged in the ideas furnished by the same. We have also noticed that these ideas, conspicuous as they are in our developed and operating consciousness, are not so much factors in our thought, independent contributions to it, as they are discriminations and excisions in its content, which, after they are all made, leave still a background of vital feeling. For the outer senses are but a portion of our sensorium, and the ideas of each, or of all together, but a portion of our consciousness.

The pleasures which accompany ideation we have also found to be unitary and vital; only just as for practical purposes it is necessary to abstract and discriminate the contribution of one sense from that of another, and thus to become aware of particular and definable impressions, so it is natural that the diffused emotional tone of the body should also be divided, and a certain modicum of pleasure or pain should be attributed to each idea. Our pleasures are thus described as the pleasures of touch, taste, smell, hearing, and sight, and may become elements of beauty at the same time as the ideas to which they are attached become elements of objects. There is, however, a remainder of emotion as there is a remainder of sensation; and the importance of this remainder—of the continuum in which lie all particular pleasures and pain—was insisted upon in the beginning.

The beauty of the world, indeed, cannot be attributed wholly or mainly to pleasures thus attached to abstracted sensations. It is only the beauty of the materials of things which is drawn from the pleasures of sensation. By far the most important effects are not attributable to these materials, but to their arrangement and their ideal relations. We have yet to study those processes of our mind by which this arrangement and these relations are conceived; and the pleasures which we can attach to these processes may then be added to the pleasures attached to sense as further and more subtle elements of beauty.

But before passing to the consideration of this more intricate subject, we may note that however subordinate the beauty may be which a garment, a building, or a poem derives from its sensuous material, yet the presence of this sensuous material is indispensable. Form cannot be the form of nothing. If, then, in finding or creating beauty, we ignore the materials of things, and attend only to their form, we miss an ever-present opportunity to heighten our effects. For whatever delight the form may bring, the material might have given delight already, and so much would have been gained towards the value of the total result.

Sensuous beauty is not the greatest or most important element of effect, but it is the most primitive and fundamental, and the most universal. There is no effect of form which an effect of material could not enhance, and this effect of material, underlying that of form, raises the latter to a higher power and gives the beauty of the object a certain poignancy, thoroughness, and infinity which it otherwise would have lacked. The Parthenon not in marble, the king's crown not of gold, and the stars not of fire, would be feeble and prosaic things. The greater hold which material beauty has upon the senses, stimulates us here, where the form is also sublime, and lifts and intensifies our emotions. We need this stimulus if our perceptions are to reach the highest pitch of strength and acuteness. Nothing can be ravishing that is not beautiful pervasively....

... The beauty of material is thus the groundwork of all higher beauty, both in the object, whose form and meaning have to be lodged in something sensible, and in the mind, where sensuous ideas, being the first to emerge, are the first that can arouse delight.[20]

11. *In Santayana's view, beauty of form arises from a conscious synthesis of distinguishable parts into a unified whole which gives pleasure, not only as a unified whole but as a relationship, a harmony, of parts. The character of parts and the methods used to unite them account for the variety of forms. Santayana finds two kinds of beauty of form in works of art: beauty of useful form and beauty of ornament.*

The most remarkable and characteristic problem of aesthetics is that of beauty of form. Where there is a sensuous delight, like that of colour, and the impression of the object is in its elements agreeable, we have to look no farther for an explanation of the charm we feel. Where there is expression, and an object indifferent to the senses is associated with other ideas which are interesting, the problem, although complex and varied, is in principle comparatively plain. But there is an intermediate effect which is more mysterious, and more specifically an effect of beauty. It is found where sensible elements, by themselves indifferent, are so united as to please in combination....

...Unity would thus appear to be the virtue of forms; but a moment's reflection will show us that unity cannot be absolute and be a form; a form is an aggregation, it must have elements, and the manner in which the elements are combined constitutes the character of the form. A perfectly simple perception, in which there was no consciousness of the distinction and relation of parts, would not be a perception of form; it would be a sensation. Physiologically these sensations may be aggregates and their values, as in the case of musical tones, may differ according to the manner in which certain elements, beats, vibrations, nervous processes, or what not, are combined; but for consciousness the result is simple, and the value is the pleasantness of a datum and not of a process. Form, therefore, does not appeal to the unattentive; they get from objects only a vague sensation which may in them awaken extrinsic associations; they do not stop to survey the parts or to appreciate their relation, and consequently are insensible to the various charms of various unifications; they can find in objects only the value of material or of function, not of form.

Beauty of form, however, is what specifically appeals to an aesthetic nature; it is equally removed from the crudity of formless stimulation and from the emotional looseness of reverie and discursive thought. The indulgence in sentiment and suggestion, of which our time is fond, to the sacrifice of formal beauty, marks an absence of cultivation as real, if not as confessed, as that of the barbarian who revels in gorgeous confusion.

The synthesis, then, which constitutes form is an activity of the mind; the unity arises consciously, and is an insight into the relation of sensible elements separately perceived. It differs from sensation in the consciousness of the synthesis, and from expression in the homogeneity of the elements, and in their common presence to sense.

The variety of form depends upon the character of the elements and on the variety of possible methods of unification. The elements may be all alike, and their only diversity be numeral. Their unity will then be merely the sense of their uniformity. Or they may differ in kind, but so as to compel the mind to no particular order in their unification. Or they may finally be so constituted that they suggest inevitably the scheme of their unity; in this case there is organization in the object, and the synthesis of its parts is one and pre-determinate....

Beauty of form is the last to be found or admired in artificial as in natural objects. Time is needed to establish it, and training and nicety of perception to enjoy it. Motion or colour is what first interests a child in toys, as in animals; and the barbarian artist decorates long before he designs. The cave and wigwam are daubed with paint, or hung with trophies, before any pleasure is taken of their shape; and the appeal to the detached senses, and to associations of wealth and luxury, precedes by far the appeal to the perceptive harmonies of form. In music we observe the same gradation; first, we appreciate its sensuous and sentimental value; only with education can we enjoy its form. The plastic arts begin, therefore, with adventitious ornament and with symbolism. The aesthetic pleasure is in the richness of the material, the profusion of the ornament, the significance of the shape—in everything, rather than in the shape itself.

We have accordingly in works of art two independent sources of effect. The first is the useful form, which generates the type, and ultimately the beauty of form, when the type has been idealized by emphasizing its intrinsically pleasing traits. The second is the beauty of ornament, which comes from the excitement of the senses, or of the imagination, by colour, or by profusion or delicacy of detail. Historically, the latter is first developed, and applied to a form as yet merely useful. But the very presence of ornament attracts contemplation; the attention lavished on the object helps to fix its form in the mind, and to make us discriminate the less from the more graceful. The two kinds of beauty are then felt, and, yielding to that tendency to unity which the mind always betrays, we begin to subordinate and organize these two excellences. The ornament is distributed so as to emphasize the aesthetic essence of the form; to idealize it even more, by adding adventitious interests harmoniously to the intrinsic interest of the lines of structure.[21]

12. *The sense of beauty may also arise through feelings pleasurably associated with an object. When this occurs there is*

beauty of expression. Santayana finds two terms in all expression: (1) the expressive thing (i.e. the object perceived), and (2) the thing expressed (i.e. the object suggested). The union of these two terms constitutes expression.

We have found in the beauty of material and form the objectification of certain pleasures connected with the process of direct perception, with the formation, in the one case of a sensation, or quality, in the other of a synthesis of sensations or qualities. But the human consciousness is not a perfectly clear mirror, with distinct boundaries and clear-cut images, determinate in number and exhaustively perceived. Our ideas half emerge for a moment from the dim continuum of vital feeling and diffused sense, and are hardly fixed before they are changed and transformed, by the shifting of attention and the perception of new relations, into ideas of really different objects. This fluidity of the mind would make reflection impossible, did we not fix in words and other symbols certain abstract contents; we thus become capable of recognizing in one perception the repetition of another, and of recognizing in certain recurrences of impressions a persistent object. This discrimination and classification of the contents of consciousness is the work of perception and understanding, and the pleasures that accompany these activities make the beauty of the sensible world.

But our hold upon our thoughts extends even further. We not only construct visible unities and recognizable types, but remain aware of their affinities to what is not at the time perceived; that is, we find in them a certain tendency and quality, not original to them, a meaning and a tone, which upon investigation we shall see to have been the proper characteristics of other objects and feelings, associated with them in our experience. The hushed reverberations of these associated feelings continue in the brain, and by modifying our present reaction, colour the image upon which our attention is fixed. The quality thus acquired by objects through association is what we call their expression. Whereas in form or material there is one object with its emotional effect, in expression there are two, and the emotional effect belongs to the character of the second or suggested one. Expression may thus make beautiful by suggestion things in themselves indifferent, or it may come to heighten the beauty which they already possess. . . .

Expression then differs from material or formal value only as habit differs from instinct—in its origin. Physiologically, they are both pleasurable radiations of a given stimulus; mentally, they are both values incorporated in an object. But an observer, looking at the mind historically, sees in the one case the survival of an experience, in the other a reaction of an innate disposition. This experience, moreover, is generally rememberable, and then the extrinsic source of the charm which expression gives becomes evident even to the consciousness in which it arises. A word, for instance, is often beautiful simply by virtue of its meaning and associations; but sometimes this expressive beauty is added to a musical quality in the word itself. In all expression we may thus distinguish two terms; the first is the object actually presented, the word, the image, the expressive thing; the second is the object suggested, the further thought, emotion, or image evoked, the thing expressed.

These lie together in the mind, and their union constitutes expression. . . .

The value of the second term must be incorporated in the first; for the beauty of expression is as inherent in the object as that of material or form, only it accrues to that object not from the bare act of perception, but from the association with it of further processes, due to the existence of former impressions. We may conveniently use the word "expressiveness" to mean all the capacity of suggestion possessed by a thing, and the word "expression" for the aesthetic modification which that expressiveness may cause in it. Expressiveness is thus the power given by experience to any image to call up others in the mind; and this expressiveness becomes an aesthetic value, that is, becomes expression, when the value involved in the associations thus awakened are incorporated in the present object. . . .

These reflections may make less surprising to us what is the most striking fact about the philosophy of expression; namely, that the value acquired by the expressive thing is often of an entirely different kind from that which the thing expressed possesses. The expression of physical pleasure, of passion, or even of pain, may constitute beauty and please the beholder. Thus the value of the second term may be physical, or practical, or even negative; and it may be transmuted, as it passes to the first term, into a value at once positive and aesthetic.[22] . . .

13. *Santayana concludes his discussion of the sense of beauty by reminding us that any description of beauty is bound to be artificial: felt beauty is indescribable; its meaning, ineffable. Still, in the sense of beauty we find the realization of perfection through a perfect correspondence of our senses and our imagination, and a final satisfaction of our reason which craves unity.*

We have now studied the sense of beauty in what seems to be its fundamental manifestations, and in some of the more striking complications which it undergoes. In surveying so broad a field we stand in need of some classification and subdivision; and we have chosen the familiar one of matter, form, and expression, as least likely to lead us into needless artificiality. But artificiality there must always be in the discursive description of anything given in consciousness....

Beauty as we feel it is something indescribable: what it is or what it means can never be said. By appealing to experiment and memory we can show that this feeling varies as certain things vary in the objective conditions; that it varies with the frequency, for instance, with which a form has been presented, or with the associates which that form has had in the past. This will justify a description of the feeling as composed of the various contributions of these objects. But the feeling itself knows nothing of composition nor contributions. It is an affection of the soul, a consciousness of joy and security, a pang, a dream, a pure pleasure. It suffuses an object without telling why; nor has it any need to ask the question. It justifies itself and the vision it gilds; nor is there any meaning in seeking for a cause of it, in this inward sense. Beauty exists for the same reason that the object which is beautiful exists, or the world in which that object lies, or we that look upon both. It is an experience: there is nothing more to say about it....

But we,—the minds that ask all questions and judge of the validity of all answers,—we are not ourselves independent of this world in which we live. We sprang from it, and our relations in it determine all our instincts and satisfactions. This final questioning and sense of mystery is an unsatisfied craving which nature has her way of stilling....

This satisfaction of our reason, due to the harmony between our nature and our experience, is partially realized already. The sense of beauty is its realization. When our senses and imagination find what they crave, when the world so shapes itself or so moulds the mind that the correspondence between them is perfect, then perception is pleasure, and existence needs no apology. The duality which is the condition of conflict disappears. There is no inward standard different from the outward fact with which that outward fact may be compared. A unification of this kind is the goal of our intelligence and of our affection, quite as much as of our aesthetic sense; but we have in those departments fewer examples of success. In the heat of speculation or of love there may come moments of equal perfection, but they are very unstable. The reason and the heart remain deeply unsatisfied. But the eye finds in nature, and in some supreme achievements of art, constant and fuller satisfaction. For the eye is quick, and seems to have been more docile to the education of life than the heart or the reason of man, and able sooner to adapt itself to the reality. Beauty therefore seems to be the clearest manifestation of perfection, and the best evidence of its possibility. If perfection is, as it should be, the ultimate justification of being, we may understand the ground of the moral dignity of beauty. Beauty is a pledge of the possible conformity between the soul and nature, and consequently a ground of faith in the supremacy of the good.[23]

14. *Finally, Santayana envisages an ideal rational life in which art can fulfill its proper function as an instrument of happiness and the artist, no longer alienated from his society, can represent its highest creative expression.*

The value of art lies in making people happy, first in practising the art and then in possessing its product. This observation might seem needless, and ought to be so; but if we compare it with what is commonly said on these subjects, we must confess that it may often be denied and more often, perhaps, may not be understood. Happiness is something men ought to pursue, although they seldom do so; they are drawn away from it at first by foolish impulses and afterwards by perverse laws. To secure happiness conduct would have to remain spontaneous while it learned not to be criminal; but the fanatical attachment of men, now to a fierce liberty, now to a false regimen, keeps them barbarous and wretched. A rational pursuit of happiness—which is one thing with progress or with the Life of Reason—would embody that natural piety which leaves to the episodes of life their inherent values, mourning death, celebrating love, sanctifying civic traditions, enjoying and correcting nature's ways. To discriminate happiness is therefore the very soul of art, which expresses experience without distorting it, as those political or metaphysical tyrannies distort it which sanctify unhappiness. A free mind, like a creative imagination, rejoices at the harmonies it can find or make between man and nature; and, where it finds none, it solves the conflict so far as it may and then notes and endures it with a shudder.

A morality organised about the human heart in an ingenuous and sincere fashion would involve every fine art and would render the world pervasively beautiful—beautiful in its artificial products and beautiful in its underlying natural terrors. The closer we keep to elementary human needs and to the natural agencies that may satisfy them, the closer we are to beauty. Industry, sport, and science, with the perennial intercourse and passions of men, swarm with incentives to expression, because they are everywhere creating new moulds of being and compelling the eye to observe those forms and to recast them ideally. Art is simply an adequate industry; it arises when industry is carried out to the satisfaction of all human demands, even of those incidental sensuous demands which we call aesthetic and which a brutal industry, in its haste, may despise or ignore....

Art, in its nobler acceptation, is an achievement, not an indulgence. It prepares the world in some sense to receive the soul, and the soul to master the world; it disentangles those threads in each that can be woven into the other. That the artist should be eccentric, homeless, dreamful may almost seem a natural law, but it is none the less a scandal. An artist's business is not really to cut fantastical capers or be licensed to play the fool. His business is simply that of every keen soul to build well when it builds, and to speak well when it speaks, giving practice everywhere the greatest possible affinity to the situation, the most delicate adjustment to every faculty it affects. The wonder of an artist's performance grows with the range of his penetration, with the instinctive sympathy that makes him, in his mortal isolation, considerate of other men's fate and a great diviner of their secret, so that his work speaks to them kindly, with a deeper assurance than they could have spoken with to themselves. And the joy of his great sanity, the power of his adequate vision, is not the less intense because he can lend it to others and has borrowed it from a faithful study of the world.

If happiness is the ultimate sanction of art, art in turn is the best instrument of happiness. In art more directly than in other activities man's self-expression is cumulative and finds an immediate reward; for it alters the material conditions of sentience so that sentience becomes at once more delightful and more significant. In industry man is still servile, preparing the materials he is to use in action. In action itself, though he is free, he exerts his influence on a living and treacherous medium and sees the issue at each moment drift farther and farther from his intent. In science he is an observer, preparing himself for action in another way, by studying its results and conditions. But in art he is at once competent and free; he is creative. He is not troubled by his materials, because he has assimilated them and may take them for granted; nor is he concerned with the chance complexion of affairs in the actual world, because he is making the world over, not merely considering how it grew or how it will consent to grow in future. Nothing, accordingly, could be more delightful than genuine art, nor more free from remorse and the sting of vanity. Art springs so completely from the heart of man that it makes everything speak to him in his own language; it reaches, nevertheless, so truly to the heart of nature that it cooperates with her, becomes a parcel of her creative material energy, and builds by her instinctive hand. If the various formative impulses afoot in the world never opposed stress to stress and made no havoc with one another, nature might be called an unconscious artist. In fact, just where such a formative impulse finds support from the environment, a consciousness supervenes. If that consciousness is adequate enough to be prophetic, an art arises. Thus the emergence of arts out of instincts is the token and exact measure of nature's success and of mortal happiness.[24]

NOTES

1. On the life of Santayana, see his autobiography, *Persons and Places*, 3 vols. (New York, Charles Scribner's Sons, 1944, 1945, 1955). Also see Daniel Cory (ed.), *The Letters of George Santayana* (New York, Charles Scribner's Sons, 1955). For further material, consult our "Guide to Supplementary Reading."

2. This is not literally true, however. On the development of American aesthetics prior to Santayana's work, see William Knight, *The Philosophy of the Beautiful* (New York, Charles Scribner's Sons, 1905), Vol. I, Chap. XIII.

3. George Santayana, *The Sense of Beauty, Being the Outlines of Aesthetic Theory* (New York, Charles Scribner's Sons, 1896), pp. 3–4. All subsequent quotations and selections from this work will be taken from this edition, to be cited as S. B.

4. S. B., p. 7.

5. S. B., p. 18.

6. S. B., pp. 267–268.

7. S. B., p. 52.

8. George Santayana, "A Brief History of My Opinions," in Paul Arthur Schilpp (ed.), *The Philosophy of George Santayana* (Evanston and Chicago, Library of Living Philosophers, Northwestern University Press, 1940), p. 20.

9. George Santayana, "The Mutability of Aesthetic Categories," *The Philosophical Review*, XXXIV (May, 1925), p. 284, footnote.

10. George Santayana, *The Idler and His Works*, edited by Daniel Cory (New York, George Braziller, 1957), pp. 11–12.

11. S. B., p. 14.

12. S. B., pp. 35–37.

13. S. B., pp. 37–40.

14. S. B., pp. 40–42; pp. 43–44.

15. S. B., pp. 44–45; pp. 47–49.

16. S. B., pp. 49–51; p. 52.

17. S. B., pp. 53–54; pp. 55–57; pp. 58–59; p. 62.

18. S. B., pp. 65–66; pp. 68–70.

19. S. B., pp. 73–75.

20. S. B., pp. 76–78; p. 81.

21. S. B., p. 82; pp. 96–97; pp. 163–164.

22. S. B., pp. 192–193; p. 195; pp. 197–198; p. 201.

23. S. B., p. 266; pp. 267–268; pp. 269–270.

24. George Santayana, *The Life of Reason; or, The Phases of Human Progress: Reason in Art* (New York, Charles Scribner's Sons, 1905), pp. 222–224; pp. 228–230.

QUESTIONS AND TOPICS FOR FURTHER STUDY

1. What defects does Santayana find in past attempts to define the sense of beauty? What is his own procedure in undertaking this task?

2. How does Santayana distinguish aesthetic pleasure from physical or bodily pleasure? Why does he object to defining aesthetic pleasure in terms of disinterested enjoyment?

3. What would be Santayana's opinion of someone who, judging something to be beautiful, claimed that everyone else ought to find it equally beautiful?

4. Explain what Santayana means by the "objectification of pleasure." Does he conceive of the sense of beauty as being entirely subjective?

5. Explain how vital functions, sexual instincts, and social feelings contribute to the sense of beauty, according to Santayana. Give examples of works of art that might illustrate his views.

6. Why does Santayana consider sight to be "perception *par excellence*"? In what way is form "the synthesis of the seen"?

7. Why does Santayana consider sensuous material to be more fundamental to aesthetic experience than form? What are the distinguishing characteristics of form, in his view?

8. What are the two terms in expression, according to Santayana? How does expressive value differ from material and formal value in a work of art? Discuss Santayana's conception of expression with reference to some specific works of art.

9. Explain what Santayana means by the statement that "Beauty is a pledge of the possible conformity between the soul and nature, and consequently a ground of faith in the supremacy of the good." How is this statement related to his view that art is the best instrument of happiness?

10. Topics for further study: (a) philosophical influences on Santayana's early aesthetic theory; (b) Santayana's conception of the sublime; (c) the Tragic and the Comic in Santayana's aesthetic theory; (d) differences in Santayana's and Croce's views of artistic expression; (e) Santayana's later views on beauty.

GUIDE TO SUPPLEMENTARY READING

(Works marked with asterisks are available in paperbound editions.)

I. PRIMARY SOURCES

Santayana, George, *The Sense of Beauty (New York, Dover Publications, 1955).

———*Reason in Art, Volume IV of The Life of Reason (New York, Collier Books, 1962).

———"What Is Aesthetics?" and "An Aesthetic Soviet" in Justus Buchler and Benjamin Schwartz (eds.), Obiter Scripta: Lectures, Essays and Reviews (New York, Charles Scribner's Sons, 1936).

———"Croce's Aesthetics," in Daniel Cory (ed.), The Idler and His Works and Other Essays (New York, George Braziller, 1957).

———"The Mutability of Esthetic Categories," The Philosophical Review, XXXIV (May, 1925), 281–291.

II. SECONDARY WORKS

Ames, Van Meter, "Santayana at One Hundred," *Journal of Aesthetics and Art Criticism*, XXII (Spring, 1964), 243–247.

Arnett, Willard E., *Santayana and the Sense of Beauty* (Bloomington, Indiana University Press, 1955).

——"Santayana and the Fine Arts," *JAAC*, XVI (September, 1957), 84–95.

Ashmore, Jerome, "Santayana's Mistrust of Fine Arts," *JAAC*, XIV (March, 1956), 339–347.

Boas, George, "Santayana and the Arts," in Paul Arthur Schilpp (ed.), *The Philosophy of George Santayana* (Evanston and Chicago, Library of Living Philosophers, Northwestern University Press, 1940).

Gilbert, Katharine E., "Santayana's Doctrine of Aesthetic Expression," in *Studies in Recent Aesthetic* (Chapel Hill, University of North Carolina Press, 1927).

Howgate, George Washburne, *George Santayana* (Philadelphia, University of Pennsylvania Press, 1938).

Pepper, Stephen C., *The Basis for Criticism in the Arts* (Cambridge, Mass., Harvard University Press, 1946). Chap. 2.

Singer, Irving, *Santayana's Aesthetics: A Critical Introduction* (Cambridge, Mass., Harvard University Press, 1957).

CHAPTER 11

Intuition, Expression, and Art

CROCE

Few philosophers of the twentieth century can compare with Benedetto Croce (1866–1952) in erudition, productiveness, influence, and service as a cultural leader to his country and to the world.[1] And few have stimulated so much interest and controversy in aesthetics. Born in a small town in Abruzzi, Italy, Benedetto grew up in Naples, where his father owned an estate. His mother, a lover of art and literature, encouraged his early passion for books and learning. At the age of nine, Benedetto enrolled in a Catholic boarding school, where he distinguished himself by his high spirits and high grades, began to write his first scholarly essays, and passed through a religious crisis (precipitated by a priest's lectures on philosophy of religion) which resulted in a rejection of religious dogmas. A turning point in young Croce's life and an experience which left him emotionally scarred occurred in 1883 when he was buried alive and his parents and only sister were killed in an earthquake at Casamicciola. Injured and depressed, he afterwards went with his brother to live in Rome with a cousin, a powerful politician. At first he was so miserable in Rome that he considered suicide, and although he was enrolled as a law student at the University of Rome, he had little interest in the political life surrounding him. Independent scholarly research was his main interest and solace. During the second year in Rome, however, he found a rational faith to satisfy his spiritual longings in the rationalistic moral philosophy expounded by the Herbartian professor, Antonio Labriola, at the University of Rome.

Returning to Naples in 1886, Croce continued his antiquarian and historical studies and began to publish works on Neapolitan history and culture. Later, he traveled in pursuit of knowledge in England, France, Spain, and Germany. Increasingly he became interested in the philosophy of history and art; his first important philosophical essay, which appeared in 1893, was entitled "History Subsumed Under the General Concept of Art." This essay, along with an essay on literary criticism which immediately followed it, gave Croce a sense of personal liberation, convincing him that at last he had found his true mission in life as a thinker. Afterwards he pursued his specialized historical research and delved deeply into a study of economic theory—he was for a time a Marxist—but his interests turned more and more to the fundamental problems of philosophy. Vico, De Sanctis, and Hegel[2] were the thinkers who influenced him most as he gradually developed his own "Philosophy of Spirit," which was published during the first decade of this century in three main parts: *Aesthetic* (1902), *Logic* (1909), and *Philosophy of the Practical* (economics and ethics) (1909). (Later, in 1917, a fourth part, *History: Its Theory and Practice*, was added.) Also during this period, he collaborated with another Italian philosopher, Giovanni Gentile (who was later to become an important spokesman for Fascism), in starting and directing a review, *La Critica*, which served continuously as a cultural forum for forty years (1903–1943).

Croce's contributions to his nation's cultural life did not go unrecognized or unrewarded. In 1910 he received a lifetime appointment as Senator of the Kingdom. From 1920 to 1921 he was asked to serve as Minister of Education. Even during the dictatorship of Benito Mussolini, Croce's immense prestige made him sacrosanct, and he was allowed to continue his work relatively unhampered, in spite of his well-known opposition to Fascism. When Italy was invaded by the Allies in the Second World War and Mussolini fell from power, Croce re-emerged as a powerful spokesman of unity, freedom, and hope for his fellow countrymen. After the war had ended, the aged philosopher founded an institute for historical studies in his home, where he continued to seek and to share knowledge up until his death at the age of eighty-six.

Aesthetics, for Croce, is the philosophical science of art, or (as he also defines it), the whole of philosophy as it concerns itself with the understanding of art. The basic question, then, which the philosopher as aesthetician, or the aesthetician as philosopher, must

ask is "What is art?" Croce may seem at times to be more concerned with saying what art is *not* than with affirming what it *is*.
He always insists that art is not to be confused with logic, with
history or economics, with physics or mathematics, with the play
of fancy, with feeling in its immediacy, with instruction or
oratory.[3] And in his *Essence of Aesthetic* (1921), he points out
that art can never be understood when it is viewed as a physical
fact, as a utilitarian act, as a moral activity, or as a form of conceptual knowledge.[4] But Croce's philosophy of art is far more than
a series of negations, for, as he reminds us, negations are, after all,
relations, and as we think our way through mistaken (but not
completely erroneous) notions of art, which can be viewed as
"eternal stages of the search for truth," we are coming closer to
discovering art's essential nature by seeing it in its "ideal connections."[5] Then, and only then, can we grasp the full significance
of a simple yet profound truth: Art is intuition.

And what is intuition? For Croce it is not an instinctive knowing,
or a grasp of a self-evident truth, or any kind of mystical apprehension of a higher realm of being. It is rather an inner vision
of an image; an immediate knowledge through the imagination of
an individual thing in its concreteness; the lowest and most fundamental grade of mental activity.[6] Or, one may simply say that
intuition is expression, for to know directly and fully the image
or nexus of images constituting a work of art is to express or to
intuit inwardly that work of art. To say that one *knows* but
cannot express, that one intuits but cannot formulate, is, according
to Croce, to feign aesthetic vision when there is none.[7] The genuine
work of art is not something outwardly present, something existing
"objectively" in an external world, a physical fact. A physical
fact, when analyzed, turns out to be a scientific abstraction, and
art is precisely that which is concrete, immediate, unanalyzable.
Beauty cannot be measured or weighed like a piece of marble, or
counted or divided like the words on a page or the acts in a
script, or reduced to numerical relations like geometrical figures;
for beauty is inner material—impressions or feelings—*fused* into
an image of contemplation: it *is* inner expression or form. Art
cannot be a matter of technique; it is a matter of poetical, feeling-
impregnated images: lyrical intuition. And, like the spirit of which
it is a form, it is eternal and omnipresent.

This spirit of which Croce so often speaks is not a transcendent
or supernatural reality; it is rather the immanent conscious activity

in all its concreteness; it is the all-inclusive life of mind, outside of which there is nothing. Within spirit, distinctions may be made, but there are no divisions or separations. The philosopher, in studying the nature of spirit, finds it to be either *theoretical* or *practical* as it manifests itself in either *thought* or *action*. The theoretical spiritual activity can further be distinguished as knowledge of individuals by intuition (aesthetics) and knowledge of universals by concepts (logic); the practical activity also can be distinguished as *economical* (related to desiring individual things) and *ethical* (related to willing of universal ends). This gives us the four categories of being, and the only ones essential to understanding the whole realm of spirit; it also gives us the all-important concepts which determine the meaning and value of life: The Beautiful, the True, the Useful, and the Good. These grades of being may seem to be progressively higher as we move from aesthetics to logic, or from economics to ethics: thought seems to presuppose intuition, as will seems to presuppose desire. But, since all things in spirit are organically interrelated, each moment or grade really presupposes all the rest. As Croce puts it in *The Philosophy of the Practical*, "philosophy is a circle and a unity and every point of it is intelligible only in relation to all others."[8] Convinced of the coherence and organic unity of spirit, Croce elaborates a system of philosophy which has sometimes been characterized as an absolutistic spiritual monism, or as idealistic humanism.

Since art, as intuition-expression, constitutes one of the categories or grades of spirit, it can have no types, kinds, varieties, techniques, ends, modes or degrees, characters or categories.[9] This is why Croce in his first *Aesthetic* proposes to drop from aesthetics much of the content traditionally associated with it. Banished from the domain of aesthetics, therefore, are rhetorical categories, such as "simple" and "ornate," "proper" and "metaphorical," pseudo-aesthetic concepts such as "tragic" and "comic," "sublime" and "ridiculous," the so-called "objective conditions of the beautiful," artistic "technique," as well as all technical or supposedly aesthetic theories of the different arts, and, finally, all classifications of arts. Croce also believes that the terms "beautiful" and "ugly" are not really useful to aesthetics, since the attempt to define such terms often leads aestheticians away from their primary task of understanding art as expression. However, as long as we understand and accept the basic truth that art is intuition-expression, Croce has no objection to our using "beauty" to refer to expression and "ugly" to refer to unsuccessful expression.[10] For, whereas a beautiful work is a perfect unity, a complete fusion of parts into a whole, an ugly work is an incompletely fused multiplicity. But while some things are absolutely beautiful (i.e. perfectly expressive), nothing is absolutely ugly (i.e. lacking in expressiveness).[11]

Although he continued to identify artistic intuition and expression throughout his life, Croce also continued to develop and sometimes to modify his aesthetic views after the completion of his first *Aesthetic* as he confronted new problems, attained new insights through solving them, and widened his knowledge of art.[12] To emphasize the emotional content of expression, he later focused attention on "lyrical intuition." Still later he stressed "cosmic intuition," the artistic expression of the totality of reality. Finally, in his last major work on poetry, *La Poesia* (1936), he modified further some of his earlier views and made a sharp distinction between poetry and literature. He gave an excellent statement of his aesthetics "in a nutshell" in an article for the *Encyclopaedia Britannica* from which the following selections are taken. Here his views are stated more maturely and less dogmatically than they were in his early *Aesthetic*, but with no less vigor and conviction.

Intuition, Expression, and Art

1. *Croce begins by stating and illustrating his basic conviction that a genuine poem consists of a complex of images and a feeling which are fused into an indivisible unity, a "lyrical intuition." The nature of poetry is, he goes on to explain, purely aesthetic, not practical. And what is true of poetry is, he believes, also true of the other arts; they, too, are to be understood in terms of lyrical expression and not in terms of any extraneous considerations.*

If we examine a poem in order to determine what it is that makes us feel it to be a poem, we at once find two constant and necessary elements: a complex of *images*, and a *feeling* that animates them. Let us, for instance, recall a passage learnt at school: Virgil's lines (*Aeneid*, iii, 294, *sqq.*), in which Aeneas describes how on hearing that in the country to whose shores he had come the Trojan Helenus was reigning, with Andromache, now his wife, he was overcome with amazement and a great desire to see his surviving son of Priam and to hear of his strange adventures. Andromache, whom he meets outside the walls of the city, by the waters of a river renamed Simois, celebrating funeral rites before a cenotaph of green turf and two altars to Hector and Astyanax; her astonishment on seeing him, her hesitation, the halting words in which she questions him, uncertain whether he is a man or a ghost; Aeneas's no less agitated replies and interrogations, and the pain and confusion with which she recalls the past—how she lived through scenes of blood and shame, how she was assigned by lot as slave and concubine to Pyrrhus, abandoned by him and united to Helenus, another of his slaves, how Pyrrhus fell by the hand of Orestes and Helenus became a free man and a king; the entry of Aeneas and his men into the city, and their reception by the son of Priam in this little Troy, this mimic Pergamon with its new Xanthus, and its Scaean Gate whose threshold Aeneas greets with a kiss—all these details, and others here omitted, are images of persons, things, attitudes, gestures, sayings, joy and sorrow; mere images, not history or historical criticism, for which they are neither given nor taken. But through them all there runs a feeling, a feeling which is our own no less than the poet's, a human feeling of bitter memories, of shuddering horror, of melancholy, of homesickness, of tenderness, of a kind of childish *pietas* that could prompt this vain revival of things perished, these playthings fashioned by a religious devotion, the *parva Troia*, the *Pergama simulata magnis*, the *arentem Xanthi cognomine rivum*: something inexpressible in logical terms, which only poetry can express in full. Moreover, these two elements may appear as two in a first abstract analysis, but they cannot be regarded as two distinct threads, however intertwined; for, in effect, the feeling is altogether converted into images, into this complex of images, and is thus a feeling that is contemplated and therefore resolved and transcended. Hence poetry must be called neither feeling, nor image, nor yet the sum of the two, but "contemplation of feeling" or "lyrical intuition" or (which is the same thing) "pure intuition"—pure, that is of all historical and critical reference to the reality or unreality of the images of which it is woven, and apprehending the pure throb of life in its ideality. Doubtless, other things may be found in poetry besides these two elements or moments and the synthesis of the two; but these other things are either present as extraneous elements in a compound (reflections, exhortations, polemics, allegories, etc.), or else they are just these image-feelings themselves taken in abstraction from their context as so much material, restored to the condition in which it was before the act of poetic creation. In the former case, they are non-poetic elements merely interpolated into or attached to the poem; in the latter, they are divested of poetry, rendered unpoetical by a reader either unpoetical or not at the moment poetical, who has dispelled the poetry, either because he cannot live in its ideal realm, or for the legitimate ends of historical enquiry or other practical purposes which involve the degradation—or rather, the conversion—of the poem into a document or an instrument....

What has been said of "poetry" applies to all the other "arts" commonly enumerated; painting, sculpture, architecture, music. Whenever the artistic quality of any product of the mind is discussed, the dilemma must be faced, that either it is a lyrical intuition, or it is something else, something just as respectable, but not art. If painting (as some theorists have maintained) were the imitation or reproduction of a given object, it would be, not art, but something mechanical and practical; if the task of the painter (as other theorists have held) were to combine lines and lights and colours with ingenious novelty of invention and effect, he would be, not an artist, but an inventor; if music consisted in similar combinations of notes, the paradox of Leibniz and Father Kircher would come true, and a man could write music without being a musician; or alternatively we should have to fear (as Proudhon did for poetry and John Stuart Mill for music) that the possible combinations of words or notes would one day be exhausted, and poetry or music would disappear. As in poetry, so in these other arts, it is notorious that foreign elements sometimes intrude themselves; foreign either *a parte objecti* or *a parte subjecti*, foreign either in fact or from the point of view of an inartistic spectator or listener. Thus the critics of these arts advise the artist to exclude, or at least not to rely upon, what they call the "literary" elements in painting, sculpture and music, just as the critic of poetry advises the writer to look for "poetry" and not be led astray by mere literature. The reader who understands poetry goes straight to this poetic heart and feels its beat upon his own; where this beat is silent, he denies that poetry is present, whatever and however many other things may take its place, united in the work, and however valuable they may be for skill and wisdom, nobility of intellect, quickness of wit and pleasantness of effect. The reader who does not understand poetry loses his way in pursuit of these other things. He is wrong not because he admires them, but because he thinks he is admiring poetry.[13]

2. *In order to make his definition of art clearer, Croce proceeds to distinguish art, as lyrical intuition, from other forms of activity and production with which it is sometimes confused—philosophy, history, natural science, the play of fancy, feeling in its immediacy, instruction and oratory, etc. By making these rather sharp distinctions, he is not only excluding these other forms of activity from the aesthetic domain; he is also showing, he believes, the true relations of art as an activity of mind or spirit to other mental or spiritual activities. The true artist does not feel and create without thinking, willing, and acting, any more than the man of practical affairs thinks, wills, and acts without feeling and having some degree of aesthetic experience.*

By defining art as lyrical intuition we have implicitly distinguished it from all other forms of mental production. If such distinctions are made explicit, we obtain the following negations:

1. *Art is not philosophy*, because philosophy is the logical thinking of the universal categories of being, and art is the unreflective intuition of being. Hence, while philosophy transcends the image and uses it for its own purposes, art lives in it as in a kingdom. It is said that art cannot behave in an irrational manner and cannot ignore logic; and certainly it is neither irrational nor illogical; but its own rationality, its own logic, is a quite different thing from the dialectical logic of the concept, and it was in order to indicate this peculiar and unique character that the name "logic of sense" or "aesthetic" was invented. The not uncommon assertion that art has a logical character, involves either an equivocation between conceptual logic and aesthetic logic, or a symbolic expression of the latter in terms of the former.

2. *Art is not history*, because history implies the critical distinction between reality and unreality; the reality of the passing moment and the reality of a fancied world: the reality of fact and the reality of desire. For art, these distinctions are as yet unmade; it lives, as we have said, upon pure images. The historical existence of Helenus, Andromache and Aeneas makes no difference to the poetical quality of Virgil's poem. Here, too, an objection has been raised: namely that art is not wholly indifferent to his-

torical criteria, because it obeys the laws of "verisimilitude"; but, here again, "verisimilitude" is only a rather clumsy metaphor for the mutual coherence of images, which without this internal coherence would fail to produce their effect as images, like Horace's *delphinus in silvis* and *aper in fluctibus*.

3. *Art is not natural science*, because natural science is historical fact classified and so made abstract; nor is it *mathematical science*, because mathematics performs operations with abstractions and does not contemplate. The analogy sometimes drawn between mathematical and poetical creation is based on merely external and generic resemblances; and the alleged necessity of a mathematical or geometrical basis for the arts is only another metaphor, a symbolic expression of the constructive, cohesive and unifying force of the poetic mind building itself a body of images.

4. *Art is not the play of fancy*, because the play of fancy passes from image to image, in search of variety, rest or diversion, seeking to amuse itself with the likenesses of things that give pleasure or have an emotional and pathetic interest; whereas in art the fancy is so dominated by the single problem of converting chaotic feeling into clear intuition, that we recognize the propriety of ceasing to call it fancy and calling it imagination, poetic imaginaton or creative imagination. Fancy as such is as far removed from poetry as are the works of Mrs. Radcliffe or Dumas *père*.

5. *Art is not feeling in its immediacy.*—Andromache, on seeing Aeneas, becomes *amens, diriguit visu in medio, labitur, longo vix tempore fatur*, and when she speaks *longos ciebat incassum fletus;* but the poet does not lose his wits or grow stiff as he gazes; he does not totter or weep or cry; he expresses himself in harmonious verses, having made these various perturbations the object of which he sings. Feelings in their immediacy are "expressed" for if they were not, if they were not also sensible and bodily facts ("psychophysical phenomena," as the positivists used to call them) they would not be concrete things, and so they would be nothing at all. Andromache expressed herself in the way described above. But "expression" in this sense, even when accompanied by consciousness, is a mere metaphor from "mental" or "aesthetic expression" which alone really expresses, that is, gives to feeling a theoretical form and converts it into words, song and outward shape. This distinction between contemplated feeling, or poetry, and feeling enacted or endured, is the source of the power, ascribed to art, of "liberating us from the passions" and "calming"

us (the power of *catharsis*), and of the consequent condemnation, from an aesthetic point of view, of works of art, or parts of them, in which immediate feeling has a place or finds a vent. Hence, too, arises another characteristic of poetic expression—really synonymous with the last—namely its "infinity" as opposed to the "finitude" of immediate feeling or passion; or, as it is also called, the "universal" or "cosmic" character of poetry. Feeling, not crushed but contemplated by the work of poetry, is seen to diffuse itself in widening circles over all the realm of the soul, which is the realm of the universe, echoing and re-echoing endlessly: joy and sorrow, pleasure and pain, energy and lassitude, earnestness and frivolity, and so forth, are linked to each other and lead to each other through infinite shades and gradations; so that the feeling, while preserving its individual physiognomy and its original dominating motive, is not exhausted by or restricted to this original character. A comic image, if it is poetically comic, carries with it something that is not comic, as in the case of Don Quixote or Falstaff; and the image of something terrible is never, in poetry, without an atoning element of loftiness, goodness and love.

6. *Art is not instruction or oratory:* it is not circumscribed and limited by service to any practical purpose whatever, whether this be the inculcation of a particular philosophical, historical or scientific truth, or the advocacy of a particular way of feeling and the action corresponding to it. Oratory at once robs expression of its "infinity" and independence, and, by making it the means to an end, dissolves it in this end. Hence arises what Schiller called the "non-determining" character of art, as opposed to the "determining" character of oratory; and hence the justifiable suspicion of "political poetry"—political poetry being, proverbially, bad poetry.

7. As art is not to be confused with the form of practical action most akin to it, namely instruction and oratory, so *a fortiori*, it must not be confused with other forms directed to the production of certain effects, whether these consist in pleasure, enjoyment and utility, or in goodness and righteousness. We must exclude from art not only meretricious works, but also those inspired by a desire for goodness, as equally, though differently, inartistic and repugnant to lovers of poetry. Flaubert's remark that indecent books lacked *vérité*, is parallel to Voltaire's gibe that certain "poésies sacrées" were really "sacrées, car personne n'y touche.[14]..."

The "negations" here made explicit are obviously, from another point of view, "relations"; for the various distinct forms of mental activity cannot be conceived as separate each from the rest and acting in self-supporting isolation. This is not the place to set forth a complete system of the forms or categories of the mind in their order and their dialectic; confining ourselves to art, we must be content to say that the category of art, like every other category, mutually presupposes and is presupposed by all the rest: it is conditioned by them all and conditions them all. How could the aesthetic synthesis, which is poetry, arise, were it not preceded by a state of mental commotion? *Si vis me flere, dolendum est*,[15] and so forth. And what is this state of mind which we have called feeling, but the whole mind, with its past thoughts, volitions and actions, now thinking and desiring and suffering and rejoicing, travailing within itself? Poetry is like a ray of sunlight shining upon this darkness, lending it its own light and making visible the hidden forms of things. Hence it cannot be produced by an empty and dull mind; hence those artists who embrace the creed of pure art or art for art's sake, and close their hearts to the troubles of life and the cares of thought, are found to be wholly unproductive, or at most rise to the imitation of others or to an impressionism devoid of concentration. Hence the basis of all poetry is human personality, and, since human personality finds its completion in morality, the basis of all poetry is the moral consciousness. Of course this does not mean that the artist must be a profound thinker or an acute critic; nor that he must be a pattern of virtue or a hero; but he must have a share in the world of thought and action which will enable him, either in his own person or by sympathy with others, to live the whole drama of human life. He may sin, lose the purity of his heart, and expose himself, as a practical agent, to blame; but he must have a keen sense of purity and impurity, righteousness and sin, good and evil. He may not be endowed with great practical courage; he may even betray signs of timidity and cowardice; but he must feel the dignity of courage. Many artistic inspirations are due, not to what the artist, as a man, is in practice, but to what he is not, and feels that he ought to be admiring and enjoying the qualities he lacks when he sees them in others. Many, perhaps the finest, pages of heroic and warlike poetry are by men who never had the nerve or the skill to handle a weapon. On the other hand, we are not maintaining that the possession of a moral personality is enough to make a poet or an artist. To be a *vir bonus*[16] does not make a man even an orator, unless he is also *dicendi peritus*.[17] The *sine qua non* of poetry is poetry, that form of theoretical synthesis which we have defined above; the spark of poetical genius without which all the rest is mere fuel, not burning because no fire is at hand to light it. But the figure of the pure poet, the pure artist, the votary of pure Beauty, aloof from contact with humanity, is no real figure but a caricature.

That poetry not only presupposes the other forms of human mental activity but is presupposed by them, is proved by the fact that without the poetic imagination which gives contemplative form to the workings of feeling, intuitive expression to obscure impressions, and thus becomes representations and words, whether spoken or sung or painted or otherwise uttered, logical thought could not arise. Logical thought is not language, but it never exists without language, and it uses the language which poetry has created; by means of concepts, it discerns and dominates the representations of poetry, and it could not dominate them unless they, its future subjects, had first an existence of their own. Further, without the discerning and criticizing activity of thought, action would be impossible; and if action, then good action, the moral consciousness, duty. Every man, however much he may seem to be all logical thinker, critic, scientist, or all absorbed in practical interests or devoted to duty, cherishes at the bottom of his heart his own private store of imagination and poetry; even Faust's pedantic *famulus*, Wagner, confessed that he often had his "grillenhafte Stunden."[18] Had this element been altogether denied him, he would not have been a man, and therefore not even a thinking or acting being. This extreme case is an absurdity; but in proportion as this private store is scanty, we find a certain superficialty and aridity in thought, and a certain coldness in action.[19]

3. *Croce does not believe that his doctrine that art is lyrical intuition goes against the ordinary conception of art. Although it is an a priori* concept, *art manifests itself in individual works which could not exist without its creative activity. Out of reflection on art, aesthetics, the science of art or of intuition-expression, has developed. This science Croce conceives to be non-dogmatic, perpetually developing, and necessarily philosophical.*

The concept of art expounded above is in a sense the ordinary concept, which appears with greater or less clarity in all statements about art, and is constantly appealed to, explicitly or implicitly, as the fixed point round which all discussions on the subject gravitate: and this, not only nowadays, but at all times, as could be shown by the collection and interpretation of things said by writers, poets, artists, laymen and even the common people. But it is desirable to dispel the illusion that this concept exists as an innate idea, and to replace this by the truth, that it operates as an *a priori* concept. Now an *a priori* concept does not exist by itself, but only in the individual products which it generates. Just as the *a priori* reality called Art, Poetry or Beauty does not exist in a transcendent region where it can be perceived and admired in itself, but only in the innumerable works of poetry, of art and of beauty which it has formed and continues to form, so the logical *a priori* concept of art exists nowhere but in the particular judgments which it has formed and continues to form, the refutations which it has effected and continues to effect, the demonstrations it makes, the theories it constructs, the problems and groups of problems, which it solves and has solved. The definitions and distinctions and negations and relations expounded above have each its own history, and have been progressively worked out in the course of centuries, and in them we now possess the fruits of this complex and unremitting toil. Aesthetic, or the science of art, has not therefore the task (attributed to it by certain scholastic conceptions) of defining art once for all and deducing from this conception its various doctrines, so as to cover the whole field of aesthetic science; it is only the perpetual systematization, always renewed and always growing, of the problems arising from time to time out of reflection upon art, and is identical with the solutions of the difficulties and the criticisms of the errors which act as stimulus and material to the unceasing progress of thought. This being so, no exposition of aesthetic (especially a summary exposition such as can alone be given here) can claim to deal exhaustively with the innumerable problems which have arisen and may arise in the course of the history of aesthetics; it can only mention and discuss the chief, and among these, by preference, those which still make themselves felt and resist solution in ordinary educated thought; adding an implied "et cetera," so that the reader may pursue the subject according to the criteria set before him, either by going again over old discussions, or by entering into those of to-day, which change and multiply and assume new shapes almost daily. Another warning must not be omitted: namely that aesthetics, though a special philosophical science, having as its principle a special and distinct category of the mind, can never, just because it is philosophical, be detached from the main body of philosophy; for its problems are concerned with the relations between art and the other mental forms, and therefore imply both difference and identity. Aesthetics is really the whole of philosophy, but with special emphasis on that side of it which concerns art. Many have demanded or imagined or desired a self-contained aesthetics, devoid of any general philosophical implications, and consistent with more than one, or with any, philosophy; but the project is impossible of execution because self-contradictory. Even those who promise to expound a naturalistic, inductive, physical, physiological or psychological aesthetics—in a word, a non-philosophical aesthetics—when they pass from promise to performance surreptitiously introduce a general positivistic, naturalistic or even materialistic philosophy. And anyone who thinks that the philosophical ideas of positivism, naturalism, and materialism are false and out of date, will find it an easy matter to refute the aesthetic or pseudo-aesthetic doctrines which mutually support them and are supported by them, and will not regard their problems as problems still awaiting solution or worthy of discussion—or, at least, protracted discussion. For instance, the downfall of psychological associationism (or the substitution of mechanism for *a priori* synthesis) implies the downfall not only of logical associationism but of aesthetics also, with its association of "content" and "form," or of two "representations," which (unlike Campanella's *tactus intrinsecus*,[20] effected *cum magna suavitate*[21]) was a *contactus extrinsecus*[22] whose terms were no sooner united than they *discedebant*.[23] The collapse of biological and evolutionary explanations of logical and ethical values implies the same collapse in the case of aesthetic value. The proved inability of empirical methods to yield knowledge of reality, which in fact they can only classify and reduce to types, involves the impossibility of an aesthetics arrived at by collecting aesthetic facts in classes and discovering their laws by induction.[24]

4. *Croce now presents his most characteristic and controversial aesthetic doctrine: intuition and expression are identical. Although this doctrine may at first seem paradoxical, he believes that it accords both with common sense and true philosophy. For to be*

*capable of intuiting something clearly and fully is also to be
capable of giving it (at least inwardly) a clear and full expression.
But we must be careful, Croce points out, not to confuse expression, which is the same as intuition, with communication,
which is different. While we may be quite capable of intuiting-
expressing an image, we may not (and do not have to) choose
to embody it in a so-called external, physical thing. And when we
do choose to do this we pass from the strictly aesthetic into the
practical sphere, the sphere of artistic technique, which is not
properly the concern of aesthetics, the science of intuition-
expression. Genuine artistic expression is, according to Croce's
idealism, primarily, and exclusively, an inner, formative spiritual
activity which is not dependent upon matter or physical things
(mere abstractions in his view) for its reality and significance.*

One of the first problems to arise, when the work of art is
defined as "lyrical image," concerns the relation of "intuition" to
"expression" and the manner of the transition from the one to the
other. At bottom this is the same problem which arises in other
parts of philosophy: the problem of inner and outer, of mind and
matter, of soul and body, and, in ethics, of intention and will,
will and action, and so forth. Thus stated, the problem is insoluble;
for once we have divided the inner from the outer, body from
mind, will from action, or intuition from expression, there is no
way of passing from one to the other or of reuniting them, unless
we appeal for their reunion to a third term, variously represented
as God or the Unknowable. Dualism leads necessarily either to
transcendence or to agnosticism. But when a problem is found to
be insoluble in the terms in which it is stated the only course
open is to criticize these terms themselves, to inquire how they
have been arrived at, and whether their genesis was logically
sound. In this case, such inquiry leads to the conclusion that the
terms depend not upon a philosophical principle, but upon an
empirical and naturalistic classification, which has created two
groups of facts called internal and external respectively (as if
internal facts were not also external, and as if an external fact
could exist without being also internal), or souls and bodies, or
images and expressions; and everyone knows that it is hopeless
to try to find a dialectical unity between terms that have been
distinguished not philosophically or formally but only empirically
and materially. The soul is only a soul in so far as it is a body;

the will is only a will in so far as it moves arms and legs, or is action; intuition is only intuition in so far as it is, in that very act, expression. An image that does not express, that is not speech, song, drawing, painting, sculpture or architecture—speech at least murmured to oneself, song at least echoing within one's own breast, line and colour seen in imagination and colouring with its own tint the whole soul and organism—is an image that does not exist. We may assert its existence, but we cannot support our assertion; for the only thing we could adduce in support of it would be the fact that the image was embodied or expressed. This profound philosophical doctrine, the *identity of intuition and expression* is, moreover, a principle of ordinary common sense, which laughs at people who claim to have thoughts they cannot express or to have imagined a great picture which they cannot paint. *Rem tene, verba sequentur;* [25] if there are no *verba*, there is no *res*. This identity, which applies to every sphere of the mind, has in the sphere of art a clearness and self-evidence lacking, perhaps, elsewhere. In the creation of a work of poetry, we are present, as it were, at the mystery of the creation of the world; hence the value of the contribution made by aesthetics to philosophy as a whole, or the conception of the One that is All. Aesthetics, by denying in the life of art an abstract spiritualism and the resulting dualism, prepares the way and leads the mind towards idealism or absolute spiritualism. . . .

Objections to the identity of intuition and expression generally arise from psychological illusions which lead us to believe that we possess at any given moment a profusion of concrete and lively images, when in fact we only possess signs and names for them; or else from faulty analysis of cases like that of the artist who is believed to express mere fragments of a world of images that exists in his mind in its entirety, whereas he really has in his mind only these fragments, together with—not the supposed complete world, but at most an aspiration or obscure working towards it, towards a greater and richer image which may take shape or may not. But these objections also arise from a confusion between *expression* and *communication,* the latter being really distinct from the image and its expression. Communication is the fixation of the intuition-expression upon an object metaphorically called material or physical; in reality, even here we are concerned not with material or physical things but with a mental process. The proof that the so-called physical object is unreal, and its resolution into terms of mind, is primarily of interest for our general philosophical conceptions, and only indirectly for the elucidation of aesthetic questions; hence for brevity's sake we may let the metaphor or symbol stand and speak of matter or nature. It is clear that the poem is complete as soon as the poet has expressed it in words which he repeats to himself. When he comes to repeat them aloud, for others to hear, or looks for someone to learn them by heart and repeat them to others in a *schola cantorum*, or sets them down in writing or in printing, he has entered upon a new stage, not aesthetic but practical, whose social and cultural importance need not, of course, be insisted upon. So with the painter; he paints on his panel or canvas, but he could not paint unless at every stage of his work, from the original blur or sketch to the finishing touches, the intuited image, the line and colour painted in his imagination, preceded the brush-stroke. Indeed, when the brush-stroke outruns the image, it is cancelled and replaced by the artist's correction of his own work. The exact line that divides expression from communication is difficult to draw in the concrete case, for in the concrete case the two processes generally alternate rapidly and appear to mingle, but it is clear in idea, and it must be firmly grasped. Through overlooking it, or blurring it through insufficient attention, arise the confusions between *art* and *technique*. Technique is not an intrinsic element of art but has to do precisely with the concept of communication. In general it is a cognition or complex of cognitions disposed and directed to the furtherance of practical action; and, in the case of art, of the practical action which makes objects and instruments for the recording and communicating of works of art; e.g., cognitions concerning the preparation of panels, canvases or walls to be painted, pigments, varnishes, ways of obtaining good pronunciation and declamation and so forth. Technical treatises are not aesthetic treatises, nor yet parts or chapters of them. Provided, that is, that the ideas are rigorously conceived and the words used accurately in relation to them it would not be worth while to pick a quarrel over the use of the word "technique" as a synonym for the artistic work itself, regarded as "inner technique" or the formation of intuition-expressions. The confusion between art and technique is especially beloved by impotent artists, who hope to obtain from practical things and practical devices and inventions the help which their strength does not enable them to give themselves.[26]

5. We must not forget that the work of art is not, for Croce, a physical thing, but a mental creation or (for the appreciator) a re-creation. The physical thing which we sometimes (mistakenly) refer to as an art object is only a relatively permanent practical instrument produced by the artist in order to communicate his original intuition-expression to us. Without it, however, we could not re-create the artist's lyrical intuition, the real work of art, in our own minds. Since genuine art consists of this inner, unitary mental process, it is impossible to divide or to differentiate various arts upon meaningful aesthetic grounds. Croce also points out that the so-called natural beauties are only existing physical things which can serve as stimulants to poetic imagination.

The work of communicating and conserving artistic images, with the help of technique, produces the material objects metaphorically called *"artistic objects"* or *"works of art"*: pictures, sculptures and buildings, and, in a more complicated manner, literary and musical writings, and, in our own times, gramophones and records which make it possible to reproduce voices and sounds. But neither these voices and sounds nor the symbols of writing, sculpture and architecture, are works of art; works of art exist only in the minds that create or recreate them. To remove the appearance of paradox from the truth that beautiful objects, beautiful things, do not exist, it may be opportune to recall the analogous case of economic science, which knows perfectly well that in the sphere of economics there are no naturally or physically *useful* things, but only demand and labour, from which physical things acquire, metaphorically, this epithet. A student of economics who wished to deduce the economic value of things from their physical qualities would be perpetuating a gross *ignoratio elenchi.*[27]

Yet this same *ignoratio elenchi* has been, and still is, committed in aesthetic, by the theory of special *arts*, and the limits or peculiar aesthetic character of each. The divisions between the arts are merely technical or physical, according as the artistic objects consist of physical sounds, notes, coloured objects, carved or modelled objects or constructed objects having no apparent correspondence with natural bodies (poetry, music, painting, sculpture, architecture, etc.). To ask what is the artistic character of each of these arts, what it can and cannot do, what kinds of images can be expressed in sounds, what in notes, what in colours, what in lines, and so forth, is like asking in economics what things are entitled by their physical qualities to have a value and what are not, and what relative values they are entitled to have; whereas it is clear that physical qualities do not enter into the question, and anything may be desired or demanded or valued more than another, or more than anything else at all, according to circumstances and needs. Even Lessing found himself slipping down the slope leading to this truth, and was forced to such strange conclusions as that actions belonged to poetry and bodies to sculpture; even Richard Wagner attempted to find a place in the list for a comprehensive art, namely Opera, including in itself by a process of aggregation the powers of all the arts. A reader with any artistic sense finds in a single solitary line from a poet at once musical and picturesque qualities, sculpturesque strength and architectural structure; and the same with a picture, which is never a mere thing of the eyes but an affair of the whole soul, and exists in the soul not only as colour but as sound and speech. But when we try to grasp these musical or picturesque or other qualities, they elude us and turn into each other, and melt into a unity, however we may be accustomed to distinguish them by different names; a practical proof that art is one and cannot be divided into arts. One, and infinitely varied; not according to the technical conceptions of the several arts, but according to the infinite variety of artistic personalities and their states of mind.

With this relation (and confusion) between artistic creations and instruments of communication or *objets d'art* must be connected the problem of *natural beauty*. We shall not discuss the question, raised by certain aestheticians, whether there are in nature other poets, other artistic beings, beside man; a question which ought to be answered in the affirmative not only out of respect for the song-birds, but, still more, out of respect for the idealistic conception of the world as life and spirituality throughout; even if (as the fairy-tale goes) we have but the magic herb which when we put it in our mouth, gives us the power of understanding the language of animals and plants. The phrase *natural beauty* properly refers to persons, things and places whose effect is comparable to that of poetry, painting, sculpture and the other arts. There is no difficulty in allowing the existence of such "natural *objets d'art,*" for the process of poetic communication may take place by means of objects naturally given as well as by means of objects artificially produced. The lover's imagination creates a woman beautiful to him, and personifies her in Laura; the pilgrim's imagination creates the charming or sublime landscape, and embodies it in the scene of a lake or a mountain; and these creations of theirs are sometimes shared by more or less wide social circles, thus becoming the "professional beauties" admired by everyone and the famous "views" before which all experience a more or less sincere rapture. No doubt, these creations are mortal; ridicule sometimes kills them, satiety may bring neglect, fashion may replace them by others; and—unlike works of art— they do not admit of authentic interpretation. The bay of Naples, seen from the height of one of the most beautiful Neapolitan villas, was after some time described by the Russian lady who owned the villa as *une cuvette bleue*,[28] whose blue encircled by green so wearied her that she sold the villa. But even the *cuvette bleue* was a legitimate poetical creation.[29]

6. *Although Croce is willing to admit the utility of classificatory concepts and categories in dealing with the so-called art objects in the practical sphere, he is firm in rejecting the relevance of such devices to the aesthetical understanding of art as lyrical intuition.*

Effects at once greater and more detrimental upon the criticism and historical study of art and literature have been produced by a theory of similar but slightly different origin, the theory of *literary and artistic kinds*. This, like the foregoing, is based on a classification in itself justifiable and useful. The foregoing is based on a technical or physical classification of artistic objects; this is based on a classification according to the feelings which form their content or motive, into *tragic, comic, lyrical, heroic, erotic, idyllic, romantic* and so on, with divisions and subdivisions. It is useful in practice to distribute an artist's work, for purposes of publication, into these classes, putting lyrics in one volume, dramas in another, poems in a third and romances in a fourth; and it is convenient, in fact, indispensable, to refer to works and groups of works by these names in speaking and writing of them. But here again we must deny and pronounce illegitimate the transition from these classificatory concepts to the poetic laws of composition and aesthetic criteria of judgment, as when people try to decide that a tragedy must have a subject of a certain kind, characters of a certain kind, a plot of a certain kind and a certain length; and, when confronted by a work, instead of looking for and appraising its own poetry, ask whether it is a tragedy or a poem, and whether it obeys the "laws" of one or other "kind." The literary criticism of the 19th century owed its great progress largely to its abandonment of the criteria of kinds, in which the criticism of the Renaissance and the French classicists had always been entangled, as may be seen from the discussions arising out of the poems of Dante, Ariosto and Tasso, Guarini's *Pastor fido*, Corneille's *Cid*, and Lope de Vega's *comedias*. Artists have profited by this liberation less than critics; for anyone with artistic genius bursts the fetters of such servitude, or even makes them the instruments of his power; and the artist with little or no genius turns his very freedom into a new slavery.

It has been thought that the divisions of kinds could be saved by giving them a philosophical significance; or at any rate one such division, that of lyric, epic and dramatic, regarded as the three moments of a process of objectification passing from the lyric, the outpouring of the ego, to the epic, in which the ego detaches its feeling from itself by narrating it, and thence to the drama, in which it allows this feeling to create of itself its own mouthpieces, the *dramatis personae*. But the lyric is not a pouring-forth; it is not a cry or a lament; it is an objectification in which the ego sees itself on the stage, narrates itself, and dramatizes itself; and this lyrical spirit forms the poetry both of epic and of drama, which are therefore distinguished from the lyric only by external signs. A work which is altogether poetry, like *Macbeth* or *Antony and Cleopatra*, is substantially a lyric in which the various tones and successive verses are represented by characters and scenes.

In the old aesthetics, and even to-day in those which perpetuate the type, an important place is given to the so-called categories of beauty: the *sublime*, the *tragic*, the *comic*, the *graceful*, the *humorous* and so forth, which German philosophers not only claimed to treat as philosophical concepts, but developed by means of that dialectic which belongs only to pure or speculative concepts, philosophical categories. Thus they arranged them in an imaginary progress culminating now in the Beautiful, now in the Tragic, now in the Humorous. Taking these concepts at their face value, we may observe their substantial correspondence with the concepts of the literary and artistic kinds; and this is the source from which, as excerpts from manuals of literature, they have found their way into philosophy. As psychological and empirical concepts, they do not belong to aesthetics; and as a whole, in their common quality, they refer merely to the world of feelings, empirically grouped and classified, which forms the permanent matter of artistic intuition.[30]

NOTES

1. On Croce's life, see *Benedetto Croce: An Autobiography*, translated by R. G. Collingwood (Oxford, Clarendon Press, 1928); Cecil Sprigge, *Benedetto Croce: Man and Thinker* (New Haven, Yale University Press, 1952), and Gian N. G. Orsini, *Benedetto Croce: Philosopher of Art and Literary Critic* (Carbondale, Ill., Southern Illinois University Press, 1961), pp. 293–298.

2. See Croce's discussion of Hegel, Vico, and De Sanctis in Part II of his *Aesthetic as Science of Expression and General Linguistic*, translated by Douglas Ainslie, revised edition (New York, Noonday Press, 1953). For a fuller account of his views on Hegel, see his work *What Is Living and What Is Dead of the Philosophy of Hegel*, translated by Douglas Ainslie (London, Macmillan, 1915). For comparisons of Croce's aesthetic views with those of Vico and De Sanctis, see two articles by Angelo A. de Gennaro, "Croce and Vico," *Journal of Aesthetics and Art Criticism*, XXII (Fall, 1963), 43–46, and "Croce and De Sanctis," *JAAC*, XXIII (Winter, 1964), 227–231.

3. Benedetto Croce, "Aesthetics" in *Encyclopaedia Britannica*, 14th edition, 1929. Although this article is considered to be one of the most satisfactory statements of Croce's own aesthetics, it contains a rather biased account of the history of aesthetics.

4. Benedetto Croce, *The Essence of Aesthetics*, translated by Douglas Ainslie (London, William Heinemann, 1921).

5. Benedetto Croce, *Aesthetic as Science of Expression and General Linguistic*, translated by Douglas Ainslie (London, Macmillan, 1909), p. 386. This first edition of Ainslie's translation of Croce's *Aesthetic* contains in an appendix Croce's important lecture "Pure Intuition and the Lyrical Character of Art" which he delivered before the Third International Congress of Philosophy held in Heidelberg, Sept. 2, 1908.

6. One of the clearest and best explanations of what Croce meant by "intuition" is given by Gian N. G. Orsini in *Benedetto Croce: Philosopher of Art and Literary Critic*, cited above, Chap. 2.

7. Benedetto Croce, *Aesthetic as Science of Expression and General Linguistic*, translated by Douglas Ainslie, revised edition (New York, Noonday Press, 1953), pp. 8–9.

8. Benedetto Croce, *Philosophy of the Practical*, translated by Douglas Ainslie (London, Macmillan, 1913), p. 442.

9. See Croce's *Aesthetic as Science of Expression and General Linguistic*, cited above, Part I, Chaps. IX and XII.

10. Ibid., pp. 78–79.

11. Ibid., p. 79.

12. The various stages in the later development of Croce's aesthetic theory are discussed by Gian N. G. Orsini in *Benedetto Croce: Philosopher of Art and Literary Critic*, cited above, Chaps. XI–XIII.

13. Benedetto Croce, "Aesthetics," *Encyclopaedia Britannica,* [14th edition] (London, Chicago, Toronto, Encyclopaedia Britannica, c. 1929–1941), Vol. I, 263–264.

14. "Sacred, because no one touches it."

15. Croce has quoted part of the famous line from Horace's *Art of Poetry* in which the aspiring poet is told that if he wants his reader to weep, he must first feel grief himself.

16. Good man.

17. Skilled in speaking.

18. "Whimsical hours."

19. Croce, "Aesthetics," cited above, pp. 264–265.

20. Influence from the inside.

21. With great pleasantness.

22. Contact from the outside.

23. Were drawing apart.

24. Croce, "Aesthetics," cited above, pp. 265–266.

25. Grasp the idea, the words will follow.

26. Croce, "Aesthetics," cited above, pp. 266–267.

27. Ignorance of the point at issue, or the logical fallacy which arises from an attempt to win an argument by proving a point not at issue.

28. A blue washbowl.

29. Croce, "Aesthetics," cited above, p. 267.

30. Ibid., pp. 267–268.

QUESTIONS AND TOPICS FOR FURTHER STUDY

1. Explain Croce's definition of poetry. What do the other arts have in common with poetry?

2. How does Croce distinguish art from philosophy, history, natural science, and other modes of thought and action? Why does he think these distinctions are necessary?

3. Explain why Croce believes that "poetry not only presupposes the other forms of human mental activity but is presupposed by them"?

4. What is Croce's view of the tasks of aesthetics? Why, in his view, is it a necessarily philosophical science?

5. Explain the meaning of Croce's statement that "intuition is only intuition in as far as it is, in that very act, expression." What is his view of the distinction between expression and communication? Why is this distinction so important to his aesthetic theory?

6. Why does Croce believe that art is not a matter of technique? Under what conditions would he consider it meaningful to refer to "artistic technique"?

7. How does Croce distinguish the art object from the genuine work of art? Why does he object to the theory of special arts? What would be his criticism of Lessing's attempt to define the limits of poetry and painting?

8. Explain Croce's view of natural beauty. What does he mean by "natural *objets d'art*"?

9. Of what use is the theory of literary and artistic kinds, according to Croce? Why does he think that such a theory can sometimes be misleading?

10. Topics for further study: (a) the metaphysical basis of Croce's aesthetics; (b) Croce and Santayana on artistic expression; (c) Croce's approach to literary criticism; (d) Croce's view of the identity of linguistics and aesthetics; (e) some recent critics of Croce's aesthetics.

GUIDE TO SUPPLEMENTARY READING

(Works marked with asterisks are available in paperbound editions.)

I. PRIMARY SOURCES

Croce, Benedetto, *Aesthetic as Science of Expression and General Linguistic, translated by Douglas Ainslie (New York, Noonday Press, 1952).

———The Essence of Aesthetic, translated by Douglas Ainslie (London, William Heinemann, 1921).

———*My Philosophy: Essays on the Moral and Political Problems of Our Time, selected by R. Klibansky and translated by E. F. Carritt (New York, Collier Books, 1962). Chaps. 20, 21, 22.

———"Aesthetics," in Encyclopaedia Britannica, 14th edition, 1929.

II. SECONDARY WORKS

Abercrombie, Lascelles, "Communication versus Expression in Art," British Journal of Psychology, 14 (1923), 68–78.

Bertocci, Angelo, "Croce's Aesthetic in Context," The Personalist, XXXVIII (1957), 248–259.

Bosanquet, Bernard, "Croce's Aesthetic," Proceedings of the British Academy, (1919–1920), 261–288.

Brown, Merle E., "Croce's Early Aesthetics: 1894–1912," Journal of Aesthetics and Art Criticism, XXII (Fall, 1963), 29–41.

Carr, Herbert Wildon, The Philosophy of Benedetto Croce: The Problem of Art and History (London, Macmillan, 1917).

Carritt, Edgar F., *The Theory of Beauty* (New York, Barnes and Noble, 1962), Chap. VIII.

———"Croce and his Aesthetic," *Mind*, 62 (1953), 452–465.

Cock, Albert A., "The Aesthetic of Benedetto Croce," *Proceedings of the Aristotelian Society*, 15 (1914–1915), 164–198.

De Gennaro, Angelo A., **The Philosophy of Benedetto Croce* (New York, Citadel Press, 1961).

———"The Drama of the Aesthetics of Benedetto Croce," *JAAC*, XV (September, 1956), 117–121.

Gilbert, Katharine E., "The One and the Many in Croce's Aesthetic," in *Studies in Recent Aesthetic* (Chapel Hill, University of North Carolina Press, 1927).

Hospers, John, "The Croce-Collingwood Theory of Art," *Philosophy*, 31 (1956), 291–308.

Mayo, Bernard, "Art, Language, and Philosophy in Croce," *Philosophical Quarterly*, 5 (1955), 245–260.

Nahm, Milton C., "The Philosophy of Aesthetic Expression: The Crocean Hypothesis," *JAAC*, 13 (1955), 458–468.

Orsini, Gian N. G., *Benedetto Croce: Philosopher of Art and Literary Critic* (Carbondale, Ill., Southern Illinois University Press, 1961).

———"Theory and Practice in Croce's Aesthetics," *JAAC*, XIII (March, 1955), 300–313.

Piccoli, Raffaello, *Benedetto Croce: An Introduction to His Philosophy* (New York, Harcourt, Brace & Co., 1922).

Roditi, Edouard, "The Growth and Structure of Croce's Philosophy," *JAAC* (Spring, 1942), 14–29.

Seerveld, Calvin G., *Benedetto Croce's Earlier Aesthetic Theories and Literary Criticism* (Kampen, Holland, J. H. Kok, 1958).

Simoni, Frederic S., "Benedetto Croce: A Case of International Misunderstanding," *JAAC*, XI (September, 1952), 7–14.

Sprigge, Cecil, *Benedetto Croce: Man and Thinker* (New Haven, Yale University Press, 1952).

Wasiolek, Edward, "Croce and Contextualist Criticism," *Modern Philology*, 57 (1959), 44–54.

Wimsatt, William K., Jr., and Cleanth Brooks, *Literary Criticism: A Short History* (New York, Alfred A. Knopf, 1957). Chap. 23.

Zink, Sidney, "Intuition and Externalization in Croce's Aesthetic," *Journal of Philosophy*, XLVII (1950), 210–216.

CHAPTER 12

Creative Vision and Symbolic Form

FRY AND CASSIRER

Aesthetic formalism is the theory that the aesthetic appreciation of a work of art necessarily involves focusing attention on the work's form—its structural design, its integrated pattern, its ordered relations—rather than on its content or matter, or on what it supposedly represents, or on the emotion or idea it may evoke in the appreciator. Since aesthetic formalists have often disagreed as to what exactly should be included in the conception and analysis of form, their theories have differed considerably one from another in the history of aesthetics.[1] Plato is sometimes called a precursor of aesthetic formalism in that he recognized that aesthetic pleasure can be derived from the contemplation of formal elements.[2] But Kant is usually given credit for having provided the germinal ideas of modern formalist theories by pointing out in his *Critique of Judgment* that aesthetic pleasure has to do only with the form of an object as it is judged aesthetically and, further, by distinguishing between purely formal or "free" beauty and beauty dependent upon concepts, "adherent" beauty.[3] Drawing its inspiration not so much from Kant as from his follower, Johann Friedrich Herbart (1776–1841), formalism became a fully articulated aesthetic theory, with vocal proponents and opponents, in Germany during the latter half of the nineteenth century.[4]

According to Herbart's teaching, the main task of aesthetics is to indicate the "elementary aesthetic relations" which account for the power of works of art.[5] No single element is beautiful taken in isolation from the whole in which it plays a significant part; formal relations, not material contents, are fundamental to aesthetic experience. Herbart's formalism was further developed and staunchly defended by Robert Zimmermann (1824–1898), often called the "father of formalist aesthetics." Defining aesthetics as "the science of forms," Zimmermann directed his attention thereafter to the knowledge and evaluation of aesthetic forms. The aesthetician, he held, should always be concerned primarily with the *how*, not with the *what* of aesthetic apprehension. It is only form that matters. The noisy war which ensued in German aesthetic circles between Zimmermann, supported by a flock of faithful formalists, and the still orthodox content-oriented Hegelians may seem today to have been for the most part a war over a vast but barren territory of meaningless abstractions.[6] But several fruitful and meaningful results emerged from the form–content controversies. The Viennese music critic Eduard Hanslick (1825–1904) was stimulated to work out a strictly formalist aesthetics of music based on his conviction that "the essence of music is sound and motion." [7] Deeper explorations into the nature of form in the visual arts, undertaken by the art critic Conrad Fiedler (1841–1895) and the sculptor Adolf von Hildebrand (1847–1921),[8] led to the formulation of the highly influential conception of "pure visibility," according to which feelings and associations must be completely banished from the mind of the aesthetic contemplator if he is to really "see" the work of art, pictured as though "at-a-distance."

Having reached a high level of development in the nineteenth century, aesthetic formalism found new and able champions in the twentieth century, especially in Germany, France, England, and the United States.[9] Among the important recent formalists were the English painter and art critic Roger Fry and the German philosopher Ernst Cassirer. Both of these thinkers attempted to give a more adequate analysis and interpretation of aesthetic form. Each brought to his analysis a wealth of detailed knowledge of art, Fry through his experience as a practicing painter and through his extensive study of painting, sculpture, and architecture of various periods and cultures, Cassirer through his intensive research into the various forms of man's symbolic expression in art as well as in language, mythology, science, religion, and history. As Fry is primarily concerned with the visual arts in his analysis of form, and refers usually to these by way of illustration and validation, his perspective is narrower than Cassirer's. Cassirer's perspective, on the other hand, is more traditionally philosophical;

he attempts to explain artistic creation and appreciation with reference to a theory of knowledge and reality and to place art in the whole system of human activities. Moreover, the aesthetic theory of each of these thinkers was stimulated by quite different preoccupations, Fry's from an effort to understand the "emotional elements of design" and the different functions of form and content in works of art, and Cassirer's from an awareness of the importance of art as one aspect of man's "ideal" world of symbolic expression. Fry and Cassirer also differ strikingly in another way. Whereas Fry rarely speaks of other aesthetic theories but draws his materials directly from his own contemplation and creation of works of art, Cassirer's thought is deeply rooted in the aesthetic thought of the past. A historian of a period in aesthetics as well as a philosopher,[10] he draws from other thinkers—from Baumgarten, Lessing, Kant, Schiller, Goethe, Shaftesbury, Diderot, and numerous others—as he undertakes to formulate his own views on art. Because of their rich endowments and also because of their different perspectives, both Fry and Cassirer were able to contribute something unique and important to the development of formalist aesthetics and to the more complete understanding of works of art.

FRY

To those who knew and admired him, Roger Fry (1866–1934) was remarkable for his intellectual and moral integrity, his open-mindedness, his passionate love of art, his exquisite sensibility, and his sheer genius in verbalizing his aesthetic perceptions.[11] These qualities, exemplified so clearly in his writing and lecturing, made Fry a powerful force in British aesthetics and art criticism. The son of an eminent Quaker judge, he was born in London and attended a Quaker school there before going on to Cambridge University. Although while he was at the University he distinguished himself for his work in the natural sciences, his most intense interest was in painting, to which he decided to devote himself exclusively, despite his parents' opposition, upon his graduation in 1888. After spending some time in Italy and France studying Renaissance art, Fry returned to London, where he kept up his painting, became a member of the New English Art Club, and began to write art criticism and to give lectures on the history and appreciation of art. In 1896 he married Helen Coombe, a painter, but his marital happiness was short-lived as his wife became mentally ill a year later while they were living in Rome. From 1905 to 1910 he served as Director of the Metropolitan Museum of Art in New York. Continual disagreements with one of the museum's trustees, Pierpont Morgan, eventually made his position intolerable. Back in England, Fry stirred up a furor in 1910 by organizing the first exhibition of Post-Impressionist painting. During the First World War one of his main interests was in establishing and supervising the Omega workshops in order to help young artists and artisans produce and sell their works. After the war, he became known to a wider audience through the publication of a number of important works, including *Vision and Design* (1919), *Transformations* (1926),[12] *Flemish Art* (1927), *Cezanne* (1927), *The Characteristics of French Art* (1932), and *Reflections on British Painting* (1934). The last decade of his life was happy and productive: his wife having been permanently hospitalized, he established a liaison with another woman; he traveled to Spain and Greece to expand further his knowledge of art; and in 1933 he accepted the position of Slade Professor of Art at Cambridge, a position he had long desired. He had already begun a series of lectures on art history in Cambridge when he had a fall and had to be hospitalized.[13] While he was recuperating in a London hospital, he had a heart failure and died. His body later was cremated.

Fry's aesthetics, as he himself recognized, is not so much a coherent system as it is a series of systematic attempts to comprehend and to give order to his aesthetic impressions, mainly of the visual arts, at various stages in his lifetime exploration of the world of art.[14] He never feels that he—or anyone—can explain completely the ultimate nature of art or can discover absolutely valid standards for judging particular works of art; he is therefore content to present his theoretical conclusions not as dogmas but only as empirically grounded hypotheses which, having served him well, might conceivably serve others in understanding and appreciating works of art. No matter how convincing these conclusions may seem to him at the time to be, he is willing, should they turn out not to gibe with further experiences, to modify or perhaps even to discard them, though with some natural regret that in the meantime he has been mistaken in his view. This attitude explains the characteristic provisional quality, the tentativeness, with which Fry usually presents his points of view.

Three of the important influences which affected the development of Fry's aesthetic theories, to which he himself pays homage in looking back over his "aesthetic evolution," were his reading of Tolstoy's *What Is Art?*, his discovery of Post-Impressionist painting, and his acquaintance with Clive Bell, the formulator of the theory of "significant form." Tolstoy's insistence that art should not be concerned with the creation of beauty but rather with the expression and communication of emotion struck Fry as a message of liberation from which he drew the inspiration for his own early expressionist theory, without however retaining the moralistic tone and intent of Tolstoy.[15] At this stage, Fry conceived the task of aesthetics to be three-fold: it involved a consideration of the artist's emotional experience, of his communication of this experience by means of the "emotional elements of design"—rhythm of line, mass, space, light and shade, and color—and of the spectator's re-creation of the emotion from the contemplation of the design. Later, however, when he had become acquainted with the works of the Post-Impressionists, particularly with those of Cezanne, he became increasingly aware of the importance of purely formal relations in works of art, relations which seemed to have little if any connection with the artist's everyday emotional experiences but very much to do with the artist's unique aesthetic vision. Fry now put emphasis on the experience of formal values rather than on emotional expression. This revision brought him close to the views of his friend, Clive Bell, who in *Art* defended the thesis that a work of art expresses a "unique kind of emotion" through its "significant form," by which Bell referred to the "relations and combinations of lines and colors" capable of moving the perceiver aesthetically.[16] Fry never went quite so far as Bell, however, who, holding representation to be completely irrelevant to significant form, envisaged a purely nonrepresentational kind of painting. Still, Fry greatly admired Bell's attempt "to isolate the purely aesthetic feeling" from other feelings and for his emphasis on the fundamental formal values inherent in a work of art which Fry, like Bell, considered to be much more important to aesthetic appreciation than other elements, such as the work's resemblance to life.[17]

Formal design and creative vision are fundamental themes running throughout Fry's mature aesthetics. In his essay "The Artist's Vision," he distinguishes and characterizes four different kinds of vision.[18] The first of these, practical or biological vision, is concerned solely with recognizing things in order to put them to use or to label them. The second kind of vision, "curiosity vision," is awakened by objects which stimulate imagination or awaken disinterested contemplation because of their novelty or peculiarity. Aesthetic vision, the third kind of vision, is more intense, disinterested, and biologically functionless than either of the first two; it is concerned not with the utility or oddity of an object but with its harmony of form and color. Finally, there is creative vision, the detached and impassioned vision unique to the artist by means of which he is able to perceive the rhythmic patterns, the inherent designs, and the unexpected relations in things. Whatever stimulates this unusually intense vision—it matters not whether it be a man's head or a pumpkin—engages the artist's rapt attention as something which may be transformed into a work of art.[19] This creative vision Fry refers to elsewhere as "great imaginative organization."

Fry's aesthetic theory, as it is formulated in its final form in his posthumously published Last Lectures, reaffirms the importance of the communicative function of art—its usefulness in imparting "the quality and quiddity" of human experiences—without, however, reducing the importance of formal values in works of art. A work of art is "a transmitting medium," a liaison, between the artist and the spectator; it is not an "isolated, static phenomenon" but "a potentiality" by means of which feelings can be communicated.[20] Fry's main concern now is with what we can get from works of art—the full, rich, significant feelings which can be evoked in us by them—rather than what the works are in themselves. He thinks that we can isolate the emotion-evoking qualities in works of art and, by comparing these qualities, can gain insight into aesthetic experience. The qualities selected for comparison by Fry in his Last Lectures are sensibility—the feeling of texture or the evidence of the artist's sensitivity to the textural qualities of the form—and vitality—"the idea of an inner energy expressing itself in the form."[21] The intelligibility of a work of art, Fry argues, is not to be understood in terms of ordinary formal logic but in terms of "a logic of the senses." Just as the color-blind or tone-deaf person cannot appreciate colors and sounds, so cannot the "form-blind" understand visual arts.[22] Art is for the artist as for the appreciator a "purely free and biologically gratuitous (or useless) spiritual activity."[23] In the course of his last reflections on art, Fry calls attention to the unconscious factors which may be influential in the creation and appreciation of works of art; he also speculates further on the ultimate nature of pure form; and he reinterprets the qualities of ancient art in ways that are both provocative and enlightening.

To the very end of his career, Fry was still apparently "troubled by aesthetics," as his friend Clive Bell noted,[24] but because he was troubled, because his brilliant probing intellect always demanded at least a partially satisfactory explanation of his most passionate aesthetic experience, Fry's "aesthetic evolution," as recorded in his works, remains one of the most fascinating and rewarding to study in the history of aesthetics. And almost everything Fry wrote is capable of imparting that joy he felt in exploring the domain of aesthetic experience.

Creative Vision and Formal Design

1. *In an early formulation of his views on aesthetics, Fry rejects the theory of art which attempts to explain art in terms of its connections with real life and argues that art is to be understood in terms of its connections with the imaginative life, in which sensations and emotions are contemplated and enjoyed for their own sake, independently of practical and moral considerations. Art, as imaginative, emotional expression, finds its true justification, Fry believes, not on moral or religious grounds but on purely aesthetic grounds alone; for it enriches the life of man by making possible at the level of imagination a clarification of perception and emotion.*

That the graphic arts are the expression of the imaginative life rather than a copy of actual life might be guessed from observing children. Children, if left to themselves, never, I believe, copy what they see, never, as we say, "draw from nature," but express, with a delightful freedom and sincerity, the mental images which make up their own imaginative lives.

Art, then, is an expression and a stimulus of this imaginative life, which is separated from actual life by the absence of responsive action. Now this responsive action implies in actual life moral responsibility. In art we have no such moral responsibility—it presents a life freed from the binding necessities of our actual existence. . . .

Now the imaginative life has its own history both in the race and in the individual. In the individual life one of the first effects of freeing experience from the necessities of appropriate responsive action is to indulge recklessly the emotion of self-aggrandisement. The day-dreams of a child are filled with extravagant romances in which he is always the invincible hero. Music—which of all the arts supplies the strongest stimulus to the imaginative life, and at the same time the least power of controlling its direction—music, at certain stages of people's lives, has the effect merely of arousing in an almost absurd degree this egoistic elation, and Tolstoy appears to believe that this is its only possible effect. But with the teaching of experience and the growth of character the imaginative life comes to respond to other instincts and to satisfy other desires, until, indeed, it reflects the highest aspirations and the deepest aversions of which human nature is capable.

In dreams and when under the influence of drugs the imaginative life passes out of our own control, and in such cases its experiences may be highly undesirable, but whenever it remains under our own control it must always be on the whole a desirable life. That is not to say that it is always pleasant, for it is pretty clear than mankind is so constituted as to desire much besides pleasure, and we shall meet among the great artists, the great exponents, that is, of the imaginative life, many of whom the merely pleasant is very rarely a part of what is desirable. But this desirability of the imaginative life does distinguish it very sharply from actual life, and is the direct result of that first fundamental difference, its freedom from necessary external conditions. Art, then, is, if I am right, the chief organ of the imaginative life; it is by art that it is stimulated and controlled within us, and, as we have seen, the imaginative life is distinguished by the greater clearness of its perception, and the greater purity and freedom of its emotion.

First with regard to the greater clearness of perception. The needs of our actual life are so imperative, that the sense of vision bcomes highly specialised in their service. With an admirable economy we learn to see only so much as is needful for our purposes; but this is in fact very little, just enough to recognise and identify each object or person; that done, they go into an entry in our mental catalogue and are no more really seen. In actual life the normal person really only reads the labels as it were on the objects around him and troubles no further. Almost all the things which are useful in any way put on more or less this cap of invisibility. It is only when an object exists in our lives for no other purpose than to be seen that we really look at it, as for instance at a China ornament or a precious stone, and towards such even the most normal person adopts to some extent the artistic attitude of pure vision abstracted from necessity.

Now this specialisation of vision goes so far that ordinary people have almost no idea of what things really look like, so that oddly enough the one standard that popular criticism applies to painting, namely, whether it is like nature or not, is one which most people are, by the whole tenour of their lives, prevented from applying properly. The only things they have ever really *looked* at being other pictures; the moment an artist who has looked at nature brings to them a clear report of something definitely seen by him, they are wildly indignant at its untruth to nature. This has happened so constantly in our own time that there is no need to prove it. . . .

But though this clarified sense perception which we discover in the imaginative life is of great interest, and although it plays a larger part in the graphic arts than in any other, it might perhaps be doubted whether, interesting, curious, fascinating as it is, this aspect of the imaginative life would ever by itself make art of profound importance to mankind. But it is different, I think, with the emotional aspect. We have admitted that the emotions of the imaginative are generally weaker than those of actual life. The picture of a saint being slowly flayed alive, revolting as it is, will not produce the same physical sensations of sickening disgust that a modern man would feel if he could assist at the actual event; but they have a compensating clearness of presentment to the consciousness. The more poignant emotions of actual life have, I think, a kind of numbing effect analogous to the paralysing influence of fear in some animals; but even if this experience be not generally admitted, all will admit that the need for responsive action hurries us along and prevents us from ever realising fully what the emotion is that we feel, from co-ordinating it perfectly with other states. In short, the motives we actually experience are too close to us to enable us to feel them clearly. They are in a sense unintelligible. In the imaginative life, on the contrary, we can both feel the emotion and watch it. When we are really moved at the theatre we are always both on the stage and in the auditorium.

Yet another point about the emotions of the imaginative life—since they require no responsive action we can give them a new valuation. In real life we must to some extent cultivate those emotions which lead to useful action, and we are bound to appraise emotions according to the resultant action. So that, for instance, the feelings of rivalry and emulation do get an encouragement which perhaps they scarcely deserve, whereas certain feelings which appear to have a high intrinsic value get almost no stimulus in actual life. For instance, those feelings to which the name of the cosmic emotion has been somewhat unhappily given find almost no place in life, but, since they seem to belong to certain very deep springs of our nature, do become of great importance in the arts.

Morality, then, appreciates emotion by the standard of resultant action. Art appreciates emotion in and for itself.[25] . . .

2. *While Fry acknowledges his debt to Tolstoy for having previously defined art as the expression and communication of emotion, he believes that Tolstoy went astray when he passed moral judgment on the emotions expressed in works of art. For the task of the aesthetician is, Fry holds, to judge works of art on the basis of their intrinsic merits, not on the basis of extrinsic considerations such as their moral usefulness or their religious significance. He therefore devotes his attention to an attempt at determining the expressive aesthetic qualities of works of art, chiefly those qualities related to design or form, which can account for the unique capacity art possesses for satisfying the needs of the imaginative life.*

If, then, an object of any kind is created by man not for use, for its fitness to actual life, but as an object of art, an object subserving the imaginative life, what will its qualities be? It must in the first place be adapted to that disinterested intensity of contemplation, which we have found to be the effect of cutting off the responsive action. It must be suited to that heightened power of perception which we found to result therefrom.

And the first quality that we demand in our sensations will be order, without which our sensations will be troubled and perplexed, and the other quality will be variety, without which they will not be fully stimulated.

It may be objected that many things in nature, such as flowers, possess these two qualities of order and variety in a high degree, and these objects do undoubtedly stimulate and satisfy that clear disinterested contemplation which is characteristic of the aesthetic attitude. But in our reaction to a work of art there is something more—there is the consciousness of purpose, the consciousness of a peculiar relation of sympathy with the man who made this thing in order to arouse precisely the sensations we experience. And when we come to the higher works of art, where sensations are so arranged that they arouse in us deep emotions, this feeling of a special tie with the man who expressed them becomes very strong. We feel that he has expressed something which was latent in us all the time, but which we never realised, that he has revealed us to ourselves in revealing himself. And this recognition of purpose is, I believe, an essential part of the aesthetic judgment proper.

The perception of purposeful order and variety in an object gives us the feeling which we express by saying that it is beautiful, but when by means of sensations our emotions are aroused we demand purposeful order and variety in them also, and if this can only be brought about by the sacrifice of sensual beauty we willingly overlook its absence.

Thus, there is no excuse for a china pot being ugly, there is every reason why Rembrandt's and Degas' pictures should be, from the purely sensual point of view, supremely and magnificently ugly.

This, I think, will explain the apparent contradiction between two distinct uses of the word beauty, one for that which has sensuous charm, and one for the aesthetic approval of works of imaginative art where the objects presented to us are often of extreme ugliness. Beauty in the former sense belongs to works of art where only the perceptual aspect of the imaginative life is exercised, beauty in the second sense becomes as it were super-sensual, and is concerned with the appropriateness and intensity of the emotions aroused. When these emotions are aroused in a way that satisfies fully the needs of the imaginative life we approve and delight in the sensations through which we enjoy that heightened experience because they possess purposeful order and variety in relation to those emotions. . . .

Let us now see how the artist passes from the stage of merely gratifying our demand for sensuous order and variety to that where he arouses our emotions. I will call the various methods by which this is effected the emotional elements of design.

The first element is that of the rhythm of the line with which the forms are delineated.

The drawn line is the record of a gesture, and that gesture is modified by the artist's feeling which is thus communicated to us directly.

The second element is mass. When an object is so represented that we recognise it as having inertia we feel its power of resisting movement, or communicating its own movement to other bodies, and our imaginative reaction to such an image is governed by our experience of mass in actual life.

The third element is space. The same-sized square on two pieces of paper can be made by very simple means to appear to represent either a cube two or three inches high, or a cube of hundreds of feet, and our reaction to it is proportionately changed.

The fourth element is that of light and shade. Our feelings towards the same object become totaly different according as we see it strongly illuminated against a black background or dark against light.

A fifth element is that of colour. That this has a direct emotional effect is evident from such words as gay, dull, melancholy in relation to colour.

I would suggest the possibility of another element, though perhaps it is only a compound of mass and space: it is that of the inclination to the eye of a plane, whether it is impending over or leaning away from us.

Now it will be noticed that nearly all these emotional elements of design are connected with essential conditions of our physical existence: rhythm appeals to all the sensations which accompany muscular activity; mass to all the infinite adaptations to the force of gravity which we are forced to make; the spatial judgment is equally profound and universal in its application to life; our feeling about inclined planes is connected with our necessary judgments about the conformation of the earth itself; light again, is so necessary a condition of our existence that we become intensely sensitive to changes in its intensity. Colour is the only one of our elements which is not of critical or universal importance to life, and its emotional effect is neither so deep nor so clearly determined as the others. It will be seen, then, that the graphic arts arouse emotions in us by playing upon what one may call the overtones of some of our primary physical needs. They have, indeed, this great advantage over poetry, that they can appeal more directly and immediately to the emotional accompaniments of our bare physical existence.

If we represent these various elements in simple diagrammatic terms, this effect upon the emotions is, it must be confessed, very weak. Rhythm of line, for instance, is incomparably weaker in its stimulus of the muscular sense than is rhythm addressed to the ear in music, and such diagrams can at best arouse only faint ghost-like echoes of emotions of differing qualities; but when these emotional elements are combined with the presentation of natural appearances, above all with the appearance of the human body, we find that this effect is indefinitely heightened.[26] . . .

3. *In a later discussion of aesthetic theory, Fry moves even closer to the strictly formalist position that everything except the perception of purely formal relations is irrelevant to a genuine appreciation of art. Here he defends the uniqueness of the aesthetic experience against such critics as I. A. Richards who argue that this experience does not differ in kind from ordinary experience. Fry's own experiences with various works of art have convinced him that the distinctive aesthetic emotion cannot be aroused by the mere representation of objects or by the attempt to evoke the emotions of actual life; it can only be aroused, he believes, by the structural design or by what Clive Bell calls the "significant form" of the work of art.*

In approaching once again the general problem of Esthetics I wish to enforce two things: one, that such attempts at any general theory that I make are tentative efforts to make clear to myself the principles involved in exercising the critical faculty on works of art, and secondly that the problem is far too complicated, for me, at all events, to approach it by any other than an experimental method. The experiments have to be made by the inquirer and mainly on himself, by watching, with such honesty and detachment as he can command, his own reactions. That honesty is, of course, very difficult to come at, since in this matter we are all excessively auto-suggestible and apt to discover, with suspicious facility, whatever our predisposition of mind may have led us to desire and anticipate. The only guarantee that the inquirer can give under such circumstances is to lay his cards on the table and invite the reader to see whether his own reactions in any given case coincide. It is this that in the following pages I have tried to do.

The general notion which, in an essay in "Vision and Design,"[27] I had tentatively put forward was to the effect that whenever we make a favourable esthetic judgment—whenever we say that a work of art is beautiful—we imply by that statement that it is of such a kind as to produce in us a certain positive response, and that if we compare in our minds responses experienced in turn in face of different works of art of the most diverse kinds—as, for instance, architectural, pictorial, musical or literary—we recognise that our state of mind in each case has been of a similar kind, we see in all these different experiences a general similarity in our attitude, in the pattern of our mental disposition, and further that the attitude common to all these experiences is peculiar to them and is clearly distinguishable from our mental attitude in other experiences. I therefore suggested that we might conveniently label this kind of mental disposition the specifically esthetic state of mind.

That position has been very vigorously and brilliantly attacked of late, notably by Mr. Richards in his "Principles of Criticism,"[28] and I shall have occasion to take some of his objections to the view outlined above as the basis for further investigations into the nature and ends of pictorial design.

And as this proceeding will lead me into a controversial attitude upon the points at issue, I take this opportunity to express my admiration of a great part of this work. Mr. Richards has arrived at a point of view which seems to me fertile and full of possibilities. He has opened up many striking new perspectives for the critic to explore, and I fully share his desire to do away with metaphysical entities and absolutes in esthetic discussion. Moreover, I take to heart, in so far as I may have offended in that direction, his wise protest against assuming any state of mind to be unanalysable. But all the same, as I shall have occasion to show, I cannot feel that he has solved certain questions as completely and decisively as he claims.

According to Mr. Richards our response to a work of art is of a similar nature to our response to other situations. He says: "When we look at a picture, or read a poem, or listen to music, we are not doing something quite unlike what we were doing on our way to the Gallery or when we dressed in the morning."[29] That is to say, the responses to a work of art are the same responses as those of ordinary life and only differ in the manner in which the objects are presented to us, as, for example, the difference between our response to a real tree and what we recognise as a tree in a picture.[30] Now I hope to show certain reasons why we should regard our responses to works of art as distinct from our responses to other situations.

The question is, no doubt, made extremely difficult owing to the fact that many structures which profess to be works of art do not even aim at provoking the special kind of response which I hope to describe. And that many works which do provoke that special response also evoke at the same time many of the responses of ordinary life.

It is necessary, therefore, for me to put up a preliminary hypothesis of the existence of pure and impure works of art—a distinction which Mr. Richards has the good fortune to be able to ignore.

It nowise invalidates this conception if such a thing as an absolutely pure work of art has never been created: the contention is that some works approximate much more nearly than others to this ideal construction. I cannot deny that the position I am trying to maintain is dangerously exposed. If it is to be held at all it must be held with regard to works of art of all kinds. And this is no easy matter. The idea of a special kind of experience, a special disposition of the mind, may seem plausible enough with regard to our experience of certain peculiarly abstract musical constructions or even of certain kinds of architecture. It becomes far less plausible the moment representation of actual forms comes in, as in painting or sculpture, still less when, as in poetry, the novel or the drama, the very stuff of which these are constructed, namely words, calls up images and memories of things and emotions of actual life.

And yet this must be faced if the idea of a special esthetic experience is to have any meaning. It would be fatal if in the case of any work of art on which we pass a favourable esthetic judgment we had to admit that the experience was of an altogether different kind from that which we had before others. We cannot hold our theory for music and architecture and drop it for poetry and drama.

Now the crucial fact which appears to me to arise from the comparison of a number of these experiences which are the subject of our inquiry is that in all cases our reaction to works of art is a reaction to a relation and not to sensations or objects or persons or events. This, if I am right, affords a distinguishing mark of what I call esthetic experiences, esthetic reactions, or esthetic states of mind.

Let us examine this in more detail. Our emotional reactions are not, I say, about sensations. This may at first sight appear paradoxical, because the arts seem to be peculiarly preoccupied with agreeable sensations, with relatively pure colours and pure sounds. But it is not difficult to see that, however valuable a predisposing and accompanying condition of aesthetic apprehension such agreeably pure sensations may be, they are not essential, nor have we any difficulty in distinguishing between our response to sensations and our response to works of art. Those responses to sensation may be very rich and complex and tinged with emotion, but they are distinct. Thus a smell may, as Proust has admirably shown, produce a very profound response. By its associations in memory it may even excite a more poignant state of mind than many works of art, but we easily distinguish it from our feeling about a work of art. The evocations of smell are indeed so powerful that they would doubtless form the basis for an art similar to music in its deep emotional evocations, if only different perfumes could be perceived in relation one to another. It is this impossibility alone that deprives us of yet another art.

It is true that in nearly all works of art agreeable sensations form the very texture of the work. In music pleasurable quality of sound is the object of deliberate research, but it is by no means evident that this is essential. Some effects of modern music suggest that relations of more noises not in themselves agreeable can arouse esthetic pleasure, and many great composers have worked in sound textures which were generally proclaimed harsh and disagreeable. If it be said that though disagreeable to the audiences they had been found agreeable by the composer, we are none the less faced with the fact that his contemporaries did, after all, accept his work for its esthetic quality even whilst the sound-texture appeared unpleasing; although under stress of that esthetic satisfaction the unpleasure gradually changed to pleasure.

For vision, as for hearing, there are simple pleasant sensations and simple indifferent or even unpleasant sensations, notably with regard to colour. Pure, brightly luminous colours have a strong physiological effect of a pleasing kind. This is especially marked in children, but long after we have ceased to stop in front of the chemist's windows to gaze at lights seen through blue and red solutions we are still aware of the attraction. But when we come to arrangements of colour in a work of art all these sensational effects may be overridden by our emotions about colour relations. Some works of the greatest colourists are built up of elements each of which is devoid of any specially pleasurable quality, and they may even be, to particular observers, positively unpleasant, although that displeasure is immediately swamped by the pleasure which results from their interrelation.

In literature there is no immediate sensual pleasure whatever, though it may be a favourable predisposing condition for poetry to be spoken by a beautiful voice. There is, of course, the pleasure of rhythmic utterance, but this is already concerned with relations, and even this is, I believe, accessory to the emotion aroused by rhythmic changes of states of mind due to the meanings of the words.

In architecture materials are often chosen for the comparatively simple sensual pleasure which their surfaces arouse. But we distinguish at once between this pleasure and those emotions which are generated by our apprehension of architectural plasticity. Before too many buildings on which polished marble and gilt bronze are lavished our pleasure in these appearances is more than counterbalanced by the painful absence of esthetic purpose. The ensuing reflections on the waste of so much precious material cause them to become actually a source of mental pain.

The esthetic emotion, then, is not an emotion about sensations, however necessary a responsive sensualism may be for our apprehension of esthetic wholes. Nor is it an emotion about objects or persons or events. Here we touch the crux of the esthetic experience for the greater number of people who are accustomed to rely almost exclusively on their interest in, or emotion about, the persons or events called to mind by the imagery of the fine arts. Landscape, for such, is just reminiscence or revelation of pleasant natural scenes; portraiture interests by the beautiful or fascinating ladies and the celebrated gentlemen it presents; figure painting avails by its attractive or provocative nudes; literature by its exciting events or its imagined wish fulfilments. In fact, the vast mass of so-called works of art are designed primarily to arouse these interests and emotions even though in doing this some esthetic appeals may supply an accompaniment.

These observations appear to me to have made out a very fair *a priori* case for the existence in all esthetic experiences of a special orientation of the consciousness, and, above all, a special focussing of the attention, since the act of esthetic apprehension implies an attentive passivity to the effects of sensations apprehended in their relations. We have no need for our purposes to create the hypothesis of any mysterious or specific faculty.

There is no need to imagine that the state of mind here indicated is unanalysable; probably it may be resolved into different factors, none of which is peculiar to this state. The same mental faculties and aptitudes as enter into play in esthetic apprehension no doubt are employed elsewhere. What matters for us is that there should be a constant and recognisable pattern of the mental disposition in such situations. I believe that this is so, and that the pattern is distinct enough for us to say, in contradiction to Mr. Richards, that when we are in the picture gallery we are employing our faculties in a manner so distinct from that in which we employed them on the way there, that it is no exaggeration to say we are doing a quite different thing. On the way there our conscious attention must frequently have been directed to spotting and catching the right 'bus, or detecting the upright flag of a distant taxicab or, at least, avoiding collisions on the pavement or recognising our friends. I exclude the case of those who being artists themselves may, in the course of their walk, have been preoccupied with distilling from their diverse visual sensations some vague sketches and adumbrations of possible harmonic combinations. Such, and such alone, might, I think, be said to have been similarly occupied on their way to and within the gallery.

If I am right, then it is not impossible to draw a fairly sharp dividing line between our mental disposition in the case of esthetic responses and that of the responses of ordinary life. A far more difficult question arises if we try to distinguish it from the responses made by us to certain abstract mental constructions such as those of pure mathematics. Here I conceive the emotional states due to the apprehension of relations may be extremely similar to those aroused by the esthetic apprehension. Perhaps the distinction lies in this, that in the case of works of art the whole end and purpose is found in the exact quality of the emotional state, whereas in the case of mathematics the purpose is the constatation of the universal validity of the relations without regard to the quality of the emotion accompanying apprehension. Still, it would be impossible to deny the close similarity of the orientation of faculties and attention in the two cases.[31] . . .

CASSIRER

The son of a wealthy merchant of Breslau, Ernst Cassirer (1874–1945) studied at the Universities of Berlin, Leipzig, Heidelberg, and, finally, at the University of Marburg, where he came under the influence of the Neo-Kantian philosopher Hermann Cohen and received his doctorate in philosophy.[32] Afterwards he married and settled down in Berlin for several years to a life of philosophical research and writing. Having completed the first two volumes of a major work on epistemology, *The Problem of Knowledge*, in 1908 he accepted a teaching position at the University of Berlin. During the next ten years he distinguished himself as a brilliant teacher of philosophy, continued his research and writing, and, when the First World War came, served in the German civil service. After the end of the war, he accepted a professorship at the newly founded University of Hamburg, and began work on what was to be his *magnum opus, The Philosophy of Symbolic Forms*.[33] Although Cassirer was elected rector of the University in 1930, when Hitler became dictator of Germany the Jewish philosopher decided to emigrate. He resigned his position and left Germany in 1933. First he taught at Oxford for two years, then at the University of Goeteborg in Sweden for six years. In 1941 he came to the United States as visiting professor of philosophy at Yale University. Deciding to remain in this country, he accepted a permanent position at Columbia University, where he taught until his death. His last works were *An Essay on Man* (1944), which was the first book he ever wrote in English, and *The Myth of the State*, a work published posthumously in 1946. A philosopher of staggering erudition and soaring imagination, Cassirer was also a man of remarkable versatility and culture who impressed some who knew him as an ideal example of the Kantian man of good will.

Like Immanuel Kant, by whom he was profoundly influenced, Ernst Cassirer was very much interested in investigating the concepts and presuppositions involved in the scientific cognition of the world. He was equally interested in exploring the realm of human values. But he went beyond Kant in not limiting his attention primarily to the spheres of scientific knowledge, morality, and aesthetics; he was led from his own "critique of reason" to a "critique of culture."[34] In his *Philosophy of Symbolic Forms* he attempts to explain the functions of language, of myth and religion, and of knowledge generally in building up man's cultural world, a world in which passive impressions are transformed into expressions of the human spirit through the "dynamism of forms." As his major philosophical task, Cassirer undertakes to work out a "morphology of the human spirit" and to present a "phenomology of human culture." And in accomplishing this task, he delineates the entire "architectural structure" of man's "ideal" world, the world of symbolic forms.

Cassirer thinks that the task he sets for himself is of crucial importance in the twentieth century, for during this century there has occurred a "crisis in man's knowledge of himself."[35] In his *Essay on Man* he surveys the answers which have been and are presently given to the question "What is Man?" and finds "a complete anarchy of thought." No approach, empirical or introspective, has provided a coherent and consistent interpretation of the whole world of human culture. So far we have lacked the integrating concept, the intellectual focal point, around which the various specialized fields of knowledge of man can be organized, and without a general rational "frame of reference" to guide us in thinking about human nature it will remain enigmatical. But Cassirer thinks that he has found "the magic key" to explain the nature of man.[36] This "key" is the principle of symbolism. It makes more sense to him to define man as a symbol-using animal than as a rational animal. For man not only attains knowledge through reason, he also attains meanings through symbols. His intellect needs not just concepts and images, it also needs symbols.[37] Like the other animals man receives and interprets stimuli and effects changes in his physical environment; but unlike the other animals man also creates a symbolic universe in order to interpret and to organize his experience, giving it in the process a deeper and a richer significance. Man lives and moves and has his being not only in a physical environment but also in a symbolic environment composed of language, mythology, religion, science, history, and art. He is thus able to converse continuously with himself, to envelop himself in a multidimensional reality which is his own creation.[38] By studying the symbolic system which man as a symbol-using animal, *animal symbolicum*, has created, Cassirer thinks that the philosopher can find the previously missing focal point of human culture.

A study of the nature of art can shed, Cassirer believes, a great deal of light on human nature. Art, in his view, is neither an imitation of nature nor an expression of human emotions; it is rather an ideal reconstruction of reality and an expression of the inner "dynamic process" of human life.[39] Art testifies to the fact that man can know an intelligible world not just through concepts and thoughts but also through intuitions and sensations.[40] When we enter into this world we move through new dimensions of reality and learn to see through the "constructive eye" of the artist. We experience new modes of perception more complex, various, and richer than those of ordinary sense perception. Under the guidance of the artist we are able to perceive the inexhaustibility of the world as it is perceived aesthetically. Not that the artist has invented the forms which he presents to us in his works; these forms are constitutive of the nature of things.[41] But what the artist does is to present them to us sensuously in such a way that their clarity, their universality, and their versatility are apparent, allowing us to discover for the first time, as it were, the immediate structural elements inherent in our sensuous experience.[42] This is why art can be such a powerful instrument in understanding the nature of human nature and in exploring the ideal world of culture.

In order to be an artist, Cassirer holds, a man must possess a high degree of sensitivity to "the dynamic life of forms" which awakens within him "a corresponding dynamic process."[43] He must be inventive and constructive and capable of animating or personifying the world around him. But that is not enough. Along with great powers of perceiving and feeling, he must possess also the imaginative power of objectifying, of embodying, his perceptions and feelings in external sensuous forms.[44] Here Cassirer's viewpoint is essentially that of Fry. Creative vision is basically the power to grasp the lines and colors, rhythms and designs, the "architectonic structure" of sensuous experience and to re-present them in artistic form. Also like Fry, he would reject metaphysical explanations of artistic imagination (e.g. Hegel's), which make it too mysterious, as well as reductive empirical explanations (e.g. Taine's), which make it far too simple. The forms with which the artist's imagination is preoccupied are means of constructing and of giving order and meaning to his own and to his fellow man's experiences. Through these forms, he integrates diverse elements into structural wholes; he transforms objects into symbols; and creates a new world for contemplation, enjoyment, and exploration.

Turning to a consideration of aesthetic appreciation, Cassirer lays stress on its dynamic quality, its constructive aspect, its synthesis of subjective and objective elements. He agrees with Dewey that the appreciator of a work of art has before him a demanding task rather than a merely passive pleasure. There is no such thing as "easy" beauty.[45] The genuine work of art, which is always more than a plaything, can never be fully understood and appreciated until an effort is made to reconstruct, to relive the process by which it was created. The appreciator must understand the work through a "logic of feeling." He contemplates it, to be sure, but in doing so is absorbed in its dynamic formal aspects. He must experience, Cassirer points out, not just the emotion, but the motion in a work of art, otherwise he will not experience the sense of inner freedom or "self-liberation" which art can bring.[46] In doing all this, in bringing his energies to bear on the work of art, in imaginatively reconstructing the process objectified in the work, in understanding its forms to be not transcendent essences but immanent functional principles, the appreciator can experience the lasting satisfaction which comes when a work of art reveals itself for what it truly is, a symbolic expression of a distinctly human world.

Art as Symbolic Form

*1. Cassirer takes issue with theorists such as Croce who identify
expression with intuition or emotion without giving due attention
to the constructive process by means of which an artist's intuition or emotion is externalized in sensuous form. After explaining why, to the contrary, he holds that embodiment of emotion
in an objective, coherent structure is essential to the creation of a
work of art, Cassirer proceeds to explain how in the process of
artistic creation an artist discovers and exemplifies in his works the
forms of things.*

Art is indeed expressive, but it cannot be expressive without
being formative. And this formative process is carried out in a
certain sensuous medium. "As soon as he is free from care and
fear," writes Goethe, "the demigod, creative in repose, gropes
round him for matter into which to breathe his spirit." In
many modern aesthetic theories—especially that of Croce and
his disciples and followers—this material factor is forgotten or
minimized. Croce is interested only in the fact of expression, not
in the mode. The mode he takes to be irrelevant both for the
character and for the value of the work of art. The only thing
which matters is the intuition of the artist, not the embodiment of
this intuition in a particular material. The material has a technical
but not an aesthetical importance. Croce's philosophy is a philosophy of the spirit emphasizing the purely spiritual character of
the work of art. But in his theory the whole spiritual energy is
contained and expended in the formation of the intuition alone.
When this process is completed the artistic creation has been
achieved. What follows is only an external reproduction which
is necessary for the communication of the intuition but meaningless with respect to its essence. But for a great painter, a great
musician, or a great poet, the colors, the lines, rhythms, and
words are not merely a part of his technical apparatus; they are
necessary moments of the productive process itself.

This is just as true of the specifically expressive arts as of the
representative arts. Even in lyrical poetry emotion is not the

only and decisive feature. It is of course true that the great lyrical poets are capable of the deepest emotions and that an artist who is not endowed with powerful feelings will never produce anything except shallow and frivolous art. But from this fact we cannot conclude that the function of lyrical poetry and of art in general can be adequately described as the artist's ability "to make a clean breast of his feelings." "What the artist is trying to do," says R. G. Collingwood, "is to express a given emotion. To express it, and to express it well, are the same thing. . . . Every utterance and every gesture that each one of us makes is a work of art." [47] But here again the whole constructive process which is a prerequisite both of the production and of the contemplation of the work of art is entirely overlooked. Every gesture is no more a work of art than every interjection is an act of speech. Both the gesture and the interjection are deficient in one essential and indispensable feature. They are involuntary and instinctive reactions; they possess no real spontaneity. The moment of purposiveness is necessary for linguistic and artistic expression. In every act of speech and in every artistic creation we find a definite teleological structure. An actor in a drama really "acts" his part. Each individual utterance is a part of a coherent structural whole. The accent and rhythm of his words, the modulation of his voice, the expressions of his face, and the postures of his body all tend to the same end—to the embodiment of human character. All this is not simply "expression"; it is also representation and interpretation. Not even a lyric poem is wholly devoid of this general tendency of art. The lyric poet is not just a man who indulges in displays of feeling. To be swayed by emotion alone is sentimentality, not art. An artist who is absorbed not in the contemplation and creation of forms but rather in his own pleasure or in his enjoyment of "the joy of grief" becomes a sentimentalist. Hence we can hardly ascribe to lyric art a more subjective character than to all the other forms of art. For it contains the same sort of embodiment, and the same process of objectification. "Poetry," wrote Mallarmé, "is not written with ideas, it is written with words." It is written with images, sounds, and rhythms which, just as in the case of dramatic poetry and dramatic representation, coalesce into an indivisible whole. In every great lyrical poem we find this concrete and indivisible unity.

Like all the other symbolic forms art is not the mere reproduction of a ready-made, given reality. It is one of the ways leading to an objective view of things and of human life. It is not an imitation but a discovery of reality. We do not, however, discover nature through art in the same sense in which the scientist uses the term "nature." Language and science are the two main processes by which we ascertain and determine our concepts of the external world. We must classify our sense perceptions and bring them under general notions and general rules in order to give them an objective meaning. Such classification is the result of a persistent effort toward simplification. The work of art in like manner implies such an act of condensation and concentration. When Aristotle wanted to describe the real difference between poetry and history he insisted upon this process. What a drama gives us, he asserts, is a single action ($\mu\iota\alpha\ \pi\rho\tilde{\alpha}\xi\iota\varsigma$) which is a complete whole in itself, with all the organic unity of a living creature; whereas the historical has to deal not with one action but with one period and all that happened therein to one or more persons, however disconnected the several events may have been.

In this respect beauty as well as truth may be discribed in terms of the same classical formula: they are "a unity in the manifold." But in the two cases there is a difference of stress. Language and science are abbreviations of reality; art is an intensification of reality. Language and science depend upon one and the same process of abstraction; art may be described as a continuous process of concretion. In our scientific description of a given object we begin with a great number of observations which at first sight are only a loose conglomerate of detached facts. But the farther we proceed the more these individual phenomena tend to assume a definite shape and become a systematic whole. What science is searching for is some central features of a given object from which all its particular qualities may be derived. If a chemist knows the atomic number of a certain element he possesses a clue to a full insight into its structure and constitution. From this number he may deduce all the characteristic properties of the element. But art does not admit of this sort of conceptual simplification and deductive generalization. It does not inquire into the qualities or causes of things; it gives us the intuition of the form of things. But this too is by no means a mere repetition of something we had before. It is a true and genuine discovery. The artist is just as much a discoverer of the forms of nature as the scientist is a discoverer of facts or natural laws. The great artists of all times have been cognizant of this special task and special gift of art. Leonardo da Vinci spoke of the purpose of painting and sculpture in the words *"saper vedere."* According to him the painter and sculptor are the great teachers in the realm of the visible world. For the awareness of pure forms of things is by no means an instinctive gift, a gift of nature. We may have met with an object of our ordinary sense experience a thousand times without ever having "seen" its form. We are still at a loss if asked to describe not its physical qualities or effects but its pure visual shape and structure. It is art that fills this gap. Here we live in the realm of pure forms rather than in that of the analysis and scrutiny of sense objects or the study of their effects.[48]

2. Cassirer finds Plato's and Tolstoy's views on the role of emotion in art to be mistaken since they fail to take into account the basic fact that art is formative. Through its various media art intensifies, transforms, and interprets passions and emotions until they acquire a new and higher significance. Aristotle was closer to an understanding of the nature of art in his doctrine of catharsis, which Cassirer reinterprets in light of his own views so as to show more clearly how passions can be ordered and liberated when they are given aesthetic form.

From Plato to Tolstoi art has been accused of exciting our emotions and thus of disturbing the order and harmony of our moral life. Poetical imagination, according to Plato, waters our experience of lust and anger, of desire and pain, and makes them grow when they ought to starve with drought. Tolstoi sees in art a source of infection. "Not only is infection," he says, "a sign of art, but the degree of infectiousness is also the sole measure of excellence in art." But the flaw in this theory is obvious. Tolstoi suppresses a fundamental moment of art, the moment of form. The aesthetic experience—the experience of contemplation—is a different state of mind from the coolness of our theoretical and the sobriety of our moral judgment. It is filled with the liveliest energies of passion, but passion itself is here transformed both in its nature and in its meaning. Wordsworth defines poetry as "emotion recollected in tranquillity." But the tranquillity we feel in great poetry is not that of recollection. The emotions aroused by the poet do not belong to a remote past. They are "here"—alive and immediate. We are aware of their full strength, but this strength tends in a new direction. It is rather seen than immediately felt. Our passions are no longer dark and impenetrable powers; they become, as it were, transparent. . . . The great painters show us the forms of outward things; the great dramatists show us the forms of our inner life. Dramatic art discloses a new breadth and depth of life. It conveys an awareness of human things and human destinies, of human greatness and misery, in comparison to which our ordinary existence appears poor and trivial. All of us feel, vaguely and dimly, the infinite potentialities of life, which silently await the moment when they are to be called forth from dormancy into the clear and intense light of consciousness. It is not the degree of infection but the degree of intensification and illumination which is the measure of the excellence of art.

If we accept this view of art we can come to a better understanding of a problem first encountered in the Aristotelian theory of catharsis. We need not enter here into all the difficulties of the Aristotelian term or into the innumerable efforts of the commentators to clear up these difficulties. What seems to be clear and what is now generally admitted is that the cathartic process described by Aristotle does not mean a purification or a change in the character and quality of the passions themselves but a change in the human soul. By tragic poetry the soul acquires a new attitude toward its emotions. The soul experiences the emotions of pity and fear, but instead of being disturbed and disquieted by them it is brought to a state of rest and peace. At first sight this would seem to be a contradiction. For what Aristotle looks upon as the effect of tragedy is a synthesis of two moments which in real life, in our practical existence, exclude each other. The highest intensification of our emotional life is thought of as at the same time giving us a sense of repose. We live through all our passions feeling their full range and highest tension. But what we leave behind when passing the threshold of art is the hard pressure, the compulsion of our emotions. The tragic poet is not the slave but the master of his emotions; and he is able to transfer this mastery to the spectators. In his work we are not swayed and carried away by our emotions. Aesthetic freedom is not the absence of passions, not Stoic apathy, but just the contrary. It means that our emotional life acquires its greatest strength, and that in this very strength it changes its form. For here we no longer live in the immediate reality of things but in a world of pure sensuous forms. In this

world all our feelings undergo a sort of transubstantiation with
respect to their essence and their character. The passions themselves are relieved of their material burden. We feel their form
and their life but not their encumbrance. The calmness of the
work of art is, paradoxically, a dynamic, not a static calmness.
Art gives us the motions of the human soul in all their depth
and variety. But the form, the measure and rhythm, of these
motions is not comparable to any single state of emotion. What we
feel in art is not a simple or single emotional quality. It is
the dynamic process of life itself—the continuous oscillation
between opposite poles, between joy and grief, hope and fear,
exultation and despair. To give aesthetic form to our passions is
to transform them into a free and active state. In the work of
the artist the power of passion itself has been made a formative power.[49]

3. *Cassirer does not think that aesthetic hedonism provides a
satisfactory explanation of the nature and value of aesthetic experience. Although aesthetic experiences may indeed bring intense
pleasure, their common denominator is not pleasure but rather
symbolic form. Santayana's view of beauty as "pleasure objectified" is therefore misleading, Cassirer holds, unless it is interpreted
in quite a different sense than Santayana, as a hedonist, probably
intended it.*

In contemporary thought the theory of aesthetic hedonism has
found its clearest expression in the philosophy of Santayana.
According to Santayana beauty is pleasure regarded as a quality
of things; it is "pleasure objectified." But this is begging the
question. For how can pleasure—the most subjective state of our
mind—ever be objectified? Science, says Santayana, "is the response
to the demand for information, and in it we ask for the whole
truth and nothing but the truth. Art is the response to the demand
for entertainment, . . . and truth enters into it only as it subserves
these ends." [50] But if this were the end of art we should be bound
to say that art, in its highest achievements, fails to attain its real
end. The "demand for entertainment" may be satisfied by much
better and cheaper means. To think that the great artists worked
for this purpose, that Michelangelo constructed Saint Peter's
Cathedral, that Dante or Milton wrote their poems, for the sake

of entertainment, is impossible. They would undoubtedly have subscribed to Aristotle's dictum that "to exert oneself and work for the sake of amusement seems silly and utterly childish."[51] If art is enjoyment it is not the enjoyment of things but the enjoyment of forms. Delight in forms is quite different from delight in things or sense impressions. Forms cannot simply be impressed on our minds; we must produce them in order to feel their beauty. It is a common flaw of all the ancient and modern systems of aesthetic hedonism that they offer us a psychological theory of aesthetic pleasure which completely fails to account for the fundamental fact of aesthetic creativeness. In aesthetic life we experience a radical transformation. Pleasure itself is no longer a mere affection; it becomes a function. For the artist's eye is not simply an eye that reacts to or reproduces sense impressions. Its activity is not confined to receiving or registering the impressions of outward things or to combining these impressions in new and arbitrary ways. A great painter or musician is not characterized by his sensitiveness to color or sounds but by his power to elicit from his static material a dynamic life of forms. Only in this sense, then, can the pleasure we find in art be objectified. To define beauty as "pleasure objectified" contains, therefore, the whole problem in a nutshell. Objectification is always a constructive process. The physical world—the world of constant things and qualities—is no mere bundle of sense data, nor is the world of art a bundle of feelings and emotions. The first depends upon acts of theoretical objectification, objectification by concepts and scientific constructs; the second upon formative acts of a different type, acts of contemplation.[52]

4. *Cassirer now explains how the symbolic language of art differs from ordinary language. Art expresses to us the living forms of things and the dynamic properties of our inner life; it does not, like ordinary discourse, explain things in terms of concepts or aid us in utilizing them. But even though the knowledge we gain from art may be nonconceptual and nonutilitarian, it is nonetheless valuable in the education of aesthetic perception and feeling.*

Science gives us order in thoughts; morality gives us order in actions; art gives us order in the apprehension of visible, tangible, and audible appearances. Aesthetic theory was very slow indeed to recognize these fundamental differences. But if instead of seeking a metaphysical theory of beauty we simply analyze our immediate experience of the work of art we can hardly miss the mark. Art may be defined as a symbolic language. But this leaves us only with the common genus, not the specific difference. In modern aesthetics the interest in the common genus seems to prevail to such a degree as almost to eclipse and obliterate the specific difference. Croce insists that there is not only a close relation but a complete identity between language and art. To his way of thinking it is quite arbitrary to distinguish between the two activities. Whoever studies general linguistics, according to Croce, studies aesthetic problems—and vice versa. There is, however, an unmistakable difference between the symbols of art and the linguistic terms of ordinary speech and writing. These two activities agree neither in character nor purpose; they do not employ the same means, nor do they tend toward the same ends. Neither language nor art gives us mere imitation of things or actions; both are representations. But a representation in the medium of sensuous forms differs widely from a verbal or conceptual representation. The description of a landscape by a painter or poet and that by a geographer or geologist have scarcely anything in common. Both the mode of description and the motive are different in the work of a scientist and in the work of an artist. A geographer may depict a landscape in a plastic manner, and he may even paint it in rich and vivid colors. But what he wishes to convey is not the vision of the landscape but its empirical concept. To this end he has to compare its form with other forms; he has to find out, by observation and induction, its characteristic features. The geologist goes a step farther in this empirical delineation. He does not content himself with a record of physical facts, for he wishes to divulge the origin of these facts. He distinguishes the strata by which the soil has been built up, noting chronological differences; and he goes back to the general casual laws according to which the earth has reached its present shape. For the artist all these empirical relations, all these comparisons with other facts, and all this research into causal relations do not exist. Our ordinary empirical concepts may be, roughly speaking, divided into two classes according as they have to do with practical or theoretical interests. The one class is concerned with the use of things and with the question "What is that for?" The other is concerned with the causes of things and with the question "Whence?" But upon entering the realm of art we have to forget all such questions. Behind the existence, the nature, the empirical properties of things, we suddenly discover their forms. These forms are no static elements. What they show is a mobile order, which reveals to us a new horizon of nature. Even the greatest admirers of art have often spoken of it as if it were a mere accessory, an embellishment or ornament, of life. But this is to underrate its real significance and its real role in human culture. A mere duplicate of reality would always be of a very questionable value. Only by conceiving art as a special direction, a new orientation, of our thoughts, our imagination, and our feelings, can we comprehend its true meaning and function. The plastic arts make us see the sensible world in all its richness and multifariousness. What would we know of the innumerable nuances in the aspect of things were it not for the works of the great painters and sculptors? Poetry is, similarly, the revelation of our personal life. The infinite potentialities of which we had but a dim and obscure presentiment are brought to light by the lyric poet, by the novelist, and by the dramatist. Such art is in no sense mere counterfeit or facsimile, but a genuine manifestation of our inner life.

So long as we live in the world of sense impressions alone we merely touch the surface of reality. Awareness of the depth of things always requires an effort on the part of our active and constructive energies. But since these energies do not move in the same direction, and do not tend toward the same end, they cannot give us the same aspect of reality. There is a conceptual depth as well as a purely visual depth. The first is discovered by science; the second is revealed in art. The first aids us in understanding the reasons of things; the second in seeing their forms. In science we try to trace phenomena back to their first causes, and to general laws and principles. In art we are absorbed in their immediate appearance, and we enjoy this appearance to the fullest extent in all its richness and variety. Here we are not concerned with the uniformity of laws but with the multiformity and diversity of intuitions. Even art may be described as knowledge, but art is knowledge of a peculiar and specific kind. We may well subscribe to the observation of Shaftesbury that "all beauty is truth." But the truth of beauty does not consist in a theoretical description or explanation of things; it consists rather in the "sympathetic vision" of things. The two views of truth are in contrast with one another, but not in conflict or contradiction. Since art and science move in entirely different planes they cannot contradict or thwart one another. The conceptual interpretation of science does not preclude the intuitive interpretation of art. Each has its own perspective and, so to speak, its own angle of refraction. The psychology of sense perception has taught us that without the use of both eyes, without a binocular vision, there would be no awareness of the third dimension of space. The depth of human experience in the same sense depends on the fact that we are able to vary our modes of seeing, that we can alternate our views of reality. *Rerum videre formas* is a no less important and indispensable task than *rerum cognoscere causas*. In ordinary experience we connect phenomena according to the category of casuality or finality. According as we are interested in the theoretical reasons or the practical effects of things, we think of them as causes or as means. Thus we habitually lose sight of their immediate appearance until we can no longer see them face to face. Art, on the other hand, teaches us to visualize, not merely to conceptualize or utilize, things. Art gives us a richer, more vivid and colorful image of reality, and a more profound insight into its formal structure. It is characteristic of the nature of man that he is not limited to one specific and single approach to reality but can choose his point of view and so pass from one aspect of things to another.[53]

NOTES

1. For general discussion and criticism of aesthetic formalism see Hunter Mead, *Introduction to Aesthetics* (New York, Ronald Press, 1952), Chap. 13, and F. E. Sparshott, *The Structure of Aesthetics* (Toronto, University of Toronto Press, 1963), Chaps. XII, XIII.

2. Plato, *Philebus*, 51.

3. Kant, *Critique of Judgment*, Sec. 16; see above, p. 138.

4. On the development of German formalism during this period, see Ernest K. Mundt's article, "Three Aspects of German Aesthetic Theory," *Journal of Aesthetics and Art Criticism*, XVII (March, 1959), 287–310.

5. Selections from Herbart's discussions of aesthetics are included in E. F. Carritt, *Philosophies of Beauty* (New York, Oxford University Press, 1931), pp. 151–158.

6. Benedetto Croce gives a brief account of the "war" in Part I, Chap. XVII of his *Aesthetic* . . . translated by Douglas Ainslie (New York, Noonday Press, 1953), pp. 370–374.

7. Eduard Hanslick, *On the Beautiful in Music*, translated by Gustav Cohen (New York, Liberal Arts Press, 1957), p. 48.

8. See Conrad Fiedler, *On Judging Works of Visual Art*, translated by H. Schaeffer-Simmern, 2nd edition (Berkeley, University of California Press, 1957) and Adolf Hildebrand, *The Problem of Form in Painting and Sculpture*, translated by Max Meyer and Robert M. Ogden (New York, Stechert, 1907).

9. Allowing for wide divergences in interpretation of form and its relations to other aspects of aesthetic experience, we may mention the following: Alois Riegl, Heinrich Wölfflin, Wilhelm Worringer, Ernst Cassirer in Germany; Clive Bell, Roger Fry, and R. H. Wilenski in England; Etienne Souriau and Henri Focillon in France; Rhys Carpenter, Albert C. Barnes, Elijah Jordan, and Susanne Langer in the United States. The Italian aesthetician Luigi Pareyson should also be mentioned.

10. Cassirer traced the development of eighteenth-century aesthetics in Chap. VII of his *Philosophy of the Enlightenment*.

11. As Virginia Woolf records in her admirable biography, *Roger Fry* (London, Hogarth Press, 1940), upon which the following account is based.

12. *Vision and Design* and *Transformations* are composed for the most part of Fry's previous articles, essays, and lectures.

13. The lectures were later edited by Sir Kenneth Clark and published posthumously as *Last Lectures* (London, Cambridge University Press, 1939). In his survey of world art, Fry had gotten as far as Roman art, having discussed already Egyptian, Mesopotamian, Negro, American, Chinese, Indian, and Greek art.

14. See his "Retrospect" in *Vision and Design* (New York, Meridian Books, 1957), pp. 284–286.

15. See Fry's remarks on Tolstoy in his "Retrospect," cited above, pp. 292–293, and in his "Essay in Aesthetics," in the same volume, pp. 27–29.

16. Clive Bell, *Art* (London, Chatto & Windus, 1914), Chap. I.

17. Bell's views are discussed briefly by Fry in his "Retrospect" in *Vision and Design*, cited above, pp. 295–296. On Bell's aesthetics, see the chapter on him in Solomon Fishman, *The Interpretation of Art* (Berkeley, University of California Press, 1963), and a recent issue of *The British Journal of Aesthetics*, Vol. V, No. 2 (April, 1965), which contains five articles on Bell.

18. See "The Artist's Vision" in *Vision and Design*, previously cited, pp. 47–54.

19. Ibid., p. 52.

20. See *Last Lectures* (Boston, Beacon Press, 1962), pp. 15–16.

21. Ibid., p. 45.

22. Ibid., p. 30.

23. Ibid., p. 37. "Spiritual," as Fry points out, is not used here in any supernatural sense; it refers simply to those "faculties and activities" not essential to human existence as such.

24. See Clive Bell's *Old Friends: Personal Recollections* (London, Chatto & Windus, 1956), pp. 62–91.

25. The preceding selections are from Roger Fry's "An Essay in Aesthetics" in *Vision and Design* (New York, Meridian Books, 1957); pp. 20–21; pp. 23–25; pp. 26–27.

26. Fry, *Vision and Design*, pp. 29–31; pp. 33–35.

27. Fry is referring to "An Essay in Aesthetics." In another essay, *The Artist and Psycho-Analysis* (London, Hogarth Press, 1924), he made the distinction between "pure" and "impure" art to which he will refer in the present discussion.

28. I. A. Richards, *Principles of Criticism* (London, Kegan Paul, 1924).

29. Richards, *Principles of Criticism*, p. 16.

30. Ibid, p. 110.

31. The preceding selection is taken from "Some Questions on Esthetics" in Roger Fry's *Transformations, Critical and Speculative Essays on Art* (London, Chatto & Windus, 1926), pp. 1–6. In the rest of his essay, Fry attempts to support his argument by referring to the aesthetic interpretation of literature and representational painting.

32. The following account of Cassirer's life is based on the biography by Dimitry Gawronsky, "Ernst Cassirer: His Life and Work" in Paul A. Schilpp (ed.), *The Philosophy of Ernst Cassirer* (New York, Tudor Publishing Company, 1949), pp. 3–37.

33. *Die Philosophie der symbolischen Formen* was published in Berlin by Bruno Cassirer in three volumes over a six year period: Vol. I, *Die Sprache* (1923); Vol. II, *Das mythische Denken* (1925); and Vol. III, *Phänomenologie der Erkenntnis* (1929). All three volumes have been translated into English by Ralph Manheim and have been published by Yale University Press in a paperbound as well as a hardbound edition.

34. See *The Philosophy of Symbolic Forms*, Manheim translation (New Haven, Yale University Press, 1953), Vol. I, p. 80.

35. See the first chapter of *An Essay on Man, An Introduction to a Philosophy of Human Culture* (New Haven and London, Yale University Press, 1944), (to be cited henceforth as "E. M.").

36. E. M., p. 35.

37. E. M., p. 57.

38. E. M., p. 25.

39. E. M., p. 149.

40. E. M., p. 146.

41. E. M., p. 145.

42. E. M., p. 157.

43. E. M., p. 151.

44. E. M., p. 154.

45. E. M., p. 165.

46. E. M., p. 149.

47. R. G. Collingwood, *The Principles of Art* (Oxford, Clarendon Press, 1938), pp. 279, 282, 285.

48. This selection and the selections which follow are taken from Chap. IX, "Art," of *An Essay on Man*. The preceding selection is from pp. 141–144.

49. E. M., pp. 146–149.

50. *The Sense of Beauty* (New York, Charles Scribner's Sons, 1896), p. 22.

51. Aristotle, *Nicomachean Ethics*, 1776^b 33.

52. E. M., pp. 159–160.

53. E. M., pp. 168–170.

QUESTIONS AND TOPICS FOR
FURTHER STUDY

1. Explain how the imaginative life is distinguished from actual life, according to Fry. Why does he consider art to be "the chief organ of the imaginative life"?

2. What similarities do you find in Fry's, Kant's, and Vernon Lee's views of the nature of aesthetic contemplation? How do you account for these similarities?

3. Explain the various "emotional elements of design" mentioned by Fry, and illustrate them by referring to a painting of your choice.

4. What is the point at issue in Fry's and Richards' views of aesthetic experience? What argument does Fry give to substantiate his own view? Do you find his argument convincing? Why or why not?

5. What suggestions does Fry make for interpreting arts other than painting according to his formalist position?

6. What are the main differences between art, language, and science, according to Cassirer? Explain why he believes that an artist can be as much of a discoverer as a scientist.

7. What criticisms are presented by Cassirer against Croce's, Tolstoy's, and Santayana's approaches to aesthetics?

8. How does Cassirer re-interpret the meaning of Aristotle's theory of catharsis? Explain why he holds that "the calmness of the work of art is, paradoxically, a dynamic not a static calmness."

9. What similarities and differences do you find in Fry's and Cassirer's views of the nature of the work of art? Which of the two thinkers offers, in your opinion, a more adequate general theory of art?

10. Topics for further study: (a) the conception of vitality in Fry's aesthetics; (b) Fry's view of the function of color in artistic form; (c) Fry's views on form in sculpture; (d) Cassirer's view of the relation of art to language; (d) Cassirer on artistic and scientific imagination.

GUIDE TO SUPPLEMENTARY READING

(Works marked with asterisks are available in paperbound editions.)

FRY

I. PRIMARY SOURCES

Fry, Roger, *Vision and Design* (New York, Meridian Books, 1957).
——*Transformations, Critical and Speculative Essays on Art* (New York, Doubleday Anchor Books, 1956).
——*Last Lectures*, with an Introduction by Kenneth Clark (Boston, Beacon Press, 1962).

II. SECONDARY WORKS

Buermeyer, Laurence, "The Esthetics of Roger Fry," in John Dewey et al., *Art and Education, A Collection of Essays.* (Merion, Penna., Barnes Foundation Press, 1929), pp. 230–244.

Fishman, Solomon, *The Interpretation of Art* (Berkeley and Los Angeles, University of California Press, 1963). Chapter on Roger Fry.

Hannay, Howard, *Roger Fry and Other Essays* (London, George Allen & Unwin, 1937). Chap. I.

Johnstone, J. K., *The Bloomsbury Group* (New York, Noonday Press, 1963). Chap. III.

Lang, Berel, "Significance or Form: The Dilemma of Roger Fry's Aesthetic," *Journal of Aesthetics and Art Criticism,* XXI (Winter, 1962) 167–176.

Stolnitz, Jerome, *Aesthetics and Philosophy of Art Criticism, A Critical Introduction* (Boston, Houghton Mifflin Co., 1960). Chap. 6.

Weitz, Morris, *Philosophy of the Arts* (New York, Russell & Russell, 1964). Chap. 1.

CASSIRER

I. PRIMARY SOURCES

Cassirer, Ernst, *An Essay on Man, An Introduction to a Philosophy of Human Culture* (New Haven, Yale University Press, 1944).
———*The Philosophy of the Enlightenment*, translated by Fritz C. A. Keolln and James P. Pettegrove (Boston, Beacon Press, 1955). Chap. VII.

II. SECONDARY WORKS

Gilbert, Katharine E., "Cassirer's Placement of Art," in Paul A. Schilpp (ed.), *The Philosophy of Ernst Cassirer*, cited above, pp. 607–630.
Hartman, Robert S., "Cassirer's Philosophy of Symbolic Forms," in Paul A. Schilpp (ed.), *The Philosophy of Ernst Cassirer* (New York, Library of Living Philosophers, Tudor Publishing Co., 1949), pp. 291–333.
Hendel, Charles W., "Introduction" to Ernst Cassirer, *The Philosophy of Symbolic Forms*, translated by Ralph Manheim (New Haven, Yale University Press, 1953), Vol. I, pp. 1–65.
Langer, Susanne, *Philosophy in a New Key, a Study in the Symbolism of Reason, Rite, and Art* (New York, New American Library, 1948).
Reichardt, Konstantin, "Ernst Cassirer's Contribution to Literary Criticism," in Paul A. Schilpp (ed.), *The Philosophy of Ernst Cassirer*, cited above, pp. 663–688.
Slochower, Harry, "Ernst Cassirer's Functional Approach to Art and Literature," in Paul A. Schilpp (ed.), *The Philosophy of Ernst Cassirer*, cited above, pp. 633–659.

CHAPTER 13

Art, Experience, and Rebellion

DEWEY AND CAMUS

The view that art grows out of human experience and can develop into an instrument indispensable to the transformation of man and his world has been a recurrent theme in the literature of aesthetics, especially in the writings of Plato and Aristotle, Schiller and Goethe, Véron and Guyau, Tolstoy and Plekhanov, and Morris and Ruskin. In recent times few thinkers have orchestrated this theme as well as John Dewey in America and Albert Camus in France. Although they differed markedly in cultural background, philosophical methodology, and ultimate commitment, Dewey and Camus were similar in several respects in their treatment of art. As humanists, both were greatly disturbed by the impoverishment of cultural life by various forms of materialism, and each sought ways of overcoming the sense of alienation experienced by workers and artists and of restoring the vital continuity between work and creation. Both thinkers, considering art to be essential to the good life, were opposed to esoteric and nihilistic approaches to art which tend to separate the artist from his public. Both rejected, on the one hand, a totalitarian restriction of artistic creation and, on the other hand, a total lack of restraint and of moral responsibility on the part of the artist. Absent from Dewey's perspective are the tormenting sense of the absurd, the passionate nostalgia, the joyful agony which often appear in Camus's perspective. But if Dewey's treatment of art is less intense and dramatic than Camus's, it is much more extensive and systematic. Whatever be their comparative merits and shortcomings, Dewey's effort to explain art as experience and Camus's to explain it as rebellion are two of the most conscientious and impressive efforts yet made to relate art to its creator, to its public, and to its total environment.

DEWEY

John Dewey (1859–1952) was born and spent his early years in Burlington, Vermont, where he attended public schools and received his undergraduate training in philosophy at the University of Vermont.[1] Later, as a graduate student in philosophy at Johns Hopkins University he became an enthusiastic convert to Hegelianism, which through its idealistic integration of knowledge and experience brought him both intellectual and emotional satisfaction. After receiving his Ph.D. in 1884, he taught for nine years at the University of Michigan, married, and in 1894 moved on to the University of Chicago, where he taught philosophy, psychology, and pedagogy. At Chicago he founded, with the help of his brilliant wife, Alice Chipman, a new elementary school, "The Laboratory School," in which he was able to try out some of his pedagogical theories. By this time Dewey had "drifted away from Hegelianism" and, influenced by William James's biological approach to psychology, was developing his own interpretation of pragmatism, which he called "instrumentalism." For he now conceived of ideas not in Hegelian terms but as tools useful in solving problems, as instruments to be tried and tested in and through action. Disagreement with the university administration over the future of his school, which had become a breeding ground for progressive ideas, led Dewey to resign his position in 1904 and to accept another, this time at Columbia University. Columbia became his permanent base for the rest of his academic career. That career, however, was never "strictly academic." Along with teaching, it included the writing of more than thirty books[2] and innumerable articles, participation in founding and directing professional organizations, involvement in political and social affairs, as well as lecturing and traveling in foreign countries. At the age of seventy-eight, he went to Mexico as head of a commission to investigate Soviet charges against Leon Trotsky; at eighty-seven, having been a widower for many years, he married again. By the time he died, at the age of ninety-two, he had already become world famous as America's greatest philosopher, the father of progressive education, and one of the greatest living exemplars of Western liberal ideas.[3]

The philosophy of art which Dewey first presented in *Experience and Nature* (1925) and later developed more fully in *Art as Experience* (1934) contains the dominant themes which characterized Dewey's entire philosophic enterprise.[4] Among these themes are: (1) an empirical, scientific approach to the formulation and solution of all problems; (2) an emphasis on the natural, evolutionary development of all existing things; (3) a view of experience as a two-way process of doing and undergoing, in which man continuously adjusts himself to his environment and his environment to himself; (4) an appreciation of the material and sensuous conditions that make life and culture possible; (5) a constant reference to the organic context, the interrelated whole, in which any activity or achievement takes place; (6) a delight in the immediate qualities and limitless possibilities of growing experience, leading to a sense of "heightened vitality," energetic participation, and increased communication; (7) an adherence to the doctrine of the continuity of means and ends, necessitating a vigorous opposition to compartmentalisms in thought or in action; (8) a definition of intelligence in terms of the dynamic facility to solve problems rather than in terms of static faculties; (9) an appeal for the reconstruction of all existing institutions, so that they can better meet the growing needs of "whole individuals" in their "unified vitality"; and (10) a vigorous defense of freedom of action, investigation, and speech springing from a rational faith in democracy, science, and education.

These themes recur throughout Dewey's discussion of the problems of aesthetics as he pursues his major task of showing the continuity of aesthetic experience with ordinary experience. Art cannot be understood, he holds, by considering it to be something esoteric, something unrelated to the "events, doings and sufferings" of everyday living,[5] or by going to museums to admire objects that have been segregated from the activities by means of which they were created, or by studying "the theory of the beautiful."[6] All such approaches result in "compartmental pigeon-holeing," and give little if any real insight into the origin of art and the meaning of aesthetic experience. Because of the obstructions set up by faulty approaches, we must take a detour around objects of art in order to reach a sound understanding of art, but this detour will lead us eventually back to the main road of human experience, along which artistic construction and aesthetic appreciation can move unimpeded.[7] "Products of art" are, according to Dewey, only physical things, potential "works of art."[8] A complex interaction of agent with object is necessary to bring the real "work of art" into existence. And in the process, experience is clarified, intensified, and transformed; experience "in the raw" becomes aesthetic experience. For this to take place, for art to grow out of experience, materials and energies must be organized, natural rhythms must be brought to satisfying fulfillment; meanings "funded"; relations integrated; qualities "fused"; and life-experience given form. No less creative a process is involved in aesthetic appreciation: the perceiver must recreate the actual "work of art" by interacting with the artist's product, by effecting an imaginative reconstruction of the artist's own experience.[9]

Dewey's examination of art as a form of experience led him to consider it to be of supreme importance to life and philosophy. For in his view, art is not a "beauty parlor of civilization"[10] but a means of promoting civilization through its ability to break down barriers between human beings. It is "more moral than moralities"[11] because it extends rather than restricts the limits of feeling and imagination. Since art can express meanings rather than merely state them, it can restore the necessary union and vital continuity of man with life and nature. How art expresses meanings is a problem central in Dewey's aesthetics. In his view, the expressive aesthetic activity is certainly not the same as a mere emotional discharge which lacks a medium to give it material embodiment and formal significance.[12] The act of expression involves a continuous modification and transformation of "outer" or physical and "inner" or mental materials which are organically related.[13] The means through which an aesthetic effect is achieved are not external to the effect but essential to it: the means are media incorporated in the end, in the work of art.[14] This view, that means are continuous with ends and cannot be separated from them without destroying the organic relatedness of experience, is fundamental to Dewey's entire philosophy. Because art shows so clearly the coalescence of means (as media) and ends, a study of it can aid the philosopher, he believes, in overcoming the dualisms—mind and matter, thought and feeling, learning and doing, freedom and control, etc.—which plague modern thought and lead to the compartmentalization of life.[15]

Experience as Art and Art as Experience

1. *Dewey is opposed to the view, stemming from Greek philosophy, that theoretic contemplation is superior to practical
production and that art, being a form of production, is an inferior
mode of human activity. Art is, in Dewey's view, the ideal form
of all activity; it marks the culmination of a natural process carried
on through consummatory fulfillment. Such a view of art, Dewey
believes, provides a basis for overcoming dualistic thinking and
for understanding all phases of conscious experience.*

If Greek philosophy was correct in thinking of knowledge as
contemplation rather than as a productive art, and if modern
philosophy accepts this conclusion, then the only logical course is
relative disparagement of all forms of production, since they are
modes of practice which is by conception inferior to contemplation. The artistic is then secondary to the esthetic: "creation," to
"taste," and the scientific *worker*—as we significantly say—is
subordinate in rank and worth to the dilettante who enjoys the
results of his labors. But if modern tendencies are justified in
putting art and creation first, then the implications of this position
should be avowed and carried through. It would then be seen that
science is an art, that art is practice, and that the only distinction
worth drawing is not between practice and theory, but between
those modes of practice that are not intelligent, not inherently and
immediately enjoyable, and those which are full of enjoyed
meanings. When this perception dawns, it will be a commonplace
that art—the mode of activity that is charged with meanings
capable of immediately enjoyed possession—is the complete culmination of nature, and that "science" is properly a handmaiden
that conducts natural events to this happy issue. Thus would
disappear the separations that trouble present thinking: division of
everything into nature *and* experience, of experience into practice
and theory, art *and* science, of art into useful *and* fine, menial
and free.

Thus the issue involved in experience as art in its pregnant sense
and in art as processes and materials of nature continued by direc-

tion into achieved and enjoyed meanings, sums up in itself all the issues which have been previously considered. Thought, intelligence, science is the intentional direction of natural events to meanings capable of immediate possession and enjoyment; this direction—which is operative art—is itself a natural event in which nature otherwise partial and incomplete comes fully to itself; so that objects of conscious experience when reflectively chosen, form the "end" of nature. The doings and sufferings that form experience are, in the degree in which experience is intelligent or charged with meanings, a union of the precarious, novel, irregular with the settled, assured and uniform—a union which also defines the artistic and the esthetic. For wherever there is art the contingent and ongoing no longer work at cross purposes with the formal and recurrent but commingle in harmony. And the distinguishing feature of conscious experience, of what for short is often called "consciousness," is that in it the instrumental and the final, meanings that are signs and clews and meanings that are immediately possessed, suffered and enjoyed, come together in one. And all of these things are preëminently true of art.[16]

2. When experience fails to become art—"productive activity possessed of immanent and directly enjoyed meaning"—*the result may be to separate living into extremes of mere routine, on the one hand, or of capricious impulse on the other. Objecting to the usual distinction between useful and fine art, Dewey points out that the former is not merely instrumental and the latter consummatory. All genuine art is simultaneously instrumental and consummatory.*

The limiting terms that define art are routine at one extreme and capricious impulse at the other. It is hardly worth while to oppose science and art sharply to one another, when the deficiencies and troubles of life are so evidently due to separation between art and blind routine and blind impulse. Routine exemplifies the uniformities and recurrences of nature, caprice expresses its inchoate initiations and deviations. Each in isolation is unnatural as well as inartistic, for nature is an intersection of spontaneity and necessity, the regular and the novel, the finished and the beginning. It is right to object to much of current practice on the ground that it is routine, just as it is right to object to

much of our current enjoyments on the ground that they are
spasms of excited escape from the thraldom of enforced work.
But to transform a just objection against the quality of much of
our practical life into a description and definition of practice is
on the same plane as to convert legitimate objection to trivial
distraction, senseless amusement, and sensual absorption, into a
Puritanical aversion to happiness. The idea that work, productive
activity, signifies action carried on for merely extraneous ends,
and the idea that happiness signifies surrender of mind to the
thrills and excitations of the body are one and the same idea. The
first notion marks the separation of activity from meaning, and
the second marks the separation of receptivity from meaning. Both
separations are inevitable as far as experience fails to be art:—when
the regular, repetitious, and the novel, contingent in nature fail
to sustain and inform each other in a productive activity possessed
of immanent and directly enjoyed meaning.

Thus the theme has insensibly passed over into that of the relation of means and consequence, process and product, the instrumental and consummatory. Any activity that is simultaneously
both, rather than in alternation and displacement, is art. Disunion
of production and consumption is a common enough occurrence.
But emphasis upon this separation in order to exalt the consummatory does not define or interpret either art or experience. It
obscures their meaning, resulting in a division of art into useful
and fine, adjectives which, when they are prefixed to "art," corrupt
and destroy its intrinsic significance. For arts that are merely useful
are not arts but routines; and arts that are merely final are not arts
but passive amusements and distractions, different from other
indulgent dissipations only in dependence upon a certain acquired
refinement or "cultivation"....

... Anyone, who reflects upon the commonplace that a measure
of artistic products is their capacity to attract and retain observation with satisfaction under whatever conditions they are approached, while things of less quality soon lose capacity to hold
attention becoming indifferent or repellent upon subsequent
approach, has a sure demonstration that a genuinely esthetic object
is not exclusively consummatory but is causally productive as well.
A consummatory object that is not also instrumental turns in time
to the dust and ashes of boredom. The "eternal" quality of great
art is its renewed instrumentality for further consummatory
experiences.

When this fact is noted, it is also seen that limitation of fineness of art to paintings, statues, poems, songs and symphonies is conventional, or even verbal. Any activity that is productive of objects whose perception is an immediate good, and whose operation is a continual source of enjoyable perception of other events exhibits fineness of art. There are acts of all kinds that directly refresh and enlarge the spirit and that are instrumental to the production of new objects and dispositions which are in turn productive of further refinements and replenishments. Frequently moralists make the acts *they* find excellent or virtuous wholly final, and treat art and affection as mere means. Estheticians reverse the performance, and see in good *acts* means to an ulterior external happiness, while esthetic appreciation is called a good in itself, or that strange thing an end in itself. But on both sides it is true that in being preëminently fructifying the things designated means are immediate satisfactions. They are their own excuses for being just because they are charged with an office in quickening apprehension, enlarging the horizon of vision, refining discrimination, creating standards of appreciation which are confirmed and deepened by further experiences. It would almost seem when their non-instrumental character is insisted upon as if what was meant were an indefinitely expansive and radiating instrumental efficacy.[17]

3. *Dewey contrasts his naturalistic theory of art with the theory, which he considers "esoteric," that holds art to be a unique activity with an occult origin and ineffable significance. The latter theory, Dewey holds, can make no sense of aesthetic experience because it distorts the relationship between emotion and subject matter in art.*

There are substantially but two alternatives. Either art is a continuation, by means of intelligent selection and arrangement, of natural tendencies of natural events; or art is a peculiar addition to nature springing from something dwelling exclusively within the breast of man, whatever name be given to the latter. In the former case, delightfully enhanced perception or esthetic appreciation is of the same nature as enjoyment of any object that is consummatory. It is the outcome of a skilled and intelligent art of dealing with natural things for the sake of intensifying, purifying, prolonging and deepening the satisfactions which they spontaneously afford. That, in this process, new meanings develop, and that these afford uniquely new traits and modes of enjoyment is but what happens everywhere in emergent growths.

But if fine art has nothing to do with other activities and products, then of course it has nothing inherently to do with the objects, physical and social, experienced in other situations. It has an occult source and an esoteric character. It makes little difference what the source and the character be called. By strict logic it makes literally no difference. For if the quality of the esthetic experience is by conception unique, then the words employed to describe it have no significance derived from or comparable to the qualities of other experiences; their signification is hidden and specialized to a degree. Consider some of the terms which are in more or less current use among the critics who carry the isolation of art and the esthetic to its limit. It is sometimes said that art is the expression of the emotions; with the implication that, because of this fact, subject-matter is of no significance except as material through which emotion is expressed. Hence art becomes unique. For in works of science, utility and morals the character of the objects forming this subject-matter is all-important. But by this definition, subject-matter is stripped of all its own inherent characters in art in the degree in which it is genuine art; since a truly artistic work is manifest in the reduction of subject-matter to a mere medium of expression of emotion.

In such a statement emotion either has no significance at all, and it is mere accident that this particular combination of letters is employed; or else, if by emotion is meant the same sort of thing that is called emotion in daily life, the statement is demonstrably false. For emotion in its ordinary sense is something called out *by* objects, physical and personal; it is response *to* an objective situation. It is not something existing somewhere by itself which then employs material through which to express itself. Emotion is an indication of intimate participation, in a more or less excited way in some scene of nature or life; it is, so to speak, an attitude or disposition which is a function of objective things. It is intelligible that art should select and assemble objective things in such ways as to evoke emotional response of a refined, sensitive and enduring kind; it is intelligible that the artist himself is one capable of sustaining these emotions, under whose temper and spirit he performs his compositions of objective materials. This procedure may indeed be carried to a point such that the use of objective materials is economized to the minimum, and the evocation of the emotional response carried to its relative maximum. But it still remains true that the origin of the art-process lay in emotional responses spontaneously called out by a situation occurring without any reference to art, and without "esthetic" quality save in the sense in which all immediate enjoyment and suffering is esthetic. Economy in use of objective subject-matter may with experienced and trained minds go so far that what is ordinarily called "representation" is much reduced. But what happens is a highly funded and generalized representation of the formal sources of ordinary emotional experience.[18]

4. *Dewey's approach to the construction of an aesthetic theory begins not with the works of art themselves but rather with the everyday human experiences without which works of art would never come into existence. His major task is to show the continuity of aesthetic experience and other kinds of experience.*

By one of the ironic perversities that often attend the course of affairs, the existence of the works of art upon which formulation of an esthetic theory depends has become an obstruction to theory about them. For one reason, these works are products that exist externally and physically. In common conception, the work of art is often identified with the building, book, painting, or statue in its existence apart from human experience. Since the actual work of art is what the product does with and in experience, the result is not favorable to understanding. In addition, the very perfection of some of these products, the prestige they possess because of a long history of unquestioned admiration, creates conventions that get in the way of fresh insight. When an art product once attains classic status, it somehow becomes isolated from the human conditions under which it was brought into being and from the human consequences it engenders in actual life-experience.

When artistic objects are separated from both conditions of origin and operation in experience, a wall is built around them that renders almost opaque their general significance, with which esthetic theory deals. Art is remitted to a separate realm, where it is cut off from that association with the materials and aims of every other form of human effort, undergoing, and achievement. A primary task is thus imposed upon one who undertakes to write upon the philosophy of the fine arts. This task is to restore continuity between the refined and intensified forms of experience that are works of art and the everyday events, doings, and sufferings that are universally recognized to constitute experience. Mountain peaks do not float unsupported; they do not even just rest upon the earth. They *are* the earth in one of its manifest operations. It is the business of those who are concerned with the theory of the earth, geographers and geologists, to make this fact evident in its various implications. The theorist who would deal philosophically with fine art has a like task to accomplish.

If one is willing to grant this position, even if only by way of temporary experiment, he will see that there follows a conclusion at first sight surprising. In order to understand the meaning of artistic products, we have to forget them for a time, to turn aside from them and have recourse to the ordinary forces and conditions of experience that we do not usually regard as esthetic. We must arrive at the theory of art by means of a detour.[19] ...

5. *To consider art as continuous with experience does not, Dewey points out, denigrate art. On the contrary, recognition that art can grow out of experience should enhance one's appreciation of what is accomplished consciously in and through art.*

It is mere ignorance that leads then to the supposition that connection of art and esthetic perception with experience signifies a lowering of their significance and dignity. Experience in the degree in which it *is* experience is heightened vitality. Instead of signifying being shut up within one's own private feelings and sensations, it signifies active and alert commerce with the world; at its height it signifies complete interpenetration of self and the world of objects and events. Instead of signifying surrender to caprice and disorder, it affords our sole demonstration of a stability that is not stagnation but is rhythmic and developing. Because experience is the fulfillment of an organism in its struggles and achievements in a world of things, it is art in germ. Even in its rudimentary forms, it contains the promise of that delightful perception which is esthetic experience. ...

Experience is the result, the sign, and the reward of that interaction of organism and environment which, when it is carried to the full, is a transformation of interaction into participation and communication. Since sense-organs with their connected motor apparatus are the means of this participation, any and every derogation of them, whether practical or theoretical, is at once

effect and cause of a narrowed and dulled life-experience. Oppositions of mind and body, soul and matter, spirit and flesh all have
their origin, fundamentally, in fear of what life may bring forth.
They are marks of contraction and withdrawal. Full recognition,
therefore, of the continuity of the organs, needs and basic impulses of the human creature with his animal forbears, implies
no necessary deduction of man to the level of the brutes. On the
contrary, it makes possible the drawing of a ground-plan of
human experience upon which is erected the superstructure of
man's marvelous and distinguishing experience. What is distinctive
in man makes it possible for him to sink below the level of the
beasts. It also makes possible for him to carry to new and unprecedented heights that unity of sense and impulse, of brain and
eye and ear, that is exemplified in animal life, saturating it with
the conscious meanings derived from communication and deliberate
expression. . . .

Art is thus prefigured in the very processes of living. A bird
builds its nest and a beaver its dam when internal organic pressures
coöperate with external materials so that the former are fulfilled
and the latter are transformed in a satisfying culmination. We may
hesitate to apply the word "art," since we doubt the presence of
directive intent. But all deliberation, all conscious intent, grows
out of things once performed organically through the interplay
of natural energies. Were it not so, art would be built on quaking
sands, nay, on unstable air. The distinguishing contribution of man
is consciousness of the relations found in nature. Through consciousness, he converts the relations of cause and effect that are
found in nature into relations of means and consequence. Rather,
consciousness itself is the inception of such a transformation. . . .
Art is the living and concrete proof that man is capable of restoring
consciously, and thus on the plane of meaning, the union of sense,
need, impulse and action characteristic of the live creature. The
intervention of consciousness adds regulation, power of selection,
and redisposition. Thus it varies the arts in ways without end. But
its intervention also leads in time to the *idea* of art as a conscious
idea—the greatest intellectual achievement in the history of
humanity.[20]

6. *While to live is to experience continuously, sometimes
moments of experience are composed into a unity, given a self-
sufficient and individualized quality, felt as a rhythmic consumma-*

tion and closure. When this occurs, as it so often does in art and in other areas of experience, we have had an experience.

Experience occurs continuously, because the interaction of live creature and environing conditions is involved in the very process of living. Under conditions of resistance and conflict, aspects and elements of the self and the world that are implicated in this interaction qualify experience with emotions and ideas so that conscious intent emerges. Oftentimes, however, the experience had is inchoate. Things are experienced but not in such a way that they are composed into *an* experience. There is distraction and dispersion; what we observe and what we think, what we desire and what we get, are at odds with each other. We put our hands to the plow and turn back; we start and then we stop, not because the experience has reached the end for the sake of which it was initiated but because of extraneous interruptions or of inner lethargy.

In contrast with such experience, we have *an* experience when the material experienced runs its course to fulfillment. Then and then only is it integrated within and demarcated in the general stream of experience from other experiences. A piece of work is finished in a way that is satisfactory; a problem receives its solution; a game is played through; a situation, whether that of eating a meal, playing a game of chess, carrying on a conversation, writing a book, or taking part in a political campaign, is so rounded out that its close is a consummation and not a cessation. Such an experience is a whole and carries with it its own individualizing quality and self-sufficiency. It is *an* experience. . . .

In such experiences, every successive part flows freely, without seam and without unfilled blanks, into what ensues. At the same time there is no sacrifice of the self-identity of the parts. A river, as distinct from a pond, flows. But its flow gives a definiteness and interest to its successive portions greater than exist in the homogenous portions of a pond. In an experience, flow is from something to something. As one part leads into another and as one part carries on what went before, each gains distinctness in itself. The enduring whole is diversified by successive phases that are emphases of its varied colors.

Because of continuous merging, there are no holes, mechanical junctions, and dead centers when we have *an* experience. There are pauses, places of rest, but they punctuate and define the quality of movement. They sum up what has been undergone and prevent its dissipation and idle evaporation. Continued acceleration is breathless and prevents parts from gaining distinction. In a work of art, different acts, episodes, occurrences melt and fuse into unity, and yet do not disappear and lose their own character as they do so—just as in a genial conversation there is a continuous interchange and blending, and yet each speaker not only retains his own character but manifests it more clearly than is his wont....

In short, art, in its form, unites the very same relation of doing and undergoing, outgoing and incoming energy, that makes an experience to be an experience. Because of elimination of all that does not contribute to mutual organization of the factors of both action and reception into one another, and because of selection of just the aspects and traits that contribute to their interpenetration of each other, the product is a work of esthetic art. Man whittles, carves, sings, dances, gestures, molds, draws and paints. The doing or making is artistic when the perceived result is of such a nature that *its* qualities *as perceived* have controlled the question of production. The act of producing that is directed by intent to produce something that is enjoyed in the immediate experience of perceiving has qualities that a spontaneous or uncontrolled activity does not have. The artist embodies in himself the attitude of the perceiver while he works....

For to perceive, a beholder must *create* his own experience. And his creation must include relations comparable to those which the original producer underwent. They are not the same in any literal sense. But with the perceiver, as with the artist, there must be an ordering of the elements of the whole that is in form, although not in details, the same as the process of organization the creator of the work consciously experienced. Without an act of recreation the object is not perceived as a work of art. The artist selected, simplified, clarified, abridged and condensed according to his interest. The beholder must go through these operations according to his point of view and interest. In both, an act of abstraction, that is of extraction of what is significant, takes place. In both, there is comprehension in its literal signification—that is, a gathering together of details and particulars physically scattered into an experienced whole.[21] ...

7. *Dewey attempts to differentiate distinctively aesthetic experiences from intellectual or practical experiences which may have aesthetic qualities. In aesthetic experiences there is a heightened interest in the factors that constitute* an *experience—in the experience's omnipresent form, in its dynamic organization, in its rhythmic variety and unity.*

The considerations that have been presented imply both the community and the unlikeness, because of specific emphasis, of *an* experience, in its pregnant sense, and esthetic experience. The former has esthetic quality; otherwise its materials would not be rounded out into a single coherent experience. It is not possible to divide in a vital experience the practical, emotional, and intellectual from one another and to set the properties of one over against the characteristics of the others. The emotional phase binds parts together into a single whole; "intellectual" simply names the fact that the experience has meaning: "practical" indicates that the organism is interacting with events and objects which surround it. The most elaborate philosophic or scientific inquiry and the most ambitious industrial or political enterprise has, when its different ingredients constitute an integral experience, esthetic quality. For then its varied parts are linked to one another, and do not merely succeed one another. And the parts through their experienced linkage move toward a consummation and close, not merely to cessation in time. This consummation, moreover, does not wait in consciousness for the whole undertaking to be finished. It is anticipated throughout and is recurrently savored with special intensity.

Nevertheless, the experiences in question are dominantly intellectual or practical, rather than *distinctively* esthetic, because of the interest and purpose that initiate and control them. In an intellectual experience, the conclusion has value on its own account. It can be extracted as a formula or as a "truth," and can be used in its independent entirety as a factor and guide in other inquiries. In a work of art there is no such single self-sufficient deposit. The end, the terminus, is significant not by itself but as the integration of the parts. It has no other existence. A drama or novel is not the final sentence, even if the characters are disposed of as living happily ever after. In a distinctively esthetic experience, characteristics that are subdued in other experiences are dominant; those that are subordinate are controlling—namely, the characteristics in virtue of which the experience is an integrated complete experience on its own account.

In every integral experience there is form because there is dynamic organization. I call the organization dynamic because it takes time to complete it, because it is a growth. There is inception, development, fulfillment. Material is ingested and digested through interaction with that vital organization of the results of prior experience that constitutes the mind of the worker. Incubation goes on until what is conceived is brought forth and is rendered perceptible as part of the common world. An esthetic experience can be crowded into a moment only in the sense that a climax of prior long enduring processes may arrive in an outstanding movement which so sweeps everything else into it that all else is forgotten. That which distinguishes an experience as esthetic is conversion of resistance and tensions, of excitations that in themselves are temptations to diversion, into a movement toward an inclusive and fulfilling close. . . .

The *form* of the whole is therefore present in every member. Fulfilling, consummating, are continuous functions, not mere ends, located at one place only. An engraver, painter, or writer is in process of completing at every stage of his work. He must at each point retain and sum up what has gone before as a whole and with reference to a whole to come. Otherwise there is no consistency and no security in his successive acts. The series of doings in the rhythm of experience give variety and movement; they save the work from monotony and useless repetitions. The undergoings are the corresponding elements in the rhythm, and they supply unity; they save the work from the aimlessness of a mere succession of excitations. An object is peculiarly and dominantly esthetic, yielding the enjoyment characteristic of esthetic perception, when the factors that determine anything which can be called *an* experience are lifted high above the threshold of perception and are made manifest for their own sake.[22]

CAMUS

One of the most important French literary artists of the twentieth century, Albert Camus (1913–1960) was born not in France but in Algeria, where he grew up poverty-stricken, worked hard to get an education at the Lycée and the University in Algiers, and struggled to become a writer.[23] In his youth and early manhood he developed a passionate interest in sports, literature, the theatre, and philosophy. He also developed a passionate hatred of injustice and tyranny in any form and a strong sympathy for the working classes. Having completed his academic work in 1936—his thesis was on Plotinus and St. Augustine—Camus wanted to go into teaching but was disqualified because he had tuberculosis. As an alternative, he turned to journalism and eventually went to France to work. During the Second World War, while he was secretly editing a French resistance newspaper, he became famous for his novel *The Stranger* (1942) and a philosophical essay, *The Myth of Sisyphus* (1943). After the liberation of Paris by the Allies in 1944, he won new acclaim when his underground activities became public knowledge. In the years that followed he further distinguished himself both as a creative artist and as a stringent critic of his times through several plays, among which was *Caligula* (1945), the novels, *The Plague* (1947) and *The Fall* (1956), and philosophical essays such the *The Rebel* (1953). In 1957 he received the Nobel Prize for Literature.[24] His plans for new literary and theatrical ventures were unfortunately never realized as at the age of forty-six he was killed in an automobile accident.

Although Camus was well read in philosophy and had pursued philosophical research in his university days, he never claimed to be a professional philosopher or to have formulated a system of philosophy. Dissatisfied with all systems, critical of all rigid comparmentalisms, wary of all absolutes, Camus seeks fresh answers to old problems by returning to the method of rigorous self-examination which had been characteristic of French philosophy since Montaigne, Pascal, and Descartes. Philosophy is, in his view, more of an attitude toward the universe rather than a system of values or a set of beliefs about the nature of reality. The basic philosophical problem, for him, is not the nature of reality or the nature of mind; it is the nature, the value, of life itself. Why not commit suicide if life is meaningless, if existence is absurd?[25] This is the question which Camus raises and attempts to answer in his *Myth of Sisyphus*. He seeks a way beyond nihilism, a way of living and dying with dignity despite the ultimate absurdity and futility of man's efforts to transcend his mortality.

In the course of his search for meaning, Camus discusses artistic creation which is, in his view, "the absurd joy *par excellence*."[26] For despite the fact that ultimately the artist's creations come to nothing, he does succeed in making his consciousness concrete and his experiences relatively permanent in and through his works. He recreates in his works the reality which otherwise would be ephemeral; he thus lives doubly, achieving a kind of immortality which, though illusory, offers some consolation. Knowing that some day he must die, that all his projects will eventually come to nothing and that his most passionate striving to attain absolute truth and beauty is futile, still the artist knows that as long as he is alive and free he can actualize in his work the diversity, the inexhaustible aspects of the world in which he lives. The absurd artist, the artist who has faced fully and unflinchingly the ever frightening and frustrating human predicament, can still find courage to create, even though there is no "reason" to do so and even though he must be willing to create "for nothing." From accomplishing his work, from revolting against his predicament, the artist can gain a patience, a lucidity, a disciplined freedom, and a human dignity which can make life bearable, if not fulfilled. Like Sisyphus, the Greek mythological character who was condemned by the gods for all eternity to roll a stone up a mountain only to have it fall again before it reached the top, the artist is condemned to a hopeless but heroic task.

But *The Myth of Sisyphus* does not express Camus's most mature views on art. Later, in *The Rebel*, an extensive essay on man's efforts in modern history to overcome by force the irrationality and injustice in the world and to impose upon social and political conditions a more ideal unity, he returns to the discussion of art, under the heading "Rebellion and Art."[27] Here Camus is clearer, more affirmative, and less pessimistic than in his earlier treatment of art. He now sees the work of art, a novel, for example, as an expression of its creator's "passion for unity." It is at once a means of rejecting and recreating the world. By giving his experience form, by creating an imaginary universe in which action is more orderly, more stylized, more significant than it usually is in life, the artist satisfies his own and his reader's need to possess the world more completely than would ever be possible without the aid of art.[28] For the artist, unlike the lover in the *Rubaiyat*, can indeed shatter the world to bits and remold it nearer to the heart's desire. Through his creations, he and his reader can rise above the transitory event by seeing it concretized; they can experience the satisfaction of seeing characters developed fully, thoughts articulated admirably, destinies worked out completely, and meaning imparted to the trivial and the absurd. The novelist, in Camus's view, is like a god who judges, rewards and punishes, destroys and recreates. And in the permanence of his art, at least, he even overcomes death.[29]

Because he considers art to be of such crucial importance to mankind, Camus is highly critical of much of the art of the twentieth century, which, in his opinion, has failed to meet the challenges of our time. Recent art, he holds, has thus far been dominated either by a passion for pure form, which often deteriorates into an annihilation of reality and makes a virtue of unintelligibility, or by a passion for totality, for social realism, which usually leads to a totalitarian aesthetic and a propagandistic art. Camus considers both of these passions to be expressions of the same nihilistic tendencies of our times which, in turn, are the result of the separation of work from creation and the subordination of everything to production.[30] But Camus sees a sensible alternative to these. It is rebellion rather than annihilation, imaginative control rather than brutish restriction. But the goal of rebellion, whether in art or politics, should be free creation, creation which can lead ultimately to a new form of civilization. Camus envisages a future society in which tyrants and slaves have been replaced by genuine creators who are able to achieve a new and higher cultural synthesis.[31] He remains accutely aware of the perils an artist faces today in attempting to create in an age of collective passions and social turmoil. But despite the perils, despite the fact that free creation may even turn out to be impossible in our time, the artist can, Camus is convinced, still uphold his aesthetic ideals, continuing to create in face of absurdity and despair and working toward a future in which conditions more favorable to the genuine creative spirit may prevail.

Rebellion and Art

1. *Although Camus considers art to be rebellion in its purest form, he is well aware of the strictures which have been pronounced against art by social reformers such as Plato, Tolstoy, and Marx. But to reject art outright, or to relegate it to a position inferior to the so-called practical interests is, to Camus, a kind of "ascetic insanity." This attitude is sometimes promoted by the artists themselves when they repent of what they have created.*

Art is the activity that exalts and denies simultaneously. "No artist tolerates reality," says Nietzsche. That is true, but no artist can get along without reality. Artistic creation is a demand for unity and a rejection of the world. But it rejects the world on account of what it lacks and in the name of what it sometimes is. Rebellion can be observed here in its pure state and in its original complexities. Thus art should give us a final perspective on the content of rebellion.

The hostility to art shown by all revolutionary reformers must, however, be pointed out. Plato is moderately reasonable. He only calls in question the deceptive function of language and exiles only poets from his republic. Apart from that, he considers beauty more important than the world. But the revolutionary movement of modern times coincides with an artistic process that is not yet completed. The Reformation chooses morality and exiles beauty. Rousseau denounces in art a corruption of nature by society. Saint-Just inveighs against the theater, and in the elaborate program he composes for the "Feast of Reason" he states that he would like Reason to be impersonated by someone "virtuous rather than beautiful." The French Revolution gave birth to no artists, but only to a great journalist, Desmoulins, and to a clandestine writer,

Sade. It guillotines the only poet of the times.[32] The only great prose-writer took refuge in London and pleaded the cause of Christianity and legitimacy.[33] A little later the followers of Saint-Simon demanded a "socially useful form of art." "Art for progress" was a commonplace for the whole period, and one that Hugo revived, without succeeding in making it sound convincing. Vallès alone brings to his malediction of art a tone of imprecation that gives it authenticity.

This tone is also employed by the Russian nihilists. Pisarev proclaims the deposition of aesthetic values, in favor of pragmatic values. "I would rather be a Russian shoemaker than a Russian Raphael." A pair of shoes, in his eyes, is more useful than Shakespeare. The nihilist Nekrassov, a great and moving poet, nevertheless affirms that he prefers a piece of cheese to all of Pushkin. Finally, we are familiar with the excommunication of art pronounced by Tolstoy. Revolutionary Russia finally even turned its back on the marble statues of Venus and Apollo, still gilded by the Italian sun, that Peter the Great had had brought to his summer garden in St. Petersburg. Suffering, sometimes, turns away from too painful expressions of happiness.

German ideology is no less severe in its accusations. According to the revolutionary interpreters of Hegel's *Phenomenology*, there will be no art in reconciled society. Beauty will be lived and no longer imagined. Reality, become entirely rational, will satisfy, completely by itself, every appetite. The criticism of formal conscience and of escapist values naturally extends itself to embrace art. Art does not belong to all times; it is determined, on the contrary, by its period, and expresses, says Marx, the privileged values of the ruling classes. Thus there is only one revolutionary form of art, which is, precisely, art dedicated to the service of the revolution. Moreover, by creating beauty outside the course of history, art impedes the only rational activity: the transformation of history itself into absolute beauty. The Russian shoemaker, once he is aware of his revolutionary role, is the real creator of definitive beauty. As for Raphael, he created only a transitory beauty, which will be quite incomprehensible to the new man.

Marx asks himself, it is true, how the beauty created by the Greeks can still be beautiful for us. His answer is that this beauty is the expression of the naïve childhood of this world and that we have, in the midst of our adult struggles, a nostalgia for this childhood. But how can the masterpieces of the Italian Renaissance, how can Rembrandt, how can Chinese art still be beautiful in our eyes? What does it matter! The trial of art has been opened definitely and is continuing today with the embarrassed complicity of artists and intellectuals dedicated to calumniating both their art and their intelligence. We notice, in fact, that in the contest between Shakespeare and the shoemaker, it is not the shoemaker who maligns Shakespeare or beauty, but, on the contrary, the man who continues to read Shakespeare and who does not choose to make shoes—which he could never make, if it comes to that. The artists of our time resemble the repentant noblemen of nineteenth-century Russia; their bad conscience is their excuse. But the last emotion that an artist can experience, confronted with his art, is repentance. It is going far beyond simple and necessary humility to pretend to dismiss beauty, too, until the end of time, and meanwhile, to deprive all the world, including the shoemaker, of this additional bread of which one has taken advantage oneself.[34]

2. *Camus explains how rebellion and art resemble each other in that both are attempts to reconstruct and to unify a reality which both initially reject. In composing a symphony, in making a statue, in writing a novel, or in painting a picture, an artist tries to impose order upon disorder, to unify the disparate, and to render permanent what is transitory. But while the artist rejects and denies certain aspects of the world, he affirms and exalts others. The genuine artist, Camus holds, is never an absolute nihilist.*

...In every rebellion is to be found the metaphysical demand for unity, the impossibility of capturing it, and the construction of a substitute universe. Rebellion, from this point of view, is a fabricator of universes. This also defines art. The demands of rebellion are really, in part, aesthetic demands. All rebel thought, as we have seen, is expressed either in rhetoric or in a closed universe. The rhetoric of ramparts in Lucretius, the convents and isolated castles of Sade, the island or the lonely rock of the romantics, the solitary heights of Nietzsche, the primeval seas of Lautréamont, the parapets of Rimbaud, the terrifying castles of the surrealists, which spring up in a storm of flowers, the prison, the nation behind barbed wire, the concentration camps, the empire of free slaves, all illustrate, after their own fashion, the same need for coherence and unity. In these sealed worlds, man can reign and have knowledge at last.

This tendency is common to all the arts. The artist reconstructs the world to his plan. The symphonies of nature know no rests. The world is never quiet; even its silence eternally resounds with the same notes, in vibrations that escape our ears. As for those that we perceive, they carry sounds to us, occasionally a chord, never a melody. Music exists, however, in which symphonies are completed, where melody gives its form to sounds that by themselves have none, and where, finally, a particular arrangement of notes extracts from natural disorder a unity that is satisfying to the mind and the heart.

"I believe more and more," writes Van Gogh, "that God must not be judged on this earth. It is one of His sketches that has turned out badly." Every artist tries to reconstruct this sketch and to give it the style it lacks. The greatest and most ambitious of all the arts, sculpture, is bent on capturing, in three dimensions, the fugitive figure of man, and on restoring the unity of great style to the general disorder of gestures. Sculpture does not reject resemblance, of which, indeed, it has need. But resemblance is not its first aim. What it is looking for, in its periods of greatness, is the gesture, the expression, or the empty stare which will sum up all the gestures and all the stares in the world. Its purpose is not to imitate, but to stylize and to imprison in one significant expression the fleeting ecstasy of the body or the infinite variety of human attitudes. Then, and only then, does it erect, on the pediments of teeming cities, the model, the type, the motionless perfection that will cool, for one moment, the fevered brow of man. The frustrated lover of love can finally gaze at the Greek caryatides and grasp what it is that triumphs, in the body and face of the woman, over every degradation.

The principle of painting is also to make a choice. "Even genius," writes Delacroix, ruminating on his art, "is only the gift of generalizing and choosing." The painter isolates his subject, which is the first way of unifying it. Landscapes flee, vanish from the memory, or destroy one another. That is why the landscape painter or the painter of still life isolates in space and time things that normally change with the light, get lost in an infinite perspective, or disappear under the impact of other values. The first thing that a landscape painter does is to square off his canvas. He eliminates as much as he includes. Similarly, subject-painting isolates, in both time and space, an action that normally would become lost in another action. Thus the painter arrives at a point of stabilization. The really great creative artists are those who, like Piero della Francesca, give the impression that the stabilization has only just taken place, that the projection machine has suddenly stopped dead. All their subjects give the impression that, by some miracle of art, they continue to live, while ceasing to be mortal. Long after his death, Rembrandt's philosopher still meditates, between light and shade, on the same problem.

"How vain a thing is painting that beguiles us by the resemblance to objects that do not please us at all." Delacroix, who quotes Pascal's celebrated remark, is correct in writing "strange" instead of "vain." These objects do not please us at all because we do not see them; they are obscured and negated by a perpetual process of change. Who looked at the hands of the executioner during the Flagellation, and the olive trees on the way to the Cross? But here we see them represented, transfigured by the incessant movement of the Passion; and the agony of Christ, imprisoned in images of violence and beauty, cries out again each day in the cold rooms of museums. A painter's style lies in this blending of nature and history, in this stability imposed on incessant change. Art realizes, without apparent effort, the reconciliation of the unique with the universal of which Hegel dreamed. Perhaps that is why periods, such as ours, which are bent on unity to the point of madness, turn to primitive arts, in which stylization is the most intense and unity the most provocative. The most extreme stylization is always found at the beginning and end of artistic movements; it demonstrates the intensity of negation and transposition which has given modern painting its disorderly impetus toward interpreting unity and existence. Van Gogh's admirable complaint is the arrogant and desperate cry of all artists. "I can very well, in life and in painting, too, do without God. But I cannot, suffering as I do, do without something that is greater than I am, that is my life—the power to create."

But the artist's rebellion against reality, which is automatically suspect to the totalitarian revolution, contains the same affirmation as the spontaneous rebellion of the oppressed. The revolutionary spirit, born of total negation, instinctively felt that, as well as refusal, there was also consent to be found in art; that there was a risk of contemplation counterbalancing action, beauty, and injustice, and that in certain cases beauty itself was a form of

injustice from which there was no appeal. Equally well, no form
of art can survive on total denial alone. Just as all thought, and
primarily that of non-signification, signifies something, so there is
no art that has no signification. Man can allow himself to denounce
the total injustice of the world and then demand a total justice
that he alone will create. But he cannot affirm the total hideous-
ness of the world. To create beauty, he must simultaneously
reject reality and exalt certain of its aspects. Art disputes reality,
but does not hide from it. Nietzsche could deny any form of
transcendence, whether moral or divine, by saying that transcendence drove one to slander this world and this life. But perhaps
there is a living transcendence, of which beauty carries the promise,
which can make this mortal and limited world preferable to and
more appealing than any other. Art thus leads us back to the
origins of rebellion, to the extent that it tries to give its form to
an elusive value which the future perpetually promises, but of
which the artist has a presentiment and wishes to snatch from the
grasp of history.[35] ...

3. *Rejecting both extreme formalism and extreme realism as
approaches in art, Camus argues that these are absurd concepts
which are conducive not to genuine artistic creation but to
nihilism. The genuine artist, unlike the formalist who absolutely
rejects the world and the realist who absolutely affirms it, takes
the materials provided by reality and, by means of his style, imposes upon these materials a unity and a coherence of form.*

By the treatment that the artist imposes on reality, he declares
the intensity of his rejection. But what he retains of reality in the
universe that he creates reveals the degree of consent that he gives
to at least one part of reality—which he draws from the shadows
of evolution to bring it to the light of creation. In the final analysis,
if the rejection is total, reality is then completely banished and the
result is a purely formal work. If, on the other hand, the artist
chooses, for reasons often unconnected with art, to exalt crude
reality, the result is then realism. In the first case the primitive
creative impulse in which rebellion and consent, affirmation and
negation are closely allied is adulterated to the advantage of rejection. It then represents formal escapism, of which our period has
furnished so many examples and of which the nihilist origin is

quite evident. In the second case the artist claims to give the world unity by withdrawing from it all privileged perspectives. In this sense, he confesses his need for unity, even a degraded form of unity. But he also renounces the first requirement of artistic creation. To deny the relative freedom of the creative mind more forcibly, he affirms the immediate totality of the world. The act of creation denies itself in both these kinds of work. Originally, it refused only one aspect of reality while simultaneously affirming another. Whether it comes to the point of rejecting all reality or of affirming nothing but reality, it denies itself each time either by absolute negation or by absolute affirmation. It can be seen that, on the plane of aesthetics, this analysis coincides with the analysis I have sketched on the historical plane.

But just as there is no nihilism that does not end by supposing a value, and no materialism that, being self-conceived, does not end by contradicting itself, so formal art and realist art are absurd concepts. No art can completely reject reality. The Gorgon is, doubtless, a purely imaginary creature; its face and the serpents that crown it are part of nature. Formalism can succeed in purging itself more and more of real content, but there is always a limit. Even pure geometry, where abstract painting sometimes ends, still derives its color and its conformity to perspective from the exterior world. The only real formalism is silence. Moreover, realism cannot dispense with a minimum of interpretation and arbitrariness. Even the very best photographs do not represent reality; they result from an act of selection and impose a limit on something that has none. The realist artist and the formal artist try to find unity where it does not exist, in reality in its crudest state, or in imaginative creation which wants to abolish all reality. On the contrary, unity in art appears at the limit of the transformation that the artist imposes on reality. It cannot dispense with either. This correction[36] which the artist imposes by his language and by a redistribution of elements derived from reality is called style and gives the re-created universe its unity and its boundaries. It attempts, in the work of every rebel, to impose its laws on the world, and succeeds in the case of a few geniuses. "Poets," said Shelley, "are the unacknowledged legislators of the world."

Literary art, by its origins, cannot fail to illustrate this vocation. It can neither totally consent to reality nor turn aside from it completely. The purely imaginary does not exist, and even if it did exist in an ideal novel which would be purely disincarnate, it would have no artistic significance, in that the primary necessity for a mind in search of unity is that the unity should be communicable. From another point of view, the unity of pure reasoning is a false unity, for it is not based on reality. The sentimental love story, the horror story, and the edifying novel deviate from art to the great or small extent that they disobey this law. Real literary creation, on the other hand, uses reality and only reality with all its warmth and its blood, its passion and its outcries. It simply adds something that transfigures reality.

Likewise, what is commonly called the realistic novel tries to be the reproduction of reality in its immediate aspects. To reproduce the elements of reality without making any kind of selection would be, if such an undertaking could be imagined, nothing but a sterile repetition of creation. Realism should only be the means of expression of religious genius—Spanish art admirably illustrates this contention—or, at the other extreme, the artistic expressions of monkeys, which are quite satisfied with mere imitation. In fact, art is never realistic though sometimes it is tempted to be. To be really realistic a description would have to be endless. Where Stendhal describes in one phrase Lucien Leuwen's entrance into a room, the realistic artist ought, logically, to fill several volumes with descriptions of characters and settings, still without succeeding in exhausting every detail. Realism is indefinite enumeration. By this it reveals that its real ambition is conquest, not of the unity, but of the totality of the real world. Now we understand why it should be the official aesthetic of a totalitarian revolution. But the impossibility of such an aesthetic has already been demonstrated. Realistic novels select their material, despite themselves, from reality, because the choice and the conquest of reality are absolute conditions of thought and expression.[37] To write is already to choose. There is thus an arbitrary aspect to reality, just as there is an arbitrary aspect to the ideal, which makes a realistic novel an implicit problem novel. To reduce the unity of the world of fiction to the totality of reality can only be done by means of an *a priori* judgment which eliminates form, reality, and everything that conflicts with doctrine. Therefore so-called socialist realism is condemned by the very logic of its nihilism to accumulate the advantages of the edifying novel and propaganda literature.

Whether the event enslaves the creator or whether the creator claims to deny the event completely, creation is nevertheless reduced to the degraded forms of nihilist art. It is the same thing with creation as with civilization: it presumes uninterrupted tension between form and matter, between evolution and the mind, and between history and values. If the equilibrium is destroyed, the result is dictatorship or anarchy, propaganda or formal insanity. In either case creation, which always coincides with rational freedom, is impossible. Whether it succumbs to the intoxication of abstraction and formal obscurantism, or whether it falls back on the whip of the crudest and most ingenious realism, modern art, in its semi-totality, is an art of tyrants and slaves, not of creators.[38]

4. *If formalism and realism do not provide styles conducive to genuine artistic creation, what kind of style does? According to Camus, it is a style which reflects clearly, without itself being noticeable, the artist's stylization of reality; a style which without being artificial is quite capable of expressing the distortion of reality that the artist as rebel perpetuates.*

A work in which the content overflows the form, or in which the form drowns the content, only bespeaks an unconvinced and unconvincing unity. In this domain, as in others, any unity that is not a unity of style is a mutilation. Whatever may be the chosen point of view of an artist, one principle remains common to all creators: stylization, which supposes the simultaneous existence of reality and of the mind that gives reality its form. Through style, the creative effort reconstructs the world, and always with the same slight distortion that is the mark of both art and protest. Whether it is the enlargement of the microscope which Proust brings to bear on human experience or, on the contrary, the absurd insignificance with which the American novel endows its characters, reality is in some way artificial. The creative force, the fecundity of rebellion, are contained in this distortion which the style and tone of a work represent. Art is an impossible demand given expression and form. When the most agonizing protest finds its most resolute form of expression, rebellion satisfies its real aspirations and derives creative energy from this fidelity to itself. Despite the fact that this runs counter to the prejudices of the times, the greatest style in art is the expression of the most passionate rebellion. Just as genuine classicism is only romanticism subdued, genius is a rebellion that has created its own limits. That is why there is no genius, contrary to what we are taught today, in negation and pure despair.

This means, at the same time, that great style is not a mere formal virtue. It is a mere formal virtue when it is sought out for its own sake to the detriment of reality, but then it is not great style. It no longer invents, but imitates—like all academic works— while real creation is, in its own fashion, revolutionary. If stylization must necessarily be rather exaggerated, since it sums up the intervention of man and the desire for rectification which the artist brings to his reproduction of reality, it is nevertheless desirable that it should remain invisible so that the demand which gives birth to art should be expressed in its most extreme tension. Great style is invisible stylization, or rather stylization incarnate. "There is never any need," says Flaubert, "to be afraid of exaggeration in art." But he adds that the exaggeration should be "continuous and proportionate to itself." When stylization is exaggerated and obvious, the work becomes nothing but pure nostalgia; the unity it is trying to conquer has nothing to do with concrete unity. On the other hand, when reality is delivered over to unadorned fact or to insignificant stylization, then the concrete is presented without unity. Great art, style, and the true aspect of rebellion lie somewhere between these two heresies.[39]

NOTES

1. On the life of Dewey, see the biography edited by Jane M. Dewey in Paul A. Schilpp (ed.), *The Philosophy of John Dewey* (Evanston and Chicago, Library of Living Philosophers, 1939) to which reference has been made in writing the following account.

2. Among these books were *The School and Society* (1899), *How We Think* (1910), *Democracy and Education* (1916), *Reconstruction in Philosophy* (1920), *Human Nature and Conduct* (1922), *Experience and Nature* (1925), *The Quest for Certainty* (1929), *A Common Faith* (1934), *Art as Experience* (1934) and

Logic: The Theory of Inquiry (1938). An extensive bibliography of Dewey's writings, including a number of articles pertinent to the study of his aesthetics, is included in Paul A. Schilpp (ed.), *The Philosophy of John Dewey*, cited above.

3. For an introduction to Dewey's thought, written by another philosopher who knew him well and who helped him on the manuscript of *Art as Experience*, see Sidney Hook's *John Dewey: An Intellectual Portrait* (New York, John Day Co., 1939).

4. Although at the time *Art as Experience* was published some critics expressed surprise that Dewey considered himself qualified to write a work on art, he was well prepared to deal theoretically with the arts, and with questions raised by reflection on aesthetic experience. His early study of classical Greek and German philosophers, especially of Plato, Aristotle, Kant, and Hegel, probably first aroused his interest in aesthetic problems. His work in psychology undoubtably gave him a rich fund upon which to draw in analyzing aesthetic perception, while his educational experiments developed in him an appreciation of aesthetic elements in education. He was well read in the literature of aesthetics, and capable of reviewing critically works on aesthetics by thinkers as different as Bernard Bosanquet, George Santayana, and Alfred North Whitehead. His visits to Japan and China brought him into contact with the Eastern approach to aesthetic appreciation. In Russia, he had been on the scene to witness what seemed to be a dramatic renewal in the arts accompanying a reconstruction of social institutions. For many years he was the close friend of Albert C. Barnes, an art collector and founder of an institution, The Barnes Foundation, in which Dewey's educational methods were being applied in the teaching of art appreciation. (Barnes's *The Art in Painting* is dedicated to Dewey; Dewey's *Art as Experience* is dedicated to Barnes.) Prior to writing his major work on aesthetics, Dewey had dealt with aesthetics in earlier works, notably in *Experience and Nature* (1925) and in *Philosophy and Civilization* (1931). *Art as Experience*, then, grew slowly and substantially out of a continuous and cumulative reflection on experiences that stimulated Dewey to probe deeper into the meaning of art and to explain its relevance to fuller living and understanding.

5. Dewey, *Art as Experience* (New York, Capricorn Books, G. P. Putnam's Sons, 1958), p. 3. (To be abbreviated henceforth as A. E.)

6. Among the aesthetic theories of thinkers included in the present volume, Dewey makes reference in *Art as Experience* to

Plato, Aristotle, Kant, Hegel, Schopenhauer, Tolstoy, Santayana, Vernon Lee, Roger Fry, and Croce.

7. A. E., p. 4.

8. A. E., p. 162, p. 214.

9. A. E., p. 54.

10. A. E., p. 344.

11. A. E., p. 348.

12. A. E., pp. 61–63.

13. A. E., pp. 74–75.

14. A. E., pp. 197–199.

15. Dewey, *Experience and Nature*, 2nd edition (La Salle, Illinois, The Open Court Publishing Co., 1958), 317–318.

16. *Experience and Nature*, pp. 290–291.

17. *Experience and Nature*, pp. 292–293; pp. 295–296.

18. *Experience and Nature*, pp. 315–317.

19. A. E., pp. 3–4.

20. A. E., p. 19; pp. 22–23; pp. 24–25.

21. A. E., pp. 35; pp. 36–37; p. 48; p. 54.

22. A. E., pp. 54–57.

23. On the life of Camus, see Germaine Brée's *Camus*, revised edition (New York, Harbinger Books, Harcourt, Brace & World, 1964), Chaps. 2–5, to which reference has been made in preparing the following account.

24. His speech of acceptance was translated by Justin O'Brien and printed in *The Atlantic*, CCI, 5 (May, 1958), pp. 3–5.

25. Camus, *The Myth of Sisyphus and Other Essays* (New York, Vintage Books, Alfred A. Knopf, 1955), pp. 3–5.

26. See *The Myth of Sisyphus*, pp. 69–87, "Absurd Creation."

27. Camus, *The Rebel*, translated by Anthony Bower (New York, Vintage Books, Alfred A. Knopf, 1956), Part IV, "Rebellion and Art."

28. *The Rebel*, pp. 262–263.

29. *The Rebel*, p. 264.

30. *The Rebel*, pp. 272–273.

31. *The Rebel*, pp. 274–276.

32. André Chénier. (ED). [Note by editor of *The Rebel*.]

33. François René Chateaubriand. (ED.) [Note by editor of *The Rebel*.]

34. The Rebel, pp. 253–255. [Note by editor of *The Rebel*.]

35. *The Rebel*, pp. 255–258.

36. Delacroix notes—and this is a penetrating observation—that it is necessary to correct the "inflexible perspective which (in reality) falsifies the appearance of objects *by virtue of precision*." [Camus's note]

37. Delacroix demonstrated this again with profundity: "For realism not to be a word devoid of sense, all men must have the same minds and the same way of conceiving things." [Camus's note]

38. *The Rebel*, pp. 268–271.

39. *The Rebel*, pp. 271–272.

QUESTIONS AND TOPICS FOR FURTHER STUDY

1. Explain how Dewey conceives art to grow out of experience. Why does he think that a consideration of the meaning of art is of such crucial importance to the philosopher?

2. Why does Dewey object to the usual distinction between useful and fine arts? What is his view of the relation between the "instrumental" and the "consummatory" in art and in other activities?

3. What criticisms would Dewey bring against Fry's conception of a unique aesthetic emotion? What is Dewey's view of the role of emotion in aesthetic experience?

4. Why does Dewey consider the existence of works of art to be an obstruction to aesthetic theory? By what "detour" does he propose to reach an adequate theory of art?

5. Explain what Dewey means by "*an* experience." Give some examples from your own experiences which you think have the characteristics he mentions. According to Dewey, how

does *an* aesthetic experience differ from other experiences having aesthetic qualities?

6. Explain why Camus considers art to be rebellion in its purest form. Why, in his view, is it impossible for an artist to be a nihilist?

7. Why does Camus object to extreme formalism and extreme realism as approaches to art? To what extent do his views on these approaches agree with those of Dewey's?

8. Why is style so important to the artist, according to Camus? What are the characteristics of great style, in his opinion?

9. What are some of the criticisms Camus brings against contemporary art? What changes are necessary, in his opinion, in order to make possible better art in the future?

10. Topics for further study: (a) Dewey's conception of artistic expression; (b) Dewey's views of the role of the arts in a reconstructed society; (c) comparison of Dewey's and Croce's approach to aesthetics; (d) some recent criticisms of Dewey's aesthetic theory; (e) Camus's aesthetics of the novel; (f) Camus and Aristotle on the aesthetic effects of drama.

GUIDE TO SUPPLEMENTARY READING

(Works marked with asterisks are available in paperbound editions.)

DEWEY

I. PRIMARY SOURCES

Dewey, John, *Art as Experience (New York, Capricorn Books, G. P. Putnam's Sons, 1958).

———*Experience and Nature (New York, Dover Publications, 1958). Chap. 9.

II. SECONDARY WORKS

Ames, Van Meter, "John Dewey as Aesthetician," *Journal of Aesthetics and Art Criticism*, XII (December, 1953), 145–168.

Boas, George, "Communication in Dewey's Aesthetics," *JAAC*, XII (December, 1953), 177–183.

Croce, Benedetto, "Dewey's Aesthetics and Theory of Knowledge," *JAAC*, XI (September, 1952), 1–6.

——"On the Aesthetics of Dewey," *JAAC*, VI (March, 1948), 203–209 (including Dewey's rejoinder).

Edman, Irwin, "Dewey and Art," in Sidney Hook (ed.), *John Dewey, Philosopher of Science and Freedom* (New York, Dial Press, 1950), pp. 47–65.

Gauss, Charles E., "Some Reflections on John Dewey's Aesthetics," *JAAC*, XIX (Winter, 1960), 127–132.

Geiger, George R., *John Dewey in Perspective* (New York, Oxford University Press, 1958). Chap. 2.

Gotshalk, D. W., "On Dewey's Aesthetics," *JAAC*, XXIII (Fall, 1964), 131–138.

Grana, Cesar, "John Dewey's Social Art and the Sociology of Art," in Robert N. Wilson (ed.), *The Arts in Society* (Englewood Cliffs, N.J., Prentice-Hall, 1964), pp. 175–190.

Jacobson, Leon, "Art as Experience and American Visual Art Today," *JAAC*, XIX (Winter, 1960). 117–126.

Kallen, Horace M., *Art and Freedom* (New York, Duell, Sloan and Pearce, 1942). Vol. II, Chap. 32.

Pepper, Stephen C., "Some Questions on Dewey's Esthetics," in Paul A. Schilpp (ed.), *The Philosophy of John Dewey* (Evanston and Chicago, Library of Living Philosophers, 1939), pp. 371–389. (For Dewey's rejoinder see pp. 549–554.)

——"The Concept of Fusion in Dewey's Aesthetic Theory," *JAAC*, XII (December, 1953), 169–176.

Shearer, E. A., "Dewey's Esthetic Theory," *Journal of Philosophy*, XXXII (1935), 617–627; 650–664.

Tamme, Sister Anne Mary, *A Critique of John Dewey's Theory of Art in the Light of the Principles of Thomism* (Washington, D.C., The Catholic University of America Press, 1956).

Zink, Sidney, "The Concept of Continuity in Dewey's Theory of Esthetics," *The Philosophical Review*, LII (1943), 392–400.

CAMUS

I. PRIMARY SOURCES

Camus, Albert, *The Myth of Sisyphus and Other Essays,* translated by Justin O'Brien (New York, Vintage Books, 1955). (Includes "The Artist and His Time.")

——*The Rebel; An Essay on Man in Revolt,* translated by Justin O'Brien, with a forward by Sir Herbert Read (New York, Vintage Books, 1956).

——*Resistance, Rebellion and Death,* translated by Justin O'Brien (New York, Alfred A. Knopf, 1961), pp. 237–272.

II. SECONDARY WORKS

Brée, Germaine, *Camus,* revised edition (New York, Harcourt, Brace & World, 1964). Chap. 24.

Cruickshank, John, *Albert Camus and the Literature of Revolt* (New York, Galaxy Books, 1960).

Durfee, Harold A., "Camus' Challenge to Modern Art," *JAAC,* XIV (December, 1955), 201–205.

Hanna, Thomas, *The Thought and Art of Albert Camus* (Chicago, Henry Regnery Co., 1958). Chaps. II, VIII.

King, Adele, *Albert Camus* (New York, Grove Press, 1964). Chap. III.

EPILOGUE

Although most people go through life without ever discovering that there is a subject called "aesthetics," few would find life bearable without some sort of primitive aesthetic enjoyment—the sight of a loved face, the taste of a good meal, or the feel of a comfortable resting place. As civilized beings, we might find it equally unbearable to live in a world, such as that described in George Orwell's *1984*, devoid of the aesthetic pleasures derivable from art. Fortunately, our world still contains an almost infinite variety of natural and created phenomena from which we can derive aesthetic pleasure. Most people usually take these phenomena and the pleasures associated with them for granted. Those who do not take them for granted, but who seek to understand their nature and value, are engaged in the task (whether they know it or not) that was initiated by Socrates and Plato over two thousand years ago and that has kept aesthetics ever since a going concern.

But is the task really meaningful? Is it worth the effort? Can its goal ever be attained? There are critics of aesthetics who would without hesitation answer "No!" Some of these hold that aesthetic experience is ineffable, completely beyond the reach of rational description and analysis, and that consequently aesthetics as the theoretical study of this experience is impossible. Others claim that aesthetics must be by its very nature such an abstract form of speculation that it can have little or nothing to do with real art and with "the blood and guts" of creative endeavor. Aesthetics, according to others, is only a kind of "Cloudkookooland" where "castrated creators" engage in sterile speculation as a compensation for their inability to create anything more substantial than fantastic theory. Still others are afraid to study aesthetics for fear that it might "clog up the springs of creativity" with its obscure ideas about art and beauty. Among these are some artists who would as soon have a labotomy as take a course in aesthetics, and even a book on the subject is to them, in William James' phrase, an "abomination of desolation." Aesthetics has also been criticized by poets for being too unfeeling and critical, by art critics for being too general and ill-informed, by psychologists for being unscientific, by preachers for being immoral, by economists for being useless, by politicians for being undemocratic, by philosophers for being dreary, desolate, and dull, and by students for being "anesthetics in disguise."

Even those who have "indulged" in aesthetics have not hesitated at times to berate it. Emerson referred to it as "the arid departmental post-mortem science." Santayana considered much of it to be "sheer verbiage." Irving Babbitt called it a "nightmare science." Goethe told his human tape recorder, Eckermann, one day that he could not "help laughing at the aesthetical folk . . . who torment themselves in endeavoring by some abstract words to reduce to a conception that inexpressible thing to which we give the name of beauty," and he agreed with Eckermann that aesthetics teachers "instead of helping the young poet to what he has not, confuse him about what he has." [1] (This did not prevent Goethe, however, from pontificating, sometimes at great length, about the nature of beauty or from giving advice to poets about how to make their works more beautiful.) That worshipper of perfect aesthetic form, Gustave Flaubert, poked fun at aesthetics in his satire of the bourgeois quest for knowledge, *Bouvard and Pécuchet*, by having one of his unheroic heroes, who is studying aesthetics, wonder why, if beauty be correctly defined as unity in variety, cross-eyes are not aesthetically pleasing.[2]

Our purpose here is not to defend aesthetics against its countless critics, nor to answer all of the objections which have been raised against it.[3] The reader, from his own study of the perspectives in aesthetics included in this book and from his own reflection, should already have some of the answers. But a few remarks will be made about some of the criticisms mentioned earlier. Going back to the objection that the ineffability of aesthetic experience makes aesthetics impossible, we would point out that even if the experience is ineffable this should not prevent us from being able to discuss intelligibly the conditions under which it comes about, some of the components that constitute it, its relations to other aspects of experience, and the object in which it finds satisfaction. And if we can do this, aesthetics is possible. As for aesthetics being abstract, like all theory it cannot avoid being abstract, in that it involves the use of generalizations, definitions, deductions, etc., but this does not mean that it cannot be concrete in the sense that it can refer constantly, consistently, and coherently to experience—to the sensible phenomena, whether natural or created, which it attempts to explain. Just because some metaphysically biased theories of aesthetics have lacked this coherence of theory with fact does not mean that no aesthetic theory can achieve it.

Another objection was that aestheticians engage in theorizing as a compensation for their inability to create works of art. Even if this were true about the motivation of aestheticians, it would be irrelevant to the truth or falsity of their theories. Moreover, some aestheticians have been quite able creators, and not just able creators of theories but of works of art. Lessing was an excellent playwright; Tolstoy wrote two of the world's greatest novels; Guyau and Santayana wrote poetry, some of it quite good; Roger Fry was a skilled painter; and Camus was a superb novelist and playwright. And we have mentioned only the artists-aestheticians included in this book. It would not be difficult to name many other artists who have also been interested in theorizing about their own and others' creations.[4]

But even when aestheticians do lack the skill to create works of art, as many of them apparently do, this does not mean that they lack the ability to appreciate and evaluate them or to construct theories about them. Socrates is said to have frequented artists' studios, questioning the artists about their works and helping them to get clearer conceptions of their intentions.[5] "You may scold a carpenter who has made you a bad table, though you cannot make a table," said Dr. Samuel Johnson, adding that "it is not your trade to make tables."[6] If it is not the art critics or the aesthetician's "trade" to make works of art, it is their "trade" to deal with these works theoretically, whether it be in order to analyze, interpret, and evaluate them, as the art critic does, or to study them more generally as objects capable of playing a role in bringing about aesthetic experience, as the aesthetician studies them.

Finally, a comment on the view that a study of aesthetics can stifle the artist's creativity. An artist should not study aesthetics if he is afraid it will affect his work adversely or if he lacks the inclination to theorize about art[7] There is very little evidence, however, that a study of aesthetics has ever done irreparable harm to artists. One who blamed Sir Joshua Reynolds or Victor Cousin or Taine or John Ruskin or John Dewey for his own inability to create would be suspected of rationalizing. There are in fact artists who find it interesting and helpful to generalize about art. They see their mental horizons widening as they view their own art in relation to theory. When they speculate about the motivation of artistic creativity they do not usually find that it decreases their chances of becoming "inspired." Furthermore, some of them experience great satisfaction in the realization that so many serious thinkers have over the centuries expended so much time, energy, and ink in discussing art and beauty. There are even those who claim that they feel less alone with their creative problems when they discover that some of the greatest thinkers have grappled with similar problems and have attempted to clarify and solve them. And there are a few who are able to apply in practice what they have learned in theory and become better artists. "In energetic minds," Coleridge writes in *Biographia Literaria,* "truth soon changes by domestication into power; and from directing in the discrimination and appraisal of the product, becomes influencive in the production. To admire on principle, is the only way to imitate without loss of originality." [8] In writing these lines, Coleridge was thinking of the value of literary criticism, but what he says is also apropos of aesthetics.

There are some thinkers who believe that aesthetics is still in its "Stone Age." [9] There are others who believe, more optimistically, that it is at last entering into the age of science. [10] In any case, the subject so long associated with the ivory tower has been brought out into the market place to be examined and it is attracting a lot of serious attention, especially among contemporary philosophers, some of whom previously viewed it with derision. The attention has often taken the form of the complement of criticism, but it is nonetheless attention. Logical positivists, rejecting aesthetics as a normative science, have claimed that aesthetic propositions, like metaphysical and ethical propositions, are usually without meaning since they cannot be verified or determined to be true or false by definition. [11] Value judgments (including aesthetic judgments) may express "emotive" meanings, but nothing more. Linguistic analysts have been apalled at the confusion rampant in the language of aesthetic discourse. They have tirelessly and tediously pointed out that in talking and writing about art and beauty, aestheticians have often been guilty of employing empty generalizations, misleading analogies, and highly ambiguous terms.[12] Naturalists have criticized traditional approaches to aesthetics on the grounds that their association with metaphysical idealism has only led to wooly thinking and has delayed the development of newer, empirically well-grounded scientific approaches to the field. Older aestheticians must be told the news—Hegel is dead. Traditional approaches to aesthetics have also been criticized by the existentialists, who have objected, above all, to the "essentialism" which, they hold, has been content to attain abstract rather than concrete (existential) truth about art. But art, in their view, must be understood in its relation not to metaphysical essences but to the anxiety-provoking human predicament from which it springs and to which it must constantly refer if the artist is to achieve a free and meaningful involvement in life. So proceeds the critical appraisal and transvaluation of aesthetics and its values. But if aesthetics is making progress today, it is doing so not despite its critics, but partly because of them.

Whatever be the shortcomings of aesthetics in this latter half of the twentieth century, it will probably not be used to harm mankind. In an age in which cleaner bombs and bigger and more far-ranging missiles attract so much attention, and in which men race furiously toward the moon, who can object to a little earthbound "science" which promotes only clearer conceptions and wider and more far-ranging investigations, and whose followers are content, in the main, simply to look and listen while others blast off?

NOTES

1. J. P. Eckermann, *Conversations with Goethe*, translated by John Oxenford, edited by J. K. Moorhead (London, Everyman's Library, J. M. Dent & Sons, 1930), p. 192; p. 322.

2. Gustave Flaubert, *Bouvard and Pécuchet*, translated by T. W. Earp and G. W. Stonier (New York, New Directions, 1954), p. 166.

3. On the criticisms of aesthetics and answers to them, see F. H. Sparshott, *The Structure of Aesthetics* (Toronto, University of Toronto Press, 1963), pp. 6–25, and Jerome Stolnitz, *Aesthetics and Philosophy of Art Criticism* (Boston, Houghton Mifflin, 1960), pp. 7–19.

4. To name some of them: the poets Coleridge, Baudelaire, Poe, Eliot; the painters Delacroix, Reynolds, Matisse; the musicians Debussy, D'Indy, Wagner, Stravinsky, Sessions; the architects Vitruvius, Wright, Greenough; the sculptors Rodin, Moore; the novelists Conrad, Zola, Flaubert, Henry James.

5. Xenophon, *Memorabilia*, Bk. III, Chap. 10.

6. James Boswell, *Life of Samuel Johnson* (London, Everyman's Library, J. M. Dent & Sons, 1906), Vol. I, p. 253.

7. For a discussion as to whether or not an artist should study aesthetics, see Thomas Munro, *Toward Science in Aesthetics* (New York, Liberal Arts Press, 1956), IX, "Aesthetics and the Artist," pp. 302–323.

8. Samuel Taylor Coleridge, *Biographia Literaria* (London, Everyman's Library, J. M. Dent & Sons, 1906), Chap. IV, p. 43.

9. For example, Arnold Isenberg in William Elton (ed.), *Aesthetics and Language* (Oxford, Basil Blackwell, 1959), p. 144.

10. For example, Thomas Munro in *Toward Science in Aesthetics*, cited above.

11. See A. J. Ayer, *Language, Truth and Logic* (New York, Dover Publications, 1950), pp. 113–114.

12. See William Elton (ed.), *Aesthetics and Language*, cited above, Introduction.

INDEX

459